Covers the Newest Exam!

The Cram Sheet

This Cram Sheet contains the distilled, key facts about A+. Review this information last thing before you enter the test room, paying special attention to those areas where you feel you need the most review. You can transfer any of these facts from your head onto a blank sheet of paper when you enter the test room.

MOTHERBOARDS

1. Two basic types of motherboards: AT (Advanced Technology) and XT (Extended Technology). Baby AT and ATX are form factors of the AT system board.

2. Two basic expansion buses: ISA and PCI. ISA is the Industry Standard Architecture used on XT and AT boards.

3. XT boards use an 8-bit ISA bus. In general, AT boards use a combination 8-bit/16-bit ISA bus.

4. ISA bus slots are usually very long and large, and tend to be nearer one of the edges of a motherboard.

5. PCI bus is a 32-bit/64-bit bus specification with smaller slots, generally nearer the center of a motherboard. PCI slots can sometimes be interwoven between the ISA slots: first ISA, then PCI, then ISA again, and so forth.

6. CMOS is a battery-backed chip that contains system settings, configured from a hotkey combination at startup. CMOS stores passwords. The best way to recover from a forgotten CMOS password is to disconnect the chip's power supply, thereby clearing all settings. A badly configured

CMOS (where the hardware attached is set with the wrong name) usually means a device mismatch error.

7. Jumpers are used to set the motherboard's clock speed. The clock oscillator can be tuned to a specific frequency. One Hertz (Hz) is the time it takes for the oscillator to produce One full wave. one Megahertz is one-million cycles (clock ticks). Motherboard speeds should match the fastest CPU speed.

8. Power supplies take in 110 volts (AC) and typically put out 12 and 5 volts (DC). Sometimes a voltage regulator on the system board can be set by jumpers to provide other voltages (note the 3.3 volts used by many processors).

MEMORY/PROCESSORS

9. Real mode comes from the 8088/86 processor where the chip can only address 1MB of real memory addresses. The 1MB is called "conventional memory" and can be split into low memory (IRQ tables), application memory (640K), and high memory (around 370K).

10. Protected mode started with the 80286 processor and means that one application

can run in a different area than another application, and they won't affect each other if one of them crashes.

11. Enhanced mode (386 Enhanced mode, 32-bit Protected mode), comes from the 80386 chip. All current processors can use Enhanced mode. The 32-bit 386 was the first chip that could run both Real mode and Protected mode, without resetting the system.

12. Parity is a way to test RAM chips (SIMMs and DRAM) to see if they can correctly remember data. Parity checking requires an additional circuit and logic in order to work. When a computer heats up it can change the SIMMs and cause parity errors. The POST routine can't uncover heat-related problems, since everything on the board is cool. Heat problems usually cause software problems and are uncovered using software utilities.

13. Pentium chips generally run from 66 to 200 MHz. Pentium Pro chips are usually sold in two speeds: 180 MHz and 200 MHz.

14. L1 cache (Level 1) is internal to the CPU and is usually 16K in size. L2 cache (Level 2) is an external chip or chips near the CPU and works best when it is 256K or 512K in size.

15. HIMEM.SYS is a memory manager required by Windows 95. Without HIMEM.SYS, the system can't access any more than the 1MB of conventional memory. HIMEM is loaded from the CONFIG.SYS file in everything except W95, which loads if from IO.SYS.

PERIPHERALS

16. Port connectors from the back panel of a chassis include: 9-pin male serial, 25-pin female parallel, 15-pin female video.

17. Parallel cables are usually a DB25-pin male (plugs into the female end on the chassis) connector with a 36-pin male Centronics connector at the other end.

18. SCSI cables are usually 50-pin ribbon cables. SCSI chains can have up to 7 devices and must be terminated at both ends. IDE chains can have 2 devices. SCSI is usually used for external devices like CD-ROM drives and scanners.

19. COM1 and COM3 are logically joined, while COM2 and COM4 are logically joined. COM1 and 3 use IRQ 4 while COM2 and 4 use IRQ 3.

20. COM port addresses include: com1= 03F8; com3=03E8; com2=02F8; com4= 02E8

21. LPT1 uses IRQ 7, and LPT2 uses IRQ 5.

22. IRQ14 is the primary drive controller, and IRQ15 is the secondary drive controller. When IRQ 2 cascades to IRQ 9, number 2 can't be used.

23. Laser printers use a primary corona wire to charge the drum. The drum is cleaned, charged, and written to. The image develops (by the corona charge) and pulls toner to the drum. Paper is charged and pulls toner from the drum, where it's fused by the fuser rollers. If the heat-sensor on the fuser rollers shuts down, the toner will fail to stick to the paper. Paper jams are usually caused by a bad separator pad.

24. Sectors are 512 bytes. Clusters grow to fit the size of the formatted logical drive, depending on the operating system. The FAT is 16K. The master boot record is in Sector 0, Track 0, Head 0, Cylinder 0 of the primary active partition.

25. Hard drives can have a maximum of 24 logical drives (A: and B: are floppies; C: is drive 1). Once the C: drive has been partitioned, the largest extended partition can have 23 drive letters.

26. LASTDRIVE must be set for any number of drives that go beyond the default E: drive.

27. If a keyed connector doesn't have a physical notch, the red stripe refers to Pin 1.

DOS

28. FDISK.EXE is used to create partitions.

29. FORMAT C: /S transfers the system files to the C: drive.

30. SYS C: (SYS.COM) is used to transfer system files to a corrupted disk showing "Missing or bad system files" errors.

31. An operating system is a command line, a command interpreter (processor, COMMAND.COM), and a user interface. The three critical DOS (system) files are

Are You Certifiable?

That's the question that's probably on your mind. The answer is: You bet! But if you've tried and failed or you've been frustrated by the complexity of the program, you've come to the right place. We've created our new publishing and training program, *Certification Insider Press*, to help you accomplish one important goal: to ace the A+ exam without having to spend the rest of your life studying for it.

The book you have in your hands is part of our *Exam Cram* series. Each book is especially designed not only to help you study for an exam but also to help you understand what the exam is all about. Inside these covers you'll find hundreds of test-taking tips, insights, and strategies that simply cannot be found anyplace else. In creating our guides, we've assembled the very best team of certified trainers, A+ professionals, and course developers.

Our commitment is to ensure that the *Exam Cram* guides offer proven training and active-learning techniques not found in other study guides. We provide unique study tips and techniques, memory joggers, custom quizzes, a sample test, and much more. In a nutshell, each *Exam Cram* guide is closely organized like the exam it is tied to.

To help us continue to provide the very best certification study materials, we'd like to hear from you. Write or email us (craminfo@coriolis.com) and let us know how our *Exam Cram* guides have helped you study, or tell us about new features you'd like us to add. If you send us a story about how an *Exam Cram* guide has helped you ace an exam and we use it in one of our guides, we'll send you an official *Exam Cram* shirt for your efforts.

Good luck with your certification exam, and thanks for allowing us to help you achieve your goals.

Keith Weiskamp

Keith Weiskamp
Publisher, Certification Insider Press

A+

Covers the Newest Exam!

COMPTIA CERTIFIED COMPUTER TECHNICIAN

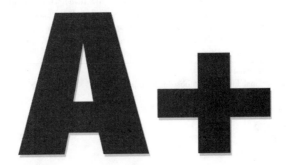

James G. Jones
Craig Landes

A+ Exam Cram

Copyright © The Coriolis Group, 1998

Limits of Liability and Disclaimer of Warranty

Trademarks

The Coriolis Group, Inc.
An International Thomson Publishing Company
14455 N. Hayden Road, Suite 220
Scottsdale, Arizona 85260

602/483-0192
FAX 602/483-0193
http://www.coriolis.com

Library of Congress Cataloging-in-Publication Data
Jones, James G.
    A+ exam cram / by James G. Jones and Craig Landes
      p. cm.
    Includes index.
    ISBN 1-57610-251-3
    1. Computer technicians—Certification. 2. Microcomputers—Maintenance and repair—Examinations—Study guides. 3. Computing Technology Industry Association—Examinations—Study guides.
I. Landes, Craig. II. Title.
TK7885.54.J66 1998
621.39'16'0288—dc21

                              98-8181
                              CIP

Printed in the United States of America
10 9 8 7 6 5 4 3 2 1

CORIOLIS

an International Thomson Publishing company

Albany, NY • Belmont, CA • Bonn • Boston • Cincinnati • Detroit • Johannesburg • London • Madrid
Melbourne • Mexico City • New York • Paris • Singapore • Tokyo • Toronto • Washington

Publisher
Keith Weiskamp

Acquisitions
Shari Jo Hehr

Marketing Specialist
Cynthia Caldwell

Project Editor
Ann Waggoner Aken

Production Coordinator
Kim Eoff

Cover Design
Anthony Stock

Layout Design
April Nielsen

About The Authors

James G. Jones

James G. Jones has over 25 years of experience in multiple aspects of the IT industry, including systems design and development, sales, education, and management. In addition to a BS in Education and an MBA in Information Technology, James has earned numerous certifications from Microsoft (Product Specialist, Systems Engineer, Trainer), Novell (Network Engineer, Network Administrator), CompTIA (A+ Certified), Bay Networks, Ascend, Shiva, and Gandalf (Certified Instructor).

Craig Landes

Craig Landes has over ten years experience in Information Technology, holding numerous positions from database programming to Manager Information Systems in the field of health care. Craig regularly helps some of today's largest consulting firms develop technical programs for clients and employees at all levels. He is currently heading the development of The National Association of Personal Systems Administrators (NAPSA), a professional organization of technology specialists servicing the over 46 million home and small business computer users.

Table Of Contents

Chapter 9
16-Bit Windows 257

Introduction

Welcome to *A+ Exam Cram!* This introduction is very much like the "Quick Setup" reference section for a software application, and we use it to give you some important insights into the exam. The purpose of this book is to get you ready to take—and pass—the 1998 Computing and Industry Trade Association's (CompTIA) A+ certification exam. In the following pages, we've outlined the CompTIA A+ certification in general, and we talk about how *Exam Cram* can optimize your knowledge of PCs and focus in on critical exam topics.

New job listings often require applicants to be A+ certified, and many individuals who complete the program qualify for increases in pay and/or responsibility. If the job requirements don't require an existing A+ certification, many corporations require that you complete the certification process within 90 days of being hired.

This book is aimed strictly at exam preparation and review. It will *not* teach you everything you need to know about a topic. Instead, it will present and dissect the question topics that you're probably going to see on the exam. We've drawn on material from CompTIA's own listing of requirements, from other preparation guides, and from the exams themselves. We've also drawn from a battery of third-party test preparation tools and from our own experience with microcomputers, going all the way back to the Altair. Our aim is to bring together as much information as possible about the revised A+ certification exams.

Our explicit purpose in writing this book is to stuff as many facts and technical answers about computers as possible into your brain before you begin the test. The A+ exam makes a basic assumption that you already have a *very* strong background of experience with PCs, hardware, and Wintel operating systems. On the other hand, we think that microcomputers are changing so fast that no one can be a total expert. We think this book is the most up-to-date analysis of the 1998 A+ exam on the market.

Depending on your experience with PCs, we recommend that you begin your studies with some classroom training or that you visit the CompTIA Web site (http://www.comptia.org) for a definition of what it means to be A+ certified. We *strongly* recommend that you install, configure, and generally "fool around" with the DOS, Windows, and Windows 95 operating environment that you'll be tested on. Nothing beats hands-on experience and familiarity when it comes to understanding the questions you're likely to encounter. Book learning is essential, but hands-on experience is the best teacher of all!

Perhaps a quick way for you to decide where you stand in relation to the current certification process is to turn to the end of the book and examine the Sample Test (Chapter 12). This is a highly accurate representation of both the test format and the types of questions you will encounter.

The New A+ Certification Program

The A+ Certification Program has been extensively revised as of July 1998 and now includes two separate exams. You will be required to pass both the PC *core* module and the DOS/Windows *specialty* module in order to receive your A+ certification. Additionally, there are a number of questions concerning customer service.

Many people feel that the two exams are so closely related that they should be combined into one. Whether or not they're eventually combined, we recommend you treat the two components as one exam. In fact, we have organized this book as if they were one exam and urge you to sign up for *both* exams at the same time. Taking both exams in one session saves you money as well.

The PC core exam tests your knowledge of microcomputer hardware, including motherboards, processors, memory, peripherals, IRQs, electronics, and buses. The Windows/DOS specialty exam tests your knowledge of the three most widely-used operating systems in the current market. Customer service questions do *not* have a pass/fail consequence, but they *do* produce a score notation on your A+ certificate. Thus, potential employers will be able to use your customer service score in an interview and hiring decision.

Taking A Certification Exam

Unfortunately, testing isn't free. You'll be charged $100 for each test you take, whether you pass or fail. It isn't necessary to take both tests at the same time, but if you do, the discounted cost of the combined tests is $165.00.

> *Note: CompTIA is evaluating the pricing of these tests, and it may change prior to your enrollment in the exam. We are sure the price will not go down, so the sooner you sign up the better.*

The United States and Canadian tests are administered by Sylvan Prometric. Sylvan Prometric can be reached at 1-800-77MICRO (1-800-776-4276), Monday through Friday, between 7:00 AM and 6:00 PM (Central Time).

To schedule an exam, you must call at least one day in advance. *To cancel or reschedule an exam*, you must call at least 12 hours before the scheduled test time (or you may be charged). When calling Sylvan Prometric, please have the following information ready for the sales representative who handles your call:

➤ Your name, organization, and mailing address

➤ The name of the exam(s) you wish to take (A+ core, and/or DOS/ Windows specialty module)

➤ A method of payment

The most convenient payment method is to provide a valid credit card number with sufficient available credit. Otherwise, payments by check, money order, or purchase order (PO) must be *received* before a test can be scheduled. If the latter methods are required, ask your sales representative for more details.

Keep in mind that if you choose to pay for your exam by a method that involves the postal service and banking system (i.e., check, PO, etc.), you'll have to call to schedule your exam much earlier than one day in advance.

Arriving At The Exam Site

On the day of your exam, try to arrive at least 15 minutes before the scheduled time slot. You must bring *two* forms of identification, one of which *must* be a photo ID. Typically, a driver's license and credit card are valid forms of identification. Insurance cards, birth certificates, state ID cards, employee identification cards, or any other legal identification can also be used. If you're not sure whether your identification is acceptable, ask the person you schedule your exam with.

You will be given a user ID code as an identification number for your test, which you enter in the computer at the time you begin your exam(s). The exam is fully computer based, and is all multiple choice. Ordinarily, your ID number is the same as your Social Security number, though it may be different. Your ID number will be used to track your session.

In The Exam Room

All exams are completely closed-book. In fact, you will not be permitted to take anything with you into the testing area other than a blank sheet of paper and a pencil provided by the exam proctors. We suggest that you *immediately write down the most critical information* about the test you're taking on the blank sheet of paper you're given. *Exam Cram* books provide a brief reference (the Cram Sheet, located in the front of the book) that lists essential information from the book in distilled form.

Each question will offer you an opportunity to mark that question for review. We strongly suggest that you mark any questions about which you have any shade of doubt. Each exam offers a generously fair amount of time to complete the questions, and by marking questions for review, you can go back without the pressure of worrying whether you'll complete the whole session.

The time you take to answer the questions is not factored into scoring your test. Your answers can be changed at any time before you terminate the session, and the review option is not tracked for scoring. Many terms and words are easy to mix up, so take time to review your work.

When you complete the exam, the software will tell you whether you've passed or failed. All tests are scored on a basis of 100 points, and results are broken into several topical areas. Even if you fail, we suggest that you ask for (and keep) the detailed report that the test administrator prints out for you. You can use the report to help you prepare for another go-round, if necessary. If you need to retake an exam, you must call Sylvan Prometric, schedule a new test date, and pay another $100 per exam.

Certification

When you've passed the core and specialty exams, you will be A+ certified. It's a good idea to save the test results you are given at the conclusion of the test, as they are your immediate proof. Official certification normally takes anywhere from four to six weeks, so don't expect to get your credentials overnight. When the package arrives, it will include a Welcome Kit, a certificate (suitable for framing), and an identification lapel pin.

As an official recognition of hard work and broad-based knowledge, A+ certification is also a badge of honor. Many organizations view certification as a necessary foundation for a career in the information technology (IT) industry.

How To Prepare For An Exam

A+ certification requires an extensive range of knowledge about the entire field of microcomputers. Preparing for network certification, Windows 95 certification, aerobics certification, or even driving certification (driver's license) is somewhat simpler. In these cases, the area you're being certified in is a limited subset of everything in that field. A+ certification, on the other hand, has no boundary limitations. Anything at all about a PC is a valid subject for testing!

By using this book in your preparation efforts, you'll be able to concentrate your efforts on the areas considered to be the most important in understanding PCs. We've "been there, done that" so to speak, and we'll point you in the right direction for your studies.

At a minimum, preparing for the A+ exams requires a good test guide (this book) and detailed reference materials addressing the information covered on the exams. We've attempted to make no assumptions whatsoever about your current knowledge and to cram between the covers of the book as much information as possible about PCs. However, our main focus is to get you through the exam. Using the self-study method, you might consider us as virtual tutors, coming to your site at your convenience and stuffing the facts between your ears.

In the past, candidates have used many individual reference books that, taken together, cover most of the required material on the exam. This avenue is still open to you, and a good professional should always have a solid reference library as a matter of course. See the "Need To Know More?" sections at the end of each chapter for our lists of recommended references.

If you like a little more structure, there are several good programs available in both a self-paced and classroom format. However, you must be sure the program you select has been developed for the revised A+ requirements released in July 1998. Consider too that the cost of structured class instruction is significantly higher than the price of this book.

The A+ certification exam is constantly being updated so as to reflect the ever-progressive developments in the microcomputer industry. The best source of current exam information is CompTIA's website at **http://www. comptia.org**. If you don't have access to the Internet, you can call or write CompTIA directly at:

Computing Technology & Industry Trade Association
450 East 22nd Street, Suite 230
Lombard, IL 60134-6158
Phone: (630) 268-1818

About This Book

Each *Exam Cram* chapter follows a regular structure, along with graphical cues about especially important or useful material. The structure of a typical chapter includes:

➤ **Opening Hotlists** Each chapter begins with lists of the terms you'll need to understand and the concepts you'll need to master before you can be fully conversant with the chapter's subject matter. We follow the hotlists with a few introductory paragraphs to set the stage for the rest of the chapter.

➤ **Topical Coverage** After the opening hotlists, each chapter covers at least four topics related to the chapter's subject.

➤ **Study Alerts** Throughout the topical coverage section, we highlight material most likely to appear on the exam by using a special Study Alert layout that looks like this:

 This is what a Study Alert looks like. A Study Alert stresses concepts, terms, software, or activities that will most likely appear in one or more certification exam questions. For that reason, we think any information found offset in Study Alert format is worthy of unusual attentiveness on your part.

Even if material isn't flagged as a Study Alert, *all* the content in this book is associated in some way to something test related. The book is focused on high-speed test preparation; you'll find that what appears in the meat of each chapter is critical knowledge.

➤ **Sidebars** When we discuss an exam topic that may be based on common knowledge among people in the IT industry, we've tried to explicitly describe the underlying assumptions of the discussion. You may have many years of experience with PCs, or you may be just starting out. Your certification shouldn't depend on "secret knowledge" that you're supposed to "just know" somehow.

Something You May Not Know

A sidebar like this is a way to step outside the flow of the discussion to provide you with "insider" information that you may not have heard before. A sidebar is a way to increase the saturation level of your knowledge and apply some "fixative" to help keep topical facts from slipping out of your ears.

➤ **Notes** This book is part of the overall reference material pertaining to computers. As such, we dip into nearly every aspect of working with and configuring PCs. Where a body of knowledge is far deeper than the scope of the book, we use Notes to indicate areas of concern or specialty training.

Note: Cramming for an exam will get you through a test. It won't make you a competent IT professional. While you can memorize just the facts you need to become certified, your daily work in the IT field will rapidly put you in water over your head if you don't know the underlying principles of computers.

➤ **Useful Knowledge Tips** We provide tips that will help build a better foundation of knowledge. Although the information may not be on the exam, it is highly relevant and will help you become a better test-taker. Many of the Customer Service scenarios, for example, are structured as tips, since the subject matter is so subjective.

This is how tips are formatted. Here's an example of a tip: You should always choose the custom or advanced option, if the setup routine offers one. In every case we've ever seen, there is a default setting for any steps in the program where you're given a choice. In situations where you don't know what you're looking at, you can choose the default. However, in places where you do know what you're looking at, you may often disagree with what some faraway programmer has decided to do to your system.

➤ **Exam Prep Questions** This section presents a series of mock test questions and explanations of both correct and incorrect answers. Each chapter has a number of Exam Prep Questions highlighting the areas we found to be most important on the exam.

➤ **Need To Know More** Every chapter ends with a section entitled "Need To Know More?" This section provides direct pointers to resources that offer further details on the chapter's subject matter. In addition, this section tries to rate the quality and thoroughness of each topic's coverage. If you find a resource you like in this collection, use it, but don't feel compelled to use all these resources. On the other hand, we recommend only resources that we have used on a regular basis, so none of the recommendations will be a waste of your time or money.

The bulk of the book follows this chapter structure, but there are a few other elements that we would like to point out:

➤ **Sample Test** A very close approximation of the 1998 A+ exam is found in Chapter 12.

➤ **Answer Key** The answers to the sample test appear in Chapter 13.

➤ **Acronym Glossary** This is a fairly extensive glossary of acronyms.

➤ **The Cram Sheet** This appears as a tear-away inside the front cover of this *Exam Cram* book. It is a valuable tool that represents a condensed and compiled collection of facts and numbers that we think you should memorize before taking the test. Because you can dump this information out of your head onto a piece of paper before answering any exam questions, you can master this information by brute force. You only need to remember it long enough to write it down when you walk into the test room.

You might even want to look at the Cram Sheet in the car or in the lobby of the testing center just before you walk in to take the exam. Keep in mind that if you take both tests together, there is a break between the core and the DOS/Windows specialty exam. The Cram Sheet is divided under headings, so you can review the appropriate parts just before each test.

Using This Book

If you're preparing for the A+ certification exam for the first time, we've structured the topics in this book to build upon one another. Therefore, the topics covered in later chapters will make more sense after you've read earlier chapters. In our opinion, many computer manuals and reference books are essentially a list of facts. Rather than simply list raw facts about each topic on the exam, we've tried to paint an integrated landscape in your imagination, where each topic and exam fact takes on a landmark status.

We suggest you read this book from front to back for your initial test preparation. You won't be wasting your time, since nothing we've written is a guess about an unknown exam. If you need to brush up on a topic or you have to bone up for a second try, use the Index or Table of Contents to go straight to the topics and questions that you need to study. After taking the tests, we think you'll find this book useful as a tightly focused reference and an essential foundation of microcomputer knowledge.

If you have a *lot* of experience with PCs and their operating systems, you may want to read those sections of the book and then try the sample test in Chapter 12. We do think, though, that because the A+ exam covers an extremely wide range of information, you would be better served by taking the time to go through the book chapter by chapter.

Contacting The Authors

We've tried to create a real-world tool that you can use to prepare for and pass the core and specialty exams. We are definitely interested in any feedback you would care to share about the book, especially if you have ideas about how we can improve it for future test-takers. We will consider everything you say carefully and will respond to all reasonable suggestions and comments.

We would like to know if you found this book to be helpful in your preparation efforts. We'd also like to know how you felt about your chances of passing the exam *before* you read the book and then *after* you read the book. Of course, we'd love to hear that you passed the exam, and even if you just want to share your triumph, we'd be happy to hear from you.

You can reach us via email at jimjones@jamesgjones.com. Please include the title of the book in your message (i.e., *A+ Exam Cram*); otherwise, we'll have to guess which book you're making suggestions about.

For up-to-date information on A+ certification, specifications, and other preparation materials, visit the Certification Insider Press Web site at www.certificationinsider.com. You're always welcome to stop by the authors' Web site, too, at www.jamesgjones.com (note the "g" in the middle).

Thanks for choosing us as your personal trainers, and enjoy the book! We'll wish you luck on the exam, but we know that if you read through all the chapters, you won't need luck—you'll ace the test on the strength of real knowledge!

A+ Certification Tests

Terms you'll need to understand:

√ Exhibit

√ Multiple-choice question formats

√ Careful reading

√ Strategy

Concepts you'll need to master:

√ Preparing to take a certification exam

√ Practicing—to make perfect

√ Budgeting your time

√ Marking for review

√ Using one question to figure out another question

√ Analyzing responses logically

√ Guessing (as a last resort)

As experiences go, test-taking isn't something most people anticipate eagerly, no matter how well they're prepared. In most cases, familiarity reduces exam anxiety. In other words, you probably wouldn't be as nervous if you had to take a second A+ certification exam as you will be taking your first one. We've taken lots of exams, and this book is partly about helping you to reduce your test-taking anxiety. This chapter explains what you can expect to see in the exam room itself.

Whether it's your first or your tenth exam, understanding the exam particulars (how much time to spend on questions, the setting you'll be in, and so on) and the testing software will help you concentrate on the material rather than on the environment. Likewise, mastering a few basic test-taking skills should help you recognize—and perhaps even outfox—some of the tricks and "gotchas" you're bound to find in A+ exam questions.

The Test Site

When you arrive at your scheduled Sylvan Prometric Testing Center, you'll be required to sign in with a test coordinator. He or she will ask you to produce two forms of identification, one of which must be a photo ID. After you've signed in and your time slot arrives, you'll be asked to deposit any books, bags, or other items you brought with you, then you'll be escorted into a closed room.

Typically, the testing room will be furnished with anywhere from one to six computers. Each workstation will be separated from the others by dividers designed to keep you from seeing what's happening on someone else's computer.

When you sign in with the exam administrators, you'll be furnished with a pen or pencil and a blank sheet of paper, or, in some cases, an erasable plastic sheet and an erasable felt-tip pen. You're allowed to write down any information you want on both sides of this sheet. As mentioned in the Introduction, you should memorize as much of the material that appears on The Cram Sheet (inside the front cover of this book) as you can and then write that information down on the blank sheet as soon as you are seated in front of the computer. You can refer to your rendition of The Cram Sheet anytime you like during the test, but you'll have to surrender the sheet when you leave the room. Keep in mind that if you've registered for both exams, you can take a break between the core and the DOS/Windows specialty exams, or you can proceed directly into the second exam. If you do take a break, you may have to turn your notes in and start over fresh on the second exam.

Most exam rooms feature a wall with a large picture window. This is to permit the test coordinator to monitor the room, to prevent test-takers from talking to one another, and to observe anything out of the ordinary that might go on.

The exam coordinator will have preloaded the A+ certification test, and you'll be permitted to start as soon as you're seated in front of the computer.

All A+ certification exams are designed to be taken within a fixed time period, and there's a countdown timer on the screen showing you the time remaining. In our opinion, the amount of time is fair and generous, and it offers ample time for reviewing your responses. Each question offers you the opportunity to "mark for review" so you can return to the question at the end of the exam.

A+ certification exams are computer generated and use a multiple-choice format. Although this may sound easy, the questions are constructed to check your mastery of basic facts and figures as well as test your ability to evaluate one or more sets of circumstances or requirements.

You might be asked to select the best or most effective solution to a problem from a range of choices, all of which technically are correct. You might be asked to select the best choice from a graphic image. You might also find questions where a series of blanks represent a list of terms used to complete a sentence. All in all, it's quite an adventure, and it involves real thinking. This book shows you what to expect and how to deal with the problems, puzzles, and predicaments you're likely to find on the test.

The Sample Test in Chapter 12 is a very close approximation of the combined exams. As you'll see, we've included a sample of every type of question as well as mimicked the phrasing style of the overall exam.

Test Layout And Design

As mentioned earlier, the questions on A+ exams are multiple choice. CompTIA has specified that the 1998 revised exam will allow only one correct response to each question. Additionally, there should be no questions requiring you to type in a phrase or series of words. Some questions will provide the information in paragraph format, and others will provide an exhibit (line drawing) and ask you to identify specific components. *Paying careful attention* is the key to success! Be prepared to toggle between a picture and a question as you work. Often, both are complex enough that you might not be able to remember all of either one.

Each question stands alone in a windowed page. The text of the question displays near the top of the screen, and the response choices are listed below the question. Each response appears next to a typical Windows radio button, where clicking on the appropriate circle turns it black. You can change your selection at any time from within the question window. The time you take to respond and the number of times you change a response are not factored into the scoring process. At the bottom of the screen, there are several option buttons allowing you to proceed to the next question or return to the previous question. When a question includes a graphic exhibit, an additional button displays and links to the graphic. Along the top of the screen is the countdown timer and a place where you can mark a question for later review.

Review Responses

When you complete the last question of the exam and press the Next button, a final screen will offer you the option to review your responses. A listing of all the question numbers, along with your chosen response letter shows on the screen, and the marked questions have a graphic indicator. When you highlight a marked question and choose Review, the software displays the selected question.

When you review a question, you'll see a window displaying the original question and your response. You can use the window to change or verify your answer. When you're satisfied with your response, you can unmark the question by clicking on the Mark For Review checkbox, or you can proceed to the next review question. At the bottom of the screen, you'll see a Review Next button, which will take you to your next marked question (bypassing unmarked questions). The number of questions you choose to review is not factored into the scoring process.

Advantages Of Marking Questions For Review

Marking questions for review offers several advantages. The obvious advantage is that you can work through the exam one time with your eye on the clock. Generally, most test-takers get a little worried about whether they'll be able to complete the exam within the time limit. *Don't worry!* If you've studied this book and you're comfortable with the Sample Test, you'll have plenty of time to complete the real exam.

A less obvious advantage of marking a question for review is that some questions are answered by other questions presented later in the exam. For instance, if one question asks you something like, "Which component charges the EP drum?" and lists a number of laser printer parts, you might get thrown off track by the phrase *EP drum*. However, a later question might ask, "Which component writes an image to the electrophotosensitive drum in a laser printer?" As you can see, the second question has provided you with information for the first question.

A third advantage of marking questions for review is that tricky phrasing can sometimes lead to a misinterpretation. For instance, you might be asked, "Of the following items, which is not part of the boot sequence?" In your first reading of the question, you might easily miss the *not* and choose a response designed to catch this kind of error. We recommend that you mark any question that uses lists in its responses.

Take Your Test Seriously

The most important advice we can give you about taking any test is this: *Read each question carefully!* Some questions are deliberately ambiguous, offering several responses that could be correct, depending on your reading of the question. Other questions use terminology in very precise ways. We use Exam Alerts and Tips throughout this book to point out where you might run into these types of questions.

We've taken numerous practice and real tests, and, in nearly every case, we've missed at least one question because we didn't read it closely or carefully enough. For example, the use of the word *requires* commonly causes test-takers to answer incorrectly. Consider Sample Question 1.

Sample Question 1

> Windows 95 requires the WIN.INI and SYSTEM.INI files during the startup process in order to load device drivers and user options.
>
> ○ a. True
>
> ○ b. False

The correct answer is b, false, because the WIN.INI file isn't *required*.

Here are some suggestions for dealing with the tendency to select an answer too quickly:

➤ *Read every word in the question!* If you find yourself jumping ahead impatiently, go back and start over.

➤ Schedule your exam on a day when you don't have a lot of other appointments and errands. This should help you feel a little more relaxed.

➤ As you read, try to rephrase the question in your own terms.

➤ When returning to a question after your initial read-through, reread every word again—otherwise, you might fall into a rut. Sometimes, seeing a question fresh after turning your attention elsewhere enables you to catch something you missed earlier. This is where the review option comes in handy.

➤ If you return to a question more than twice, try to explain to yourself what you don't understand about the question, why the answers don't appear to make sense, or what appears to be missing. If you ponder the subject for a while, your subconscious might provide the details you're looking for, or you might notice a "trick" that will point to the right answer.

Finally, try to deal with each question by thinking through what you know about hardware and software systems. By reviewing what you know (and what you've written down on your Cram Sheet), you'll often recall or understand concepts sufficiently to determine the correct answer.

Question-Handling Strategies

Based on the tests we've taken, we've noticed a couple of interesting trends in exam question responses. Usually, some responses will be obviously incorrect, and two of the remaining answers will be plausible. Remember that only one response can be correct. If the answer leaps out at you, reread the question to look for a trick—just in case.

Unfamiliar Terms

Our best advice regarding guessing is to rely on your intuition. None of the exam topics should come as a surprise to you if you've read this book and taken the Sample Test. If you see a response that's totally unfamiliar, chances are good that it's a made-up word. Recognizing unfamiliar terms can help narrow down the possible correct answers for a question. For example, Sample Question 2 shows how you can use the process of eliminating unfamiliar terms to arrive at the correct answer.

Sample Question 2

Which is the most useful tool for checking a circuit?

○ a. Differentiometer

○ b. Benchmark analyzer

○ c. Multimeter

○ d. Integrity meter

The correct answer is c. Chances are that you've at least heard of a *multimeter* before, thereby enabling you to take an educated guess at this question.

Last Minute Guesses

As you work your way through the test, the exam indicates the number of questions completed and questions outstanding. Budget your time by making sure that you've completed one-fourth of the questions one-quarter of the way through the test period. Check again three-quarters of the way through. If you're not through with the test at the five-minute mark, use the last five minutes to *guess* your way through the remaining questions.

Guesses are more valuable than blank answers, because blanks are *always* wrong. A guess has a 25 percent (one in four odds) chance of being right. If you don't have a clue regarding the remaining questions, pick answers at random, or choose all A's, B's, and so on. The important thing is to submit a test for scoring that has *some answer for every question*.

Mastering The Inner Game

In the final analysis, knowledge breeds confidence, and confidence breeds success. If you study the materials in this book carefully, review the Exam Prep questions at the end of each chapter, and take the Sample Test in Chapter 12, you should be aware of all the areas where additional studying is required.

The appendix provides a reality check in terms of how well you've retained most of the critical concepts. If you find yourself scratching your head and wondering about some of the configuration material, then make a special note to go back and read about that area in earlier chapters.

Additional Resources

By far, the best source of information about A+ certification tests comes from CompTIA. Because products and technologies—and the tests that go with them—change frequently, the best resource for obtaining exam-related information is the Internet. If you haven't already visited the CompTIA Web site, do so at **www.comptia.org**.

There's *always* a way to find what you want on the Web, if you're willing to invest some time and energy. As long as you can get to the CompTIA site (and we're pretty sure that it will stay at **www.comptia.org** for a long while yet), you have a good jump on finding what you need.

Third-Party Test Providers

Even though CompTIA offers the best information about its certification exams, there are plenty of third-party sources of information, training, and assistance, including the following:

➤ Your local college or junior college might offer an A+ certification course. Usually, these are very good courses, with a reasonable cost factor.

➤ Transcender Corporation is located at 242 Louise Avenue, Nashville, TN, 37203-1812. You can reach the company by phone at (615) 726-8779 or by fax at (615) 320-6594. Trancender's URL is **www.transcender.com**, and you can download an order form for their materials online (but it must be mailed or faxed to Transcender for purchase). We have found their practice tests to be useful, but somewhat expensive. The tests cost from $89 to $179 if purchased individually, with discounts available for packages containing multiple tests.

➤ Self Test Software is located at 4651 Woodstock Road, Suite 203-384, Roswell, GA, 30075. The company can be reached by phone at (770) 641-9719 or (800) 200-6446 and by fax at (770) 641-1489. Visit their Web site at **www.stsware.com**, where you can order their products on line. STS's tests are cheaper than Transcender's (STS's exams cost $69 when purchased individually, $59 each when two or more are purchased simultaneously), but they're otherwise quite comparable—making them a good value.

Motherboards

Terms you'll need to understand:

√ Motherboard form factors (XT, AT, ATX, LPX)

√ Bus types (ISA, EISA, VESA, MCA, PCI, PC card)

√ Basic input/output system (BIOS)

√ CMOS

√ Configuration settings

√ Volatile and nonvolatile memory

√ Serial interfaces (UART chip, COM ports, connector types)

√ Parallel interfaces

√ Data flow

√ Megahertz

√ I/O (input/output)

√ PnP (Plug 'n' Play)

√ Slots and cards

√ AC/DC conversion

Concepts you'll need to master:

√ How the motherboard controls timing

√ Process and data flow

√ Connectivity

√ System components

√ Configuration memory

This chapter will prepare you for the questions pertaining to the motherboard on the certification exam. The motherboard is the basic foundation of a computer and connects all the components of the system. Starting with the original personal computers in 1974, most PCs have since consolidated nearly all the electronic components onto a single board: the motherboard. As well as the CPU and supporting chipset, the motherboard holds the expansion bus, I/O (input/output) interfaces, drive controllers, and RAM (random access memory).

The motherboard is also called the *system board* or *planar board*. All three of these names may be used on the exam to refer to the same thing.

Functions Of The Motherboard

The motherboard, or system board, provides *connectivity* for all system components. Essentially, the motherboard is the hardware foundation to which all the connecting parts involved in the computer are attached. The motherboard does the following:

➤ Distributes power from the power supply

➤ Provides data paths for control signals and data

➤ Offers various sockets and pads for mounting components

Motherboards: Two Basic Types

Motherboards are divided into two general categories: XT and AT.

Although the XT is rarely seen today (most motherboards are AT type), you will need to know the difference between the two for the exam. Motherboards connect all the system components, thus providing connectivity. The two main types of motherboards are the XT and AT, although there are various form factors.

XT Motherboards

XT (extended technology) describes the first motherboards used in IBM PCs. They are designed around the Intel 8088 processor, which has a 16-bit internal bus and an 8-bit external bus for communicating with system components. It's important to note that when we say "16-bit" or "8-bit" bus, we're talking about a circuit with 8 or 16 separate channels that signals move through simultaneously. These channels, taken together, are called a *datapath*. The *number* of channels is also referred to as the "width" of the datapath. When multiple components can be connected to a datapath (no matter what the width), that datapath is called a *bus*. The XT motherboard has an eight-bit bus, meaning that its eight-bit datapath has eight channels.

The 8088 processor can address only 1MB (megabyte) of RAM. Consequently, the XT motherboards are *also* limited to 1MB of memory, of which only 640K can be used by application programs.

XT motherboards are configured manually using jumpers, switches, or both (no CMOS [Complementary Metal Oxide Semiconductor] was provided for XT motherboards). An XT motherboard uses an eight-bit ISA (Industry Standard Architecture) expansion bus (discussed later in this chapter).

CMOS

CMOS (Complementary Metal Oxide Semiconductor) RAM is a small, battery-backed memory bank that stores configuration settings. It eliminates many of the jumpers and switches used for configuration.

XT motherboards are relatively simple, so basic configuration changes are done manually through jumpers and switches. However, the AT allows for many more configuration options, so CMOS was provided to allow many of these settings to be configured through the keyboard.

In the days of the XT motherboards, so-called large applications required only 64K of memory, so the restrictions of the XT motherboard weren't a problem. Within a few years, the size requirements of applications increased dramatically, and the need for motherboards with more flexibility and more expansion capacity became apparent.

 XT motherboards use an eight-bit datapath and are configured with manual jumpers and switches.

AT Motherboards

AT (advanced technology) describes most of the motherboards in use today. Unlike XT motherboards, which were designed around a single type of processor, AT motherboards are designed for flexibility and expandability.

The first processor to use an AT motherboard was the Intel 80286, which used a 16-bit internal and a 16-bit external bus. The ISA bus was expanded to 16 bits and CMOS was added so that complex configurations could be set through the keyboard. These boards have since become the foundation for a long line of improved buses, sockets, and integrated components.

 AT motherboards have a datapath of at least 16-bits. However, sometimes only 8 channels are used to maintain compatibility with older expansion cards. The AT motherboard can use as few as 8 channels, but is *designed* with a minimum of 16 channels.

Clock Speed

Clock speed is a *frequency* measurement, written as MHz (megahertz), and refers to *cycles per second;* thus, one MHz refers to one million cycles per second. An oscillator, or electronic clock, is put onto a motherboard and configured through jumpers to yield a specific frequency.

The motherboard must be designed to match the speed of the oscillator, and the processor chip must be matched to the motherboard's clock speed. The frequency of the motherboard determines the processor chip's running speed. Placing a 100 MHz processor chip on a 166 MHz motherboard can lead to the chip's overheating, random lockups and glitches, and can destroy the chip.

 Newer AT motherboards are designed to run at multiple clock speeds that can be manually configured. All components on the motherboard should be rated to run at the maximum speed rating for the motherboard.

The AT-Style Form Factor

Motherboards come in various shapes, or *form factors,* and are designed with different clock speeds and transfer rate capabilities.

 Be able to distinguish between various components on a motherboard based on their general outline and their typical position.

Full-Size AT Motherboard

Primarily, the form factor of a full-size AT motherboard is its size. The full-size AT motherboard is designed around the original XT motherboard and is primarily used today for the larger internal space of a tower case. Tower cases are vertically oriented, usually standing on the floor. Full-size cases were meant for the desktop, and took up a large surface area. Originally, IBM focused on upgrading the motherboard and wasn't thinking about the physical size of the component. Full-size AT motherboards are distinguished by the following:

➤ 16-bit or more transfer buses

➤ CMOS

➤ A five-pin DIN connector for the keyboard (the so-called AT connector)

➤ A size of 12 inches wide by 13.8 inches deep, matching the original IBM XT (fitting in full-size or tower cases only)

Baby-AT Motherboard

The AT-style motherboard was so popular that it became the basis for most motherboards on the market. Computers were beginning to find their way into so many areas that space became a problem. The way in which the internal components fit together had to be changed to reduce the physical size of the PC; thus, the Baby-AT form factor was developed with the following features:

➤ The ability to fit into a smaller case (otherwise the same as the original IBM XT board)

➤ Available for every type of case except low profile and slimline

➤ Built-in CMOS

➤ A five-pin DIN connector for the keyboard

➤ Flexibility, which makes it the most popular board

LPX And Mini-LPX Motherboards

Baby-AT boards and their corresponding smaller case size arrived at the same time that a fundamental change in marketing was occurring. Customers were demanding more selection and customization. The LPX and mini-LPX motherboards were developed to meet the space and aesthetic needs of customers. These have the following features:

➤ Low-profile and slimline cases, typically referred to as "desktop" units

➤ Expansion cards that plug into a "riser card," allowing them to lie the same way as the motherboard (reducing the height of the case by the width of the card)

➤ Mini-DIN (PS/2) mouse and keyboard connectors

➤ Standard connector placement (at the back of the board) for a video, parallel port, and two serial ports

ATX Motherboard

The ATX form (released by Intel in 1995) is becoming the new standard for motherboard design. The ATX improves on four main areas: ease of use, better support for I/O, better support for processor technology, and reduced total system costs. All Pentium Pro system boards are the ATX form factor, with older Pentiums generally installed on AT boards. Features of the ATX system board include the following:

➤ I/O ports are built right into the board (as opposed to just their connectors being built-in on AT boards)

➤ An integrated PS/2 mouse connector rather than the AT DIN connector

➤ No drive overlap (board is rotated 90 degrees for access to the entire board without reaching around drives)

➤ Reduced heat with better cooling circulation (blows air into the case rather than out of the case)

➤ Placement of the CPU closer to the power supply and its cooling fan

➤ A single keyed 20-pin power supply connector

➤ 3.3V DC comes directly from the power supply, removing the need for voltage regulators to reduce voltage from 5V to 3.3V (the virtual standard voltage for today's components)

The proximity of the processor chip to the cooling fan of the main power supply removes the need for a CPU fan. The power supply fan blows air over the chip's heat sink. The tendency of Pentium chips to run hot makes the ATX a better choice for more efficient cooling.

Note: The ATX form is not physically compatible with Baby-AT cases and LPX cases and requires a different case.

NLX Form Factor

The Intel NLX specification is also gaining wide support from many system designers and is expected to replace the older LPX form factor. Eventually, the NLX form factor is expected to replace even the ATX design. The NLX form specification requires a new system design and is not compatible with the LPX form. However, the form design is more "modular," allowing for dockable motherboards that can be replaced without removing any screws.

The NLX form factor supports the new "tall memory" architecture of the Pentium II processor, along with the new AGP (accelerated graphics port).

Interestingly, the AGP is essentially the old VESA Local bus, dusted off and reintroduced under a different name. The VL bus is discussed later in this chapter.

Components Of The Motherboard

The following two images of a motherboard are for your general reference. Figure 2.1 shows an actual motherboard image. Figure 2.2 is an outlined representation of that motherboard's components.

Note: The processor and memory make up the heart of a system, so these are discussed fully in Chapters 3 and 4.

Power Supply

The power supply, although technically not a component of the motherboard, is physically attached to the computer case and connects to the motherboard through either a single, keyed connector or a set of two connectors.

The single, keyed connector was developed to eliminate the possibility of destroying a motherboard by reversing the connectors. While there is a push to

Figure 2.1   A typical motherboard.

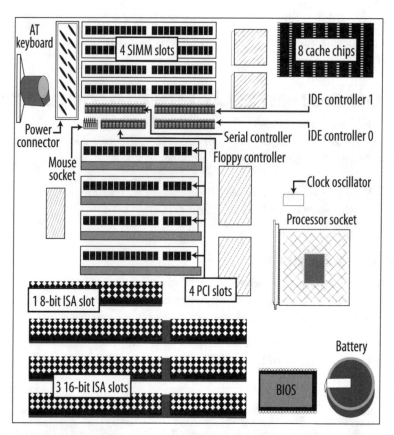

Figure 2.2 Stylized outline showing the components of the motherboard in Figure 2.1.

make the two, keyed connectors into a standard single connector, many machines still use the dual connectors (usually labeled P8 and P9). In dual and single connectors, each connector is keyed so that the connector itself can only be put in one way. However, with dual connectors, it is possible to put a connector in the wrong socket. Even though they are *keyed* correctly, the connectors are in the wrong place. Combining both connectors into one, big connector is an attempt to eliminate this possibility.

"Keying" a connector means designing the plug and the socket with matching notches. If the notches don't line up, the plug can't fit into the socket.

The power supply converts AC (alternating current: 110V in the United States) to DC (direct current) at the voltages required by the system components. Computer components usually require 24, 12, 5, and 3V DC.

The motherboard distributes power to all its system components, except for high-current components such as the fan or disk drives. These high-current components connect directly to the power supply.

 The power supply is a "swap-out," or exchange component, rather than a repair item. Voltage and current levels within a power supply can be lethal. Further, computer-grade capacitors can hold a charge even after the supply is unplugged. Always treat a power supply with respect and replace it if defective. Do not repair it!

Today's power supplies are usually rated at over 200 watts and are capable of powering almost any configuration of system components. Older computers, such as the early XTs, had power supplies rated at less than 100 watts and often failed to meet the demand of additional components.

BIOS (Basic Input/Output System)

When a PC is turned on, the processor first looks at the system BIOS (basic input/output system) to determine the system's configuration and environment. This information is stored in a nonvolatile memory chip on the motherboard. The BIOS largely determines which peripherals the system can support and as such, is updated regularly by the manufacturer.

Volatile Vs. Nonvolatile Memory

RAM is considered volatile in that once the power to the PC is turned off, the information stored in RAM vanishes.

Nonvolatile memory means that the information is retained regardless of whether power is being supplied to the main computer or memory chip. Nonvolatile memory is used in ROM BIOS chips.

CMOS settings information is usually stored in a memory chip and retained by using a small electrical charge provided by a battery installed on the motherboard. If the battery power fails, all CMOS information vanishes. Technically, CMOS is different from ROM BIOS in that the CMOS settings require some source of electrical power. Nonvolatile memory doesn't require electricity at all.

CMOS Setup Program

Access to the BIOS setup varies in different computers, with the differences coming from the BIOS manufacturers. Some of the better-known BIOS makers are Phoenix, American Megatrends (AMI), and Award. PC manufacturers license the BIOS from the BIOS manufacturers. Today, most computers use a keystroke combination, such as Ctrl+Del or F2 to access the CMOS. The keys are pressed at startup, that is, before BIOS transfers control to the operating system.

Older computers, such as some IBM PS/2 models and the original IBM AT, require a setup program stored on a special floppy disk. When you run the program on the floppy disk, you open a setup screen from which you can configure the BIOS. These configurations are stored in special files on the hard drive.

Compaq continued the idea of putting the setup program on a disk. Typically, the CMOS is on a dedicated 3-4MB, non-DOS partition on the hard drive, but it can also be run from a floppy. The CMOS setup program has to be reinstalled from a floppy disk if the hard drive is ever repartitioned. Since the non-DOS, CMOS partition exists in addition to a possible "Boot Manager" partition (used for booting multiple operating systems), difficult configuration problems can develop.

CMOS Updates

As technology advanced, a faster, easier way needed to be developed for the BIOS to take advantage of enhancements. Initially, this was accomplished by removing the BIOS chip and replacing it with an updated chip. Today, most BIOS chips are provided with Flash EEPROM (electrically erasable programmable ROM) so that upgrades can be downloaded through the Internet or a BBS (Bulletin Board Service) without the need for hardware modifications.

 BIOS determines compatibility. Modern BIOS is stored in the CMOS, whereas older BIOS was stored in a non-volatile chip, often soldered into the motherboard.

Expansion Bus

New peripheral devices, such as printers, drives, and monitors, are being developed every day. For a system to take advantage of these new developments, there needs to be a common way of connecting them to the motherboard. This common connection point is the *expansion bus*, sometimes called an I/O bus.

Components such as a video controllers, disk drive controllers, and modems are examples of components that may be connected to the expansion bus through interface cards.

The expansion bus is a set of standardized connectors (slots) located on the motherboard providing connectivity to the datapath. You might think of the expansion bus as a toll plaza on a highway. With eight tollbooths on an eight-lane highway, traffic moves fairly smoothly. This is analogous to an eight-bit bus with an eight-bit processor. However, with 8 toll booths and a 16-lane lane highway, traffic jams will occur as the traffic is funneled down from 16 lanes to 8 lanes. This is what happens when a 16-bit processor is connected to an 8-bit bus.

Although the expansion bus provides exceptional flexibility, it can also be a bottleneck as processor speed increases. The design of the expansion bus has changed almost as fast as processors in the need to improve performance.

Types Of Expansion Buses

PCs use a processor bus, a memory bus, an address bus, and an expansion bus. The motherboard segment of the exam will test your ability to distinguish between these expansion buses on the basis of their names, shapes, and general location on the board.

ISA (Industry Standard Architecture)— 8-Bit/16-Bit

The ISA bus was introduced in a 16-bit version at the same time that the 80286 processor chip was introduced. The ISA bus was the original XT specification and is still used in many modern PCs. The 16-bit ISA bus was developed specifically for the new AT motherboard, and many people call it the "AT bus." Technically, the AT form factor applies to a motherboard with a 16-bit CPU, so the AT bus nickname distinguishes the 16-bit ISA bus from the older, 8-bit ISA bus on an XT motherboard. Features of the ISA bus include the following:

➤ Supports 16-bit slots while staying compatible with earlier 8-bit cards

➤ Introduced in eight-bit format (original XT)

➤ Runs at 4.77 MHz

➤ Modified to 16 bits for the IBM PC/AT computers with 286 chips

➤ Originally ran at 6 MHz, then 8 MHz (eventually standardized at 8.33 MHz)

MCA (Microchannel Architecture)— 16-Bit/32-Bit

This 32-bit bus was created by IBM following the introduction of the 32-bit 386DX chip. It was released as a licensed architecture that the clone makers decided not to follow. Consequently, although microchannel is a faster bus, it faded into obsolescence because the clone makers decided not to pay IBM royalties for a license. Features of the MCA bus include the following:

➤ 32-bit and 16-bit

➤ ISA cards not compatible with MCA slots

➤ Supports bus mastering (any device can request unobstructed use of the bus)

Bus Mastering

If an adapter has its own built-in processor, it can operate independently from the CPU. A bus-mastering board can control the bus and act as if it were the entire system. This allows for very quick throughput, especially if the board is a hard drive controller or NIC (network interface card).

EISA (Extended Industry Standard Architecture)—32-Bit

When the clone makers (primarily Compaq) decided not to pay IBM royalties for its 32-bit MCA bus, they had to use either the ISA bus or develop one of their own. Compaq, having almost everything ready to go, then created the EISA committee, a nonprofit organization charged with controlling the development process. Features of the EISA bus specification include the following:

➤ 32-bit throughput at 8.33 MHz

➤ Automated setup

➤ Support for bus mastering

The EISA bus specification called for EISA expansion cards that are recognized by the bus. The EISA bus then reconciles potential installation conflicts with interrupts (IRQs) and addresses, making them a precursor to today's plug and play (PNP) specification. PNP uses this same process for ISA buses. The

EISA specification never became popular on desktops because very few cards were developed by the makers of hardware devices. The few cards that did become successful focused on disk array controllers and server-type network cards, thus developing a niche for EISA buses in network file servers.

VESA Local Bus—32-Bit

The VESA (Video Electronics Standards Association) local bus is often referred to as a VL (VESA local) bus. The ISA, MCA, and EISA buses are generally slow. Their slowness is because of compatibility issues involving their descent from the original XT motherboard, where the bus speed was the same as the 8088 processor's speed. The increasing load of GUIs (graphic user interfaces) and disk operations led to a modification to the bus as chips became faster than 33 MHz and 66 MHz clock speeds.

The VESA "local" bus is often simply called a VL bus. The VL bus moves some of the I/O ahead of the traditional bus, where it can access the higher-speed processor bus. Instructions move out of the CPU at a certain data width (8, 16, 32 bits). The hardware that moves these instructions first is the *processor bus*. Remember that a bus is a way to move instructions from a microprocessor to a piece of hardware, and the processor bus is one of the first connections between the CPU to the rest of the world. The processor bus is almost always the same width as the CPU's throughput. The 8088 CPU moved eight bits of data across an eight-bit processor bus, and *also* had an eight-bit expansion bus to work with.

Prior to the VESA bus, a video card would have to be inserted into one of the slots on the motherboard's main expansion bus. This led to competition with other cards for the CPU's attention. The VESA specification created a new bus that was separate from the main bus and dedicated exclusively to the CPU. This separation and exclusivity allowed for:

➤ Faster processing through eliminated competition with other cards

➤ Optimizing the bus to the processor speeds, since it wasn't tied to the speed of the main expansion bus

The VESA bus eventually gave way to the PCI bus and became a memory. Recently though, this same concept has returned in the form of the "new" accelerated graphics port. Features of the VL bus include the following:

➤ Access to the processor bus, which is local to the CPU

➤ Direct access to system memory at the speed of the processor itself

➤ 32-bit data transfer capability

➤ 128Mbps (megabits per second) to 132Mbps maximum throughput

➤ Architecture that involves hard drive interfaces, allowing throughput of approximately 8Mbps rather than the traditional 5Mbps of the typical IDE controllers

➤ Different physical makeup to prevent plugging slow cards into fast slots (sometimes the bus was built in and didn't show as an actual slot)

VL Bus Drawbacks

The VL bus was an important development in its time, but eventually the concept of local busing was absorbed into newer technology. Some reasons that the VL bus faded in to history are that it was:

➤ Inherently tied to the 486 chipset

➤ Not developed for the speed of a Pentium

➤ Specified to 66 MHz, but actually limited to around 33 MHz

➤ Sensitive to electrical current fluctuations

➤ Limited to a maximum of three cards, depending on system resources

PCI Local Bus—32/64-Bit

In 1992 (with an update in 1993), Intel initiated the PCI (Peripheral Component Interconnect) Special Interest Group, which released specifications for the PCI local bus. The PCI specifications were designed to solve the continuing problem of fast CPUs moving instructions across a bus that was narrower than the CPU's datapath. Features of the PCI bus include the following:

➤ Capable of being inserted between the CPU and the original I/O bus

➤ Does not connect to the relatively delicate processor bus (e.g., VL)

➤ Uses a new set of control chips to extend the bus

➤ Transfers data at 33 MHz at the full data width of the CPU

➤ With a 32-bit CPU, transfer bandwidth is 132Mbps; with a 64-bit CPU, transfer bandwidth is 264Mbps

➤ Operates at the same time as the CPU, without replacing it

Note: The main difference between a PCI bus and a VL bus is that the PCI bus is a specifically designed, high-speed main expansion bus to be shared by multiple devices. The VL bus was a separate bus dedicated to a single device.

PC Card (PCMCIA)

The PCMCIA (Personal Computer Memory Card Industry Association) card was introduced in 1990 to give laptop and notebook computers an expansion capability similar to that of desktop computers. Originally, the PC card was designed to store memory on a card, but many manufacturers of peripherals came to realize the implications of this for I/O devices. Because no one could remember the acronym PCMCIA, it became known as the PC card (and the acronym now reads "people can't memorize computer industry acronyms"). These credit card-size expansion boards have the following features:

➤ Currently exists in four standard types: Types I, II, III, and IV

➤ Are differentiated into types according to card thickness in millimeters: Type I is 3.3 mm, Type II is 5 mm, Type III is 10.5 mm, and Type IV is thicker than 10.5 mm but not yet standardized (as of 1998)

➤ Are included in the PNP specification

➤ Introduced the concept of combining the device and its I/O card on the card (e.g., tiny hard drives, fax modems, network cards, and memory expansion)

I/O Interfaces/Adapters

The exam likely will test you on the types of adapters and what they do. For example, there are display adapters and drive controllers, along with parallel and serial port adapters. An adapter interface is a way to connect one piece of hardware to another. If you've ever had a three-prong, grounded electrical plug that has to fit into an old two-prong wall socket, you've probably used a little, gray, "ground-lift" adapter interface. You just don't ordinarily call it an interface. Make a special note of the difference between parallel and serial interfaces.

Super I/O Chip

Today, many of the basic peripheral devices are built in to the motherboard, eliminating the need for a specific adapter slot. Usually, these include a primary and a secondary IDE controller, a floppy controller, two serial ports, and a parallel port, all of which are contained on a single chip: the super I/O chip.

Some systems add other peripherals, such as a SCSI host adapter, a video adapter, an integrated mouse port, and/or a network interface card (NIC).

Although these controllers and ports are built in, they act just like cards that plug into an expansion slot. A potential problem of this type of convenience is that it can limit the "upgradability" of a system where the original devices can't be removed. Some motherboards allow for disabling the built-in devices, but many, such as Compaq's, do not.

Monitors And Display Adapters

A video monitor, CRT (cathode ray tube), or VDT (video display tube) displays information to the user. A display adapter is either inserted into one of the PC's expansion slots or built into the motherboard. Although built-in display adapters are efficient and economical, the actual monitors have been evolving very quickly, and many users prefer the flexibility of the plug-in design. People can upgrade the amount of memory on a plug-in adapter card, but not on a built-in adapter.

Floppy And Hard Disk Controllers

Originally, these controllers almost always used an expansion slot because drives varied considerably. However, the standardization of the IDE and EIDE drives brought about the integration of these controllers with the motherboard. Today, most IDE and EIDE (as well as some SCSI) controllers are on a super I/O chip, that is built into the motherboard.

Parallel (LPT) Port—8 Bits In A Row

The parallel port interface transfers information in a sort of wave, eight bits across. You might think of the parallel transfer as an army of soldiers marching in a column eight across.

Bits, Bytes, And Baud

Bits are binary digits (zeroes and ones); eight bits make up one byte, which typically corresponds to one character (i.e., a letter or number).

Today, data rates are measured in Kbps (kilobytes per second) and Mbps (megabytes per second). The term *baud rate* refers to the number of discrete signal events per second in a data transfer, not bits per second. The term *baud* has fallen out of usage. In the early days of 300 and 1200 baud modems, the baud rate equaled the Kbps. The term held over until 14.4Kbps modems entered the market, even though it was no longer technically correct to refer to the modem speed by its baud rate.

Usually, printers are connected to the parallel port; the original DOS device name for the printer is LPT (line printer). The numbers 1, 2, and 3 were added to designate which LPT port the printer was connected to, leading to the familiar LPT1, LPT2, and LPT3 designations.

Parallel ports are available in the following types:

➤ **Unidirectional (original parallel port)** Data flows out, but can't come back in (printers could not communicate with the CPU)

➤ **Standard bidirectional** Peripherals can send status messages back to the CPU for action

➤ **ECP** Enhanced capabilities port

➤ **SPP** Standard parallel port (a setting often found in laptops and notebooks)

➤ **EPP** Enhanced parallel port (also called fast mode parallel port)

EPP and ECP ports are about 10 times faster than the standard bidirectional port.

A special parallel cable can be used to connect two computers without using a network interface card. Along with the special cable, DOS includes a program called Interlink, and Windows 95 uses Direct Cable Connection for this type of rudimentary networking.

DB25-Pin, Female Connector

All parallel ports use the standard DB25-pin female connector. Some serial cables come in DB25-pin, male connector configuration. Parallel and serial cables are not compatible.

 A trick question on the exam might be to present you with both a 25-pin male and a 25-pin female interface connector coming from the motherboard and ask you which one is the parallel connector. Remember that the female connector is *always* used for a parallel port. A 25-pin male connector could be a serial port.

Serial (COM) Ports—One Bit After Another

Serial ports—often referred to as COM1, COM2, COM3, or COM4—transfer information one bit at a time, much like ants following one another. Because only one bit moves at a time, serial ports are slower than parallel ports. If the eight-bit transfer is like an army of ants marching eight abreast in columns, the serial port interface can be thought of as "the ants go marching one by one."

COM ports got their name from the DOS device name (communication ports) and are most often used for modems, mice, and serial printing devices such as plotters. A little-known device name in DOS is the AUX (auxiliary) device, which refers to the first serial port. COM1 has replaced AUX in everyday usage.

Microprocessors work with bytes (eight-bit units). Serial devices work with bits (one-bit units). Bus connections are often involved in converting bytes to bits, or bits to bytes.

Modem

The word *modem* is really an acronym for *mod*ulator *dem*odulator, which is the way analog signals are converted to digital signals and then back again.

Computers work with digital information, whereas phone lines work mainly in analog mode. Some telephone systems are being converted to all digital as the electronic information age advances.

UART Chips

Because a computer works with bytes (eight bits) and the serial port transfers bits (one bit), a device is needed to break apart each byte into its component bits and then remember how they fit back together. That device is the UART (universal asynchronous receiver transmitter) chip.

Three Types Of UARTs

Almost every PC sold today will have a 16550A UART chip inside because so many people want a high-speed connection to the Internet. The difference between the UARTs is primarily how fast they can transfer information. The three UARTs are the following:

➤ **8250** The original chip in XTs: one-byte buffer

➤ **16450** Introduced with the AT: two-byte buffer

➤ **16550A** Popular in 486 and Pentium computers; adds 16-byte FIFO (first in, first out) buffering to eliminate data overrun when a port receives data faster than it can process that data (needed for speeds faster than 15.5Kbps)

16550AN Vs. 16550AFN

The original 16550AN had some problems limiting the buffer. This was fixed by the 16550AFN replacement chip.

The 8250 and 16540 UARTs send one interrupt to the CPU after each character is received. Adding the 16-byte buffer to the 16550A accumulates more characters without losing some of them (buffering). Another feature of the 16550A is that it uses only one interrupt to handle all the characters in the buffer. The buffer stores characters, waits for the CPU to be available, and interrupts only once at that time. This is a significant improvement in reliability with high-speed communication rates.

Windows 3.x can't take advantage of the 16550A's buffering, but Windows 95 can.

Serial Connectors

Consistency has never been a strong point in the computer industry, so you can't just assume that a serial connector has nine pins. Neither can you assume that serial connectors are always used for modems. Serial connectors can be:

➤ DB9 (nine-pin)

➤ DB25 (25-pin, male)

➤ Keyboard or mouse

9- And 25-Pin Male Connectors

Whereas many newer computers have a dedicated PS/2 motherboard mouse port (mini-DIN) for the mouse, many older computers used either a 9- or a 25-pin serial male connector.

Although the mouse is connected directly to the motherboard, it might still be using a COM port, generally either COM1 or COM2. A mouse using a serial connector can use either a serial port or an expansion slot of its own. When the mouse is installed with its own expansion card, it's often called a "bus" mouse.

If a motherboard has no serial ports available or no direct motherboard mouse port exists, you can install a bus mouse, which uses an expansion slot. This might be necessary where older software requires the use of both COM1 and COM2 and a mouse must be configured to COM3 or COM4.

Keyboard/Mouse Connector

The mouse has become an integral part of the PC world with the general acceptance of graphical user interfaces. Because almost every computer uses a mouse, the AT-class computers introduced a dedicated connector for them. These connectors are almost always either:

➤ Five-pin DIN (usually on Baby-AT motherboards)

➤ Six-pin mini-DIN (usually for PS/2- and LPX-type motherboards)

The keyboard/mouse connection might still be configured as a COM port even though it's installed as a PS/2 connector.

PnP

PnP (Plug 'n' Play) is a relatively new introduction to the operating system and computer market. Although the original concept began to show with the EISA bus, a truly workable autoconfiguration process involves more than only the operating system.

Autoconfiguration is where the computer tries to interpret any new adapter card on the expansion bus and then to integrate the peripheral without the typical resource conflicts of previous buses. Once the device has been configured, the PnP operating system will assign various system resources (e.g., memory, time slices) as long as the computer is running. The interactivity of the PnP technology allows the device to tell the operating system what it needs and the OS to give the device those resources.

One of the problems that can occur when an older, non-PnP hardware card is installed in a PnP system is that if the device is configured manually, the PnP operating system can't manage the system resources needed by the device. As far as the operating system is concerned, it doesn't "see" the device, and may assign those resources to a PnP-compliant card. This could shut the older card out of the resource pool, leaving the device it controls dead.

PnP is not only a hardware or only a software solution. Plug 'n' Play involves intercommunication between the hardware devices in the system and the operating system that controls how they work with each other. The three aspects described in the PnP industry specification are:

➤ PnP-compatible hardware

➤ PnP BIOS

➤ PnP operating system

While the technical standard describes only the three major components, Microsoft also includes a fourth component. There may be a question on the exam having to do with "PnP-aware application software," which refers to this fourth "specification."

PnP Operating Systems

The Plug 'n' Play standard is an agreement between developers of hardware, software, and operating systems regarding how to plug something into the system and have it "play" (work) automatically. As we know, the nice thing about standards (people say) is that there are so many of them! PnP is a great idea, but it doesn't always work very well. Windows 95 has made great strides in making PnP a true standard, but it hasn't happened yet. Currently, there are three operating systems claiming to be PnP-compliant, although NT 4 has only limited PnP support (NT 5 is supposed to be fully PnP-compliant). The operating systems are:

➤ Windows 95

➤ OS/2

➤ Windows NT 5

 We've seen a trick question on the exam that suggests that Windows 95 *requires* a new piece of hardware to be Plug 'n' Play. Don't be mislead by the word "required." A PnP operating system does *not* require PnP hardware. PnP hardware won't be auto-configured without a corresponding PnP operating system, but this means only that it must be configured manually. Likewise, non-PnP hardware won't be configured automatically by the operating system. It will have to be configured manually.

Universal Serial Bus (USB)

USB is a peripheral bus specification developed by the PC and telecom industry. The USB is designed to provide PnP capability to peripherals from outside the computer's case. This would eliminate the need to install an expansion card into an expansion slot and reconfigure the system. New peripheral devices can be plugged directly into the bus without either opening the case or rebooting the system. Some of the peripherals that will be designed for the USB include: telephones, modems, keyboards, CD-ROM drives, tape drives, floppy drives, joysticks, scanners, printers, and so on. As PnP becomes more accepted and more peripherals include standardized PNP BIOS, the USB (along with the NLX form factor) should make computer parts as easy to change as the clothes you wear.

Exam Prep Questions

Question 1

> Motherboards are designed to fit one of two basic form factors.
>
> ○ a. True
>
> ○ b. False

False. Motherboards are somewhat artificially divided into two types: XT and AT, with the main difference being the width of the datapath. Within the AT type of motherboard, there are numerous form factors (shapes), such as the AT, LPX, Baby AT, and ATX.

Question 2

> Many AT-type system boards can support multiple clock speeds, which are set with the DOS **Time** command.
>
> ○ a. True
>
> ○ b. False

False. Many AT system boards do support multiple clock speeds, but those speeds are usually set through jumpers and synchronize the system board speed to the processor speed. The DOS **Time** command is used to set or display the time of day.

Question 3

> The power supply (usually mounted to the case) provides what function?
>
> ○ a. Provides consistent 110-volt AC to the system board.
>
> ○ b. Converts AC to DC at the voltage required by the system board and system components.
>
> ○ c. Protects the system components from power outages.
>
> ○ d. Boosts power coming from the power utility to acceptable AC voltages for system components.

The answer is b. Computers require direct current (DC) at several voltages, including 5V+, 5V-, 12V+, and 12V-. Standard wall outlets in the United States provide 110-volt alternating current (110V AC). The power supply's main purpose is to convert alternating current at 110V AC to direct current at the voltages required by the computer.

Question 4

What type of expansion bus is included on most current AT system boards?

○ a. MCA

○ b. VESA

○ c. PCI and ISA

○ d. EISA

The answer is c. Most current AT system boards include both the PCI and the ISA buses for compatibility. The MCA bus developed by IBM never really caught on, and VESA local (VL) buses were predominantly used for video controllers prior to the adoption of the PCI bus. The EISA (extended ISA) bus became primarily a network fileserver niche-market bus.

Question 5

The ECP (expanded capabilities port) was developed to allow serial ports access to the super I/O chip found on many current AT boards.

○ a. True

○ b. False

False. ECP is a type of parallel port and is not related to serial communications. The super I/O chip found on many current AT motherboards integrates I/O functions such as serial and parallel communications on the system board, thus eliminating the need for a separate I/O expansion card.

Question 6

BIOS and operating system support for PnP (Plug 'n' Play) eliminates many of the configuration problems inherent in adding
expansion cards, but eliminates the ability to use cards without
PnP circuitry.

○ a. True

○ b. False

False. PnP requires operating system support, BIOS support, and PnP circuitry on the expansion card in order to function. However, if any or all of
these three parts of the PnP specification are missing, expansion cards can be
configured manually.

Need To Know More?

Andrews, Jean: *A+ Exam Prep*. Coriolis, Scottsdale, AZ. ISBN 1-57610-241-6. Pages 82 through 124 provide an excellent detailed description of the system board, main components, and basic operation. Pages 485 through 519 cover power supplies and electrical issues.

Freedman, Alan: *The Computer Desktop Encyclopedia*. American Management Association. ISBN 0-8144-0010-8. This is an excellent, high-level reference for terms and components you might be unfamiliar with, but does not provide sufficient depth to help you on the exam.

Karney, James: *Upgrade And Maintain Your PC*. MIS Press. ISBN 1-55828-460-5. Pages 223 through 253 review motherboards from the standpoint of repair technicians.

Messmer, Hans-Peter: *The Indispensable PC Hardware Book*. Addison-Wesley. ISBN 0-201-87697-3. Pages 449 through 554 provide detailed information on PC architectures and bus systems. Pages 557 through 648 cover support chips found on the motherboard. Although these sections go into more detail than you need for the exam, this is the resource to consult if you are having trouble understanding something or you just want to know more.

Minasi, Mark: *The Complete PC Upgrade And Maintenance Guide*. Sybex Network Press, San Francisco, CA. ISBN 0-7821-1956-5. Pages 401 through 423 cover power supplies and power-related issues in a PC.

Rosch, Winn: *Hardware Bible*. Sams Publishing. ISBN 0-672-30954-8. Pages 46 through 70 cover motherboards, pages 272 through 296 present chipsets, pages 298 through 366 discuss the expansion bus, and pages 1108 through 1143 cover power. All this information is presented at a level appropriate for the exam.

Processors

Terms you'll need to understand:

√ Microprocessor

√ Addressable memory

√ Cache

√ Clock speed

√ Internal and external bus width

√ Coprocessors

Concepts you'll need to master:

√ Integration of functions within the microprocessor

√ Internal and external buses

√ Cache operation

√ Clock cycles

√ Real vs. Protected mode

√ The MMX instruction set

At the heart of a PC is the central processing unit (CPU), often referred to as a *chip* or *processor*. The convention has been to refer to the chip by its clock speed in megahertz (MHz).

Intel is the market leader in chip manufacturing. Other companies, such as Advanced Micro Devices (AMD), Cyrix, and IBM, make compatible chips. IBM originally worked in cooperation with Intel to develop a computer (the original PC) that would take advantage of the microprocessor. AMD and Cyrix independently entered the chip-making business, and now compete strongly with Intel. IBM has also worked with Cyrix in the development of some of their new processor chips.

CPU (Central Processing Unit)

The CPU is where all the software instructions and math and logic calculations are carried out. Early CPUs allowed for the addition of a *math coprocessor*, or *floating-point unit* (FPU), where some of the more complex mathematical calculations were off-loaded to improve performance. Beginning with the 80486 family of processors , the math coprocessor was sometimes built in to the chip itself.

The CPU is the most expensive component on the motherboard and also a very delicate piece of equipment. The size of the chip, in relation to the number of transistors on it, makes it one of the marvels of engineering in today's world and also makes it extremely susceptible to ESD (electrostatic discharge, sometimes referred to as an electrical strike disaster).

Electrostatic Discharge And ESD Kits

Your body routinely builds up static electricity that discharges to the ground when you touch something conductive. This discharge is known as electrostatic discharge (ESD).

Before you touch *any* component inside a computer, you should ground yourself by touching a metal part of the chassis (e.g., the power supply casing or the metal frames of the chassis). A better way is to have an ESD kit, which consists of a wrist strap with a ground wire and a specially made floor mat also with a ground wire.

Some people think the static charge is removed by touching the metal in the chassis. This isn't always true. The charge is merely equalized. An ESD kit with floor mat is the only way to move the charge to the ground, thus fully removing the charge.

Perhaps you have heard someone suggest that you place circuit boards, system boards, and loose chips on a piece of aluminum foil. This is not a good idea because it can result in a small explosion, as many motherboards, expansion cards, and other boards have built-in lithium or nickel cadmium (NiCad) batteries. If these batteries become short-circuited, they can overheat and react violently by exploding and throwing off pieces of their metal casings.

Never place a circuit board of any kind onto conductive surfaces such as metal foil.

Locating The CPU

After you open up the PC and you're looking at the motherboard, look for the largest chip. On many modern motherboards, the CPU is inserted into a plastic holder, making it easy to spot.

Some of the newer plastic holders, or sockets, have what's called a ZIF (zero-insertion force) design. ZIF design means that you don't need a chip extractor to remove the chip and thus have less chance of breaking the connectors.

Typically, it takes about 100 pounds of insertion force to install a chip into a standard 169-pin screw machine socket. ZIF goes a long way toward reducing damaged sockets, chips, and pins.

The history of PC microprocessors is the story of increasing speed, together with external functions gradually being pulled onto the chip itself. In Table 3.1, we've outlined the model changes and important feature changes. Note that the 80486SX was the last chip without an internal floating point unit.

Processor Families

If every CPU really had its own model name, life would be much easier. The fact is, though, that marketing schemes and customer demands have made it difficult to keep all the processors and their modified versions separate.

Typically, the familiar 80X86 number and Pentium XX MHz is sufficient to separate whole lines (families) of chips. The exam will test your ability to recognize the family names of chips as well as the following:

➤ Derivative chips (SX, SL, DX)

➤ Clock speeds (internal and external) for derivative chips

➤ The presence or absence of internal floating point units (FPUs)

➤ Internal and external bus widths (datapaths)

Table 3.1	Processor history.							
Chip	Date Introduced	Internal Bus Width (Bits)	External (Data) Bus Width (Bits)	Memory	Internal Cache	External Clock (MHz)	Internal Clock (MHz)	Internal FPU
8086	Jun 78	16	16	1MB	No	5	5	No
		16	16			8	8	No
		16	16			10	10	No
8088	Jun 79	16	8	1MB	No	5	5	No
		16	8			8	8	No
80286	Feb 82	16	16	16MB	No	8	8	No
		16	16			10	10	No
		16	16			12	12	No
80386DX	Nov 85	32	32	4GB	No	16	16	No
	Feb 87	32	32			20	20	No
	Apr 88	32	32			25	25	No
	Apr 89	32	32			33	33	No
80386SX	Jun 88	32	16	4GB	No	16	16	No
	Jan 89	32	16			20	20	No
		32	16			25	25	No
		32	16			33	33	No

(continued)

Table 3.1   Processor history (continued).

Chip	Date Introduced	Internal Bus Width (Bits)	External (Data) Bus Width (Bits)	Memory	Internal Cache	External Clock (MHz)	Internal Clock (MHz)	Internal FPU
80386SL	Oct 90	32	16	32MB	8K	20	20	No
	Sep 91	32	16			25	25	No
80486DX	Apr 89	32	32	4GB	8K	25	25	Yes
	May 90	32	32			33	33	Yes
	Jun 91	32	32			50	50	Yes
80486SX	Sep 91	32	32	4GB	8K	16	16	No
	Sep 91	32	32			20	20	No
	Sep 91	32	32			25	25	No
	Sep 92	32	32			33	33	Yes
80486DX2	Mar 92	32	32	4GB		25	50	Yes
	Aug 92	32	32			33	66	Yes
80486SL	Nov 92	32	32	64MB	8K	20	20	Yes
		32	32			25	25	Yes
		32	32			33	33	Yes
80486DX4	Mar 94	32	32	4GB	8K	25	75	Yes
		32	32			33	100	Yes

(continued)

Table 3.1 Processor history (continued).

Chip	Date Introduced	Internal Bus Width (Bits)	External (Data) Bus Width (Bits)	Memory	Internal Cache	External Clock (MHz)	Internal Clock (MHz)	Internal FPU
Pentium	Mar 93	64	32	4GB	16K	60	60	Yes
P5		64	32			66	66	Yes
Pentium	Mar 94	64	32	4GB		60	90	Yes
P54C		64	32			66	100	Yes
		64	32			66	133	Yes
Pentium	Jan 96	64	32			60	150	Yes
P54C		64	32			66	166	Yes
	Jun 96	64	32			66	200	Yes
Pentium	Jan 97	64	32	4GB		66	166	Yes
P55C		64	32			66	200	Yes
Pentium	Nov 95	64	32	4GB		66	150	Yes
Pro		64	32			66	166	Yes
		64	32			66	180	Yes
		64	32			66	200	Yes

Everyone throws around the terms of bits, bytes, megabits, megabytes, and bigger numbers referring to larger amounts of storage. We've seen a few tricky questions that ask you for the exact size of a particular disk or file. A 1MB file isn't exactly 1,000 bytes, but 1,024 bytes. To avoid any possibility of confusion, Table 3.2 lists the exact number of bytes and bits in single units of each category.

8088

The first PC, introduced by IBM, contained an Intel 8088 processor chip. Although the 8086 was the first CPU in existence, the 8088 was released on the market first. IBM used the 8088 in its PC/XT computers. Features of the 8088 include the following:

➤ Runs at 4.77 MHz, or 4,770,000 cycles (ticks) per second. Each cycle represents the execution of one instruction or part of one instruction. Later, it was designed to run at 8 MHz, close to double the speed of the original.

➤ An eight-bit *external* bus can move eight bits of information into memory at one time.

➤ A 16-bit *internal* bus.

➤ The 20-bit address bus enables the chip to access 1MB of RAM (random access memory).

Note: RAM (random access memory) is where the CPU temporarily stores data. RAM and memory are discussed in depth following the discussion of CPUs.

Table 3.2   Standard terminology for bits and bytes.

Term	Number of Bits
bit	Single 0 or 1
kilobit (Kb)	1 bit x 1,024 — 1,024 bits
megabit (Mb)	1 bit x $1,024^2$ (or 1,024 x 1,024) — 1,048,576 bits (millions)
gigabit (Gb)	1 bit x $1,024^3$ — 1,073,741,824 bits (billions)
terabit (Tb)	1 bit x $1,024^4$ — 1,099,511,627,776 bits (trillions)
Byte	8 bits
Kilobyte (K)	1 byte x 1,024 — 1,024 bytes (8,192 bits, or 1,024 x 8)
Megabyte (MB)	1 byte x $1,024^2$ — 1,048,576 bytes
Gigabyte (GB)	1 byte x $1,024^3$ — 1,073,741,824 bytes
Terabyte (TB)	1 byte x $1,024^4$ — 1,099,511,627,776 bytes

➤ Typically, both the 8088 and the 8086 take an average of 12 cycles to execute an average instruction.

Real Mode

Beginning with the 80286 chip, reference to "Real mode" means that the newer chips imitate the original 8088 chip. Even in today's Windows 95 machines, running a DOS application initiates a virtual 8088 PC called a "virtual machine" (VM).

A CPU operating in Real mode, addresses memory in the original 1MB range that the 8088 could directly assign memory addresses to with its 20-bit address bus. The 286 could address a total 16MB of memory, but had to maintain backward compatibility with the many PCs and applications already on the market. Many of the applications had to be rewritten to take advantage of any memory beyond the first 1MB of conventional memory.

8086

Prior to the 8088, Intel made a somewhat faster chip: a true 16-bit chip that used 16 bits for both the internal *and* the external bus. However, at the time it was felt that people would be unwilling to pay a premium price for this capability, and the less expensive 8088 was adopted for the first PCs. Features of the 8086 include the following:

➤ Approximately 20 percent faster throughput than the 8088 because of its ability to communicate at 16 bits with the other system components

➤ 16-bit internal bus

➤ 16-bit external bus

Datapath Performance Increases

IBM could say that the 8 MHz 8086 PS/2-30 was two and a half times faster than the 4.77 MHz 8088 PC/XT because of the change in the external bus from 8 bits to 16 bits. This is one of the first indications that performance could be increased by making the datapath larger.

At this time, the Compaq Deskpro and the AT&T 6300 were using the 8086, but IBM didn't use it until it introduced the IBM PS/2-25 and PS/2-30.

Some History Of The 80186 And 80188

At first, these chips were unsuccessful because of numerous compatibility problems, but they did pave the way for the development and introduction of the 80286 by incorporating some of the system components into the CPU.

The advantage of the 80186 and 80188 is that they combined 15 to 20 system components that were used in the 8086-8088 series computers. This reduced the number of components in the system and led to the design of intelligent adapter cards, such as network adapters.

Breaking The 1MB Limit

We've seen that the 8088/86 CPU could address 1MB of memory. Software applications and the operating system rapidly took over the entire megabyte and began demanding more. Unfortunately, a number of engineering decisions had been made that would affect the PC industry all the way up until today. The 80286 CPU was a fundamental turning point in how chips access memory, and its introduction coincided with the new AT motherboard design. Many of the ways that modern PCs work with hardware and memory can be traced back to this processor.

80286

The 80286 (286) was the CPU installed in the first IBM AT and its new AT motherboard. The 286 was also used in the PS/2 models 50 and 60. Later PS/2s used the 80386 chip. The increasing market for PCs led to the emergence of many new companies that manufactured computers. These computers came to be known as *IBM clones*, which were referred to as *AT-compatible* or *AT-class* computers, leading to the standardization of the AT-type motherboard.

Features of the 286 include the following:

➤ 16MB of addressable memory

➤ High backward compatibility with the 8088 used in PC/XTs, meaning that software written for the older chip would run on the 286

➤ A Real mode and a Protected mode of operation

➤ Runs at 4.5 cycles per instruction rather than the 12 cycles of the 8088/86

➤ Available in 8 MHz, 10 MHz, 12 MHz, and 20 MHz versions (8088/86 limited to 8 MHz)

➤ Installs on motherboards restricted to a 16 MHz interface with memory and peripherals

 The 286 chip, which can address 16MB of memory, introduced the concept of Real mode along with Protected mode.

Real Vs. Protected Mode—"Swapping"

The 286 was the first chip to physically address 16MB of actual memory. In Real mode, the 286 acts essentially the same as the 8088/86 chips and can run older software with no modifications. Once again, Real mode means that the chip addresses the first 1,024 bytes of "conventional memory" by assigning real addresses to real locations in memory. The 80286 could address up to 16MB of memory, but software could use the chip to access even more memory.

As software began requiring more memory, the 286 introduced a way for software to access 1GB of memory, including virtual memory, by "swapping" code held in RAM to a disk. This enables the software to use the freed up memory and to think that it can utilize up to 1GB of RAM while not knowing about the swapping.

When the operating system and software are written for the 286 processor, the chip can run multiple programs at once, using the 286 Protected mode feature. This sparked the development of OS/2 and later the Windows 3.0 Standard mode. We will discuss Windows and its modes of operation in the DOS and Windows chapters later in this book. Make a note that even today, DOS applications running in Windows and the way that Windows manages "virtual memory" can be traced all the way back to the 80286 microprocessor.

Theoretically, Protected mode allows one program to fail without bringing down the system. The theory behind Protected mode is that what happens in one area of memory has no effect on other programs. However, before programs that run concurrently are truly safe from one another's actions, the CPU (along with other system chips) needs an operating system that can work to provide that protection.

Switching From Protected Mode To Real Mode

Virtual memory, or RAM that is swapped to a disk, is controlled by the operating system and the chip. The 286 Protected mode introduced this capability, though software development was slow to catch up.

The 286 can't switch from Protected mode to Real mode without re-setting (warm rebooting) the computer. However, it can switch from Real mode to Protected mode *without* resetting. The 386 improvement allowed switching to either mode without a system reset. This inability to come back from Protected mode without a warm reboot changed history when IBM continued to develop OS/2 for the 80286 and began to fall behind in relation to Microsoft's desire for a multi-tasking operating system (OS).

True Protected Mode

In order for a person to run more than one program at a time using RAM to store parts of each program, the CPU and operating system have to be able to keep everything separate. The separation of "running code" should allow for one program to crash (become inaccessible to the system) without causing the whole system to stop. The 80286 introduced the idea of protected separation, but it wasn't until the 80386 that this Protected mode worked consistently.

80386

The introduction of the 80386 (386) represented a fundamental change in the world of PCs. At that time, the PC was catching on and bringing major changes to the business world. The graphic interface of Windows was very demanding of processing power, and Intel was beginning to dominate the chip market. The constant demand for more speed and more power was pushing development efforts, and new chips were coming out every year.

Applications were becoming larger, requiring more memory to hold their code and data, and customers were prepared to spend more money for RAM if it would make their machine faster. The PC had hit a critical acceptance point, and the expanding market was bringing software that could work with as much memory as a chip could address. The 80386 opened the door to that memory, and finally provided enough speed for the new multitasking OSs and programs. Features of the 386 include the following:

➤ Has a full 32-bit processor (32-bit internal and external bus).

➤ Can switch between Protected mode and Real mode through software control without resetting the system, making multitasking, (more properly task-switching) more practical.

➤ Virtual Real mode (or Virtual 86 mode) allows several Real mode sessions to run concurrently in a "virtual machine."

Virtual Real Mode And The Virtual Machine (VM)

Using Virtual Real mode, the CPU can simulate the 8088/86 Real mode operations and memory addressing, while running hardware-based (80386) memory protection. This allows a true multitasking operating system to load multiple copies of DOS, while making the CPU think it's working with only one machine. There is only one physical machine present, but each copy of the DOS command processor is running in its own simulated world—a virtual machine.

If the system is using appropriate memory management software, the 386 chip can create several memory *partitions*. Each of these memory partitions can have its own copy of DOS and utilize the full range of DOS services, thereby functioning as if it were a standalone PC. When this type of organization is in place, the computer is often said to be running virtual machines. When we examine Windows, we'll see how the Virtual Machine (VM) manager is a basic component of all versions of Windows.

Microsoft Windows is a management software program that takes advantage of Virtual Real mode, and programs designed for Windows can run alongside multiple DOS programs in multiple virtual machines. Because the processor can service only one application per clock tick, Windows manages the amount of time the CPU gives to each program in *time slices*, usually measured in milliseconds. Because the 386 is so fast and time slices are so small, the multiple applications running under Windows appear to be running concurrently.

Task Switching Vs. Multithreaded Multitasking

IBM and Microsoft began rewriting DOS to run in both Real and Protected mode when software developers were slow to write programs for the 286. The results of these projects were OS/2 v1.0 and Windows 286, which could run most DOS programs in Real mode just as they had run before, but in multiple instances.

In Protected mode, OS/2 provided true multitasking (as opposed to task-switching) as well as access to the entire 1GB of *virtual memory*, and 16MB of physical address space. Microsoft Windows took advantage of something called "page frame switching" in both the 80286 and the 80386 chips to provide high-speed task-switching. The better protection built in to the 386 helped make Windows more stable.

Windows 3.0, in Standard mode, used the page frame memory-swapping capability of the 286 to switch among several running programs (tasks) without being able to run the programs concurrently. By the time software arrived on the market for Windows 3.0 Standard mode, the new 386 chip was rapidly replacing the 286 chip. Sixteen-bit Windows and the hybrid Windows 95/98 continue to use page frame task-switching. Windows NT is Microsoft's true multitasking operating system.

With the introduction of the 386, variations of the CPU began to enter the market, offering differences in performance and features to provide different price points in the consumer and business computer fields.

 The 386 is a full 32-bit processor with both a 32-bit internal bus and a 32-bit external bus. The 386 offers Virtual Real mode protection to run virtual machines. A virtual machine is a simulated PC with an 8088/86 CPU that can only address 1MB of RAM.

386DX

The 80386 processor is made of CMOS material, which reduces the chip's power requirements and allows software configuration of the system. Generally, the DX suffix has come to mean that a chip is the full-configuration version and includes an internal math coprocessor. However, in the 386 family of chips, the DX designation means a complete, 32-bit configuration. Features of the 386DX include the following:

➤ Full 32-bit processor (32-bit internal registers, 32-bit internal data bus, and 32-bit external bus)

➤ 32-bit memory address bus

➤ Clock speeds from 16 MHz to 33 MHz (manufacturers other than Intel offer chips up to 40 MHz)

➤ Ability to address 4GB (4 billion bytes) of physical memory

With built-in memory management, the 386DX enables software to access 64TB of memory, or about one trillion bytes, so software written for the 386 chip can access 64 trillion bytes of memory. (Current estimates of the space requirements of the human mind suggest that a complete life of memories can be stored in about 15TB.)

386SX

Market forces and the dramatic increase in consumer interest led Intel to develop a chip for people who wanted 386 capability at a price closer to that of the older 286 chips. This budget-conscious buying is essentially what led to the entire line of derivative chips being developed. The 386SX can be described as follows:

➤ Restricted to a 16-bit external bus, but internally identical to the 386DX with 32-bit internal registers

➤ 24-bit memory address bus addresses only 16MB of RAM rather than the 4GB capability of the 32-bit bus

➤ Available at 16 MHz to 33 MHz

➤ Can run 386-specific software the same as a 386DX (286 chips cannot run 386 Virtual Real mode software)

➤ Not pin-compatible with 286 processor sockets on original 286 motherboards

The 386SX ended the reign of the 286 because of its better MMU (memory management unit) and the new Virtual Real mode feature. The 386DX and the 386SX can both run Windows 3.x in Enhanced mode, which is formally called 386 Enhance mode. Enhanced mode is where the Windows software takes advantage of the 80386 chip's ability to continually switch between Real mode and Protected mode.

386SL

Along with the increased market for PCs, both in business and at home, people wanted portability and a general reduction in the space that their computers were taking up. Portable computers were introduced, but didn't really excite the market the way laptop computers did.

Laptop computers came about with the development of LCD (liquid crystal display) panel technology, and began driving the research into size reduction and lower power consumption. To meet those needs, the 386SL offered the following:

➤ A low-power chip designed for laptops

➤ A cache controller designed to control a 16K to 64K external processor cache

➤ An SMI (system management interrupt) with power management features for battery conservation, including several Sleep modes

➤ Support for LIM (Lotus/Intel/Microsoft) expanded memory functions

➤ 25 MHz clock speed

82360SL Subsystem

The 82360SL I/O subsystem, offered by Intel for laptops, provided a number of common peripheral functions such as serial and parallel ports, DMA (direct memory access) controller, interrupt controller, and power-management logic for the 386SL. This process of combining I/O in a chipset eventually became common in all PCs.

80x87 Coprocessor

Starting with the Intel 80386, a major marketing push was initiated stressing the performance advantages of adding a coprocessor. This *math coprocessor* (FPU) was designated by the change of the last digit of the main CPU's number. The "87" chip was always the same speed as the primary "86" chip. For example the 33 MHz 80386 was paired with an optional 33 MHz 80387. These coprocessors had been available as far back as the 8086.

The coprocessors only affected arithmetic calculations (add, subtract, multiply, and divide) and therefore greatly speeded up spreadsheet applications. They did not necessarily speed up all applications.

This marketing campaign was so effective that when the 486 chips internalized the floating point unit, it was disabled in the SX line and a separate 487 "math coprocessor" was offered. This coprocessor, in actuality, was a fully functional 486 CPU, and when inserted in its special socket, disabled the preexisting 486.

 Remember that a coprocessor is a floating point unit (FPU) and only affects applications that do a lot of arithmetic. These math coprocessors primarily benefited the large spreadsheets that were gaining in popularity.

AMD And Cyrix

Intel dominates the chip-manufacturing business, though other companies make microprocessors. Two of the better-known chip makers are AMD and Cyrix. An interesting lawsuit came about when Intel tried to trademark the numbers

80386, 80486, and so on and discovered that it wasn't legal to do so. Intel created the Pentium name because a name can be trademarked, while a number can't.

AMD and Cyrix began producing their own versions of the Intel 386 CPUs that can be described as follows:

➤ Mostly compatible with the Intel 386 chips

➤ Can run all software designed for an Intel 386 chip

➤ Generally less expensive than Intel chips

IBM

Because IBM has a specific license to produce Intel-designed chips, the IBM processors are somewhat different than the AMD and Cyrix chips in that they use the official masks and microcode developed by Intel. IBM chips have additional features and capabilities from the Intel chips, though the "Intel inside" marketing campaign by Intel has successfully limited their usage. One of the chips offered by IBM was the Blue Lightning, a 32-bit chip comparable to the Intel 486DX.

Making Chips With A Mask

A manufacturing *mask* is the photographic blueprint for the given chip. It is used to etch the complex circuitry into a piece (chip) of silicon.

80486

With the introduction of the 386 AT-class machines and Windows 3.0, the consumer PC market began the expansion we have come to know today. More and more businesses began to move to computers, and a PC on every desktop became typical. This led to bigger, more feature-packed software that demanded faster computers, more memory, and increasing storage capacity. The GUIs of Windows and OS/2, along with huge spreadsheets, databases, and computer-aided design (CAD) led the demand for intense mathematical calculation and higher clock speeds.

The 486 processor, about twice as fast as the 386 chip, includes the following:

➤ A 32-bit internal, 32-bit external, and 32-bit memory address bus

➤ Execution of instructions at two cycles rather than the 4.5 cycles of the 386

➤ Level-1 internal cache (typical hit ratio of 90 percent to 95 percent)

➤ Burst mode

➤ Built-in synchronous math coprocessor in some versions

➤ Upgrade capability

Synchronous And Pipeline Burst Mode

A *cache* is a small area of memory that is set aside to store data that the CPU expects to call for in the immediate future. Caches can be located in RAM, on disk, or in dedicated chips. If the cache is in a separate, dedicated chip, the speed of the cache memory can be disassociated from the motherboard clock speed. This allows cache memory chips to process instructions faster than main memory in many instances.

When the CPU executes instructions, the speed that it processes those instructions is the *processing speed*. Processing only takes place inside microprocessors. Once the instructions have been executed, the results have to be stored in some kind of memory (such as DRAM, SRAM, or virtual memory). If the processor moves the results to main system memory, the timing of that movement is tied to the speed of the motherboard. Disassociating a burst mode cache from the motherboard allows the transfer of processing results between the microprocessor and the cache memory to take place at the optimal speed of the chips, rather than the motherboard.

Cache chips have been developed that include their own internal clock, making something called "synchronous burst mode" possible. Ordinarily, the CPU sends a memory address, then data to fill that address, over and over again, until the cache is full, at which time it goes back to the beginning and overwrites previously used addresses. Synchronous burst mode means that only one address needs to be sent by the CPU for a given stream of data, which is called a *burst*. The clock on the cache chip increments the address with each new byte of data, until the burst is complete.

Pipeline burst mode replaces the internal clock on a cache chip with a less expensive *register* (an internal storage area) that holds the next piece of data to be used. You might almost think of this as a cache for the cache.

A built-in math coprocessor (FPU), running synchronously with the main processor, can execute mathematical calculations faster than the earlier designs, that is, in fewer clock cycles. This makes it two to three times faster than the external 387 coprocessor.

With the advent of the 486, and its being nearly twice as fast as the 386, the graphic user interface finally came into its own. Market acceptance of the Windows GUI prompted the sale of more expensive hardware, larger hard drives, and faster video cards. This ultimately began the price competition that has brought the prices of PCs down and driven their capability continually upward.

The DX CPUs Of The 486 Family

Although all the 486 chips have a full 32-bit architecture and built-in memory cache, differences exist in their maximum speeds and pin configurations (see Table 3.3).

Processor Speed And Motherboard Clock Speed

A processor will always process instructions internally at its rated speed (16 MHz, 25 MHz, 33 MHz, 133 MHz, and so forth). Once the internal processing is completed, the CPU stores the results in memory. While the memory is often the main, system memory (RAM), it can also be separate, cache memory. If the CPU transfers processing results to main memory, the rate of that transfer is controlled by the motherboard's oscillator (clock speed). If a CPU is rated at 33 MHz, but a system board has a clock speed of 25 MHz, the transfer of processing results between the CPU and RAM takes place at 25 MHz.

A DX2/Overdrive chip runs internally at twice the clock speed of the motherboard. A DX4 can be configured to run at 2 times, 2½ times, or 3 times the motherboard clock speed. Even though the internal processing is taking place at double, triple, or quadruple the speed of the original chip, the transfer rate of the results of all that processing is still the original motherboard clock speed.

Internal (Level-1) Cache

An *internal cache* means that the area of memory being used by the CPU to store results of processing is separated from the main, system RAM. This separate memory is inside, and a part the CPU, and is not limited to the

Table 3.3	The primary categories of the 80486 processor chip.		
486SX	1x (single speed) CPU	16, 20, 25, 33, 40, 50 MHz	No floating-point unit (FPU)
486DX	1x CPU	25, 33, 50 MHz	FPU included
486DX2	2x (double speed) CPU	40, 50, 66, 80 MHz	Clock-doubled overdrive CPU with FPU included
486DX4	3x (triple speed) CPU	75, 100, 120 MHz	Clock-tripled CPU with FPU included

motherboard's clock speed. The storage capacity of internal cache memory is usually either 8K or16K. Keep in mind the main, system RAM in modern computers is often 16MB or more.

By caching data in fast cache memory, you speed up system performance. Level-1 (L1, or primary cache) is fast and is integrated into the CPU chip. On the other hand, L1 cache memory is not very large (typically 16K). Although it is useful for storing some data, it usually relies on a secondary, external (L2, or Level-2) cache for an all-around boost in system performance.

All 486 chips include an integrated, internal L1 cache with either 8K or 16K of cache memory included. The L1 cache is:

➤ Built into the processor

➤ Faster than system RAM

➤ Not tied (limited) to the motherboard clock speed

➤ Accessible with no *wait states* (when the CPU waits until the system RAM becomes available)

486DX

Each family of chips, from the original 8086 through the current Pentiums, has represented a breakthrough in technology. The 286 introduced Protected mode, and the 386 improved on that as it moved to 32-bit processing. The 486 family began pulling together various speed-enhancing components and building them right in to the chip.

The 486 differs from the 386 and 286 primarily in its integration and upgradability. *Integration* refers to the number of components that have been moved onto the chip. *Upgradability* means that the CPU can be taken off of the motherboard and replaced with a better (faster or feature-enhanced) chip.

Integration

The 486 integrated a math coprocessor (FPU or MCP), a cache controller, and cache memory into the chip. (For a detailed discussion on caches, refer to Chapter 4.)

The math coprocessor of the 486 chips is 100 percent compatible with the external 387 math coprocessor that complements the 80386 processor. However, the 486 FPU, being internally synchronized with the 486 CPU, executes instructions in half the cycles of the 387, thereby delivering twice the performance.

Upgradability

The 486 chip was designed with upgrades in mind because of the assumption that new developments would rapidly follow current technology. The double-speed overdrive processor is an example of these upgrades.

486SL Enhanced

Once again, the size constraints of the burgeoning laptop and notebook computer markets required a different version of the 486. In this case, though, the 486SL included a series of enhancements to the 486DX, and eventually was discontinued when all those enhancements were made part of the entire 486 family. Enhancements to the 486SL include the following:

➤ The SMM (System Management mode) power management feature, which includes a Sleep mode and clock-throttling, reducing power consumption for laptops. These features eventually were added to most desktop computers as well.

➤ The Suspend/Resume feature, with Instant On/Instant Off capability, allows a 486SL system to go into a suspended state (similar to screen savers) and use almost no power. The system can be brought back to where it started in about one second, eliminating the need to turn the computer off.

An advantage of the SMM system on a desktop is that the SMI (system management interrupt) is triggered when the system tries to access a peripheral device that has been powered off to save battery power. This causes the device to power up and the system to reexecute the instruction I/O, reducing "Device not ready" error messages.

486SX

Once again, customers on a budget were looking for the advantages of the 486 at the price of the now-obsolete 386 processor. The fact that the 486SX had its internal math coprocessor disabled led many people to assume that "SX" meant "no FPU." However, as we saw with the 386 this isn't always true.

Note: The 386SX had a 16-bit external bus rather than the full 32-bit external bus of the DX.

Specifications for the 486SX include the following:

➤ Essentially identical to the 486DX but does not include the internal FPU

➤ 1,185,000 transistors, down from 1.2 million (initially, the SX was a "flawed" DX chip that simply ran slower, but eventually the SX got its own manufacturing mask)

➤ Two times faster than a 386DX with the same clock speed

The 486SX has the full 32-bit architecture of the 486DX, including pin compatibility with the DX. The primary distinction between the SX and DX in the case of a 486, is the 486SX's lack of a functional FPU. The 386SX, on the other hand, was a 16-bit external bus version of a 32-bit 386DX chip.

486DX2/Overdrive

The 486DX2 speed-doubled chip that Intel released as a new chip was also released to retail consumers as an Overdrive or Upgrade chip. Originally, it was available only in a pin configuration that was designed to fit the 486SX system performance upgrade socket. However, shortly after Intel released the chip, it provided another version of the 486DX2 for upgrading original 486DX systems. The difference was essentially a single pin, from 169 pins on the SX to 168 on the DX. The only part of the DX2 that doesn't run at double speed is the external bus. The DX2 can execute instructions in one cycle rather than in the two cycles of the DX.

Pentium Processors

In October 1992 (shipped in March 1993), a chip that Intel had code-named the P5 (fifth generation of chips) took the name Pentium and broke from the 80X86 tradition. This was because, as mentioned earlier, a number can't be trademarked.

Features of the Pentium include the following:

➤ 32-bit address bus, the same 4GB memory addressing as in the 386DX and 486 chips

➤ 64-bit data bus, transferring twice as much data I/O as a 486 with the same clock speed

➤ 64-bit-wide memory bus

➤ Two 32-bit internal registers (data transferred to RAM at 64 bits is split into two 32-bit *packets* for internal processing, allowing compatibility with 486 chips)

➤ Two separate 8K L1 caches rather than the single 8K or 16K cache of the 486 (cache controller built into the chip)

➤ Caches can be CMOS-configured to either write-back or write-through, which improves performance of the write-through-only setting

➤ Takes advantage of Level-2 (L2, or secondary) caching, usually consisting of 256K or 512K SRAM (static RAM)

➤ Manufactured on BiCMOS (Bipolar Complementary Metal Oxide Semiconductor), which increases performance by 30 percent to 35 percent over CMOS with no size or power increase

➤ SL enhanced—once again, incorporates SMM power management, clock-throttling, and the internal memory cache

Pentium Pro-based motherboards are exclusively PCI and ISA bus architecture. The Pentium Pro chip was installed on the new ATX motherboards because of the better cooling that the ATX form factor provides by moving the CPU away from the main expansion bus.

L2 Cache

Although L2 caches can be more than 512K, increases in performance are minimal beyond 512K.

The CPU is already caching the probable next data in the internal 8K or 16K caches. However, if the data is predictable but can't fit into such a small cache, having it handy in very fast (nine nanosecond) L2 SRAM allows the CPU to continue processing without waiting for transfers from system RAM.

BiCMOS

As requirements for low-power systems continue to increase, Intel expects to return to the CMOS design. There's no performance advantage to BiCMOS at low voltages, but there is about a 10 percent increase in the complexity of manufacturing a BiCMOS chip. The BiCMOS process was used in Pentium processors with clock speeds of up to 133 MHz.

Superscalar Technology

The Pentium is entirely compatible with previous processors from Intel but adds a fundamental difference: superscalar technology. Superscaler technology is based on a *twin data pipeline,* meaning that the Pentium can execute two instructions at the same time. All previous chips execute one instruction at a time.

Superscaler technology allows the Pentium to execute two instructions per cycle (1 Hz clock tick), which moved the chip's execution factor beyond the single clock-tick barrier for the first time. Another way of looking at this is to think of the Pentium performing one instruction in 0.5 Hz (half of one cycle).

MMX Instruction Set

In late 1996, in an effort to capitalize on the expanding market for multimedia applications, Intel introduced the enhanced Pentium chip with MMX (multimedia extensions) capabilities. The MMX chips contain additional instructions (commands) and other enhancements specifically designed to handle sound, video, and graphics.

MMX technology is a set of basic, general purpose integer instructions that can be applied to a wide variety of multimedia and communications applications. MMX introduces 57 new instructions for accelerating calculations typical of audio, 2D and 3D graphics, video, speech synthesis, and voice recognition. Acceleration can be as much as eight times faster than that without MMX. This should provide an apparent 50 to 100 percent performance improvement in multimedia programs.

 MMX is a hardware technology in which the instructions are built into the system.

To take advantage of MMX, software must be written specifically for these enhancements.

Exam Prep Questions

Question 1

> The floating point unit or coprocessor was internally integrated into which Intel microprocessor?
>
> ○ a. Intel 8088
>
> ○ b. Intel 8086
>
> ○ c. Intel 80286
>
> ○ d. Intel 80386
>
> ○ e. Intel 80486

Answer e is correct. The floating point unit or coprocessor was first integrated into the Intel 80486. The unit was disabled in the Intel 80486-SX for marketing reasons but still present.

Question 2

> Which was the first Intel microprocessor to be able to address more than one megabyte of memory ?
>
> ○ a. Intel 8086
>
> ○ b. Intel 80386
>
> ○ c. Intel 80486
>
> ○ d. Intel 80286

Answer d is correct. The Intel 80286 could address 16MB of memory and was the first Intel microprocessor to break the one megabyte limit.

Question 3

> Intel used "SX" to identify microprocessors which did not have integrated coprocessors.
>
> ○ a. True
>
> ○ b. False

False. "SX" was generally used to indicate a microprocessor with reduced functionality. The Intel 80386-SX had an external bus of 16 bits as opposed to 32 bits of the Intel 80386-DX, and the Intel 80486-SX disabled the floating point unit.

Question 4

> Which is true of "Protected mode" operation?
>
> ○ a. Protected mode was introduced in the Intel 80286 microprocessor but not utilized until the release of the 80386.
>
> ○ b. Theoretically, Protected mode allows a program to fail without crashing the system.
>
> ○ c. Protected mode was a diagnostic mode introduced with the Intel 80386 microprocessor.
>
> ○ d. Protected mode is a function of the operating system, not the microprocessor.

Answer b is correct. Protected mode operation was first introduced with the Intel 80286 microprocessor and theoretically allowed multiple programs to run at the same time without affecting each other if one program were to crash.

Question 5

> Clock doubling or "Overdrive" processors speeded the operation of the entire computer and provided exceptional throughput advantages.
>
> ○ a. True
>
> ○ b. False

False. Clock doubling or "Overdrive" processors provided faster CPU operation, but did not affect the speed of the motherboard or other components connected to the CPU. Because of this, the increased speed of the CPU did not always translate to faster system performance.

Question 6

> Level-1 and Level-2 caches were provided to speed CPU operation by reducing the need of the processor to access system RAM. The difference between the two types is that the level-one cache is internal to the processor and the level-two cache is external to the processor.
>
> ○ a. True
>
> ○ b. False

True. The internal L1 cache provided 8K to 16K of fast memory to the processor while the external L2 cache provided 256K or more of memory.

Need To Know More?

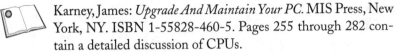 Andrews, Jean: *A+ Exam Prep.* The Coriolis Group, Scottsdale, AZ. ISBN 1-57610-241-6. Pages 87 through 99 cover processors.

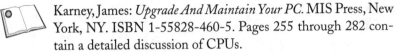 Karney, James: *Upgrade And Maintain Your PC.* MIS Press, New York, NY. ISBN 1-55828-460-5. Pages 255 through 282 contain a detailed discussion of CPUs.

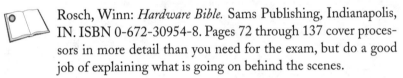 Messmer, Hans-Peter: *The Indispensable PC Hardware Book.* Addison-Wesley, Reading, MA. ISBN 0-201-87697-3. Pages 39 through 390 cover processors in great detail. The information provided here is more than you'll need for the exam. However, this is the resource to consult if you are unclear on any aspect of a CPU or memory.

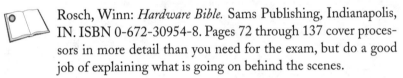 Rosch, Winn: *Hardware Bible.* Sams Publishing, Indianapolis, IN. ISBN 0-672-30954-8. Pages 72 through 137 cover processors in more detail than you need for the exam, but do a good job of explaining what is going on behind the scenes.

Memory

Terms you'll need to understand:

- √ RAM and ROM
- √ Memory address
- √ SIMM, DIMM
- √ DRAM, VRAM, SRAM
- √ EDO
- √ EPROM
- √ Cache
- √ Parity and ECC

Concepts you'll need to master:

- √ The difference between volatile and nonvolatile memory
- √ Cache memory
- √ Read-only and random access memory
- √ Accessing memory
- √ Speed of memory

This section discusses the types of physical memory used by the computer. Later, in a section devoted to DOS and Windows, we examine how the operating system and microprocessors use this memory.

Memory stores data temporarily so that the CPU can locate program instructions, data, or both. A typical instruction might be to store a character or a number in the computer's main memory. Another might be to retrieve that character when it's needed. DOS can use a maximum of 1MB of memory for applications, whereas other operating systems, such as OS/2, Unix, and Windows NT, can use more. The 1MB of memory that DOS can *use*, is different than the memory that DOS and the processor chips can *access*.

ROM—Read-Only Memory

Every computer is equipped with RAM and ROM. RAM (random access memory) is different from ROM mainly because it is *read/write* memory, whereas ROM is *read-only memory*.

RAM and ROM have certain fundamental differences:

➤ ROM chips contain vital, permanently stored information written to them by the manufacturer.

➤ ROM is nonvolatile in that the information remains stored regardless of whether an electrical current is present.

➤ ROM is nonchangeable in that it can't be written over, only read from. This is why it's called a read-only chip. Information on a ROM chip never changes. If an error occurs on the chip, the chip must be replaced.

One way to remember the difference between the two chips is to think of a school classroom with a bulletin board in a glass case and a blackboard on the wall. ROM is like the bulletin board, where hard-copy notes are placed and locked up in the glass case. At the end of the day, the notes haven't been changed in any way, and the next day they are exactly the way they were the day before.

RAM is like the blackboard. Initially, it is blank, but throughout the day, information is repeatedly written to and read from the blackboard. The information on the blackboard is repeatedly erased and new information is written to the same space. If a lot of writing and reading has occurred, there can be a buildup on the blackboard. This buildup is analogous to memory fragments, which can cause computer lock-ups. When you go home for the day, you turn off the lights, erase the blackboard, and shut the door. Whatever data is in RAM when the machine is turned off, goes away forever.

A single letter can really mess you up on the exam if you don't pay close attention. We've seen questions like, "RAM BIOS is used to permanently store instructions for a hardware device: True or False?" (False!) Keep your eyes peeled and remember that RAM sounds like RANdom. RAM is never used in BIOS since the BIOS instructions are permanent.

Programmable ROM

The most common reference to ROM is in connection with ROM BIOS. The instructions that define the motherboard and its installed I/O interfaces can't change, and must accompany the motherboard. However, sometimes the motherboard manufacturer makes changes to the instructions that can fix problems or enhance performance. The formal name for a ROM chip that can't be modified is *mask ROM* (from the chip's manufacturing mask). There are some hybrid ROM chips that do have varying capacity for change. These chips include the following.

PROM

PROM (programmable read-only memory) chips require a special type of machine called a "PROM programmer," or "PROM burner" and can be changed one time. The shipped chip is blank, and the programmer "burns in" specific instructions. From that point, the chip can't be changed.

EPROM

EPROM (erasable programmable ROM) chips use the PROM burner, but can be erased by shining ultraviolet light through a window in the top of the chip. Normal room light contains very little UV light, and EPROMs are popular inside many computers.

EEPROM

EEPROM (electrically erasable programmable ROM) chips can be erased by an electrical charge and written to using slightly higher-than-normal voltage. Additionally, EEPROM can be erased one byte at a time, rather than erasing the entire chip at once with UV light. These chips are often used to store programmable instructions in devices such as printers and other peripherals because the chip can be changed without opening up a casing.

Flash ROM

Flash ROM, sometimes called flash RAM or flash memory, stores data much like the EEPROM but uses a super-voltage charge to erase a block of data (rather than a byte). Flash ROM and EEPROM can perform read/write operations, but can only be erased a certain number of times.

RAM—Random Access Memory

RAM, sometimes referred to as *main memory,* or *main system memory,* is volatile memory. The CPU uses RAM to store data. Applications use RAM to store programming instructions and data. All PCs must have RAM to store the results of processing and data being created or modified. RAM has specific, unique locations called *memory addresses.* The CPU reads and writes information to these memory addresses.

Volatile Vs. Nonvolatile

Volatility is a technical term meaning "not permanent" and "easily changed." The dictionary defines volatile as "evaporating rapidly; passing off readily in the form of vapor."

Information in RAM, being volatile, vanishes when new information is sent to RAM in its place or when the electrical current is removed.

The speed of RAM is measured in nanoseconds (billionths of a second), whereas disk speeds are measured in milliseconds (thousandths of a second). Thus, it's fairly clear that moving data in and out of RAM memory is extremely fast—much faster than moving it to and from a disk.

Typically, a hard disk reads information at 100 reads per second, whereas a floppy disk can read at 10 reads per second. RAM can make one billion reads per second.

RAM Chips

Memory is an essential part of any computer. It is used to store both the program instructions and the data produced by the processor chips. Logically, memory can be viewed as a collection of sequential locations, each with a unique address capable of storing information of a certain size. Generally, the more RAM installed on the motherboard, the more storage room there is for applications and data. This increase in available memory can provide better performance, up to a point. Memory is used by writing data to an address, or reading data from an address.

Random Access Memory is a configuration of memory cells (or addresses) that can temporarily hold data for processing by a CPU. *Random* comes from the CPU's ability to retrieve data from and store data in any individual location (*address*) in any sequence within that memory.

DRAM—Dynamic RAM

In the world of RAM, there are two types of memory devices, differentiated according to the way they store data. These are static RAM (SRAM) and dynamic RAM (DRAM). SRAM can also refer to synchronous RAM, if the chip is being used for burst-mode caching.

Dynamic RAM, the most common type of RAM, is often referred to simply as RAM in the context of PC systems. When you hear a reference to "how much memory" a computer has, the response usually refers to DRAM.

DRAM can hold a charge (data) only for a short time, so it must be *refreshed* periodically. If the cell isn't refreshed, the data is lost—which again, is why it is called volatile.

 Notable features of DRAM include:

➤ Different DRAM chips require different refresh rates.

➤ DRAM is often referred to as "main memory."

DRAM loses its data without being refreshed and so is different than static RAM (discussed later), which can hold data without being refreshed. However, both types are volatile and require some electrical charge to hold data. SRAM usually gets that charge from the motherboard's battery.

Note: SRAM is also becoming more common as main system memory. If it is used this way, the SRAM chips receive current from the main power supply like DRAM.

Synchronous DRAM

Synchronous DRAM (SDRAM), a more recent technology, uses a clock to synchronize a memory chip's input and output signal. The clock is coordinated with the CPU clock so that the timing between the CPU and the memory chips is synchronized. Performance is enhanced by using synchronous DRAM to save time in executing commands and transmitting data. Synchronous DRAM is also used on video cards to move some of the graphics processing out of the main CPU.

VRAM—Video Memory

VRAM chips have a different design in that they have two access paths to the same memory address. It would be as though a redesigned VRAM café had a front door *and* a back door for customers. When the video controller reads memory for information, it accesses an address with one of the paths. When the CPU writes data to memory, it accesses the address from the other path. This extra circuitry requires more physical space, so VRAM chips are about 20 percent larger than DRAM chips. Though they are more expensive to make, VRAM chips can boost video performance by up to 60 percent.

SIMM—Single Inline Memory Module

A memory module is actually a grouping of memory chips (DRAM chips) put onto a printed circuit board. Once the DRAM chips have been formed into the module, or package, the module fits into a socket on the motherboard. The DRAM chips on the circuit board are placed in a line. Depending on how the chips are connected on the circuit board this module is called either a single or dual inline memory module (SIMM or DIMM).

 DRAM chips are grouped together into SIMMs, which are referred to as a chip, but are really a module (a series of chips). The SIMM is a module, whereas DRAM is a chip. Be careful when you read the questions on the exam, so that you don't accidentally agree that a SIMM is a memory chip. A good way to keep the chips separate is to remember that they have "RAM" in their name.

Don't Mix Different Types Of SIMMs

Mixing different types of SIMMs within the same memory bank prevents the CPU from accurately detecting how much memory it has. In this case, the system either will fail to boot or will boot, but fail to recognize or use some of the memory.

You can, however, substitute a SIMM with a different *speed* within the same memory bank, though only if the replacement is equal to or faster than the replaced module.

All memory taken together (from all memory banks) will be set to the speed of the slowest SIMM.

SRAM—Static RAM

L2 memory caches are usually external to the CPU and reside on static RAM (SRAM) chips. Static RAM is extremely fast (as fast as seven to nine nanoseconds and five to six nanoseconds for ultrafast SRAM). Secondary memory caches (Level-2) are usually installed in sizes of 256K or 512K, although SRAM chips are starting to become popular for main memory. Among the features of SRAM:

➤ SRAM is also used for CMOS configuration setups and requires a small amount of electricity provided by a backup battery on the system board to keep its data.

➤ Some SRAM comes in burst-mode format (containing its own clock), making it compatible with the PowerPC processors.

➤ SRAM is used on credit-card memory cards, available in 128K, 256K, 512K, 1MB, 2MB, and 4MB sizes, with battery lives of 10 or more years.

DIMM—Dual Inline Memory Modules

DIMM memory is very similar to SIMM-type memory in that it installs vertically into expansion sockets on the system board. DIMMs are also a line of DRAM chips combined on a circuit board.

The primary differences between the SIMM and the DIMM modules are as follows:

➤ DIMMs have opposing pins on either side of their board that remain electrically isolated to form two separate contacts.

➤ SIMMs have opposing pins on either side of the board, connecting, or tying together, to form a single electrical contact.

➤ DIMMs are used in modern computers that support a 64-bit or wider memory bus (typical of the Pentium and PowerPC processors).

DIP—Dual Inline Package

This DRAM chip was common when memory was soldered directly onto the system board. The pins install into holes that extend into the surface of the circuit board.

DIP switches and jumpers are so common in PCs that a common exam question will ask you for the expanded version of the acronym. DIP is short for dual inline package.

Memory Diagnostics

When a PC runs through the POST (power on self-test), commonly called a "cold boot," memory integrity is one of the first things tested. Memory integrity can be checked in two ways:

➤ Parity checking

➤ Error correction code (ECC) checking

Parity Checking

Parity is the state of either oddness or evenness assigned to a given byte of data. *Parity checking* is the way a computer uses a special set of logical rules and chips to make decisions based on the parity (state) of a particular byte. The *parity circuit* (the combined process) puts a byte in memory, then reads the byte from memory. If what it reads matches what it sent, the memory cell is okay. The parity circuit is what tells the computer how to remember what it sent, in order to compare what it reads. Until recently, parity checking has been the most common way to check the ability of memory cells to accurately hold data.

Parity works by adding one bit to every byte of data, resulting in nine bits. Remember that a byte is already eight bits. The value of the bit (1 or 0) is determined at the time the data is written to DRAM. The 1 or 0 is assigned to the byte depending on whether the byte is made up of an odd or even number of 1s.

 Remember that computers think in binary bits and bytes. The Binary computer language uses "words" composed of 1s and 0s.

In the parity method of checking memory integrity, a single *parity bit* is stored in DRAM along with every eight bits of data. The two types of parity are:

➤ Odd parity

➤ Even parity

Odd/Even Parity

If a given byte has an even number of 1s (even parity), the parity bit is turned on. In technical terminology "on" is represented by the number 1. If that byte has an odd number of 1s (odd parity), the parity bit is turned off (represented by 0). The parity bit and its corresponding byte are written to memory. When the CPU calls on memory for the data, the data is intercepted by the parity circuit before it gets to the CPU. In odd parity checking, the parity circuit reads the parity bit and the following decision process takes place:

➤ If the parity bit is 0, the system checks to see whether an odd number of 1s is present. If so, the data is considered valid and the parity bit stripped from the data. The remaining eight bits are passed through to the CPU.

➤ If the parity bit is 1, the system checks to see whether an even number of 1s are present. If so the data is considered invalid, and the circuit generates a parity error.

Even parity works the same way, except the meaning of the 1 or 0 parity bit is reversed. The difference in even parity is that when the parity circuit sees a 0, the system checks to see whether an *even* number of 1s is present.

For exam purposes, remember that parity checking uses an extra bit attached to a byte. The extra bit is set to either 1 or 0, depending on whether the byte is made up of an even or odd number of 1s or 0s.

Memory Controller

A PC must have memory to store data resulting from calculations and logical processes. An essential component of every PC is a *memory controller,* located between the CPU and the memory itself. The memory controller performs the following functions:

➤ Oversees the movement of data in and out of memory

➤ Determines which type (if any) of data-integrity checking is supported

Which type of data-integrity checking is supported is determined by the person purchasing the computer. The customer can choose ECC (error correction code) parity checking, or nothing, depending mainly on cost benefits. Because of the cost associated with checking for memory accuracy:

➤ High-end computers (e.g., file servers) typically use an ECC-capable memory controller.

➤ Midrange desktop business computers typically are configured to support parity checking.

➤ Low-cost home computers often have nonparity memory (no parity checking, or fake parity).

Note: Parity checking is limited in the sense that it can only detect an error. It can't repair or correct the error because the circuit can't detect which one of the eight bits is invalid. Additionally, if multiple bits are wrong but the result is odd or even parity, the circuit will pass the invalid data. (The odds of this happening are very small, and parity errors rarely occur.)

Fake Or Disabled Parity

Some computer manufacturers will install a less expensive "fake" parity chip that simply sends a 1 or a 0 to the parity circuit to supply parity on the basis of which parity state is expected. Regardless of whether the parity is valid, the computer is fooled into thinking that *everything* is valid. This method means there is no connection whatsoever between the parity bit being sent and the associated byte of data.

A more common way to reduce the cost of SIMMs is to simply disable the parity completely, or build a computer without any parity checking capability installed. Some of today's PCs are being shipped this way and make no reference to the disabled or missing parity. The SIMMs must be specified by the purchaser as having parity capabilities and the motherboard must be configured to turn parity on.

ECC—Error Correction Code

ECC, which uses a special *algorithm* (mathematical logic), works with the memory controller to add *error correction code* bits to each data bit when they're sent to memory. When data is requested by the CPU, the memory controller decodes the error correction bits and determines the validity of their attached data bit. The main difference between parity and ECC is that:

➤ ECC is capable of detecting and correcting one-bit errors.

➤ Some ECC, depending on the type of memory controller, can also detect the unusual two-, three-, and four-bit memory errors.

Until recently, ECC was used mainly in high-end, expensive computers. Intel has been working on chipsets that support both ECC and parity (see the following discussion of EOS).

Remember that ECC can *detect* multi-bit errors, but can *correct* only single-bit errors. Parity checking can detect that the overall byte coming out of memory doesn't match what was sent into memory, but can't correct anything.

Why Memory Becomes Corrupted

Most DRAM chips in SIMMs or DIMMs require a parity bit for two reasons:

➤ Alpha particle strikes can disturb memory cells with ionizing radiation, resulting in lost data.

➤ When reading DRAM, the cell's storage mechanism shares its charge with the bit line through a transistor. This creates a small voltage differential that can be sensed during read access and influenced by other, nearby, bit-line voltages along with other electrical noise.

EDO—Extended Data Output

Technically, data is stored in a memory address as an electrical charge. If a charge is present, it represents a binary 1. The CPU charges an address when it writes data to memory. Until EDO memory, the way data was read from memory involved an electrical discharge at the address. A complex process (using a lot of RAM) would charge and discharge addresses throughout the memory every time the CPU sent a write or read instruction.

The time it takes between the discharge of electricity from a particular location, until that location is capable of holding a new charge is called a *wait state* (typically 10 nanoseconds). EDO (extended data output) memory allows a memory address to hold a piece of data for multiple reads. In other words, rather than reading a data bit by the discharge process, EDO memory uses a different method. EDO memory doesn't discharge a memory address until a new bit of data is written to that particular location.

EDO memory is faster than previous types of memory because it doesn't produce as many wait states. If a process uses the same bit of data many times, the computer doesn't have to charge an address, discharge the address, and wait for the address to become usable again. Because of this, some manufacturers claim that a computer with EDO memory doesn't require an SRAM secondary cache. However, even with EDO, overall system performance can benefit from an included L1 and L2 cache.

Theoretically, EDO RAM should be able to boost the system's performance by nearly 60 percent, but in fact the performance boost is closer to 15 percent.

Cache (RAM) Memory

Cache (pronounced *cash*) is derived from the French word *cacher*, to hide.

A cache attempts to predict which instruction or information is about to be used. This is done using an algorithm that is based on probabilities and proximity. For example, when you open a book and look at, say, page 22, logic dictates that you'll look at the top of the page; then at the middle of the page, then at the bottom of the page, and then at the top of the next page.

A cache is like an expectation. For example, if you expect to see a piece of information and that information is right beside you, you can access it much faster than you could have had you been surprised to find that you needed it and then had to look for it. That's how computer caching operates.

Cache memory is a type of high-speed memory that is designed to speed up the processing of memory instructions by the CPU. Typically (as in L2) a memory cache is a separate SRAM chip that runs much faster than a DRAM chip. Because of this, the CPU can access cache memory much faster than it can main memory. For example, on a 100 MHz system board:

➤ Cache memory runs at about nine nanoseconds.

➤ Main memory runs at about 80 nanoseconds.

Caching is also commonly used in Web browsers. Here, pages that you call up are stored on the local hard drive, in a cache *file*. This type of file contains information that the computer expects to find next in a process. In addition, linked pages are downloaded so that they reside on the hard drive, where they can be accessed much faster than by downloading.

Cache Memory Controller

A cache memory controller contains the algorithms (logical instructions) that make the predictions as to which instructions will be needed next by the CPU. Generally, the next instruction will be the adjacent one, and the controller places that instruction in cache memory. When the CPU looks for the next instruction, the chances are good that it will find it in cache memory faster than in main memory.

The Memory Hierarchy And Caches

Because memory size is always increasing, more time is needed to decode increasingly wider addresses and to find the information stored in the ever-increasing size of the storage device. The strategy used to remedy this problem is called *memory hierarchy*. Memory hierarchy works because of the way that memory is stored in addresses, that is, in terms of the proximity of one instruction or data byte to the next instruction or data byte.

A hierarchical memory structure contains many levels of memory that usually are defined by access speed. A small amount of very fast memory (SRAM) is usually allocated adjacent to the CPU to match up with the speed and memory bus of the CPU. As the distance from the

CPU increases, the performance and size requirements for the memory are relaxed. Parts of the memory hierarchy include registers, caches, main memory, and disk.

When a memory reference is made, the processor looks in the memory at the top of the hierarchy. If the desired data is in the higher hierarchy, it wins. Otherwise, a so-called miss occurs, at which time the requested information must be brought up from a lower level of hierarchy.

Typically, memory space is divided into chunks, or blocks. At the cache level, a chunk is called a *cache block* or a *cache line*. At the main memory level, a chunk is referred as a *memory page*. A miss in the cache (i.e., the desired data isn't in the cache memory) is called a *cache miss*. A miss in the main memory is called a *page fault*. When a miss occurs, the whole block of memory containing the requested missing information is brought in from the lower, slower hierarchical level. Eventually, the information is looked for on the hard disk—the slowest storage media. If the current memory hierarchy level is full when a miss occurs, some existing blocks or pages must be removed for a new one to be brought in.

SMARTDRV.SYS and SMARTDRV.EXE are DOS program utilities that provide disk caching. The efficiency of a cache is reported as its *hit ratio*. To send an efficiency report to the screen, issue the command **SMARTDRV /S** from a DOS command prompt.

L1 And L2 Cache Memory

We have seen how technology moves toward consolidating components whenever a speed or cost efficiency might be improved. Super I/O (input/output) chipsets have combined different adapters into a single package, and processors have moved in the same direction. At one time, caches were outside the chips, but new developments paved the way to move the cache inside the chip. Caches are referred to as:

➤ Internal (inside the CPU housing)

➤ External (outside the CPU housing)

Modern computers might contain several sublevels of cache. For example, the Intel 80486 and Pentium systems have a small, built-in 16K cache on the CPU called L1 (Level-1), or *primary cache*. Another level of cache is L2 (Level-2), or *secondary cache*. The L2 cache is a separate, integrated unit of memory one step lower to the L1 cache in the memory hierarchy.

Several chips combined into a single-chip *package* are sometimes referred to as an MCM, or multi-chip module. The L1 and L2 cache package is a multi-chip module in that the two types of memory are physically separate, but are combined into an integrated package of components. The L1 (in the CPU) and L2 (separate chip) memory isn't on a single, integrated circuit board like a SIMM, but the MCM is a module in that the two memory components are installed as one feature.

As the L1 and L2 caches are a built-in module, there could potentially be a level-3 (L3) cache on the motherboard, where the CPU and memory chips reside.

Cache memory generally is categorized as follows:

➤ L1 (Level-1), or primary cache

➤ L2 (Level-2), or secondary cache, usually either 256K SRAM or 512K

 Be sure to remember that primary (L1) cache is internal to the processor, and secondary (L2) cache is external. Up until the 486 family of chips, the CPU had no internal cache, so *any* external cache was designated as the primary memory cache. The 80486 introduced a 16K internal L1 cache. The Pentium family added an external L2 SRAM secondary cache of 256K or 512K.

Exam Prep Questions

Question 1

> AT system boards use random access memory to store system settings and power that memory with a battery to prevent data loss at power down.
>
> ○ a. True
>
> ○ b. False

False. RAM memory is volatile and loses all of its data without a source of power. AT system boards commonly use nonvolatile CMOS to store system settings. CMOS memory uses very little current and can be powered for extended periods of inactivity by a small battery on the system board.

Question 2

> SIMMs of different capacity and speed can be used on a system board provided each bank of memory has the same capacity SIMMs and the speed of the SIMMs meets or exceeds processor and system board requirements.
>
> ○ a. True
>
> ○ b. False

True. SIMMs of different capacity can be used on a system board provided they are placed in different memory banks. The speed of the memory should always exceed board and processor requirements.

Question 3

> DIMMs and SIMMs are interchangeable, provided speed and capacity requirements are observed.
>
> ○ a. True
>
> ○ b. False

False. SIMMs and DIMMs look similar and both use edge connectors. However, DIMMS use both sides of the connector to support a 64-bit or wider memory bus.

Question 4

> Parity chips on SIMMs no longer provide a useful purpose and
> have been largely removed.
>
> ○ a. True
> ○ b. False

False. Parity chips allow memory to be tested during the POST and moni-
tored during the computer's operation. Some manufacturers have eliminated
them or bypassed their function to cut costs. This allows less expensive SIMMs
to be used, but at the expense of reliability.

Question 5

> Intel 486 and Pentium microprocessors integrate some memory into
> the processor to improve throughput. What is this memory called?
>
> ○ a. Processor resident pipeline
> ○ b. L2 cache
> ○ c. Pipeline cache
> ○ d. L1 cache

Answer d is correct. Intel 486 and Pentium processors have a small amount of
memory directly integrated directly into the chip to increase throughput. This
memory is called an L1 cache. Often this memory is used in conjunction with
an additional dedicated SRAM memory chip on the system board. The second
chip is called an L2 cache or secondary cache.

Question 6

> Which of the following choices best describes what is meant by
> cache memory:
>
> ○ a. A place where instructions are stored about the opera-
>   tions of a device or application
> ○ b. Extended memory that can be made accessible with the
>   SMARTDRV /ON command
> ○ c. Memory that holds applications and data that the CPU
>   isn't running
> ○ d. Memory that holds data that the CPU will search first

The correct answer is d. Instructions for the operation of a device must be available every time the computer is turned on. These instructions are stored in non-volatile ROM BIOS chips. SMARTDRV is a program utility that can use part of a logical drive as a cache, and has nothing to do with making extended memory accessible. There is no /ON switch for the program. Memory containing applications and data is called system memory or main memory, regardless of whether or not a loaded application is running. The CPU runs an application that creates or modifies data.

The CPU will look in fast cache memory first, and if it fails to find the necessary data it will look in main memory. If it fails to find what it needs in main memory, the CPU will look on the disk.

Need To Know More?

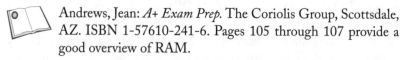 Andrews, Jean: *A+ Exam Prep*. The Coriolis Group, Scottsdale, AZ. ISBN 1-57610-241-6. Pages 105 through 107 provide a good overview of RAM.

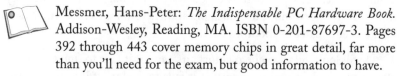 Messmer, Hans-Peter: *The Indispensable PC Hardware Book*. Addison-Wesley, Reading, MA. ISBN 0-201-87697-3. Pages 392 through 443 cover memory chips in great detail, far more than you'll need for the exam, but good information to have.

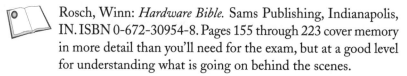 Minasi, Mark: *The Complete PC Upgrade and Maintenance Guide*. Sybex Network Press, San Francisco, CA. ISBN 0-7821-1956-5. Pages 361 through 398 present memory from the perspective of a repair technician.

Rosch, Winn: *Hardware Bible*. Sams Publishing, Indianapolis, IN. ISBN 0-672-30954-8. Pages 155 through 223 cover memory in more detail than you'll need for the exam, but at a good level for understanding what is going on behind the scenes.

Peripherals: Input Devices

Terms you'll need to understand:

√   Resistor, capacitor, ohms

√   Electrostatic discharge

√   Mice and input devices

√   Pixels, CCD, dpi

√   Cascaded IRQ

Concepts you'll need to master:

√   Hexadecimal numbering

√   IRQs and interrupt lines

√   DMA and DMA channels

√   Electricity, voltage potentials, and circuits

√   Polling, or scanning for input

√   Image resolution in pixels and dots per inch

√   Optical resolution

Human beings use computers to do work, the result of which must be understandable to other human beings. Machines communicate and process in binary machine language, but the results of all that processing must be turned into something that people can understand. Not only that, but the tools that people need to communicate with the computer must be designed for the people who use it.

On one side of the equation are the ways that people talk with machines. This requires *input devices,* such as keyboards, mice, scanners, and modems. The other side of the equation is the way that machines talk to people. This requires *output devices,* such as printers, video displays, modems, and speakers. If the motherboard and the CPU make up the basic computer, anything other than these is a *peripheral device* of some kind.

Finally, because RAM doesn't retain information when the power's turned off, there must be some way to store work in progress, finished work, and the ways of getting that work done (i.e., applications). This requires *storage devices.*

For our purposes, we separate the motherboard, CPU, and processing from everything outside that core system. All devices that can make a connection to the CPU are called peripheral devices. Commonly, only devices that aren't critical to the operations of a computer are peripherals. Although a monitor, keyboard, and mouse are considered part of the system, for now we address them as peripheral devices.

Getting a signal into the computer (i.e., to the CPU for processing) generally involves some sort of input device. Although operating systems and applications software can be considered on both the input and the output side of the equation, we don't commonly call software a peripheral. Hardware-based input devices include:

➤ Keyboards

➤ Mice, trackballs, light pens, digitizing tablets, and other pointing devices

➤ Scanners

➤ Touch-screen video screens

➤ Modems

IRQs—Interrupt Requests

Before we go any further, we want to take a moment to go over IRQs, DMAs, and how computers use a base-16 numbering system (hexadecimal). We've seen that when the CPU is busy with a process, any new request for processing must interrupt the process already in progress. These interruptions are provided for by the ROM BIOS on both the motherboard and on many devices. The operating system also understands interrupts and uses part of low memory to store something called the *interrupt vector table*.

If you think of the CPU as the Wizard of Oz, then IRQ (interrupt request) lines are like an 8- or a 15-lane yellow brick road. To take pressure off the CPU, IBM created a chip called an *interrupt controller*, which is analogous to that weird gatekeeper to the Emerald City.

When a piece of hardware sends an interrupt to the busy CPU, it tries to interrupt whatever the CPU is doing by sending an IRQ down its own IRQ line. An IRQ is a signal from a piece of hardware (e.g., a mouse) indicating that it needs the CPU to do something. The IRQ signals (Dorothy and pals) run along the IRQ lines (the yellow brick road) to an interrupt controller (that bizarre gatekeeper), which assigns priorities to incoming IRQs (puts them in the waiting room) and then delivers them to the CPU (the wizard).

Because the interrupt controller expects signals from only one hardware device per IRQ line, an *IRQ conflict* occurs when two devices try to use the same IRQ line, much like two cars using the same lane at the same time. When that happens, computers usually crash; the gatekeeper loses his mind, and you're left in the poppy fields! This is why assigning IRQs to new hardware as you install it is so important—and why it can be such a pain when it goes wrong. A technical term for *pain* is *major aggravation*.

The original PC and XT interrupt controller chip could handle eight IRQs at once. The AT motherboard (by daisy-chaining two chips), can handle 15 IRQs at once. All in all, there are 16 IRQ lines—IRQ 0 through IRQ 15.

Make a note that the AT controllers began using interrupts 9-15, leaving the XT controllers the 0-8 lines. Because of this, the old IRQ 2 is often borrowed by the new IRQ 9 using something called "cascading." You should know the term for the exam.

Hexadecimal Numbering

The decimal, hexadecimal, and binary numbering systems all start with zero. Our habit is to think of the "first" of something as being number 1, but in the world of computers and technology you'll need to become accustomed to that first thing being number 0.

If you remember your high school math, the number of digits that can fit into the units (ones) column is called the base. Decimal comes from the Latin "ten" and allows 10 digits in the ones column (0-9). Decimal numbering is also called *base-10*. When you have more than 10 digits, you cross over to the tens column.

In regular counting, we would start with a one and go to a nine. When we added one more number, we would put a zero in the ones column, and a one in the tens column, making a 10. In computer math, we start with zero. When we get to the end of the allowed numbers in the ones column we go back to the beginning, put down a zero, and move a one to the tens column.

Binary Numbers

Binary refers to *base-2* numbers, in that there are only two units before you begin using the tens column. In base-2 numbering, you can only have a zero and a one in the ones column. There is no two, and you have to go to the tens column instead. One moves to the left of the zero after two digits, just as one moves to the left of zero after 10 digits in base-10 numbers (decimal).

There's actually no 10 symbol in decimal numbering either. The word we use to describe a one in the tens column and zero in the ones column is *ten*. Ten is the same word in any base of numbering, but we get to that 10 by more or fewer numbers in the ones column. In base-3 numbers we would count zero, one, two, ten.

Text counting in binary would be: zero, one, ten, eleven, one hundred, one hundred and one, one hundred and ten, one hundred and eleven, and one thousand. The same sequence in symbols would be 0, 1, 10, 11, 100, 101, 110, 111, and 1000, respectively. Because binary has only ones and zeros, there's no such thing as a two. The two is replaced by what we think of as a 10.

The largest eight-bit binary number is 11111111, which is made up of eight "ones," and converts to 255 in decimal. By amazing coincidence, the last character in the ASCII keyboard character translation table, is 255—a blank space. On the other hand, decimal/binary zero is also a space, so maybe it's not that incredible.

Base-16 Numbering

Hexadecimal (hex) is *base-16* numbering, where numbers in the ones column must go beyond 10 digits all the way to 16 digits. This requires the use of letters, since decimal numbering (base-10) has only 10 available digits: 0, 1, 2, 3, 4, 5, 6, 7, 8, 9, before making a 10. Hexadecimal (often abbreviated as Hex, H, or h) adds A, B, C, D, E, and F.

Counting a full sequence would be 0, 1, 2, 3, 4, 5, 6, 7, 8, 9, (no ten), A (replaces 10), B (11), C, D, E, and F. The F represents the "tens" column crossover point, just like the nine does in decimal numbers. In this case, 15 (the F) is the sixteenth digit and the last that can fit in the ones column. Don't forget that zero was the first digit.

Following F (in base-16) would come a "tens unit," so the next number is 10. The sequence continues as 11, 12, 13, 14, 15, 16, 17, 18, 19, 1A, 1B, 1C, 1D, 1E, 1F, and then another tens unit, making 20.

Hexadecimal numbering allows for cramming more information into a smaller space. For example, the decimal 255 (three bits) becomes FFh (two bits) in Hex. Observe that the small "h" following the number references this number as a hexadecimal number.

 Be sure to remember that computer memory addresses are usually written in hexadecimal notation. Hex notation can be 10h, 10H, &H10, or &h10, where the first two formats are most common. Therefore, decimal 255 is typically written as FFh in hexadecimal format.

DMA Channels

There are a number of semi-intelligent chips working together with the CPU. In the past, these chips have been outside the CPU, but they're beginning to be incorporated into the CPU chipset (super I/O chip) more frequently. The interrupt controller, which handles IRQs, is one of these chips. Another peripheral chip is the *DMA controller* (direct memory access). Like IRQs, DMA channels are limited in number, and you can only allocate one channel to one device.

The CPU is extremely fast, and until recently it calculated far faster than applications could handle the results. However, the CPU could easily be loaded down if it were to send data about storing something on a hard drive and then had to wait around for the very slow hard drive to report back. This movement of data from slow disk to fast memory ordinarily would need to pass through some very small memory registers in the CPU. To offload this sort of drudge work and avoid bottlenecks in processing, the DMA controller was developed.

The DMA controller is like a highway bypass. It bypasses the CPU registers and moves information directly into and out of RAM (thus "direct memory"). The DMA controller chip is capable of taking over control of the system, but first it must request control from the microprocessor. When this happens the CPU makes itself appear as though it has been removed from the circuit.

When the hard drive needs to access RAM for addresses or instructions, those requests don't have to interrupt the CPU. Fewer interruptions means more work (just like in real life) and better system performance.

Originally, there was only one DMA controller on a motherboard. The system worked so well that a second one was added. Each controller allows four channels, and today we have eight DMA channels available on most systems.

Basic Electronics

Before we move into keyboards, this is a good place to review some of the essential elements of electricity. The 1998 A+ exam has some questions relating to your understanding of basic electricity and you should know about the following terms and devices:

➤ Voltage

➤ Amperage

➤ Ohms

➤ Resistors

➤ Capacitors

➤ Multimeters

Electricity

Electricity is actually a flow of electrons. The electrons can be flowing in one direction (direct current, DC) or changing direction back and forth (alternating current, AC). Both types of flow have unique benefits. Voltage is a measure of the pressure pushing electrons through a medium such as a wire and is often called "potential." Current is the actual number of electrons moving through wire and is measured in "amps." Lastly, "watts" are the product of volts multiplied by amps and are often called a measure of work.

 You won't need to be overly concerned with the definition of electrical measurements, but you do need to be familiar with the terms as outlined above.

Electrons repel each other, which is why a device or substance holding an abundance of electrons will discharge to a device or material with few electrons. When you rub your feet across a wool carpet, you can build up a charge of electrons in yourself that will discharge to a doorknob when you touch it. If you see a spark, the discharge was at over 650 volts, which brings up two important facts. First, as little as 35 volts can destroy the semiconductors used in computers. That's right, you would not even feel the spark that destroyed a $200 CPU! This is why electrostatic discharge (ESD) is a concern, and must be prevented while handling components. Secondly, it is current as measured in amps, that is of the most danger to life forms (that's you). You can zap the doorknob all day long with static electricity at 650+ volts from your finger, but short out a 12V car battery with your body, and you may not get up! That is why old electricians say, "Volts jolt, mills [milliamps] kill."

> *Note: All technicians know they should ground themselves while working on computers. There are many ESD kits available that provide safe, efficient grounding. However, to avoid the cost of an ESD kit, some young technicians have been known to ground themselves with a metal strap (few old technicians have participated in this practice). Bad idea! ESD kits have a resistor in the grounding strap to limit current flow in the event of a short. A metal strap is a perfect conductor and in the event of a short, your body is part of the path.*

Basic Electrical Components

There are hundreds of basic electrical components, but fortunately only two will be present on the exam: resistors and capacitors.

Resistors

Resistors resist the flow of electricity and are measured in ohms. Some resistors, called potentiometers or "pots," can vary resistance. A good example of a potentiometer is the volume control on a radio. The volume control can be turned to vary resistance, which directly affects the current flowing to the speakers, and as such controls the volume.

Capacitors

Capacitors store a quantity of electrons for a short period of time. Large capacitors, as used in power supplies, can store a huge charge and are capable of delivering a nasty shock even after the power cord has been disconnected. We have seen the tip of a screwdriver vaporized by accidentally shorting the terminals of a capacitor. Replace the word "screwdriver" with "finger" and you can see why power supplies are given a great deal of respect.

Multimeters

Again, there are hundreds of test instruments. Fortunately you will only be asked about multimeters on the A+ exam. You will not be tested on the use of a multimeter, but you will need to know what it is.

At one time there were individual meters to measure electrical values; voltmeters measured electrical potential, ohmmeters measured resistance, and so on. Often one instrument was used for direct current and a different one was needed for alternating current. Today, most of these instruments have been combined into one instrument called a multimeter. Most multimeters are small, portable, and can measure ohms, volts, and amps for both direct current and alternating current. They are simply the most versatile test instrument you can have.

Keyboards

Arguably, the most important peripheral component is the keyboard. Without a keyboard there's not much anyone can do with a computer unless it's a remote terminal, and even then the computer controlling the remote must have a keyboard. Most PCs check to see whether a keyboard is attached during the POST process and generate a keyboard error message if a keyboard can't be found. We discuss the POST at length in Chapter 8.

Warning: Don't Fry The Keyboard!

Always turn the computer *off* before plugging in or unplugging a keyboard. Failing to do so can seriously damage the motherboard because the computer is constantly scanning for the state of the keyboard.

A keyboard has a set of keys with language symbols for the human operator. When an operator presses a key, a microprocessor in the keyboard interprets the signal generated as a digital code that can be sent to the computer. Depending on how an electronic signal is generated by the key, there are two basic types of keyboards: switches and capacitive.

Switch Technology

Most computers use a mechanical switch for every key on the keyboard. If the switch fails, the key must be replaced. The switch makes a momentary mechanical connection and sends a signal to the keyboard's microprocessor. The keys are located in a grid called a *keyboard matrix;* when a key is pressed, the keyboard processor identifies it by its matrix location. The processor can also determine how long a key has been pressed and, with a small 16-byte buffer, can handle multiple key presses.

Once the key and the press have been identified, the processor converts this information into a *scan code*. Each key has its own code for both the depression and the key-press combinations (e.g., Ctrl+Home and Shift+B). Common varieties of key switches are:

➤ Pure mechanical

➤ Foam element

➤ Rubber dome

➤ Membrane

Debouncing

Most keys will bounce somewhat when you press them, leading to several high-speed contracts (in mechanical and dome-type switches). Keyboards also generate some amount of electrical noise whenever you press a key, which the CPU could interpret as something you meant to do. To clean up the noise, and to help the keyboard processor determine real key presses from noise, the processor constantly scans the keyboard, looking at the state of every key. This constant scanning is why you should never plug a keyboard in or unplug it while the power is on.

Typically, debouncing waits for two scans before deciding that a key is legitimately depressed. Usually key bounce is far faster than a human being can press a key twice.

Pure Mechanical

This is exactly what it sounds like: a purely mechanical switch with metal contacts and a spring. A small clip and spring combination provides an audible feedback sound of a "click" along with some resistance feedback. Mechanical switches are durable, usually self-cleaning, and normally have a life of around 20 million keystrokes (making them second in longevity to the capacitive switch). The tactile and audible feedback help touch typists.

Foam Element

Many older keyboards, such as the Keytronics brand and others, use a switch that is based on a mechanism using a plunger, foam, and foil. The key cap has a spring beneath it and a plastic stem reaching down through the keyboard faceplate. A piece of compressible foam is attached at the bottom of the stem, and a foil contact is attached under the foam. Contacts on the keyboard circuit board are closed when the foil bridges them. The spring under the key cap pushes the key back up after the key press.

The foam reduces bounce but at the same time gives the keyboard a "mushy" feel that tends to hinder touch typists. These keyboards sometimes resort to sending a clicking sound to the PC speaker to provide audible feedback.

The main problem with the foam switch is that the foil becomes dirty with corrosion, leading to intermittent key strikes. However, they can be disassembled and cleaned, or the foil can be replaced.

Rubber Dome

This improvement on the foam element switch replaces the spring with a rubber dome, similar to half of a handball with a carbon button contact on the underside of the dome. The carbon resists corrosion better than the foil of the foam switch. When the key is pressed, the dome begins to collapse, then it "snaps through" like the hardball. This provides tactile feedback while pushing the carbon contact down to a pair of contacts on the circuit board. Releasing the key allows the rubber to re-form, pushing the key back up. An additional benefit is that the dome forms a seal, protecting the contacts from dust and dirt.

There are few moving parts in a rubber dome switch, making it reliable, inexpensive, and therefore popular. The only problem is that they don't provide enough tactile feedback for the touch typist.

Membrane Sheet

A simplified version of the rubber dome, the membrane switch places all the keys together on what looks like a single-sheet rubber dome. This limits key travel, making membrane switches impractical for touch typists. However, because the keys and membrane are sealed together, it makes the keyboard practically spill- and dust-proof.

Membrane keyboards are used in commercial and industrial environments in which simple data entry is the only operation (e.g., cash registers).

Capacitive Technology

Capacitive switches are the most expensive keyboards. They're the only non-mechanical keyboards currently in use. Capacitive switch keyboards last longer and resist dust and dirt even better than the rubber dome keyboards. Additionally, they offer the highest level of tactile feedback of any switch.

The capacitive switch doesn't rely on metal contacts; rather, it puts two plastic plates inside a switch housing that is designed to sense changes in the capacitance of a circuit. The upper plate is connected to the key plunger (stem); as the key moves downward, the distance between the two plates changes the capacitance. This change is detected by the keyboard's circuitry.

Usually, a mechanism provides tactile feedback and a strong click when the upper plate crosses a center point. The click and the sense of movement provided by the over-center point make these keyboards exceptionally well suited for touch typists. However, they are expensive.

Because of the enclosed housing and the lack of metal contacts, the capacitive switch is essentially corrosion free and immune to dust and dirt. The switch is highly resistant to bounce because not a single strike is produced by closing a contact. They are the most durable keyboard, being rated around 25 million or more keystrokes.

Keyboard/Mouse Connectors

The two basic types of connectors for keyboard cables are five-pin DIN (AT style) and six-pin mini-DIN (PS/2 style). As the cost of keyboards is low, a customer might decide simply to replace it if it fails.

IBM brand-name enhanced keyboards use a cable that plugs into the keyboard with an SDL (shielded data link). The other end plugs into the PC, making cable replacement easy. Until recently, most other keyboards have required that you open the keyboard case to access the other end of the cable. Some new keyboards offer a connector to the keyboard case, similar to a telephone connector.

If you always remember that not much in the computer industry is consistent, you can generally differentiate the two connectors by the motherboard form factors that they connect with. Regardless of how one end attaches to the keyboard case, the other end usually plugs into the PC with either:

➤ Five-pin DIN connectors (usually connected to AT and Baby-AT motherboards)

➤ Six-pin mini-DIN (PS/2-style) connectors (usually connected to LPX low-profile PCs)

The only way to really be sure is to look at the connection socket on the computer itself.

Mice And Trackball Devices

People might think that the mouse was invented and developed by Apple. In fact, it was invented in 1964 at Stanford University and then was applied by Xerox to an experimental computer system called the Alto.

Xerox didn't think there was much money to be made from so-called X-Y position indicator for a display system technology (along with graphic interfaces, laser printing, and small computer networks). Therefore, in 1979, Apple had a chance to both popularize the mouse and take most of the innovative scientists away from Xerox. The story of how Xerox pretty much gave away most of its modern computer industry technology is legendary.

Apple's Lisa computer was really the first system that capitalized on mouse technology, but it listed for $10,000, so we had to wait a while for the Macintosh. From that point on, the PC/Mac argument began, but mice became a standard part of the PC.

How A Basic Mouse Works

Inside a mouse or trackball, two thin rollers are set at a right angle to each other. The rollers are attached to a notched wheel mechanism called an *encoder*. The rollers touch the rubberized ball; as the ball moves, the friction turns the rollers and therefore the encoder.

The encoder wheels have very small notches on their edges and fine contact points where they touch the wall of the mouse. By calculating the number of times a contact is made from both encoders, the system can calculate where to put the pointer or cursor on the screen.

Types Of Mice

Mice come in many shapes and sizes, but essentially a mouse is a case with a rolling ball underneath it. Turning it upside down, as a case with a ball on top, makes it into a *trackball*. For convenience we use the term *mouse*, but the following discussion applies to trackballs as well. With the mouse, the case moves the ball. With the trackball, the case stays in one place and your fingers move the ball.

Both a mouse and a trackball have:

➤ A case that fits in the hand

➤ A roller ball that translates movement

➤ Control buttons (typically two, but possibly one or three)

Generally, a mouse or a trackball requires some sort of software program (a device driver) to tell either the operating system or an application how to relate the physical hardware movement to an on-screen pointer. Either the device driver is loaded (installed) with special software or it is built into the operating system (e.g., OS/2 and Windows 95).

How a mouse tracks the movement of the ball distinguishes types of mice physically. A basic mouse is mechanical in that the encoder's wheels and contacts are metal and make physical movements.

Optical

An optical mouse has no moving parts, and it works in conjunction with a reflective mouse pad. As the mouse moves, a beam of light bounces from the inside of the casing to the reflective pad and then back onto a sensor inside the mouse. The sensor calculates the changes in the light beam to define the X-Y coordinates of the screen cursor.

Optomechanical

These mice are a hybrid of mechanical and optical mice. They use a rubber ball, but instead of contacts with the encoder they use a photo-interrupter disk. The X-Y calculations are performed by counting the interruptions to a beam of light rather than by making contacts with a mechanical wire.

 The serial cable for a mouse can be any length, but usually it's between four and six feet. The cable also provides the small amount of power required by the mouse. The connector interface can be done in one of four ways:

➤ Serial connector

➤ Dedicated motherboard mouse connector

➤ Combination serial and PS/2 motherboard port

➤ Expansion card interface (bus mouse)

Scanners

By now, you should be thinking of *input* as anything that sends or helps one send information to the CPU. We sometimes think of input devices as being only mice or keyboards, but suppose you want to send a picture to the hard drive? To do this, information must be sent to the CPU through an adapter interface; the DMA controller likely will take over some of the details of transferring data to the disk because it's good at that sort of thing.

Simply stated, a scanner is a device that converts an analog image—a pattern—to digital information. On the other hand, a photocopier or a camera transfers an analog image to paper (still in analog form) or to film, respectively. An image can be a graphic, an alpha character, a bar code, a fingerprint, a retina, or any other pattern stored on a solid material.

Sending a picture to the hard drive is another way of getting data into the system. Because the scanner is off the motherboard, but used for bringing data into the system, it too is an input peripheral device. Scanners invariably require some sort of expansion card or interface. Some scanners use a SCSI interface and work with an existing parallel port, though this often means a reduction in the speed of scanning.

Scanners capture an image optically by using a light source and capturing the reflection. Some scanners capture a magnetic pattern. MICR (Magnetic Ink Character Recognition) is based on magnetic information. Other specialized scanners capture transparencies using a light source, but don't capture reflection. A slide-transparency scanner works this way.

CCDs And Resolution

A typical scanner uses a series of photosensitive cells called CCDs (charge-coupled devices) mounted in a fixed row. Each CCD registers whether light is present. Therefore, the point (or spot) of light being registered by one CCD is the pixel equivalent of a dot on a piece of paper. The smaller the physical size of the CCD in the scanner, the more *dots per inch* of image can be acquired. An important quality measurement for a scanner is its resolution in optical dots per inch. For more information on dots and resolution, see Chapter 7.

Any image or pattern can be broken down into a number of discrete areas, or *pixels* (picture units). The smaller the areas, the finer the resolution. A CCD roughly corresponds to one picture unit. Shrinking the size and sensitivity of the CCD provides finer resolution.

The *optical resolution* of a scanner is the one-to-one ratio of a physical CCD with a single dot. Software enhancement (*interpolation*) is a way to add pixels beyond a scanner's capability to scan a picture area. When software is used to change the image clarity, we refer to software resolution, interpolated resolution, or enhanced resolution.

Horizontal resolution depends on how closely the CCDs are placed in a single row. The smaller the CCDs, the closer they can fit together, and the higher the number of pixels in a row. In the rating of 300×600 *optical* dpi, the first number (300) applies to horizontal placement, in this case, 300 CCDs in a row.

The second number in the optical rating (in this example, 600) refers to vertical movement and how slowly the light source and mirror mechanism move from the top to the bottom of the image. A slower speed means smaller incremental steps. Again, the smaller the increments, the finer the resolution.

Today, most scanners found on the shelves of so-called computer superstores have an optical resolution of 250×400 or 300×600 dpi. While high-resolution 600×600 or even 1200×1200 dpi scanners are relatively inexpensive, the amount of memory and storage space a 1200 dpi image requires is more than a typical person is willing to work with. For high resolution scanning, most people and businesses use a specialty business (service bureau) and send their images out to be scanned.

Analog Vs. Digital

The difference between the analog world of the brain and the digital world of computers equates to the difference between physical matter and symbols and is directly connected to the issue of measurement.

Analog information has a potentially infinite number of settings—states, conditions, or values—that can't be stored in a profile and recalled. Analog information (the world of perceptions) varies with respect to time, and we can't encode all the different analog values as digital—only some of them. The digital process can arbitrarily *approximate* the analog, and because of this variability, whatever digital value is assigned represents only that specific state at that specific moment.

Digital values, on the other hand, are either on or off—one or zero, yes or no. In physical reality, the analog concept of *up* can mean many things, with infinite increments of direction and distance relative to gravity. In the digital world, an immediate question is, "How far up?" From a digital perspective, an immediate problem is that the initial starting point (or state) varies constantly and has a significant effect on the next or ending state.

Because analog is essentially infinite, it includes the presence of noise: random information from random sources. Digital information never varies, has no noise, and always has an exact initial and ending state.

An example of analog versus digital is the concept of two, or two-ness. The human, analog mind understands the abstract concept of two and applies it to sets of, for example, two apples, two people, and two fingers, expanding outward to the set of two in all existence. The digital computer understands only a specific two, in a specific situation, in a specific context, and in a specific state.

A computer can assign a value of two when it's told to, but can't hold the infinite values of all potentialities in the *set* of two. This is a complex point of research in artificial intelligence, pattern recognition, robotics, and graphics resolution. Experiments designed to develop an analog computer "mind" seem to be having better results in robotics than in the digital paradigm.

An analog brain interprets a newspaper image as a pattern with shades of gray. Magnifying the image shows the underlying digital format of the same image composed of only black dots on a white field. The separation values of the dots, along with their sizes and even the yes/no value of a dot's existence, are exact values and can be considered digital information.

Scanner Connections

The two most popular ways to connect a scanner to the system board are through the parallel port and by using a SCSI adapter card. The primary difference between the two is the data transfer rate. A parallel port moves eight bits of information at a time, whereas an internal interface card transfers at bus speeds. Therefore, parallel ports are slower than internal card adapters.

Some sheet-fed scanners are built into keyboards, interfacing with a processor in the keyboard casing and borrowing the keyboard cable to transfer data.

Installing an internal SCSI adapter is another exercise in IRQ/DMA conflicts. Also, some inexpensive scanners don't provide ASPI (advanced SCSI programming interface) support, which is necessary if you want to run the scanner on the same SCSI bus as other peripherals (see the section "SCSI" in Chapter 6). Scanners and sound cards are legendary for their installation and configuration difficulties.

A parallel port interface gives the scanner portability because it can be plugged into practically any computer. The SCSI interface is important because it means that the scanner will work with a wide variety of hardware and software. As is often the case, the user needs define the interface.

Handheld scanners are very small and portable and connect through their own interface cable, which also provides power to the scanner.

Summary Of Input Devices

There are many ways other than a mouse and keyboard to get information and data into a computer. Pointing devices reflect the human sense of touch, where we virtually touch the CPU on a virtual shoulder. Pointing devices such as mice, trackballs, pointing sticks (Trackpoint), and touch pads use a mechanical or optical helper to put a pointer (cursor indicator) on the screen. Virtual reality hardware, light pens, and touch screens let us directly point and touch.

Scanners are like the sense of vision, where we interface our eyesight with the computer, entering images and patterns. We store visual information not only as graphics but also in bar codes and the magnetic spectrum. Scanners, a computer's "eyes," are categorized as flatbed, sheet-fed, handheld, drum, and 3D. Scanners use CCDs to convert analog information to digital values.

Continuing our metaphor, voice and sound digitizers are the computer's sense of hearing, where audible music and communications are stored in the computer. Sound cards, microphones, speakers, and software provide file storage for voice notes and music. (Presumably, some day we'll store olfactory and taste information as we move steadily toward full immersion and sense-around virtual environments.)

Microsoft's MSD.EXE (Microsoft Diagnostics) can provide a rudimentary report of the existing state of the system, including IRQs. MSD.EXE, discussed further in Chapter 11, is a small utility program that comes with MS-DOS and Windows. Although MSD can produce simple reports, a third-party diagnostics utility is almost always better. MSD often reports either the wrong device or the default device on an IRQ, regardless of what device actually uses the IRQ.

Windows 95 includes HWDIAG.EXE as a Windows hardware diagnostics utility (in the \OTHER\MISC\HWTRACK folder on the setup CD-ROM), and will run MSD in a window. The Windows 95 Device Manager is another place to find some details on IRQs, and provides the best device management reporting without resorting to other applications. The reputable third-party diagnostics programs can report almost anything on a system, including DMA channels.

Before installing a new device, you should have a listing of open IRQs. Sound cards and SCSI interface scanners are difficult to install because of IRQ/DMA conflicts with other devices. IRQs, DMA channels, and I/O ports should first be configured on the card, following the manufacturer's instructions.

Exam Prep Questions

Question 1

> Why does the CPU constantly scan the keyboard?
>
> ○ a. To record the last keystroke in the event the keyboard is unplugged
>
> ○ b. To allow the keyboard to be unplugged without generating erroneous data
>
> ○ c. To eliminate erroneous data generated by key bounce
>
> ○ d. To allow multiple character repeat

Answer c is correct. Most keys will "bounce" just a bit when you press them, leading to several high-speed contacts (in mechanical and dome-type switches). Keyboards also generate some amount of electrical noise whenever you press a key, which the CPU could interpret as something you meant to do. To clean up the noise, and to help the keyboard processor determine real key presses from noise, the processor constantly scans the keyboard, looking at the state of every key. This constant scanning is why you should never plug a keyboard in or unplug it while the power is on.

Typically, debouncing waits for two scans before deciding that a key is legitimately depressed. Usually key bounce is far faster than a human being can press a key two times.

Question 2

> What kind of keyboard is considered nonmechanical?
>
> ○ a. Foam element
>
> ○ b. Capacitive
>
> ○ c. Membrane
>
> ○ d Rubber dome

Answer b is correct. The capacitive switch doesn't rely on metal contacts, but instead, puts two plastic plates inside a switch housing designed to sense changes in capacitance of a circuit. The upper plate is connected to the key plunger (stem) and as the key moves downward, the distance between the two plates changes the capacitance. The change is detected by the circuitry of the keyboard.

Question 3

Why is an optical mouse different from other types of mice?

- ○ a. Optical mice do not require a cable connecting them to the PC.
- ○ b. Optical mice have no moving parts.
- ○ c. Optical mice do not require the use of a mouse pad.
- ○ d. The friction ball in an optical mouse rarely requires cleaning.

Answer b is correct. An optical mouse has no moving parts and works in conjunction with a reflective mouse pad. As the mouse is moved, a beam of light is bounced from the inside of the casing to the reflective pad, then back onto a sensor inside the mouse. The sensor calculates the changes in the light beam to define the X-Y coordinates of the screen cursor.

Question 4

Most optical scanners use photosensitive devices called _____ to convert the scanned image into a machine-readable format.

- ○ a. Quartz tube emitters
- ○ b. Light-emitting diodes
- ○ c. Electro-optical couplers
- ○ d. Charge-coupled devices

Answer d is correct. A typical scanner uses a series of photosensitive cells called charge-coupled devices, or CCDs, mounted in a fixed row. Each CCD registers whether there is light or no light—on or off. The point or spot of light being registered by one CCD is the "pixel" equivalent of a dot on a piece of paper.

Question 5

> What basic electrical component can store a charge for a short period of time?
>
> ○ a. Resistor
>
> ○ b. Capacitor
>
> ○ c. Transistor
>
> ○ d. Diode

Answer b is correct. Capacitors store a quantity of electrons for a short period of time. Large capacitors, as used in power supplies, can store a huge charge and are capable of delivering a nasty shock even after the power cord has been disconnected.

Question 6

> What is the unit of measure for resistance?
>
> ○ a. Ohm
>
> ○ b. Amp
>
> ○ c. Farad
>
> ○ d. Volt

Answer a is correct. Resistors resist the flow of electricity and are measured in ohms.

Need To Know More?

Andrews, Jean: *A+ Exam Prep*. The Coriolis Group, Scottsdale, AZ. ISBN 1-57610-241-6. A good overview of keyboards can be found on pages 172-174 and pointing devices on pages 179-181.

Bigelow, Stephen: *Troubleshooting, Maintaining, & Repairing Personal Computers*. TAB Books, New York, NY. ISBN 0-07-912099-7. Detailed information from a break-fix standpoint can be found on the following pages: keyboards pages 489-497, mice pages 591-597, joysticks pages 484-487, and sound boards pages 781-789.

Karney, James: *Upgrade and Maintain Your PC*. MIS Press, Indianapolis, IN. ISBN 1-55828-460-5. Input devices are covered on pages 483-538.

Messmer, Hans-Peter: *The Indispensable PC Hardware Book*. Addison-Wesley, Reading, MA. ISBN 0-201-87697-3. There is more information provided here than you need for the test exam, but if you want to get in deep here it is. Input devices are discussed on pages 910-918.

Minasi, Mark: *The Complete PC Upgrade & and Maintenance Guide*. Sybex Network Press, San Francisco, CA. ISBN 0-7821-1956-5. Here is your source for information on peripherals from a repair standpoint. Sound boards are on pages 961-974 and input devices are on pages 927-936.

Rosch, Winn: *Hardware Bible*. Sams Publishing, Indianapolis, IN. ISBN 0-672-30954-8. Again, there is far more information here than you need for the exam. Input devices can be found on pages 635-695, and sound boards are on page 939.

Peripherals: Storage Devices

6

Chapter 5 looks at the way data can be entered into a PC system. We also know that new information tends to go into memory, using the PC's RAM. If we want to keep the results of our input, we need a place to put all that data from memory once the power shuts down. We also know that without a steady supply of power, RAM loses any data. Software applications must be stored somewhere so that they are available on a regular basis. Work and new information created with and by software programs must also be stored somewhere for continuity, sharing, and output.

The most common way to store information and data in a computer system is on a disk of some type. The original floppy disks were inexpensive, easy to use, and could be shared between computers. Today we have hard disks, CD-ROMs, floppy disks, tape drives, removable hard disks, and network file servers. The A+ exam primarily tests for your knowledge of hard disks. We will discuss all peripheral storage devices to provide a framework for the specifics involving nonremovable media (hard disks).

Floppy disk refers to a round, flimsy, bendable piece of Mylar coated with magnetic material and in a protective jacket. The protective jacket has changed from somewhat floppy on 5¼-inch disks to rigid on 3½-inch disks.

The first *minifloppy* disk, which we know as the 5¼-inch disk, followed the original 8-inch disks used prior to 1974. The floppy disk drive was developed by Alan Shugart of Shugart Associates, who also developed the Shugart Associates Systems Interface (SASI). Later, SASI was renamed SCSI (small computer systems interface) when the American National Standards Institute (ANSI) committee approved the interface in 1986.

Shugart left his company (for some reason) right before the market release of the 5¼-inch floppy drive, and he never profited fully from the disks, which became the standard for the original PCs. However, in 1979 Shugart resurfaced in a partnership with Finis Conner when they founded Seagate Technology and created the 5¼-inch hard drive.

Shugart created the floppy disk, hard disk, SCSI drive, and controller interface that are still used in most PCs today. The Shugart ST-506/412 interface was the accepted standard for all PC hard disks and stood as the basis for ESDI and IDE interfaces.

Floppy Disks And Drives

Floppy disk drives (or simply *floppy drives*) fit into locations near the front of the PC's case called *drive bays*. These bays have a knockout piece of plastic in the front panel of the PC case, which can be removed. After the drive is installed, the faceplate of the drive blends in with the front of the computer. Floppy drives are recognized by their thin slots and either a push button or a rotating knob that's used to eject a disk.

Floppy drives are available as either 5¼-inch or 3½-inch sizes, defined by the size of the disk being used in the drive. The 5¼-inch floppy drives have, for the most part, become obsolete, though you can find combination drives with both capabilities in one unit. The original PC disks used only one side for data storage and were referred to as *single-sided, single density*. Almost any disk you find today uses both sides for data storage and therefore are called *double-sided, double density*.

All disks, including floppy disks, are divided into *tracks*, *sectors*, and *clusters* by a formatting process defined by the operating system. The disks are available in different *densities* using one or two sides of the disk. Floppy disks originally used eight tracks, then changed to nine tracks.

The number of sides used on a disk, along with its density, is still referred to today by the abbreviations DS (double-sided), LD (low density), and HD (high density). The four main disk formats are often referred to by the amount of data that can be stored on the disk. Until recently, the four typical sizes/densities have been:

➤ **360K** 5¼-inch double (dual) density (DS, DD)

➤ **1.2MB** 5¼-inch high density (DS, HD)

➤ **720K** 3½-inch double density (DS, DD)

➤ **1.44MB** 3½-inch high density (DS, HD)

> *Note: The IBM 2.9MB floppy disk developed for OS/2 distribution is referred to as "extra" density. Microsoft also has a proprietary disk formatting process for storing 1.7MB on a typical floppy. Microsoft disks are referred to as distribution media format (DMF). Windows 95 can read all normal sizes, along with the extra sizes, though neither the 2.8MB nor 1.7MB formats are supported by DOS.*

A modern dual-density floppy drive can read both densities of disks and can be either 5¼-inch or 3½-inch. Combination drives provide a slot for both of the physical sizes. A typical 5¼-inch drive reads both 360K and 1.2MB disks, just as a 3½-inch drive reads 720K and 1.4MB disks. Modern drives can also physically read the 1.7 and 2.8MB drives, with proper software support. Although the larger capacities can be read by the drives, it's not so easy to format a disk to this capacity, which helps protect against software piracy.

Floppy Drive Components

Inside a floppy drive are many of the same general components used in a hard drive. We'll discuss these basic disk components here, rather than waiting until the segment on hard drives.

 Remember hexadecimal numbering and the fact that the first cylinder and track on a disk is cylinder 0, track 0. The exam sometimes uses the informal term *head* in place of the technical term *cylinder*. The boot sector could also be said to be on *head* 0, track 0.

Most floppy drives have two *read–write heads,* which is how most disks can be dual sided. The first head (head 0) is actually the bottom one, whereas the second head (head 1) is the top one. The original PCs used single-sided disks, but the need for more storage quickly changed the design.

Read/Write Heads

Read/write heads are the hardware pieces that actually change the magnetic state of the disk surface. When the state is changed by the head, it *writes* to the disk. When the existing state is sent back to the CPU, the head *reads* from the disk.

The read/write heads are moved back and forth over the disk (or platters on a hard disk), going from edge to center and back again. The heads move over *tracks* that are created on the disk by low-level *formatting* (usually performed by the manufacturer). Computer disks are not read like the old vinyl music records (disks), where the disk spins and a needle picks up analog information from a single, very long groove on each side of the disk.

Head Actuator

Moving the read/write heads is done by a stepper motor called a *head actuator.* The motor is also controlled by a *disk controller.* The disk controller works with the operating system and ROM BIOS so that the PC can move the read/write heads to the correct location on a disk to find specified data (files).

Both the read and the write heads are built into the same mechanism and move together. The heads are made of soft iron materials with electromagnetic coils. Each head is a combination read-write head, and the separate read and write heads are centered within two *tunnel erase heads.* These erase heads are used to erase information from the disk.

When a track of information is produced, the trailing, tunnel erase heads erase the outer edge of the track, making the data stand out cleanly on the disk. This forces the data to be confined in a narrow "tunnel" in the middle of the track and prevents peripheral magnetic interference from nearby tracks of data. The process also removes fading magnetic changes trailing off to the sides of the written data, which could lead to some confusion during reading.

The two heads are spring loaded and physically touch the surface of the disk to read or write data. Meanwhile, the floppy disk is spinning at 300 rpm (revolutions per minute), which is the speed of all floppy drives, including 3½-inch drives, 5¼-inch low-density drives, and 2.8MB extended-density drives. The exception is the 5¼-inch high-density drive, which is the only drive that spins at 360 rpm.

Because the time needed to read data is so short and the disks are spinning relatively fast, friction isn't a problem. Some diskette makers coat their disks with Teflon to reduce friction even further. However, this will eventually lead to some residue buildup on the drive heads and require cleaning.

Spindle Motor

To get the disk spinning at 300 rpm, the spindle motor works very much like the old record players. Older floppy drives used a belt-driven system that made them unreliable and their speed inconsistent. The belts wear and slip over time, making them even more unreliable.

Just as record players evolved from belt driven to direct drive, so did computer floppy drives. The direct-drive motor has no belts, so the spindle doesn't slip, making for very consistent speed.

Newer disk drives use automatic torque compensation to provide greater spin force for sticky disks (or less force when needed) and have very little slippage and therefore rarely need adjustment. Older drives require periodic adjustment. However, with a typical 3½-inch drive costing around $30, it's often simpler and cheaper to simply replace the drive.

Logic Board

The drive mechanism is attached to one or more *logic boards* (printed circuit boards) located underneath the main housing. This circuit board has the controls for the head actuator, spindle motor, disk sensors, and any other drive components.

All floppy drives use the standard SA-400 (Shugart Associates) interface, so most floppy drives will work with any computer, right out of the box. Depending on the installation context (e.g., switching the A: and B: drives), a CMOS setting might need to be changed.

This is one of those exceedingly rare moments when the industry (except for Apple) has followed a single standard. Unfortunately, some companies (e.g.,

Compaq) have taken to designing an unusual drive bay to require the customer to remain committed to brand-name devices. While any drive may work, installing a non-Compaq drive in a Compaq machine may be prevented due to exclusive designs for attachment rails or sizes.

Although logic boards can fail, it's usually cheaper to simply replace the drive. With the trend toward CD-ROM distribution and high-capacity removable media, floppy disks and drives are close to becoming throwaway commodities. Huge (100MB or more) application suites and software "bloat" have mostly relegated 1.44MB disks to distributing device drivers or shareware programs.

Floppy Connectors

Almost every disk drive has two connectors: one for electrical power and one for control/data signals. These connectors are fairly well standardized across the industry and across drives.

The power connector is usually a four-pin inline connector. This power connector can be in either large or small style; generally, the 5¼-inch drives use the large and all other drives use the small style.

Typically, the control cable connector is a 34-pin design and either an edge connector or a pinhead connector. Because these cables have so many wires running through them, they're designed to be flat to supply flexibility and save space. They're usually called *ribbon cables* because of their similarity to a ribbon. Again, the 5¼-inch drives use the larger-edge connector and 3½-inch drives the smaller, pinhead connector.

An exception to this rule is in some of the older IBM PS/2 systems, which used a 34- or 40-pin connector that provided both power and control/data signals along the same cable.

 Don't be confused by the smaller floppy drive ribbon cables and the typical 50-pin SCSI ribbon cable.

Floppy Drive Configuration

On floppy drives, just like hard drives, some jumper settings need to be configured. One difference between floppy drives and hard drives is that floppies are designated A: or B: and hard drives as *master* or *slave*. The specific things to check or set with a floppy drive are:

➤ Drive select jumper

➤ Media sensor jumper

➤ Disk change-line jumper

➤ Terminating resistors

Drive Select Jumper

The drive select jumper defines the *unique drive number*. In the overall scheme of drives and controllers (i.e., hard, floppy, and CD drives), every drive must have its own drive number. The drive select jumper defines the floppy as drive 0 or drive 1. (Remember, computer numbers start with 0.)

Drive 0 does not necessarily correspond to drive A:, just as drive 1 does not necessarily correspond to drive B:. This is because IBM wired its system to make installing preconfigured drives as easy as possible.

 One of the fundamental things you must remember for the exam is that IBM (and all clone makers) designed drive A: and drive B: into every system. All PCs continue to set aside two drives (A: and B:) for the basic floppy drives. The C: drive is *always* drive 3. Any additional drives take on whatever is the next consecutive letter of the alphabet.

Media Sensor Jumper

You've seen the small hole in the upper right corner on the back of a 3½-inch disk. On a high-density disk, there's another hole on the upper left corner with a place for a sliding piece of plastic. When this hole is covered, it locks the disk and prevents any writing to it, making it *write protected*.

> *Note: Write protection makes it physically impossible to write data to the disk. This is a way to guarantee that a virus program can't be placed on the disk. There's no way to write-protect RAM, but a virus in memory won't be able to transfer to a write-protected disk.*

The hole in the upper right corner is for the media sensor. If a hole in the disk exists, a light beam makes contact with a photo sensor, and the system knows there's a high-capacity, 1.44MB disk in the drive. Extended-capacity 2.8MB disks have a hole in a different location of the disk jacket, so a newer multicapacity floppy drive actually has two media sensors: one for 1.44MB and one for 2.8MB disks. (1.7MB disks use 21 sectors per track rather than 18, and don't require a special media sensor.)

Low-density 720K disks have no hole in the media sensor position, so the media sensor light fails to make contact with the photo sensor. This led to an interesting scheme whereby a special hole-punch tool was marketed for converting cheaper 720K disks to 1.44MB disks. The reformatted disk eventually becomes unstable because of the density of the magnetic structure of low-density disks. This leads to a rapid degradation of the format and catastrophic loss of data. (On the other hand, placing a piece of tape over the media sensor hole on a 1.44MB disk will fool the drive into thinking that it has a 720K disk that can be formatted with no data loss.)

Disk Change-Line Jumper

The AT system uses pin 34 to carry a signal called the *diskette change line,* or DC (not to be confused with direct current electricity). This signal is used to tell the system whether a disk is the same disk, still in the drive since the last time a disk access was requested.

The control signal is a pulse sent to the controller (to a status register) that changes once on insertion and once on ejection. When the controller sends a pulse to the drive and the drive responds with information that the heads have moved, the system knows that a disk has been inserted. If a change signal isn't received between accesses, the controller assumes that the same disk is in the drive. This allows information that is stored in RAM (having been read from the floppy) to be used without rereading the disk.

A common error among Windows users is to insert a disk and call up File Manager or Windows Explorer and then replace the disk and become agitated when the files seem to have disappeared. The F5 (refresh) option forces Windows to reread the disk and get the proper directory structure.

By keeping the directory information and file allocation table in RAM, the AT-class system makes using a floppy disk much faster than it otherwise would be. The system doesn't have to reread the disk for every process. This is particularly useful with COMMAND.COM.

On a dual-floppy PC, the DOS command processor might load into memory, and then the original disk would be removed. If only the loaded parts of COMMAND.COM were needed, DOS would read from memory. When a command required DOS to reread the disk, a "missing command interpreter" message would be generated when DOS couldn't find COMMAND.COM any more. Placing COMMAND.COM on a RAM drive and resetting the COMSPEC= environment variable was a way to solve that problem. (RAM drives and COMMAND.COM are discussed in Chapters 8 and 11.)

Terminating Resistors

A technical fact of electronic media or cables that carry a signal of any type is that it must be terminated properly at each end with *terminator resistors,* which you can think of as a bus. To maintain error-free data travel along the bus, the terminating resistors absorb any signal that reaches the end of the cable. This prevents the signal from "bouncing back" along the cable and crashing into other signals traveling along the bus.

 Remember that electronic cables or media that carry data or signals are essentially a *bus*. To prevent errors caused by signals bouncing back along the bus from the ends of the cable, a terminating resistor *must* be at both ends. These are called *terminators*. Terminators absorb signals to keep them from reflecting back along the cable.

SCSI cables, floppy disk cabling systems, and Ethernet LAN cables require a terminator at both ends. Terminators are resistors, not capacitors. If a terminator is missing from either end of a network cable, interference may cause connection problems and data transfer problems.

Because a terminator can be built into a device, a controller, or both, a floppy drive cable system often has a terminating resistor built in to the controller.

Controllers

We've seen that an I/O interface is a way to convert instructions from a human being or a device to events involving other devices. We also know that interfacing involves the expansion bus and other buses on the motherboard (e.g., parallel and serial ports). Most PCs have some amount of peripheral control right on the motherboard. To distinguish this rudimentary control from the more sophisticated I/O control of later PCs, we refer to various *controllers*.

Controllers are components that contain additional microprocessors and logic, and work through a connection with the motherboard BIOS. Depending on the age of the computer, controllers take on more or less of the actual management of their specific type of peripheral. A SCSI drive controller, for instance, can work directly with a multitasking operating system, bypassing the CPU and allowing for faster access to the disk.

> *Note: Controllers don't usually have a ROM BIOS chip. The motherboard BIOS contains instructions for working with different types of controllers. The peripherals that the controller manages may have their own BIOS chips. Peripherals can be Plug 'n' Play. Controllers are part of the motherboard system platform and aren't referred to as PnP controllers.*

There are different controllers for different peripherals. A typical PC can have a keyboard controller, floppy drive controller, and hard disk controllers. There are also memory, IRQ, DMA, and video controllers. With all these controllers working around the CPU, you can imagine the number of instructions flying around the motherboard circuitry. The places where those instructions often cross over to other devices are the buses.

You might think of a controller as a traffic cop working at a busy intersection. Traffic laws define the general way that the traffic flows through the intersection. At certain times traffic is so heavy that it speeds things up to have a thinking human being in the intersection, who can override the standard laws with individual decisions. Peripheral controllers help speed up overall performance by taking local control of traffic involving their devices.

Chaining Devices

When peripheral controllers began taking over management of various devices, the devices were also changed to allow for more than one to access the same controller. Rather than add more and more sockets to the controllers, a "pass-through" connection was added to the device. These devices have an input and an output connector, and when more than one device is connected together in this way, we call it a *daisy chain*.

Most PCs use a floppy controller that allows up to two drives to be connected with a single cable. The drive *farthest* from the controller must have the terminating resistor jumper set (enabled) to act as the other end terminator. If a second drive is in the middle of the cable, that drive must have the terminator jumper removed (or disabled) for it to work.

 Typical floppy drive controllers for IBM PCs and clones allow a maximum of two floppy drives to be connected with a single cable. On the exam, you'll likely be tested on how many devices can be attached to certain types of cable interfaces. For example, SCSI allows up to seven devices. An IDE or EIDE controller allows two devices.

Floppy Disk Controller

More modern systems have a floppy disk controller and a hard disk controller built into the motherboard. The older AT computers often had an adapter card with both controllers attached to it. On PC- and XT-class computers, a separate controller card used an expansion slot.

A peripheral device requires access to the CPU at some point in a given event. To access the CPU, the device uses an interrupt (IRQ). Drive controllers use interrupts in the same way that serial (COM) and parallel (LPT) ports do. Because almost every PC has a hard disk, the ROM BIOS includes a default IRQ for the hard disk, the floppy drives, and the basic ports.

Remember that IRQ 14 is usually assigned to the primary disk controller. IRQ 15 is assigned by default to any secondary disk controller. The obsolete XT used IRQ 5 for its disk controller, so modern PCs tend to assign a secondary parallel port (LPT2) to IRQ 5 instead.

Fixed Disks/Hard Drives

The cheapest way to store information in a computer system is on magnetic tape. However, the inconvenience and slow speeds involved in working with tape machines make a fixed disk much more convenient. With hard disks costing so little these days and with their much faster access speeds, the preferred storage device is an internal, nonremovable storage media, or *hard disk*.

The hard disk is called a *fixed disk drive* because you don't remove it except to permanently replace it. (Presumably, once it's replaced, it's fixed.) Many people call it a *hard drive* because the platters aren't flexible and floppy, and in fact you can replace it like any other drive. The technical name given by the IBM PC Institute is a DASD (direct access storage device).

Although the disk, drive mechanisms, drive controller, and cable/interface subsystem are separate components, familiar language joins them together as the *hard drive* or simply the *drive*. In the following discussion, we often refer to fixed disks as either the hard drive or the drive. Many disks are partitioned with a single, primary, active partition making them the C: drive. Because the C: drive and the fixed disk are so often the same thing, we also refer to the C: drive.

Be very careful that you don't confuse a physical disk and a logical drive. While many people call the fixed disk a hard drive, the physical disk can contain anywhere from 1 to 24 logical drives. Additionally, a system can have more than one physical disk, where each disk can have many logical drives. Tricky exam questions can trip you up by asking whether a fixed disk can contain 23 or 24 drives. (See Chapters 8 and 11 for more information on FDISK.)

Later in this chapter, when we discuss high-capacity removable storage media, we refer to them as *removable drives*. These include the Iomega Zip and Jaz drives, which are designed to be quickly disconnected. Removable drives offer the advantage of a removable disk with storage capacity similar to a fixed disk.

Inside A Hard Drive

A hard drive has many internal components and consists mainly of several plates of highly electroconductive metal spaced extremely close together. These plates are called *platters*. A spindle motor, connected to the plates at their centers, spins the platters. Each platter has a read-write head for each side of each platter. The heads are attached to an actuator arm under each platter to move the heads back and forth over the disk.

> *Note: Assigning the boot sector to head 0, cylinder 0, track 0, sector 0 explicitly points to the first platter and first cylinder. Either the head 0 or cylinder 0 can be dropped in common usage.*

Hard disks spin at thousands of revolutions per minute (e.g., 5,200 rpm), making them dramatically faster than floppy disks. The disk drive also has a circuit board and connectors to transfer data and supply power to the drive. Although we speak of a single disk, you can see in Figure 6.1 that, technically, a hard drive has a number of physical disks.

When the CPU requests data from the disk, the platters rotate and the heads move back and forth over them. The back-and-forth movement allows for random access of the data rather than being made to read sequential data (like a tape cassette). You can see the advantage of random access—back-and-forth movement over a spinning disk—when you try to read data from a tape backup and must wait for the tape to wind forward to the right place before you read the data.

Sequential reading means that if you have a file stored somewhere on a tape, the tape machine must spin through the entire length of tape before it gets to the beginning of that file. A hard drive, on the other hand, skips over whole platters and tracks and goes directly to the first cluster of a file.

Random access means that if a section (cluster) of a platter is near a read-write head and available for storage, the head can begin storing a file immediately. A tape must have enough room to store the complete file from beginning to end. A hard drive can also store pieces of a file in many different sections. If a tape doesn't have space for a complete file, either we have to wait to spin all the way through the tape to the end of used space, or we must use a new tape.

Physical Formatting

Initially, a fixed disk is magnetized (physical, or low-level formatting) by creating magnetic tracks and cylinders on the plates of the disk. Low-level formatting is usually done by the manufacturer. Tracks and cylinders are characterized by the following:

➤ **Tracks** Concentric, circular paths placed on both sides of the platter. They are identified by number, starting with track 0.

➤ **Cylinders** A set of all the tracks on all sides of all the platters located the same distance from the center of the stack of platters.

Figure 6.1   A typical hard drive, showing the platters and spindle.

If you were to take an apple corer and smash it down on a hard drive (not recommended), it would cut through one cylinder. The edge of the corer would be like the width of one track. Each track is subdivided into sectors that store a fixed amount of data. Sectors are usually formatted to store 512 bytes of data. Binary data is stored in the sectors using various combinations of zeros and ones. The zeros are nonmagnetized and the ones are magnetized areas.

 A way to remember the difference between sectors and clusters is that the formatting process adjusts the size of file clusters. Perhaps files can clutter up a disk, and clutter sounds like cluster? Sectors never change size, and the exam always uses 512 bytes for a sector size.

Over time, the magnetic coating of the platters begins to deteriorate, preventing them from holding a magnetic pattern. When this happens, the heads can't read or write data from a sector. Reformatting the disk or using certain software programs such as SCANDISK or Norton Disk Doctor will label the sector as a *bad sector*. Note that even with modern engineering, most brand-new disks have some number of bad sectors that are marked as unusable by the manufacturer during physical formatting.

After physical formatting, the operating system performs *logical formatting*, which we cover in the discussion of FDISK.EXE in Chapters 8 and 11.

Hard Drive Interfaces

Probably the most important and most confusing attribute of a hard drive is the type of interface controller it uses. Conspiracy theorists are fond of saying that much of modern technology comes from aliens visiting Earth in UFOs. If SCSI technology is any indication, hard drive interfaces might very well have come from outside our solar system.

Hard drives have such a huge responsibility in a PC that a lot of attention has been focused on how to make the drives more intelligent. We've seen that controllers can take on a lot of the management for a particular type of device, and hard drive controllers are in constant development. Hard drive controllers include:

➤ IDE (integrated drive electronics), EIDE (extended IDE), and XT IDE (extended technology IDE)

➤ SCSI (small computer systems interface)

➤ ESDI (enhanced small device interface)

➤ ST-506/412 (Seagate Technologies 506/412. Remember the story of Alan Shugart of floppy fame? Don't worry, it's not an exam topic.)

> The exam will cover the IDE and SCSI interfaces for the most part. The ATA IDE bus and the PCI bus show up as well.

Part of what makes understanding drive controllers difficult is that each *controller* interface has even more acronyms and descriptive words used for different *features*. Some of these acronyms include:

➤ ATA (AT attachment IDE)

➤ MCA (micro channel architecture IDE)

➤ Fast SCSI

➤ Wide SCSI

➤ Ultra SCSI

IDE

The interface you'll usually find in today's computers is the IDE controller. Strictly speaking, IDE refers to *any* drive that has a built-in controller. The actual interface bus is the ATA, referring to the AT-class motherboards. The ATA IDE is a 16-bit ISA motherboard interface; others are the XT IDE (8-bit ISA and the MCA IDE (16-bit microchannel).

> A confusing area of the exam centers on the difference between IDE and ATA. Make a note that IDE is basically the drive controller, while ATA is an interface (bus) between the controller and the drive. The confusion arises when you're given multiple choices and have to remember which acronym applies to what feature. ATA, XT, and MCA all describe an IDE controller.

ATA IDE

The ATA IDE combination was first developed by Compaq, CDC, and Western Digital, who decided to use a 40-pin keyed connector with a 5¼-inch form factor. The keyed connector is designed to be plugged in only one way; it cannot be plugged in backward. (Plugging in a drive backward can damage both the drive and its related circuits.) These original drives were physically large but could hold only 40MB of data. ATA IDE 5¼-inch drives were put into Compaq 386 systems (the first highly successful clones) with a Western Digital controller. Compaq created Conner Peripherals as its drive manufacturing subsidiary (Conner was later sold).

The IDE drive (with its built-in controller) plugs into a bus connector on the motherboard or on an expansion card. These drives are easy to install and require a minimum amount of cabling because the controller is on the drive unit. Because fewer parts are involved, signal paths are shorter, improving the reliability of the drive.

Shorter Data Paths Improve Data Reliability

Because of the physical properties of wire, especially cheap ribbon cable wires, signals traveling along a piece of wire are subject to various types of degradation. Electromagnetic interference and structural resistance (not to mention signals bouncing back from improperly terminated cables) make a trip from the CPU to the drive heads a risky business for any given byte of data. The shorter the path, the more likely that data byte will arrive safely.

Another advantage of the integrated controller is that the manufacturer doesn't need to worry about compatibility issues with the drive. This makes the overall hard drive unit easier and cheaper to build and makes it cheaper to sell, which is another reason that so many IDE drives are being used in the field.

 Make a note that ATA IDE drives use a 40-pin keyed connector. The cable is 40 wires wide and carries all signals to and from the controller. The controller is built into the drive. The cable should be a maximum of 18 inches long. Some connectors don't use a physical notch for keying, in which case the ribbon cables have matching colored stripes to indicate the correct orientation. SCSI connectors are generally 50-pin connectors.

The ATA Specification

The original XT IDE was *nonintelligent,* meaning that the drive simply responded to the controller commands with no optimization and feedback capabilities. The original Western Digital 1003 controller was very similar to the previous ST-506/412. The XT IDE drives were low-level formatted by the manufacturer, and a list of the drive defects and optimizations was written to a file and saved on the disk. If you low-level formatted the drive, you wiped out the file and lost any optimization capabilities.

A controller works with the ROM BIOS on a motherboard. Major configuration incompatibilities occurred because there were many manufacturers making different controllers, each with different ways of controlling their drives. In 1989, ATA IDE was accepted as the ANSI standard, ending most of these compatibility issues. Older IDE drives (built before 1989) can have problems working with a new drive added to the system. However, a hard drive's mean time before failure is around five years in modern drives, so this situation is becoming more and more rare.

ATA is an ongoing set of specifications. Each development is aimed at increasing the access speed between the software, the operating system, the CPU, and the drive. The first ATA specs were introduced in March 1989 as the ANSI standard. In 1994, ATA-1 was approved by the institute, and in 1995, ATA-2 was approved.

The ATA standard defines, for example, the signals on the 40-pin connector, the functions and timing of signals, and cable specifications. In addition, the ATA specification:

➤ Provides a way for two drives (each with its own controller) to interface with the same bus

➤ Creates the master drive (drive 0) and secondary (slave) drive (drive 1) hierarchy

All IDE drives must respond to the original eight commands of the WD1003 (Western Digital 1003) controller. These eight commands are built into just about every IBM-compatible ROM BIOS, making IDE drives very easy to install.

The ATA specification added a number of optional commands to improve capabilities and performance. A few of those commands are used by almost all IDE drives today, Identify Drive being the most important.

The Identify Drive command allows any program (including system BIOS) to read from a 512-byte block of data that describes the details of the drive, including model number, operating parameters, and serial number. This command is used by many computers' BIOS to automatically configure the drive in CMOS.

Remember that autoconfiguration in a CMOS file is different than Plug 'n' Play. PnP uses a combination of system BIOS, operating system, and device BIOS. Autoconfiguration coming from the Identify Drive command only applies to CMOS.

The PCI Bus

Think back for a moment to the intersection with the traffic cop. Recall too, that a bus is like a toll plaza where traffic moves through the toll booths and back onto the highway. Data bits and bytes are traffic and everything in a computer is involved with data moving through intersections and plazas. In early computers, the intersections and toll plazas handled memory access and data processing all at the same speeds. CPUs were slow, and printers, modems, and disks worked at about the same speed as the CPU. Everyone used the same road system.

Gradually, CPUs started getting faster, and data moving around in RAM and across the microprocessor began moving faster and faster. The problem was that I/O processing by printers and peripherals didn't need to travel that fast. Monitors were showing signs that video processing might have to get faster, but everything was held to about the same speed because everything was still using the same set of roads—the ISA bus.

Over time, the memory bus was pulled into the overall chipset around the CPU, and the ISA bus lost some of its video transfer to the VESA local bus— the VL bus. Compaq introduced a design change that split the ISA bus into two parts. One part of the bus was for slow peripherals such as printers and modems, and the other part was for faster components like hard disks. Everyone was becoming confused and looking for some sort of standardization when Intel released the PCI specification in 1992.

The PCI specification is really a way to connect various types of processor chips together. If you think of different types of roads being developed for cars, trucks, pedestrians, or bikes, then the PCI specification isn't really a specific road so much as the rules for how to build *all* roads. Once a device takes on the PCI specification, it can work with the specific set of roads designed for it. In other words, a so-called PCI bus can work with an old ISA card and slow down or work with the new ATA-2 EIDE controller and go very fast.

In a way similar to the IDE controller and ATA specification, the PCI specification allows developers and manufacturers to follow a set of rules for connecting their device's chips to whatever might be encountered in a PC. Rather than having to rebuild a device and hope it be compatible with everything in the market, PCI takes care of the compatibility as long as the new device follows the PCI rules. The ISA bus continues to be available for compatibility with very old components and for slow peripherals. New devices are becoming faster and faster and, to some extent, are taking over access to RAM directly.

If you think of the CPU as being the grandfather involved in giving everyone in a family permission to do everything, then modern PCs are growing up. Rather than waiting for the motherboard's grandpa chipset to tell everyone how to do everything, the grown-up devices and controllers are working with memory on their own (direct memory access) and only going to the CPU for central processing—a real central processing unit.

The PCI bus isn't really a bus so much as a way for many devices that can think for themselves to connect. ATA isn't really an interface so much as a way for drive controllers to join the overall family of chips in the PC.

 PCI cards come in two sizes: full-size and short. The full-size card is about 12.2 inches long, while the short PCI card is about 6.8 inches long. The cards can have varying numbers of pins, but the physical bus connector is a 32-bit, 124-pin slot.

EIDE (ATA-2)

The ATA-2 specification is the same thing as EIDE (extended IDE). This extension of the original ATA added PIO (programmed I/O) modes and DMA transfer support. The PIO is available in five modes, 0 through 2 being ATA-1, with transfer rates from 3.3Mbps (megabytes per second) to 8.3Mbps.

Let's pause for a second and take another look at this alphabet soup.

➤ The underlying device we're talking about is the IDE drive controller. IDE is a form of hard drive with a built-in controller. Ordinarily, a controller is separate from the disk and tells the drive system how to operate. The IDE process puts the controller right in the housing, along with the read-write heads and the platters.

➤ Instructions get from the controller to the drive by crossing over a bus— an interface. Data transfers from the drive back to RAM across a bus. The amount of data that can move from the disk to memory is measured in Mbps—how many megabytes can move in one second.

➤ Different drives require different ways of communicating with the motherboard's BIOS. ATA is a way to standardize that communication. Part of the ATA standardization process means that IDE drives and their controllers have to be made a certain way.

➤ The first ATA specification defined most of the manufacturing process and included a way to hook two drives to a single controller.

➤ ATA and ATA-1 changed as the sophistication for controlling the hard drive increased. ATA was one set of rules, and ATA-1 was the next set of rules. ATA-2 is the third set of rules; each set building on the previous rules.

➤ ATA-2 allows even more complicated instructions to go between the controller and the hard drive. Along with the new instructions, the controller can take charge of other system features for moving data into memory even faster.

➤ One of the ways ATA-2 speeds thing up is with something called PIO, which comes in five modes. Another way the controller speeds things up is by using direct memory access (DMA).

➤ We're still talking about a hard drive with an IDE controller, but the description and capabilities of the controller keep changing. The actual performance of the disk gets better and the disk can store more data, but the connection between the disk and the rest of the system has to improve as well. The way that improvement is described is with the letters ATA.

➤ ATA is a specification—a set of rules for doing things. The specification became more complex and now includes other hardware and software pieces. PIO and DMA are two other pieces of the system that the controller can work with.

➤ In order for PIO and DMA to work correctly, a different kind of connection has to be made for the controller—a different type of bus. The PCI bus is a new type of bus that lets the ATA-2 controller work at its best.

➤ ATA-2 changed the original IDE controller so much that the industry began calling the new version an "extended" version—the extended IDE, or EIDE.

ATA-2 added PIO modes 3 (11.1Mbps) and 4 (16.6Mbps). However, in order to run in modes 3 and 4, the IDE port on the motherboard must be on a VL (VESA local) or a PCI bus. Some newer motherboards have two IDE controllers, but only the first one is connected to the PCI bus (PCI-compatible). The second controller is connected to an ISA bus and limited to PIO mode 2—something to check when buying a new computer. The manufacturers claim that the ISA connection is required because slower devices such as CD-ROM drives don't need the higher speed of the PCI bus.

Mixing fast and slow devices (such as hard disk and CD-ROM drives) on the primary controller can cause slower data transfer for the hard disk. Typically, all transfers travel at the speed of the slower device. Put only hard disks on the primary controller and make the faster of two disks the master.

The primary benefits of ATA-2 include the following:

➤ **More storage capacity** Supports drives larger than 504MB.

➤ **Faster data transfer** Achieved through PIO modes 3 and 4. If the motherboard BIOS and the IDE adapter support ATA-2, the BIOS can execute data transfers to and from the IDE drive several times faster than normal ATA.

➤ **ATAPI (ATA packet interface)** Allows extra drives such as tape drives or CD-ROM drives to connect to the ATA connector.

➤ **DMA transfer** Supports DMA channels. The drive is capable of only supporting DMA transfer features. The operating system must support it as well. Most operating systems don't support DMA transfers directly from the drive.

Enhanced IDE can remap blocks of data so that the BIOS sees more heads (though the EIDE drive sees more cylinders). Therefore, the BIOS maximum of 7.8GB becomes the maximum capacity of an EIDE drive.

Fast ATA

Standard IDE controllers typically use PIO modes 0 through 2 to transfer data to and from the processor (and don't require disk driver software because the PC's BIOS handles IDE disk controllers). However, EIDE can use PIO modes 3 and 4 and DMA, which provide faster data transfers of up to 16.6Mbps.

PIO modes 3 and 4 have been referred to as Fast ATA and frequently require additional disk device drive software and an enhanced BIOS. Ultra ATA doubles the existing performance and moves data at around 33Mbps.

The EIDE supports feedback (flow control). *Flow control* means that the PC tries to transfer data as fast as it can. By using the PC bus's I/O channel-ready signal, the disk drive can slow the transfer if it can't provide the data as fast as the PC is requesting it. To ensure that both the PC and the disk drive support flow control, the PC sends a command (strobe) to the disk drive to enable the feature.

Ultra ATA (UDMA)

In October 1996, Quantum introduced a new way to speed up data transfers from IDE hard disks, calling it Ultra DMA. Intel backed the technology and included support for the process in new chipsets. The rest of the industry and disk manufacturers followed suit, and now UDMA or Ultra ATA (same thing) is becoming standard, making EIDE drives a direct competitor to SCSI drives in terms of speed. EIDE continues to be far less expensive than SCSI (nearly half the cost).

Today's fastest high-density drives can move data into a buffer at just over 10Mbps on a sustained basis. With a transfer rate of 16.7MBps, Fast ATA should be capable of keeping the buffer from becoming full. The reason it can't has to do with the turnaround time the PC takes between the commands it issues to the drive. This command turnaround time is what causes most of the slowdown in overall performance.

The delay from command turnaround time comes from the number of commands a PC makes to a drive and depends on the size of the command requests. The requests are typically 4K in size and equivalent to the page size supported by a virtual memory operating system like Windows. It takes approximately 4 milliseconds for a drive to read a 4K instruction command. A couple of hundred microseconds here and there, and pretty soon you're talking about real time!

The way this has all changed is a fascinating story, but is beyond the scope of this book. Suffice it to say that by putting some of the timing controls for sending and receiving data on the drive itself and using both the on and off strobe signals, the Ultra ATA took another function away from the PC and didn't have to wait for grandpa chipset to decide when it was time to read a file. Ultra ATA requires support from a newer version of the PCI bus and a supporting motherboard chipset.

IDE Configuration

Typically, IDE drives are available in three configurations: single, master, or slave. These configuration settings are most often controlled by jumpers on the rear of the drive. The single setting tells the drive that it's alone in the system; the drive will respond to all commands. The master setting tells the drive that a secondary drive is present; the drive will respond only to commands directed to a master drive. The slave setting tells the drive to respond only to commands directed to a secondary drive.

Before the ATA specification was approved, different OEM drives configured master/slave relationships in different ways. This can lead to problems by making older drives work together when a second drive is added to the system. Sometimes they work as master-then-slave and sometimes as slave-then-master.

Ordinarily a jumper setting is used to determine whether the drive is a master (drive C:) or a slave (drive D:). The cable select (CS) jumper is used in systems implementing cable select in which master or slave is determined by the connector cable and a special adapter.

Remember that there are often two IDE controller adapters on modern PCs, and that each adapter allows for two devices to be chained together. IDE and EIDE can have a system setup involving four physical disk drives. Whichever controller will control the primary, bootable drive will be assigned IRQ 14 by default, while the secondary controller will have a default assignment to IRQ 15.

SCSI

SCSI (pronounced "scuzzy") technology is one of the occult mysteries of the computer device kingdom. Like much of computer technology, the SCSI interface could take up a whole chapter, but the purpose here is to help you understand SCSI enough to pass the exam.

SCSI is available in three versions: SCSI-1, SCSI-2, and SCSI-3. The SCSI-3 standard is the latest published ANSI standard, having only recently become accepted. SCSI-3 is properly known as FAST-20 SCSI, but is commonly referred to as Ultra SCSI.

> *Note: Originally, the specification was going to be named Ultra SCSI, but a trademark conflict led to the FAST-20 change. To avoid confusion, we will refer to SCSI-2 and SCSI-3. The UltraStore's Ultra SCSI trademark refers to a SCSI FAST class of product.*

SCSI-3 is the next major performance advancement to the specification. The current implementation is still mostly SCSI-2. A quick overview of the various SCSI names includes:

➤ **SCSI** The original small computer system interface specification.

➤ **SCSI-2** Describes the 1994 ANSI standard, defining several connectors (both shielded and unshielded) that include one-byte-wide data bus; FAST transfer speeds; SCSI protocol for wider data transfers; and the parallel SCSI messages and a command structure.

➤ **SCSI-3** Describes the recently accepted, current ANSI standard, defining different "layers" of the standard, including physical (connectors, pin assignments, electrical specifications), protocol (description of how physical layer activity is organized into bus phases, packets, etc.), architecture (description of how command requests are organized, queued, and responded to by any protocol), primary commands (description of commands that must be supported by all SCSI devices), and device-specific commands (commands that are specific to a particular class of devices such as CD-ROMs or WORM drives). The SCSI-3 standards are layered in this manner to allow substitution of parts of the structure as new technology emerges.

➤ **SCSI FAST** Refers to timings defined in SCSI-2 for a 10 megatransfer-per-second (Mtps) transfer rate. A megatransfer refers to the rate of signals on the interface regardless of the width of the bus. (For example, a 10Mtps rate on 1-byte-wide bus results in a 10Mbps transfer rate, but the same rate on a 2-byte-wide bus results in a 20Mbps transfer rate.)

➤ **SCSI FAST-20** Refers to timings defined in the SCSI-3 physical layer for 20 Mtps transfer rate. This achieves data rates twice as fast as SCSI FAST rates.

➤ **SCSI FAST-40** Refers to timings of the SCSI-3 physical layer that achieves 40Mtps.

➤ **Ultra SCSI** An old term for the FAST-20 data rate.

➤ **SCSI WIDE** Usually refers to the two-byte-wide (68 pin) connector that is defined in the SCSI-3 parallel interface (SPI) document. SCSI WIDE was first introduced as a nonstandard SCSI-2 feature.

➤ **SCSI FAST-WIDE** Refers to a combination of FAST transfer rate with 2-byte-wide connector, which results in 20Mbps data transfer rate. Wide FAST-20 (40Mbps) and wide FAST-40 (80Mbps) is also available.

SCSI-3 is backward-compatible with previous generations of SCSI and uses the same physical environment. Cables, connectors, and terminators that support SCSI-3 can support SCSI-2. More importantly, SCSI-3 can be integrated without having to modify or change operating systems.

 Remember: Only seven devices can be daisy-chained on a SCSI-2 bus. A typical SCSI cable is commonly a 50-pin cable (the SCSI WIDE parallel interface cable is 68 pins). Both ends of the SCSI chain *must be terminated.* Exam questions will assume the SCSI-2 specification, which is still the most widely implemented.

SCSI Description

SCSI is completely different from IDE in the sense that it doesn't deal with disk drives. SCSI is not a controller/adapter like the IDE is; rather, it is a complete and separate bus that connects to the system bus through a host adapter.

A single SCSI bus can hold up to eight devices with a different SCSI ID (identification) from 0 through 7. The host adapter takes up one ID number, leaving seven for other hardware devices, such as hard drives, tape drives, CD-ROM drives, and scanners.

Don't be confused by the eight ID numbers of the total SCSI bus. Remember that the host adapter automatically takes up one ID number. The remaining daisy chain can hold only seven hardware devices.

A trick question on the exam will focus on the number of devices, but will ask you how many unique SCSI ID numbers are possible: eight ID numbers, but seven devices.

SCSI is much like IDE was before the ANSI standard in that SCSI can be implemented in too many different ways, making it a slow interface to adopt. The bus has gradually been catching on, but it faces a lot of competition from EIDE. Although the connections in particular are standardized, software device drivers that communicate between the CPU and devices haven't been standardized.

The result is that there is no standard host adapter, no standard software interface, and no standard BIOS for hard drives attached to a SCSI adapter. Each piece of SCSI hardware has its own proprietary host adapter, and the software for that adapter won't work with another manufacturer's host adapter.

Historical Interfaces

The original SCSI bus (before IDE) was designed to use the ST-506/412 controller. When IDE came into being, its similarity to the original Western Digital WD1003 controller made changing the BIOS quick and easy.

SCSI registers are very different from IDE, so the bus would have required a completely different BIOS in the PC, but this didn't happen. At the time, hard drives could be used only with DOS, until Adaptec and Future Domain developed adapters that could work with other operating systems.

The speed of the SCSI bus over IDE and the ability to connect the new hard drives to other operating systems made it a good choice for network servers and high-end systems. IBM began to integrate SCSI support with an adapter card or an adapter built into the motherboard, and other manufacturers followed suit.

SCSI provides a standard interface for all types of computers. The IDE or EIDE disk and its ISA bus is specific to IBM-compatible and Intel-compatible PCs. However, SCSI is now used by Macintosh computers, RISC workstations, minicomputers, and even some mainframes. Additionally, SCSI has always supported a mixture of disks, tapes, and CD-ROM drives.

Note: The old IBM-compatible designation has faded with the growth of Microsoft Windows and the predominance of Intel processors. A machine that derives from the IBM design and runs Windows on an Intel-compatible motherboard is referred to as a "Wintel" machine.

People say that Apple invented the SCSI interface, but, as we've seen, it actually came from Alan Shugart. It just wasn't applied to PCs because the hard drives (also developed for PCs) were easier to install with IDE. The desire to use an internal hard drive in computers other than PCs forced non-IBM vendors to work out the SCSI bus technology.

An IDE or EIDE disk must be mounted inside the computer. There is no standard provision for the IDE ribbon cable to run to external devices. For a while there were kits on the market that would allow a connection to an external IDE drive via the parallel port, but the wide acceptance of Iomega's Jaz and Zip drives have relegated these kits to novelty status.

SCSI devices can be internally connected, but can also be external to the computer, where they can be mounted in individual boxes or mounted together in larger, tower enclosures. Newer devices use a smaller 50-pin SCSI connector with two rows of 25 pins; the SCSI-2 standard specifies this as the preferred connector. This is frequently known as a 50-pin mini-"D" shell (MDS50) connector.

SCSI-2 is an improved, ANSI-accepted version of SCSI-1. SCSI-1 and SCSI-2 are basically the same because no industry patrol exists to verify that manufacturers really make what they say they make in terms of claiming standard 1 or standard 2. SCSI-2 hardware will work on a SCSI-1 adapter, but won't have the extra features of SCSI-2. The bottom line is that:

➤ SCSI-1 introduced the seven-device limit to a daisy chain.

➤ SCSI-1 was very strict about termination. SCSI-1 required a 132-ohm passive terminator, which didn't work well with today's high-speed transfer rates and sometimes caused data errors when more than one device was on a chain.

➤ SCSI-1 has a cable limit of 6 meters (about 19 feet).

➤ SCSI-1 could send only one command at a time.

➤ SCSI-2 lowers the terminator resistance and uses an active (voltage-regulated) terminator. The lower impedance (measured in ohms) improves reliability.

➤ SCSI-2 included the CCS original 18 common commands, rewrote some other old commands, and added specific support for more than only hard drives: CD-ROM, DAT (digital audiotape), floptical, removable disk, tape, magneto-optical, WORMS (discussed shortly), and scanners. Some drives might require third-party software drivers.

➤ SCSI-2 supports bus-mastering controllers (onboard CPU/DMA controller).

➤ SCSI-2 supports multitasking environments by sending up to 256 commands to a device at one time. In turn, the device stores the commands in a buffer and then reorders them for efficiency.

> An important thing to remember about the SCSI specification is that the bus allows devices other than a hard drive to be connected to the same cable. The bus also allows computers that aren't IBM compatible to use hard drives that were developed specifically for IBM-type PCs.
>
> A typical exam question might ask for the most common way to connect an external drive of some kind. The SCSI bus can connect peripheral devices outside the computer's case—external devices such as tape backup drives, CD-ROM drives, and additional hard drives.
>
> The IDE and EIDE controller specification only allows two devices in a chain and does not support external devices.

SCSI Configuration

The main thing to remember about configuring a SCSI device is that the host adapter and every device must have a SCSI ID number between 0 and 7. Usually, the host adapter is factory set at 7—the highest priority ID—leaving room for seven more devices. Always remember that technical numbering begins with 0.

The ID is set in much the same way as master/slave jumpers are set on an IDE hard drive. For no reason at all, and instead of making it simple, SCSI manufacturers use binary numbers represented by three jumpers. Binary 000 is SCSI ID 0, whereas binary 100 is SCSI ID 4. Just to be diabolical, some manufacturers reverse the jumper settings so that ID 4 could just as easily be 001.

Something else to remember is simply that the cable must be terminated at both ends. Because the host adapter is usually at one end, it most often has built-in termination. Just make sure that the termination is enabled.

If the host adapter is in the middle of the chain, you'll need to remember to buy and install terminators at both ends of the cable. Buy the highest quality FPT terminators, and you'll have no need to worry about data errors.

Hard Drive Configuration

After you've installed the IDE, EIDE, or SCSI drive, it still won't be ready to run without going back to the motherboard and making sure that the drive is recognized properly in the BIOS. The IDE drives are usually autoconfigured because the controller is on the drive, and they're mostly standard. Today, almost every BIOS can query the IDE drive and derive its settings.

As we've stated, SCSI manufacturers have opted for their own closed architectures, so that almost every adapter is different. The immediate problem this presents is lack of autoconfiguration. Be sure to keep the reference manual for any SCSI device because this is the only place to find which BIOS settings are required by the device.

SCSI Vs. IDE

With all the discussion of transfer rates, bus widths, and the high cost of SCSI drives, it's easy to assume that SCSI drives are better than IDE drives. Remember, though, that SCSI is a bus, not a controller.

People say that SCSI drives are faster than IDE drives. That's just not true. Hard drive speed is partly related to the interface, but mostly related to average seek time. Other parts of the drive itself, not the interface, also contribute to overall speed.

Most PCs use the IDE interface because it's inexpensive and performs reliably. Many manufacturers sell the same drive in both the IDE and the SCSI models, putting an extra chip on the SCSI circuit board. The extra chip on the IDE drive, then, is a SCSI adapter to make the drive workable on a SCSI bus. However, this extra chip requires data to go through an extra step, so the IDE model performs slightly better.

Underneath it all, though, SCSI is more intelligent than IDE even if it takes more steps to move data through the interface. One of those extra steps is the command buffering, whereby up to 256 commands can be sent by the system and rearranged by the SCSI adapter. On a system using multitasking, where several programs are running at once, the extra intelligence of the SCSI adapter boosts system performance.

Another advantage to the SCSI interface is that if bad sectors develop on the disk, a SCSI system can mark the sector bad and avoid crashing on a disk read. IDE systems require either a reformat of the disk (the FORMAT.COM command includes a check for bad sectors) or running a disk repair utility.

SCSI devices can communicate independently of the CPU and can operate at the same time. IDE devices have individual controllers that can operate only one at a time. Similar to DMA transfer, this allows SCSI devices to run a bypass around the CPU for simple device-related tasks. This bypass keeps the CPU from bogging down.

Removable Media And Drives

Many years ago, a very inexpensive notebook appeared on the market that used a stylus-based operating system, was available in various sizes, stored data in character recognition and graphic format, offered many color styles, and cost about $1 at the local stationery supply store; the stylus cost about 29¢. The main thing about these SBNs (spiral bound notebooks), as they were called, was that the stored data could be easily transported. You ripped a sheet of paper out of them and jammed it in your pants pocket!

Portability and extra storage have always been issues for computer customers, which is why 3½-inch floppies are still around. If you need to mail a file to someone, drop a copy of a file off at a service bureau, or even make backups of your hard drive, you had to use either floppy disks or a tape drive.

Dating back to the IBM mainframes and the use of magnetic tape for data storage, auxiliary tape machines have been used for storing data as backups. Prior to the recent insurgence of removable hard drives and writable CD-RW drives, backups involved the typical 10MB to 50MB of a PC's hard disk.

Tape drives are usually interfaced with a SCSI connection and an internal expansion card. The basic tape cartridge used in most home-market tape machines is the QIC (quarter-inch cartridge) format. Newer machines use DAT storage, which is a competitive technology to the CD-ROM digital storage. Tape transfer on a high-end tape system ranges from 1Mbps to 3Mbps.

The advantages of tape storage are both the capacity of the cartridges and the low costs. Current cartridges can store 7GB or more of information, and both the tape and the software used to back up original data have a high degree of error correction. The error checking of tape media results in very reliable data backup, and many networks continue to use either analog or DAT tape systems for archiving data.

The introduction of CD carousels (multiple CDs available in a single drive) and read-write technology for CDs is having a strong effect on the consumer market for tape. Redundant disk arrays, the gigabyte capacity of removable hard drives, and the downward trend in costs for removable disks may make the final advantage of tape systems the complex error-checking. However, that checking comes at a cost in terms of time, and consumers may be willing to sacrifice error-free backups to gain convenience and speed.

A CD-ROM (compact disc) is a layer of highly reflective aluminum foil sandwiched between layers of transparent plastic. Typically, the disks are either 5¼ or 3½ inches in diameter. A writing laser beam etches microscopic marks, or *pits*, in the foil. The reading laser beam bounces the reflections from the non-pitted, or flat, areas of the foil back to a photo sensor. The combination of the pits and the flat areas results in the binary 1s and 0s of digital information. The photo sensor connects to a digital-to-analog converter for music and video

CD-ROMs. For computer data, as in the case of CD-ROM data disks, the information continues straight through in digital format.

The primary drawback of the CD-ROM is that the data is burned into the foil once and becomes permanent. This original technology was called WORM (write once, read many). On the other hand, a floppy or a hard disk using magnetic storage allows a user to write information to the disk and then change that information and rewrite new information over the original.

Some CD-ROMs write in a long, single spiral groove, like the old vinyl records. This format is called CLV (constant linear velocity) recording. Other CD-ROMs, such as magneto-optical drives, work like typical floppies and hard drives, using a track and sector system. The tracks are in concentric rings around the center, and the format is called CAV (constant angular velocity) recording.

A feature of the CAV CD-ROM is that information regarding the mechanical environment is included with the data being stored. This means that the CD-ROM is constantly correcting itself for speed and signal strength, resulting in extremely reliable data reads. With the CLV CD, the spindle motor uses a mechanical process to adjust the head mechanism as it moves closer or farther from the center, keeping speed constant.

Exam Prep Questions

Question 1

> What 3½-inch floppy disk density is most common in today's applications?
>
> ○ a. 1.44MB
>
> ○ b. 1.2MB
>
> ○ c. 1.7MB
>
> ○ d. 2.8MB

Answer a is correct. 3½-inch floppy drives can be formatted in 1.7MB and 2.8MB densities, but cannot be read by DOS. 1.2MB is the standard high-density format for 5¼-inch floppy disks. 1.44MB is the most common density for 3½-inch floppy disks today.

Question 2

> How many devices can be added to a typical IDE or EIDE controller?
>
> ○ a. Seven
>
> ○ b. Four
>
> ○ c. Two
>
> ○ d. One

Answer c is correct. IDE and EIDE controllers can typically control two physical devices.

Question 3

> How many logical drives can one physical hard drive contain?
>
> ○ a. One, the primary logical drive
>
> ○ b. Two, an active and an extended logical drive
>
> ○ c. 24
>
> ○ d. 23

Answer d is correct. Be very careful that you don't confuse a physical disk and a logical drive. While many people call the fixed disk a hard drive, the physical disk can contain anywhere from 1 to 24 logical drives. Additionally, a system can have more than one physical disk, where each disk can have many logical drives. Exam questions can trip you up in terms of whether a fixed disk can contain 23 or 24 drives.

Question 4

What is the name for concentric, circular paths placed on both sides of a hard disk platter during format?

O a. Cylinders

O b. Tracks

O c. Sectors

O d. Clusters

Answer b is correct. Tracks are concentric, circular paths placed on both sides of the platter. They are identified by numbers, starting with track 0.

Question 5

How many unique SCSI ID numbers are possible on a SCSI bus?

O a. 7

O b. 2

O c. 8

O d. 24

Answer c is correct. Don't be confused by the eight ID numbers of the SCSI bus. Remember that the host adapter automatically takes up one ID number. The remaining daisy chain can hold only seven hardware devices.

Question 6

A typical CD-ROM can hold how much data?

O a. 650MB

O b. 1.54GB

O c. 7GB

O d. 1GB

Answer a is correct. A typical CD can hold 650MB of data.

Need To Know More?

Andrews, Jean: *A+ Exam Prep.* The Coriolis Group, Scottsdale, AZ. ISBN 1-57610-241-6. Pages 141 through 166 provide a good overview of floppy drives. Pages 191 through 243 give a detailed presentation of hard drive operation, and pages 244 through 249 cover removable drives.

Bigelow, Stephen: *Troubleshooting, Maintaining, and Repairing Personal Computers.* TAB Books, New York, NY. ISBN 0-07-912099-7. Detailed information from a break-fix standpoint can be found on the following pages: hard drives (pages 341–358), CD-ROM drives (pages 207–220), floppy drives (pages 310–325), and tape drives (pages 792–803).

Karney, James: *Upgrade and Maintain Your PC.* MIS Press, Indianapolis, IN. ISBN 1-55828-460-5. Hard drives are covered on pages 303 through 340.

Messmer, Hans-Peter: *The Indispensable PC Hardware Book.* Addison-Wesley, Reading, MA. ISBN 0-201-87697-3. More information is provided than you need for the exam, but this reference goes into great detail. Storage devices are discussed on pages 651 through 835.

Minasi, Mark: *The Complete PC Upgrade and Maintenance Guide.* Sybex Network Press, San Francisco, CA. ISBN 0-7821-1956-5. Here is your source for information on peripherals from a repair standpoint: hard drives (pages 427–479), CD-ROM drives (pages 1017–1047), and floppy drives (pages 753–789).

Rosch, Winn: *Hardware Bible.* Sams Publishing, Indianapolis, IN. ISBN 0-672-30954-8. Again, far more information is provided than you need for the exam: storage technology and interfaces (pages 367–482), floppy drives (pages 541–563), hard drives (pages 483–530), CD-ROM drives (pages 563–601), and tape drives (pages 603–632).

Peripherals: Output Devices

Terms you'll need to understand:

√ Video displays

√ Printers and cables

√ Dot matrix printers

√ Ink jet printers

√ Laser printer mechanics

Concepts you'll need to master:

√ Display technologies

√ Display adapters

√ Resolution

√ Interlacing

√ Printer technologies

√ Laser printing process steps

We've looked at getting data into the system and then storing that data in the system when the power is turned off. The third part of the equation is getting data back out of the system. Anything that comes out of a computer is *output*. If everything goes well, the information coming out of the computer will make sense to a human being. On the other hand, output can just as easily be meaningless garbage or noise. An *output device* is the "thing" that produces the output, and the display screen is usually the *standard output device*.

Whenever we connect something to a motherboard for the purpose of input, storage, or output, we refer to that thing as a device. When a device is outside the computer's main case, we generally call it a *peripheral device*. "Peripheral" means on the edge, or outside of an area. Standard devices include keyboards, floppy and hard drives, monitors, and mice. Peripheral devices include scanners, printers, modems, and sound cards. If it's something you have to have in order to use the computer, we normally just call it a device. If it's a device that adds to the computer, but isn't absolutely necessary, it's called a peripheral.

Overview

Output calls up the dimension of time in the sense that there's *transient output* and *final output*. Transient output is the stream of data being sent somewhere for fleeting observation or temporary storage; final output is data that moves away from the system completely and stays fixed in time. *Transient* is a fancy way of saying "just passing through."

An example of transient output is pressing a key on the keyboard and inputting a scan code to the system. The code exists only long enough to be picked up by the CPU. Additionally, you have no way to verify which code you sent because you have no way to see a translation of that code. Human perceptions don't include translating electrical pulses. The CPU accepts the code and sends it on to the video subsystem in charge of outputting a representation of that code to the screen—a letter or a number. The screen displays the output only long enough for you to act on it.

Another example of transient output is when an application is holding too much information for the installed RAM and sends part of that information to the hard disk for temporary storage. This is called a *swap file* in Windows. Once the data in the swap file has been used, it's erased by new temporary (transient) data. A swap file is somewhat similar to a *buffer*.

Imagine a faucet, a sink, and a drain at the bottom of the sink. If the water from the faucet is coming out slowly, then it goes right down the drain. The water is like a data stream coming to a modem (the drain). If the water starts pouring out of the faucet faster than it can drain, then the sink begins to fill up.

The sink is a buffer, and can only hold so much water (data). Once the sink is full, water pours over the edge onto the floor. In a buffer, data is thrown away. If there is some intelligence in the data source and the buffer, then the speed of the data stream can be adjusted so that no data will be lost. Making a bigger drain is like widening a bus or increasing the processing speed of the device.

Final output is just that: final. After you've completed inputting and the system has finished its calculating, the result (you hope) is something useful (e.g., a report, spreadsheet, or database) and something that stays put. It's time to stop working, so you need to put your work somewhere to either keep it where it is or carry it with you. When you save a file and copy it to a floppy, you're creating output from an application (the file) and output from the overall system (the copy on the floppy). Sounds from a speaker can also be considered output, that is, from a sound card.

The video monitor is the standard output device for working with a computer. The printer is the most common peripheral for creating final output. Characters on a screen are transient and change from moment to moment. A "screen capture" image of a particular set of characters at a particular moment in time can be sent to the printer. The paper with the image of what was on the screen is final output.

Video Displays

The most important output device in a computer system, in terms of output, is the monitor. Monitors have been called CRTs (cathode ray tubes), VDTs (video display terminals), CON (console), the DOS device name, or simply the screen. In this section, we refer to display monitors generically as monitors.

The two main categories of monitors on the market are CRT and LCD (liquid crystal display). A CRT is a vacuum tube with a layer of phosphor dots at the viewing end and an electron gun at the other. The gun shoots a beam of electrons at the phosphor, and the electrons glow. When we look at the glass face of the monitor, we're seeing through the glass to the backside of the phosphor layer.

Color monitors have a separate electron beam for the three primary colors in the pixel triads (discussed shortly), and different phosphorescent dots can be made to glow to create a color effect. The three primary colors of *light* used to create every other color are red, green, and blue (RGB). The primary colors of *solids* used to create the others are cyan (bluish), magenta (pinkish red), and yellow. We refer to monitors with the RGB designation and to color separation printing with a CMY abbreviation.

Note: CMY is also used in LCD panels. Solid materials reflect light and react differently from glowing light when blended together.

LCD uses a different technology. The CRT produces a beam of light, but LCD technology is passive: It relies on another source of light to pass through the crystals. If light can pass through the crystal, our eye can interpret it. When the crystal is turned off, we interpret an area of black. Each crystal can be either on or off, making it a convenient match for binary computer numbers.

LCD technology allows for a much thinner screen than the bulky CRT. This gives rise to a group of monitors referred to as *flat-panel displays* (we discuss flat-panel and LCD technology shortly).

Display Technology

The display of data involves a number of components, or *subsystems*, all of which work together to bring a visual pattern to the human eye. We saw that a typical motherboard has a video interface connector as part of the system board. We also saw that today's monitors often make use of an expansion slot in the I/O bus for a graphics accelerator card. Therefore, the display subsystem includes:

➤ A monitor

➤ A video adapter (controller)

➤ A graphics card (sometimes)

Pixel Resolution

Depending on how closely pixels can be bunched together per inch, we can say that a monitor has a resolution measurement. Technically, the word *resolution* in the context of computer video should be replaced with *pixel addressability* because we're really discussing how many pixels can be addressed in something called the video frame buffer (which you don't need to worry about for the exam). True resolution should refer to the smallest object that is capable of being displayed on the screen and therefore would be more related to dot pitch. A neurotically correct definition of resolution is "the degree of detail visible on a monitor, and therefore is related to the size of the electron beams, the degree of focus in their alignment, the arrangement of the pixel triads, and video bandwidth." But who's neurotic?

Scanners define resolution by the number of pixels per inch, as do monitors. The only difference is that scanners use one CCD per pixel and are limited by the physical size of the CCD. A CRT monitor uses lighted dots, each of which is one pixel. LCD panels use a molecular crystal as a pixel device, and gas-plasma screens use a pinpoint flash of heated gas to describe a pixel.

No matter how resolution is defined, and if we follow common terminology, the smallest piece of light or darkness that a screen can physically display is the resolution of that screen. The SVGA (super video graphics array) standard of today's monitors typically allows resolutions of 1,280 × 1,024 pixels or 1,600 × 1,200 pixels.

HHH×VVV×CCC

You've probably heard carpenters and builders talk about "two-by-fours." They're referring to a piece of wood two inches by four inches. That means measuring one pair of sides produces two inches, and measuring the other pair (at right angles) produces four inches. Almost all computer output is produced in rectangular format. The horizontal (left to right) measurement and the vertical (top to bottom) measurement is either the number of dots or pixels.

A standard VGA monitor has a resolution of 640 pixels horizontally and 480 pixels vertically. We use the "×" to mean the word "by" so the measurement is commonly written as 640×480. Because different graphics modes can also reproduce a varying number of colors, a third number has recently become popular. The third number refers to the number of colors associated with the pixel resolution. 640×480×256 means the monitor resolution is 640 pixels horizontal by 480 pixels vertical with 256 colors.

Standard VGA

Following the "great blindness epidemic" caused by CGA and EGA monitors, help came in the form of a new technology called VGA (video graphics array). Actually a superset of EGA, VGA was developed as a standard by IBM to provide higher pixel resolution and graphics capabilities. Remember that for higher and higher resolutions, the pixels have to be smaller and smaller.

The VGA standard was announced at the same time as MCGA and 8514/A, but the VGA standard became the consumer standard. VGA incorporates all the EGA modes and introduces seven subsystems:

➤ **Display memory** Consists of a set (bank) of 256K DRAM chips divided into four 64K color planes and used to store display data.

➤ **Graphics controller** Performs calculations on data being written to the display memory.

➤ **Attribute controller** Holds a color lookup table that defines the appropriate color to be displayed by a pixel for a digital value in memory.

➤ **Serializer** Converts data in display memory to a serial bitstream and sends it to the attribute controller.

➤ **Sequencer** Controls the timing on the video adapter board, turning the color planes on or off; similar to the oscillator on a motherboard.

➤ **CRT controller** Sends the synchronizing frequencies to the electron guns to control scan and refresh rates.

➤ **Graphics command language** VGA also introduced a set of simplistic, low-level graphics commands introducing the possibility of a video controller taking some of the processing away from the CPU.

➤ **Frame buffer** Essentially a way to hold data in memory before sending it to the screen.

The VGA system didn't really support any processing, so the CPU still had to manage all the new calculations and logic, making VGA very dependent on processor speed. Therefore, VGA is directly linked to the computer's processor in terms of speed comparisons. Installing the same model VGA monitor on a 386 system and a 486 system gives the appearance of making the monitor on the 486 a faster, cleaner, and sharper monitor. The dependency of the monitor on the chip's processing capabilities makes it difficult to evaluate the overall quality of the monitor itself.

Frame Buffers

Any image being sent to a monitor begins as a series of instructions programmed into an application somewhere. The application may be a drawing program or it may be a mouse device driver program that tells the computer how to display a pointer picture on the screen. The image on the monitor takes up the whole screen, and every part of the image is specifically placed on the screen in a specific location. All this is done by the application's programming working with the CPU.

You probably know that a strip of movie film contains a number of still pictures. As the film strip moves across the light source, the eye perceives movement. Each still picture on the strip is called a *frame*. The same term applies to the single picture being shown on a monitor at any given time. The difference is that some parts of the picture stay still while other parts of the picture change. This would be the case where a menu and toolbar stay constant, but a cursor and new characters are formed in different locations during typing.

The CPU sets aside an area of memory—a buffer—where it stores the information being displayed on a screen at any given time. When the CPU is ready, it lets data out of the buffer. The keyboard has a small buffer that allows you to press keys faster than the system can process the presses. If you hold a key down, you'll eventually fill the buffer, and the CPU will send an alert tone to the PC's speaker. The video system uses a buffer for image data, and the whole amount of data that will go to the screen is called the *frame buffer*.

Modern SVGA and high-resolution monitors take advantage of a separate type of memory (VRAM and DRAM) and include a more complex set of graphics instructions than the VGA standard. These instructions, working together with memory outside the main system memory, allow for faster data transfers between the CPU and the screen. The older VGA instructions were too unsophisticated for independent "intelligence" between the monitor and CPU. VGA was tied so closely to the CPU that the speed of the changes on the monitor were directly linked to the processor speed.

Early VGA circuitry was integrated onto the motherboard in a VLSI chip, and IBM developed the PS/2 display adapter to utilize the chip's functions. This adapter is just like the early VGA card and used an eight-bit expansion slot. Clone makers jumped on the bandwagon, and many third-party VGA cards were produced, some of which are still on the market.

> *Note: VLSI (very large-scale integration) is the process of placing thousands (or hundreds of thousands) of electronic components on a single chip. Modern chips almost always are VLSI or ULSI (ultra large-scale integration) chips. There is no specific dividing point between VLSI and ULSI.*

8514/A And XGA

These two standards were developed by IBM in its quest for ever-increasing resolution and the need for speed in graphic interfaces. The 8514/A adapter was developed to work with the proprietary MCA bus and provided three new graphics modes. It, too, required a VGA controller.

The 8514/A standard built on the rudimentary graphic commands that began with VGA and took over some of the processing. The 8514/A could perform some video memory transfers, draw a few lines, and calculate rectangular areas in a display image.

XGA (extended graphics adapter) followed on the heels of the 8514/A and was the first IBM video adapter that used VRAM (video RAM). The XGA specification could be configured with an additional 500K or 1MB of video memory; built on the previous set of video commands and intelligence; supported resolutions from 640×480 to 1,024×768 for graphics and 1,056×400 for text; and used a color palette of up to 65,535 colors in 640×480 mode (with additional memory installed).

SVGA And UVGA

We finally arrive at the current SVGA (super VGA) and UVGA (ultimate VGA). *Ultimate* seems a bit optimistic, given statements like "10MB of hard disk is all anyone will ever need!" However, SVGA and UVGA aren't standards, and they mean different things to different manufacturers. The common ground for standardization seems to be the VESA VGA BIOS extensions, sometimes improperly called VESA SVGA. These VESA extensions to the BIOS at least allow programmers to provide a common software interface.

SVGA technology was originally developed by third-party manufacturers as a competitive answer to IBM's 8514/A and XGA technology. Today, most video cards are called SVGA cards, meaning that any resolution higher than 640× 400 and with 16 colors is SVGA. One might say that SVGA is 800×600 mode and UVGA is 1,024×768 mode.

 Make a note that Window 95 Safe mode starts Windows 95 in the standard VGA mode, regardless of what higher resolution was last set. Standard VGA is 640×480×16 colors.

Somewhat like SCSI interfaces, SVGA is produced by many different manufacturers, all providing their own variations of commands and program interfaces, where nothing is common. Because of this individuality, most monitors used in a graphic operating environment come with software drivers designed to optimize their performance.

A video card manufacturer can provide a VESA video driver TSR that usually interprets the differences between the basic VESA VGA extensions and the proprietary SVGA extensions on the card. This gives software vendors a fighting chance of writing programs that work with most SVGA displays. Advantages of SVGA include the following:

➤ SVGA can produce millions of colors at a number of different resolutions, depending on the card and the manufacturer.

➤ The VESA resolution standards range from 640×400 to 1,280×1,024, both with 256 colors.

 Remember that modern monitors use a 15-pin D-shell connector, where the back panel of the PC has a female connector. The monitor cable has a male, 15-pin connector. Serial connectors are usually nine-pin connectors.

Screen Size

The next most popular way of differentiating monitors is by screen size. Monitors have borrowed from the television industry by measuring screen size diagonally. Until recently, typical monitor sizes were 13 and 14 inches. Today, a 15-inch or 17-inch monitor has become inexpensive enough to be part of a typical computer package. Twenty- and 21-inch monitors are readily available but expensive. Any monitor over 16 inches is called a *full-page monitor* because it can display a full page in a one-to-one ratio (1:1). A monitor that is wider than it is tall is called a *landscape monitor* and can usually display two pages side by side. A monitor that is taller than it is wide is called a *portrait monitor.*

Portrait Vs. Landscape

Silly as it may seem (and computer jargon is often pretty silly), the orientation of a page or monitor is called portrait or landscape because of the way painters turn their canvases one way or the other. A painter who was painting a person usually did the head, shoulders, and upper torso, making for a taller, narrow painting—a portrait of that person.

On the other hand, to capture the expanse of an outdoor scene, a painter would turn the canvas sideways to achieve a wide view—a landscape view of the scene.

To this day, when the paper is tall and narrow, like a letter, it has a portrait orientation. When the paper is wide and short, like a spreadsheet, it has a landscape orientation.

Image Size

The box that holds the cathode ray or the LCD panel has a physical diagonal dimension. The actual screen or panel has another size. The actual image being displayed is somewhat smaller than the physical edges of the tube/panel against the casing.

The actual area used to display the image is called the *raster.* The raster varies according to the resolution of the monitor and the internal physics of the screen. A VGA mode image of 640×480 on a 15-inch screen will display as one size, whereas an SVGA mode image of 1,024×768 is a bit different. Television monitors usually overscan the image, putting the true edge out beyond the physical edge of the screen. However, because a computer image contains information up to the edge and often beyond the raster edge, a PC monitor's image is designed to be smaller than the physical edges.

Many video adapter cards have logic to automatically resize the raster, depending on the brand name and model of the monitor. On the outside of the monitor are a number of physical controls that can manually adjust the raster and the brightness, contrast, centering position, and so on.

 We saw an interesting problem that had to do with a change to the image size on the screen. Ordinarily, if a true black border appears around the image, then either the monitor is failing, or the image controls need to be adjusted. However, if the resolution of a monitor is changed from lower to higher, it can shrink all the images on the screen. This wouldn't normally produce a black band around the entire image, though.

On an LCD panel, an image resolution change could potentially cause a black band to appear around the edge of the panel. Since the display is designed to match the number of pixels in an image, the LCD process turns on crystals based on usage, and if the resolution is set too low for the panel, the images would be too small to go all the way to the edges of the panel.

Other Classifications

There are a number of different measurements used to differentiate monitors, and some of these are important to consider when purchasing a monitor. The relative importance of the measurements depends on the expected use of the monitor. Generally, today's monitors are high-performance, high-resolution SVGA color monitors. Starting from a common level of quality, some of their listed differences include the following:

➤ **Refresh rate** The rate (cycle of time) at which each line is drawn across the screen from top to bottom. The refresh rate affects what the human eye sees as flickering on the monitor. To avoid flickering, the refresh rate must be at least 70 Hz.

➤ **Interlacing** A technique for redrawing the screen image that makes the monitor produce a higher resolution, though it slows the monitor. Most monitors sold today are noninterlaced.

➤ **Dot pitch** The space between each pixel triad, measured in millimeters. Generally, the smaller the dot pitch, the sharper the images, though a very small dot pitch can result in a loss of brightness and contrast. Typically, a good dot pitch ranges from .28 mm to .25 mm.

➤ **Convergence** Describes how clear and sharp each pixel can be displayed. Each individual color in each triad must be exactly aligned with all of the other units of the same color. The global set of all the same colors must exactly align (converge) so that they're each on top of the other. If the convergence is faulty, the image appears with blurred color edges.

➤ **Bandwidth** The range of signal frequencies that a given monitor can work with. This determines how much data it can process at a given time.

Scan/Refresh Rate

In a CRT monitor, an electron gun shoots a stream of electrons at a wall of phosphorous chemicals. Phosphors have the trait of glowing for a short time after being struck by an electron beam; however, the glow quickly fades away. The electron beam must continually restrike the chemicals to refresh the level of light.

In monochrome monitors, the phosphor can glow only in green or amber. However, when three different phosphors are arranged in a triangle, or *triad,* of dots, the electrons can be manipulated by the video card to vary which dots glow with which strength. A glowing combination of red, blue, and green light can be made to fool the eye into thinking that it sees all sorts of colors in between. We've seen that the triad of dots in an RGB monitor makes up one pixel.

Technically, dot pitch is the diagonal measurement between the centers of two neighboring triads. This works out to be the same measurement as from the center of two dots of phosphor of the same color because the arrangement of the colors in a triad is the same throughout the *matrix.* (A matrix is a grid of rows and columns, like a spreadsheet.)

These triads of dots are very small, so the inside of the CRT has many triads next to each other in a line. There are also many lines running down the inside face of the tube, forming a large matrix of triads. Take a look at the lower right corner of Figure 7.1, where you can see how a pixel is made up of three-dot triads.

The electron gun is still a kind of mechanical device, so it can only blast one triad at a time with electrons. Therefore, it takes some amount of time for the beam of electrons to sweep from the top left to the bottom right of the screen. This time is one *scan cycle.*

The video card tells the monitor how to time the period from the top line to the bottom line by sending a *scan frequency* to the monitor when the monitor is plugged in. Recall from our discussion of motherboards that frequency is measured in cycles per second and written as Hz (hertz) or MHz (megahertz). The electron beam must synchronize with the scan frequency for the timing to

Figure 7.1 Smaller pixels mean sharper resolution.

redraw the screen. *Redraw* is simply a technical term for blasting those phosphor triads with electrons a second time to make them glow again.

When the beam of electrons reaches the lowest, right set of dots, it starts over at the topmost, left set of dots. If the image hasn't changed at all, it does the whole thing over again, refreshing the image. The entire cycle from top to bottom then back to top, is called the *refresh rate.*

If you've ever watched an old movie shown on an old projector, you know that the flicker comes from the spaces between each frame as it passes the projector's beam of light. The refresh rate includes the momentary time during which the upper lines of triads are starting to fade and the electron gun is swinging into action to light them up again.

The faster the electrons can refresh the phosphors, the faster the refresh rate and the less flicker the human eye perceives. For minimum flicker, the refresh rate should be at least 70 times per second (70 Hz).

Noninterlaced And Interlaced

The conventional process of sweeping the electron beams across the pixels from top to bottom and left to right is the *noninterlaced* mode. This involves sweeping past every pixel triad, one after the other, covering the entire screen in one pass, and then beginning over again.

Interlaced mode means that the electron beam sweeps from top to bottom, but that it takes *two* passes to do so. First it refreshes the odd lines, then the even lines. Interlaced mode draws half the screen (every other line) in half the noninterlaced time, then goes back and draws the other half of the screen. Figure 7.2 demonstrates how every other row of pixels is glowing. Each row in between is black (the phosphor has lost its glow). This is an interlaced monitor in the process of redrawing a screen.

The net effect is the same amount of time but an apparent full redraw. The human eye might be able to differentiate between the very thin odd and even lines, but interlacing allows slower refresh rates to accomplish nearly the same task. This slower rate allows for cheaper manufacturing and therefore cheaper monitors.

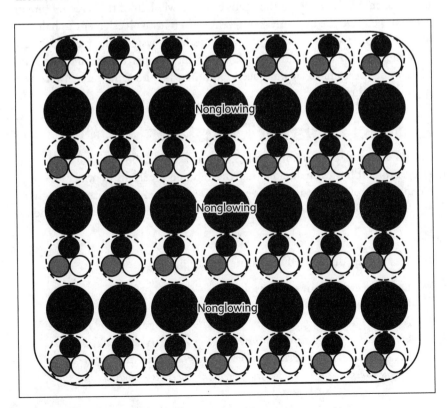

Figure 7.2   An interlaced monitor during a screen redraw.

Be sure to take your time on a question involving interlacing. Stop, think, and remember that interlacing is like weaving your *shoelaces* together. It takes two shoes, just as it takes two passes to interlace a monitor. *Noninterlaced*, is a single pass redraw.

Both modes take the same amount of time. However, given the same refresh rate, interlaced mode provides a more stable image and less flicker to the human eye. The problem is that manufacturers slow the refresh rate in interlaced monitors.

Let's say a single-pass noninterlaced process means the gun has to sweep across the whole screen 10 times per minute. The gun hits the starting point 10 times. In a two-pass interlaced process, the gun sweeps across the screen five times for the odd lines, and five times again for the even lines. The gun hits the starting point 10 times here as well. The difference is that in the two-pass process, there isn't a brightness difference between the upper half and the lower half of the screen.

In our single-pass example, it takes six seconds between the first and next glow of the top pixel. The first couple of rows have a lot of time to start fading, while the electron gun is attacking the triads on the lower half of the screen. Human eyes can perceive the brightness difference when it involves an entire half of a screen. In other words, in the two-pass interlaced system, the manufacturers slow the gun movement down, making it a bit cheaper to manufacture. The ideal would be to have an interlaced monitor with the same refresh rate as a noninterlaced monitor.

Liquid Crystal Displays

A CRT monitor, as the name implies, uses a vacuum tube to contain the beam of electrons. Physics mandates that the tube be a certain depth. Flat-panel technology brought about the *flat-panel displays* that are most often thought of as LCD monitors. However, other displays can be categorized as flat panel:

➤ LCD

➤ Gas plasma display (PDP, plasma display panel)

➤ ELD (electroluminescent display)

Note: Be advised that the term FTM (flat technology monitor) is not the same as a flat-panel display. Flat-technology monitors technically describe a CRT that uses a flat screen to reduce glare. Flat-panel displays are the typical screens used in laptops and notebooks, whereas FTMs are still tubes.

Until recently, LCD panels were almost always found on laptop or notebook computers. As color technology and the use of *active matrix* advances, full-size LCD monitors are arriving on the market. Flat-panel technology is also advancing rapidly in television and HDTV (high-definition television). The ability to control the size of the crystals (and therefore the size of the pixels) and to control each crystal directly allows for a possible way to produce very high resolutions. Potentially, LCD technology will replace cathode ray technology and bring film-quality video capability to the market.

Liquid Crystals

Liquid crystals have a fascinating property in that they exist in either a solid or a near-liquid state, depending on electrical conditions. In their near-liquid state, the crystals can pass light. Another interesting feature is that the crystals have a tendency to be straight (like a rod) in their natural state but to twist into a right angle under electrical stimulation. This combination of passing light and turning to right angles gave rise to the LCD panel.

Polarization

Have you ever used polarized sunglasses? The science used in making these glasses works on the principle that most light tends to be polarized (lined up) according to its wavelength, somewhat like iron molecules face the same direction around a magnet. The lenses of polarized glasses are constructed so that the molecules in each lens are lined up in rows leaning over at an angle. The molecules of regular glass don't line up this way. Because polarized sunglasses have this alignment property, the lenses allow only light waves traveling at the correct angle to pass—a fraction of the entire spectrum of sunlight.

If you hold a polarized lens in front of another polarized lens and rotate the first lens, all the light will gradually be blocked and the background will turn black. When the polar alignment of the one lens is 90 degrees against the other, no light passes.

LCD Panel Construction

An LCD panel is made of two polarized planes of glass placed at right angles (90 degrees) to each other. Sandwiched between the glass is a layer of liquid crystals (with that weird bending quality). Behind the back panel is a fluorescent light source that tries to get through the two misaligned panels of glass. In the default state, the light is blocked, and the panels appear black.

The Matrix

Each liquid crystal is in a matrix (rows and columns) with very thin wires leading to a set of switches along the top and side edges of the glass panels. When electrical current is sent to a specific X-Y location on the grid, the liquid crystal at that point goes into its act, bending 90 degrees and turning almost transparent.

What's so cool about this process is this: The light coming in from the back is, say, vertically aligned—straight up and down. The liquid crystal is also up and down, but the front pane of glass is horizontally aligned—left and right. When the liquid crystal becomes transparent and twists over on its side, it carries the light over sideways and then passes it through the front pane. Let there be light! We can envision all these little liquid crystals doing the Macarena dance, and when they bend down images form.

In any event, forming an image pattern always involves making a series of dots. If you can create a dot of light against a background of black, you've met the basic criterion for making an image. Depending on how often a crystal is turned on in relation to the crystals next to it, the human eye can be fooled into thinking that it sees about 16 shades of gray.

Color And Light

Over time, liquid crystals were developed that could cut out all colors of light except one. Using the CMY (cyan, magenta, yellow) process of building colors from the primary colors, the number of crystals in the matrix was tripled. Triads of three crystals (each able to pass only one primary color) were put together in the matrix, and the switches were tripled to access each subcrystal. By turning on one of the three crystals in each triad, the same effect was produced as with an electron beam and phosphors.

Because the crystals are acting only as a very tiny shutter, they can't produce light on their own. On the other hand, an actual light source doesn't need the space of an electron gun and beam. LCD panels can use a very thin light source behind them, making the entire panel far thinner than a CRT. This is why they're so often used in notebook and laptop computers.

Unless there's a light behind the panel or a very bright light reflecting through the front panel and then off the back panel, an LCD can't display anything. One problem with LCD computers is the difficulty of seeing their screens outdoors or when another light source is brighter than the back-panel light.

Twisted Nematic

LCD panels have a limited angle of viewing because of the physics of polarization and light transmission. Therefore, the types of crystals have been modified to allow light to branch off to the sides. Without getting into scientific jargon, we can see three modifications to the crystals:

1. Supertwisted nematic (also known as STND, super-twisted nematic display)

2. Double supertwisted nematic

These two modifications allow a wider viewing angle and a brighter contrast in the panels. The original crystals and the way in which they are twisted didn't let the user see the screen very well. Therefore, a third kind of crystal was developed:

3. Triple supertwisted nematic

This form of crystal allows for the color subtraction method of CMY along with added brightness and side viewing.

Passive Matrix

We've said that a matrix is a grid, much like a spreadsheet is a matrix of cells making up rows and columns. The columns have letters and the rows have numbers. If you name the X-Y coordinate B15, you're pinpointing a cell in the matrix, namely, the second column (column B) and the fifteenth row down.

As we've also seen, LCD panels have a matrix of wires. VGA resolution is 640 × 480 pixels in a matrix. Therefore, a VGA LCD panel requires 640 transistor switches along the sides and 480 along the top and bottom to produce 640 × 480 dots of lights (pixels). As in a CRT, the rows are activated sequentially, moving from top to bottom, resulting in a refresh rate and limited contrast.

Dual Scan

Some LCD panels divide the screen into a top half and a bottom half, allowing a simultaneous refresh of two rows, one in each half. On the one hand, this dual scanning process decreases the contrast, making the screen less bright. On the other hand, it consumes less power than panels that use a single refresh rate.

Either way, the response time of LCD panels is slow. It takes from 40 ms to 200 ms to move the crystal through its twist-and-relax cycle. This explains why many LCD panels show a shadowy trail when the cursor is moved and why the expected position of the cursor seems to take a moment to catch up with an actual picture of a cursor. However, passive matrix LCD panels are inexpensive to manufacture.

CSTN

A newer technology, CSTN (color supertwisted nematic), developed by Sharp Electronics, uses these color supertwisted nematic crystals in a passive matrix to produce the three primary colors. The technology is cheaper to manufacture than the color subtraction process of the active matrix and still provides color.

CSTN crystals have a faster response rate than the original crystals, with a 100 ms response and about a 140-degree viewing angle. As the name implies, they also provide color.

HPA

HPA (high performance addressing) is an addressing scheme used in a passive matrix that provides a better response rate (100 ms) and higher contrast than the conventional method. However, the technology still uses a passive matrix, so the panels aren't as crisp and fast as an active matrix panel.

HPA panels are less expensive to produce, and many computer manufacturers use them in their lower-priced notebooks.

Ferroelectric

These panels use a special type of liquid crystal that can stay polarized for a period of time after the electrical current has stopped. This reduces the refresh rate and enhances the viewing environment by almost eliminating flicker.

Ferroelectric crystals have a response rate of 100 ms, making them extremely fast, but they're also very difficult to manufacture, and therefore are very expensive. Eventually, these panels might provide active-matrix response times at passive-matrix prices.

Active Matrix

The fundamental difference between the passive and the active matrix in an LCD panel is the number of switches. The passive matrix has only one switch per column. Principles involving electrical capacitance allow a charge to be sent to a specific part of a wire, somewhere between two transistors. The active matrix gives every liquid crystal its own switch.

Putting a switch alongside every crystal in the matrix increases the speed of pinpointing a specific X-Y coordinate. This allows each crystal to be turned on and off more quickly and provides better control over how long it stays on in relation to its neighboring crystals. It also provides better control over each crystal in a triad at a grid point. Active-matrix LCD panels are basically huge integrated circuits, much like microprocessors.

The number of components in an active-matrix LCD is at least three times the number required for a passive-matrix panel. Although active-matrix LCDs are much more expensive to manufacture, they have far better contrast and response time than the passive-matrix models. The three main types of active-matrix LCD panels are:

➤ TFT (thin film transistors); each crystal is controlled by one to four transistors, depending on color triads or monochrome

➤ MIM (metal-insulator-metal)

➤ PALC (plasma addressed liquid crystal)

Because active-matrix LCD panels are manufactured mainly by the TFT process, it's not uncommon to hear people interchange the terms and call an active matrix a TFT panel.

Plasma Display Panels

A different technology for a flat-panel display is the PDP (plasma display panel). Instead of sandwiching liquid crystals, an ionized gas is placed between the panels. One panel has wires going across in rows, and the other panel has wires going up and down in columns. By combining a specific horizontal and a specific vertical wire on the two panels, a charge can be sent through the gas, making it glow as a dot of light. The type of gas determines the color of the glow.

Plasma displays are monochrome only, and most use neon gas and glow orange. Although advances are being made in colorizing gases, current technology makes these panels very expensive and provides no grayscale capability. However, the panels can be scaled to very large sizes and provide excellent brightness and contrast, making them an attractive technology for signs and public information displays.

Printers

Most people think of a printer when they hear the term *computer output*. We've seen that any device that works with data being thrown around by the CPU, its dependent chips, and memory can be thought of as an output device. A printer is a way to capture information on paper, film, transparencies, or anything that can be handled by the roller mechanism and not get stuck (sometimes even thin cloth).

In Chapter 11, we examine some of the problems with printers. For now, though, let's focus on the basic differences between printers and how they work. Printers connect to the CPU by a cable and an interface, typically either a serial interface or a parallel interface.

 You must remember the difference between a 9-pin serial interface and a 25-pin parallel interface. The confusing part is the 25-pin serial printer cable. For the exam, remember that the most common printer cable is a 25-pin male DB25 connector on one end, and a 36-pin male Centronics connector on the other. Serial interfaces (ports) use a male 9-pin connector on the back panel of the PC's chassis.

Network printers still use cabling but might have an internal NIC (network interface card), so they don't need to connect directly to a computer. New technology provides an infrared connection that does away with the cable but still uses the parallel or serial port on the computer. The four fundamental types of printers are:

➤ **Impact printers** Daisy wheel and dot matrix

➤ **Direct thermal printers** Some fax machines and inexpensive and high-portability printers

➤ **Thermal ink/color printers** Ink jet and bubble jet

➤ **Laser printers**

Printer output is by far the most common way to share information among people. The driving forces in printer technology have been the speed at which the printer can put graphics and text onto a piece of paper and the resolution of those graphics and text. Printer resolution is measured in dots per inch (dpi). Think again of that newspaper picture composed of black and white dots. The more dots in a given area, the darker the area. The smaller the dots, the sharper the edges of the area.

Dots Per Inch (dpi)

If you've ever used a computer graphics program that allows you to zoom in to an image (making an area incrementally larger or smaller), you might try visualizing the pupil of a person's eye in a photograph. If the resolution of the image is low, and you zoom in to a certain pixel level on that pupil, you'll discover that all the pixels are square. You'll also discover that only seven or eight pixel squares were used to form the pupil. This makes the pupil look like a combination of a rectangle and a cross.

If you scan that same photograph again with, say, a 1,200 dpi optical scanner and then zoom in once again to the same pixel level, you'll discover a difference. First, you'll need to zoom in a few more increments to get to the pixel squares. Second, the pupil is now made up of perhaps 25 or more pixels. Third, those pixel squares are much smaller than those in the first image.

We've seen how the smaller a series of dots used on a monitor, the sharper the resolution. This principle applies exactly the same way with printing dots. Under a microscope the dots on a printer are actually round, while the pixels in a graphic image are squares. However, the phosphorus spots on the back face of a CRT are generally round.

 Make a note that printed images resolve with dots per inch (dpi) while displayed images resolve with picture units (pixels).

Because there are so many more squares and because they're much smaller, the edges of the pupil can take them and form an actual curve rather than a rough, stepladder type of pattern. This is the same process as drawing a curve with a child's Etch-a-Sketch.

There are only two knobs on the Etch-a-Sketch, one of which moves up and down while the other moves left and right. To draw an apparent curve, you use a step-ladder process composed of vertical and horizontal movements. The smaller you make the increments of this "up-and-over" movement, the smoother the final curve will look. Likewise, the more the pins and the smaller they are, the sharper and better the printer can create a curve.

Dot matrix and laser printers work in much the same way as scanners do, that is, by placing dots into an area. The primary difference between the scanned image and the printed image is that the dots on a printer are more round than square. The roundness of the printer pixels also helps to smooth the edges of curves when the dots are very close together.

Cables

The great majority of printers sold on the market use a parallel interface. The parallel cable usually has a standard DB25 male connector on one end and a 36-pin Centronics connector on the other. If you remember that a parallel connector is 25 pins and that the back panel port connector is female, you should be able to remember that printer cables use male connectors. While there are some serial printers, we didn't see any questions on the exam pertaining to them.

Centronics

The Centronics Corporation is one of the original developers of dot matrix printers, and developed what were considered the top-of-the-line dot matrix printers at the time. The company's claim to fame was the parallel interface it developed, which became the standard printer connection. The standard Centronics connector on most printer cables is 36 pins wide.

 Don't get confused between a 36-pin Centronics connector and a 50-pin SCSI connector. We only saw the main connectors on the exam, so try to remember 9-pin, 15-pin, 25-pin, 36-pin, and 50-pin.

Paper

Although printing devices can put ink on paper, transparencies, card stock, and even cloth, paper is used the most on a day-to-day basis. High-speed *line printers* are often connected to mainframe and minicomputers and use the familiar green-bar, continuous-form paper. Green-bar computer paper is usually 11 inches by 14 inches in size. The individual environment of the personal computer, though, tends to focus on letter-size ($8^1/_2 \times 11$) or legal-size ($8^1/_2 \times 14$) paper.

The dramatic drop in the prices of laser printers has made the sheet-fed process common in the business world. At the same time, ink jet and bubble jet printers are so inexpensive and produce such high-quality output that their sheet-fed process has made continuous-feed paper mainly a specialty item.

Form Feed

Printers almost always require a piece of paper—a *form*—that they must move in front of the printing process and then out of the printer. The old printing press used human labor as a paper-feed mechanism, whereby a human being inserted paper into the press and used a letterpress to lay down a series of aligned letters on the paper. The letterpress was then raised, and the human laborer reached in and lifted off the sheet of paper. Very few people use human labor anymore and the process has become nearly obsolete.

Feeding a form *(form feed)* involves pulling a piece of paper into a printer, aligning it in front of a printing mechanism, and moving it back out of the printer. If only one piece of paper—a single form—is moved through the printer at a time, the printer is commonly said to be *sheet-fed*. If the pieces of paper are connected into one long sheet and move through the printer continuously, the printer is said to be *continuous feed*.

Continuous/Tractor Fed

Continuous-form paper is a very long, single sheet of paper with a perforated divider line every 11 (US letter) or 14 (legal) inches and with a series of holes along both sides. The perforations allow individual sheets to be separated after the print job; the holes along the sides fit over a pair of *form tractors* or a *sprocket* that rotates and then pulls the paper forward (or backward) into the printer. Today, most continuous-form paper is several sheets thick and can be pre-printed and multipart, containing blanks to be filled in with variable data.

The difference between a form tractor and a sprocket is that a form tractor is a belt that has knobs protruding from the outer surface. Oddly enough, these knobs align almost exactly with the holes in the edges of the paper. Some continuous-fed paper has been found to be intelligent; that is, it will attempt to adjust the tractor perforations (the holes along the edges) by itself, confounding some of the brightest minds in human history and jamming printers as well.

A *sprocket-feed* (also called a *pin-feed*) printer uses a less expensive plastic wheel with molded pins protruding around the edge of the wheel. Again, the pins align with the holes on the edge of the paper. Because a tractor belt has more knobs per inch than a sprocket, tractor-feed printers can work with smaller increments of movement, so line spacing can be smaller. However, the tractor belt has a tendency to slip with usage, whereas the sprocket wheel is usually glued onto a kind of axle.

Friction

An important part of the entire printing process is the physical principle of *friction*. This tendency for materials to cling to each other is responsible for our ability to walk, for vehicles to travel over roads, and for paper jams. Aside from paper jams, where friction is working against us, the pinch rollers on a printer require friction against the paper's leading edge in order to grab onto the paper and move it.

Mechanical parts that continue to move inside a machine tend to wear down and break. Friction is the primary reason for the breakdown, as the movement against other parts gradually peels off layers of material from a moving part. In order to reduce friction, we use lubricating materials of some kind. Common lubricating materials are oil or grease.

While oil is beneficial in places where constant mechanical movement can wear down a part, it becomes a detriment where friction is required. Common areas of a printer that depend on friction are:

➤ Pinch rollers

➤ Platens

➤ Tractor belts and sprockets

➤ Paper separation wheels

Consumer products have followed a trend over the years of reducing the amount of maintenance as much as possible. Other than general cleaning, many of today's printers use replaceable components instead of providing for the owner's mechanical know-how. When a part is used up (consumed) and then thrown away, we call it a *consumable*. The cost of a printer is a one-time expense. However, the overall cost of operating a printer depends on how expensive the various consumables are. Typical consumables are paper, ink cartridges, and toner cartridges.

 We saw some questions on the exam that had to do with lubricating parts of a printer. Aside from possibly using some light oil on a bidirectional print-head rail, most printers don't provide for this type of general maintenance.

When oil or grease begins to build up on surfaces that require a lot of friction, the most common way to clean them is with rubbing alcohol. Alcohol is a liquid solvent that evaporates, leaving almost no residue of any kind. Rubber wheels used in various rollers, areas under tractor belts, and sometimes the platen roller behind the paper on a dot matrix printer can benefit from cleaning with alcohol.

The solvent properties of alcohol break down oils, grease from fingers, and ink residues for removal, then evaporates cleanly, leaving a clean surface. Electrical circuits should be as clean as possible in order to minimize an accidental connection between two lines (short circuit) in the wrong place.

Note: Special cleaning kits are available that include a cleaning solvent that leaves no residue, rubber restorers for cleaning roller wheels, and pressure dusters. A blast of compressed air can blow dust out of keyboards and printers without allowing pieces of a physical duster to fall into a delicate mechanism.

Friction Feed

One of the original single-sheet, friction-feed printers was a *typewriter*. This device used a biochemical software application called the human typist to produce output and pulled a single sheet of paper through the printer with friction and rollers. Friction-feed devices rely on the friction of a *pinch roller* to catch the leading edge of a piece of paper and then draw it forward into the printer. The leading edge is the first edge (though not always the top edge) that goes into the printer. A roller mechanism then presses down on the surface of the paper, rolling it along a *paper path*. These rollers continue to turn, moving the paper along the paper path until there's no more paper to work against—usually when the paper has reached the *output tray* and the print job is complete.

Improvements on the friction-feed process led to a paper tray that can hold many sheets of paper. As the top or the bottom sheet of paper is nudged forward, the printer's pinch roller begins to turn when the printer signals that it's ready to print the next page.

Direct Thermal Printers And Paper

Thermal paper is a type of paper used mainly in small calculators, inexpensive fax machines, and some very small thermal printers designed for cash registers and laptop computers. This paper is chemically treated so that a print head can heat it in the typical dotted patterns. The print head is essentially the same as a dot matrix print head but uses heated pins to form a mark on the thermal paper rather than pressure on an ink ribbon.

Thermal paper is somewhat expensive, and it is very sensitive to ultraviolet light (i.e., sunlight), which can fade the images on the paper to the point of being illegible.

Dot Matrix

Impact printers will have a place in society as long as there are multipart forms. A typical environment for a dot matrix printer is in medical offices, where Medicare reimbursement requires a special type of form that has carbon copies attached to the front piece. Laser printers might print faster and sharper but, because laser printing uses a heat-transfer process, it can work on only one sheet of paper at a time. Thermal color printers can work on only single sheets of paper as well, which leaves impact printers alone in the field of multisheet forms.

The term *impact* applies to these printers because a mechanical device is driven forward in space and rams into the surface of the ink ribbon with great impact. The impact leaves a residue of ink on the paper when the mechanical device is withdrawn again. Impact printers can print only in portrait orientation using their built-in character sets. However, with special translation software, a print job can be converted to a graphic, and a dot matrix printer can print it landscape.

A dot matrix printer uses a print head housing a number of very small pins. The print head typically moves back and forth along a guide rail. As each line is printed the paper moves up one line. The pins in the print head are pushed toward the ribbon and paper in various combinations to form letters. The number of pins defines the quality of the letter, just as the number of dots defines printer resolution. With only nine pins, there's a limit to how many pins can form the curve at the top of, for example, the number 9. However, with 24 pins, the pins are much smaller, so more of them can be used to form the curve at the top of the number 9, resulting in a sharper-looking character.

 Make a note that dot matrix printers are distinguished by how many pins the print head uses. Common varieties are 9-pin, 18-pin, and 24-pin print heads.

Printer Ribbon

Impact printers use a ribbon that has ink on one side of it. The ribbon is pulled along and held in alignment between the print head and the paper. As the print head strikes the non - inked side of the ribbon, it presses the inked side against the paper, transferring ink in the pattern created by the print head.

Ribbons are almost always made of cloth, but some modern ribbons use a strip of plastic instead. The ribbon is connected at both ends to a reel. In a reel-to-reel mechanism, holes in each reel fit over a set of pins on the face of a horizontal sprocket, which turns and advances the ribbon incrementally. As the take-up reel turns, it draws a new segment of ribbon, with fresh ink, in front of the print head. Reel-to-reel printer ribbons were modified to be enclosed in a cartridge, making it easy to change the ribbon by simply dropping in a new cartridge and throwing away the old one.

Daisy Wheel

The daisy wheel printer is an obsolete technology that derived from the original typewriter. At the end of the mechanical typewriter era, two innovations had been introduced to make it possible to use different fonts.

One way of doing this was with a rapidly rotating ball covered with each character in a particular font. Another way was with a plastic wheel that had thin arms protruding from the center with each character at the end of an arm. Because these wheels and their arms looked like a daisy, they were called daisy wheels.

Daisy-wheel printers were essentially electric typewriters with a controller that could interface with the CPU. They were friction-feed, single-sheet printers with rudimentary controls for line spacing. Daisy-wheel printers could print only in portrait orientation.

Color Thermal Printers

Impact printers often provided a shift mechanism to move the print head up or down a small distance. The reason was that many ribbons came split into two (or sometimes three) strips: black ink above and red ink below. Some ribbons included a special "white-out" band for transferring white plastic over an incorrectly typed character. The desire for color has always been a driving force in the consumer printer market. Some impact printers even tried having all four color strips on a single ribbon.

To produce color in a small, computer-controlled printer, several methods have been explored, including wax transfer and combining colored inks. The wax transfer process is very expensive and requires special wax-composition ink and special paper. However, because the wax is melted to transfer ink to the paper, folding the final product can cause the ink to flake off.

Dye Vs. Pigment

The constant battle of bright, vivid color against the fading properties of ultraviolet light (sunlight) began with the caveman's drawing on a rock wall and continues to this day.

The two main types of ink coloring are dye and pigment, and each has its advantages and disadvantages. Dye-based ink is completely dissolved in a solution and becomes soluble again in wet conditions. Dye is very vibrant and colorful and is fairly stable, but it is susceptible to ultraviolet rays and loses optical density.

Pigments are solid particles held in suspension in a liquid that are absorbed into the paper when the solution dries. Pigments are very resistant to ultraviolet rays, but don't have the stability and vividness of dyes.

In recent years, color laser printers have arrived on the market for less than $1,000. Because the original black-and-white laser printers originally cost around $1,000, but today cost around $350, it stands to reason that within a few more years affordable color lasers will be the norm in the home and business environments.

Until color laser printers are everywhere, the most successful way to produce inexpensive color printing is through the thermal color process. An ink jet printer is much like a dot matrix printer in that characters are produced by building up a series of dots in an area of the page. However, rather than hammering a pin against a ribbon, the ink jet printer uses a bubble to force a drop of ink onto the paper, leaving a dot.

Metal Pin Impact Printing

Think about the mechanical process of impact printing with a pin-based, dot matrix printer. A rod of metal—the pin—must be held in a ready position within the print head. This is done with an electromagnet that pulls the base of the pin back against a coiled spring. A control signal from the CPU turns off the power to the magnet, and the spring gathers momentum to push the pin forward. Gradually, the pin gathers speed until it slams into the ribbon, driving the ribbon backward into the paper and stopping.

Ink is forcibly thrown from the back of the ribbon and splattered all over the paper, which is crushed between the pin, the ribbon, and the roller platen behind the paper. The ribbon and the pin exchange phone numbers and insurance information; then the electromagnet is called by the CPU, which turns on the magnetism again. The pin is hauled away by the magnetic tow truck and returned to its housing in the print head while the paper is left to recover in the hospital. The piece of ribbon moves away from the scene with only a few scratches.

All this happens very quickly from a human perspective, but at a microcosmic level it takes a lot of time. No matter how strong the spring is, it must be very small. The spring must overcome inertia in the pin, and then the electromagnet must overcome the resistance of the spring when it pulls the pin back into the head. In addition, the pins themselves must be able to withstand the carnage and "pinslaughter" of being smashed into the paper over and over again, a few million times! Let's take a moment of silence to remember those heroic pins that have paved the way to the modern day of Ink jet and laser printing. The main advantages of the thermal ink process are as follows:.

➤ Ink jet technology is faster than impact pin printing because the jet of ink has only a single mechanical step: the movement of bubbling (discussed shortly).

➤ Because a pin is constructed of metal, and ink is composed of liquid, a bubble of ink can be much smaller than a solid pin.

➤ Blowing liquid ink drops is a lot quieter than ramming a metal pin against a piece of paper and a roll bar (platen).

Ink Pixels And Resolution

We've seen that the number of dots per inch in printing is an important aspect of resolution. The pixels (picture units) sent to the printer are extremely small, so the smaller the corresponding dots, the more likely the picture will be reproduced accurately. However, the size and shape of the dots is equally important.

Advances in ink jet technology allows for the scientific break-up of a single dot into an even smaller part, in a controlled manner, to guarantee the size and spread of the broken-up original drop. These pieces of ink drop are how ink jet printers can double and almost triple the resolution of a laser printer.

However, the slight amount of drying time it takes for the ink drops to be absorbed into the paper allows a microscopic amount of capillary bleeding into the paper. This reduces the original resolution. With newer, glossy papers and appropriate drying time, a modern ink jet printer can reproduce photographic-quality resolution.

Ink Bubbles

Print heads in an ink jet printer have extremely tiny nozzles (orifices) making up the dot-laying mechanism. A hole can be engineered to be much smaller than a rod because the hole doesn't require the structural strength to withstand being smashed into a ribbon hundreds of times per minute.

Ink is held in a containing well in the print head until the CPU sends a control signal for that color of ink. The control signal generates a rapid heat increase in a thermal resistor, heating the ink and causing it to expand to form a bubble under the ink in the well. The bubble expands just enough to force a tiny drop of ink from the orifice and onto the paper.

Not only can the dot of ink be much finer than the diameter of a pin, but multiple cartridges can contain all four colors of ink. Depending on the color required, any or all of the cartridges can be told to put a drop of ink on a specific spot on the paper.

Ink jet printers work best with specially designed paper rather than ordinary paper. The porous makeup of regular paper allows for a slight capillary action in which small amounts of ink are drawn away from the original location, making the appearance fuzzy. On specially made ink jet paper, the ink stays exactly where it's placed.

Inexpensive ink jet printers once had only the three nonblack colors and used an equal combination of CMY to produce black. The blackness was not of good quality, and eventually a black ink cartridge became the norm.

Ink/Bubble Jet Vs. Piezoelectric

The problem with an ink-bubble process is that the resulting dot is a single size when it leaves the orifice, but has a tiny amount of splatter when it hits the paper—much like a raindrop hitting the ground. Another problem is that the size of the original bubble can't be precisely defined. Although the incremental differences from one bubble to the next are extremely small, they do differ.

To solve these problems, a new method of forcing the ink drop from the orifice was developed using a *piezoelectric crystal*. A piezoelectric crystal has the unusual attribute of changing size when an electrical charge is sent through it. This change in size is exactly related to the amount of charge and the size of the crystal.

By sending an exactly increasing charge across a crystal, the piezoelectric crystal contracts and pulls an exact amount of ink down from the well above it. When the charge is ended, the crystal returns to its original size, forcing the drop of ink out of the orifice.

An interesting new technology has been added that uses electronic frequencies to "bend" the drop across a cutting edge as it emerges from the orifice. By using a specific vibrational frequency and having the original drop a specific size, that ink drop can be cut into exact subdrops in a controlled splatter pattern. Combining the shatter effect with allowing a full-size drop to pass to the paper allows different size pixel drops of ink to be put on the paper, allowing for resolutions of over 1,440 dpi.

Resolution Benchmarks

When dot matrix printers came out to replace daisy wheel typewriter-type printers, the sharpness of a business letter produced by a typewriter was the benchmark. A dot matrix printer had a letter-quality mode or capability if it could produce output as clear as a typewriter.

Laser printers offered resolutions of 300 dpi and then 600 dpi, which became the benchmark. A good-quality printer was said to produce laser-quality output. Modern printers offer such high resolution that they can be compared to the analog world of color photography. The current benchmark, then, is photo-quality or photographic output. Comparing ink jet technology with laser technology results in the following observations:

➤ Modern piezoelectric printers can produce resolutions (on the proper paper) of 1,440 dpi, making them near photographic in their resolution output and number of colors.

➤ The problem with ink/bubble jet technology is the longevity of the ink cartridges in relation to their price.

➤ Ink cartridges generally output around 200 pages at high resolutions and require special paper.

➤ Laser printers might have lower resolution, but they print faster and cost less per page of output.

Laser Printers

Around 1980, when dot matrix printers were pretty much the only affordable choice for PC users, a new technology was being moved forward from the famous Xerox PARC (Palo Alto Research Complex) labs—EP (*electrophotographic*) printers—better known as the laser printer. The basic goal of a printer is to put a number of dots of color on a piece of paper in a pattern, and some schemes have tried to do this. The number, size, and color of the dots and how fast the dots can be transferred are areas of technical exploration.

Dot matrix and ink jet printers put dots on paper in *blocks*, from 7 to 64 dots at a time, depending on the number of pins or ink nozzles being used. Both these technologies move a print head along a piece of paper in a line and lay down a line of information at a time. When the line is complete, the tractor mechanism moves the paper up one line while the print head whips back across the paper to begin a new line. (Some dot matrix printers allowed printing while the print head moved in both directions, eliminating the time required for moving the print head back to a starting position.)

A laser printer still puts dots on a piece of paper. These dots are made up of tiny pieces of plastic "ink," or *toner* that are heated until they bond with the paper. However, regardless of how small those pieces of plastic are, they're still solid matter and probably can't be made smaller than a liquid dot of ink. For this reason, current ink jet printers can attain resolutions of 1,400 dpi or higher, whereas most laser printers are limited to 600 dpi.

 Laser printer toner is a near-microscopic combination of plastic resin and some organic compounds bonded to iron particles. Remember that toner powder is a combination of plastic, metal (iron), and organic compounds.

The Laser Printing Process

The 1998 A+ exam devotes a number of questions to the specific mechanics of printing with a laser printer. We suggest that you take the time to understand the step-by-step movement of paper through the printer. While the technical science behind the electrostatic and electrophotographic (EP) process may seem obscure, we found that by knowing the process we could usually puzzle out a correct response to these questions.

 Remember that EP is short for electrophotographic. The EP drum in a toner cartridge is where images are created and developed.

A fundamental difference in the way laser printers work is that a page of information is formed in RAM first and then transferred as a whole unit to the paper (much like a photocopier works). This speeds up the process of printing. On the other hand, the process requires a heating time to *fuse* (set) the image on the paper permanently. Overall, a laser printer can print a page of information faster than a line printer of any kind.

How Long Will It Last?

Remember that an ink jet printer puts ink on paper. The ink soaks into the fibers of the paper itself. A high-quality ink is designed to be resistant to ultraviolet light and won't fade or otherwise degrade. Because the ink literally is a part of the paper, it usually will last as long as the paper lasts.

Laser printing uses bits of plastic that effectively are melted onto the surface of the paper. Although the plastic is also impervious to ultraviolet light and its fading effects, the bond between the paper and the plastic is degradable. At the moment, laser-printed information hasn't been around long enough to really test its longevity against embedded ink. However, for historical and archival documents, it's worth keeping in mind that the fused bond between the paper and the plastic is an area of weakness.

A camera uses reflected light from an object to influence the molecular structure of a piece of film and capture an image. A scanner still uses reflected light that is bounced onto a CCD and transferred to a file for storage. Therefore, a laser printer is called a laser printer because it uses a laser beam to draw a "photograph" of an image onto a photosensitive drum.

The Printing Components

A laser printer is a complex grouping of subsystems, all of which interact exactly to move a blank piece of paper from the input side to the output side. In between, information is stored to the paper. The components of a laser printer are as follows:

➤ **AC/DC power supply** The main power supply takes in AC from the wall. The DC power supply converts the AC to the DC voltages typically used in a computer system.

➤ **High-voltage power supply** Electrophotography (EP) requires around 1,000 volts or more to create a static electricity charge that moves the toner particles into position.

➤ **Fusing assembly** Heat and pressure are required to fuse the plastic toner particles to the paper.

➤ **Erase lamp assembly** The laser beam writes a preliminary, or *latent,* image to the photosensitive drum before transferring the image to paper. To clear the latent image, an erase lamp resets the drum to clear.

➤ **Writing mechanism** The image in RAM must be initially written as the latent image on the drum. A laser beam is moved across the photosensitive material by the writing mechanism.

➤ **Main motor** A number of small motors drive various rollers, the drum, and mechanical processes. The main motor provides the mechanical energy needed by the submotors.

➤ **Scanner motor assembly** To move the laser beam across the photosensitive drum, a mirror and motor direct the reflected light beam.

➤ **Paper control assembly** This includes the entire process and all the mechanics of grabbing the leading edge of a piece of paper and moving it through the paper path to the output tray.

➤ **Main logic assembly** Sometimes called the ECP (electronic control package), this includes all the circuitry for communicating with the CPU, the control panel, and the internal memory of the printer.

➤ **Toner cartridge** Technically, this is the EP cartridge. The cartridge includes a number of subassemblies for cleaning, developing, and moving toner particles.

➤ **Control panel assembly** This is the user interface whereby printer controls can be entered for configuration or manual paper operations. The control panel is also where the printer communicates various internal problems to the user.

Capacitors And Resistors Electrical Shock Warning

Electricity is often expressed in terms of voltage, and many people think that the familiar 120 volts of power coming from the wall is very dangerous and can kill you. However, *amperage,* not voltage, is the dangerous part of electricity.

Cardiac arrest can be brought on by only 100 milliamperes (milliamps), or one-tenth of an amp. The typical amperage inside a printer is 1 or 2 amps. Remember, then, that the typical 2-amp fused power location is 20 times the amount of power needed to kill you. Be careful when you open up a printer!

The other side of the coin is that the internal parts of a printer are just as susceptible to ESD as are the motherboard and the computer's internal components. It's very easy to build up a 20,000 volt charge just by walking from the doorway to the printer. Always use an ESD kit when working inside a printer.

Laser Printing Steps

Laser printers depend on a whole group of systems and processes to get an image from memory onto paper. Nonlaser printers mainly use a single system to put a tiny part of a pattern onto paper, one part at a time. Therefore, the heart of the IFS (image formation system) is the photosensitive EP drum.

This drum is an extruded aluminum cylinder coated with a nontoxic organic compound that reacts to light in an unusual way: It turns light into electricity. This is called *photoconductivity.* When light touches the compound, it generates a bit of electricity that's conducted (moved) through the compound.

Figure 7.3 is a stylized representation of the various parts involved in the printing process. We didn't see any questions on the exam asking you to identify parts by letters, but we feel it may help you to keep the steps in their right order if you can visualize it.

Cleaning

Recall that latent images are like a memory of a picture. If you simply let the drum continue to accumulate images and then print them, it wouldn't take very long to have a black piece of paper because all the images would build up on top of one another. To understand this, take 5 or 10 photographic slides, put them on top of one another, and try to look through them.

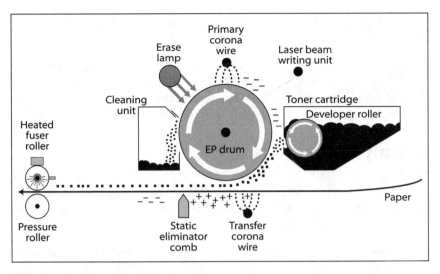

Figure 7.3   The main parts of a laser printing cycle.

To get the drum ready to accept a new image—in this case a letter to your Aunt Jane—it must be cleaned and erased. No matter how high the quality of the drum and toner, one way or another a microscopic amount of residue will stay on the drum from the previous image transfer.

A rubber cleaning blade is used to gently scrape the drum clean of any residual toner that drops into the debris cavity to the side of the cartridge and below the cleaning blade. Some cartridges allow the residual toner to be returned to the main toner supply.

 The EP drum must be clean in order to take on a new image. If you think about it logically, you can almost work out the details in your mind when you're facing a question.

Erasing

When the laser beam touches a horizontal location on the drum, it changes that point to a less negative, or relatively positive, charged spot. The image on the drum is written line by line in a series of positive dots against a negative surface until the entire image is stored on the surface of the drum. The drum surface, in its default state, has no electrical charge. The stored image is the latent image mentioned earlier.

To remove the previous page of charged dots from the drum, a series of erase lights are set up near the drum's surface. The erase lights are filtered to provide a particular wavelength that bleeds away any electrical charge from the drum.

Once the drum has been erased, it has a *neutral charge,* that is, no electrical charge at all.

An area that can be confusing during the exam is the difference between cleaning old toner particles from the EP drum, as opposed to erasing an image from the drum. Think of it this way: you erase a picture: you don't "clean" a picture.

Conditioning

The neutral surface of the drum has no sensitivity to light at this point and can't store any kind of image. The drum must be given a negative charge that's completely and evenly distributed across the entire surface of the drum. That electrical charging is called *conditioning.*

To condition the surface of the drum, an extremely powerful charge of negative electricity is swept across the surface of the drum. This voltage is in the area of -6,000 volts (negative charge) and distributed by a very thin wire called the *corona wire* located close to the drum. The drum and the corona wire have a shared ground with the high-voltage power supply, and their proximity generates the electrical field.

Corona Ionization

Essentially, the high voltage being sent through the corona wire causes a short circuit between the wire and the image drum. The air around the wire breaks down, causing a corona to form. The corona ionizes the molecules in the air surrounding the drum, and negative charges migrate to the drum surface.

Because a short circuit isn't healthy for high-voltage power supplies, a primary grid is put between the wire and the drum, allowing for a regulating process of controlled voltages—the regulating grid voltage, or typically -600 to -1,000 volts. The charge on the drum is set to this regulating voltage.

Writing

Once the negative charge has been applied to the drum, it again becomes photoconductive. When a beam of light touches the surface, it discharges a small amount of electricity, usually about -100 volts. Because the surrounding area of the drum is between -600 and -1,000 volts, this spot, or dot, is more positively charged than the surrounding area. In other words, the dot is less negatively charged. We say that it has a *relative positive charge* in that the charge is positive relative to its surroundings.

The image held in memory and sent there by the software program that wants to write something to the printer is transferred to the *writing mechanism*. This sophisticated device controls the way in which the laser beam is moved over the surface of the drum and when the beam is lit or turned off. Each time the beam is on, it produces a dot on the drum.

Developing

At this point, an invisible pattern of electrostatic charge differences is sitting on the surface of the drum. Generally, the charge is negative, but at the data points a relatively positive dot stands out from the surrounding area. Because we've started with negative charges (i.e., -600 to -1,000 volts) and the light from the laser beam has siphoned off about 100 volts, there is a high charge where the light missed and a lower charge where the light touched. The higher charge is the -600 volts, and the lower charge is the -600 volts with 100 volts siphoned off, or -500 volts.

The toner needs to be moved from the cartridge onto the drum in such a way that an image is made visible. *Visible* is a debatable term because it's pitch black inside a laser printer once the laser beam has finished writing the latent image. Nevertheless, the *toner cylinder* (sometimes called the *developer roller*) is a long metal sleeve with a permanent magnet inside of it.

The toner cylinder turns constantly in the middle of all the toner powder (the toner trough) and attracts particles of toner to the metal sleeve. Again, the high-voltage power supply sends current, this time through the toner cylinder, and charges the toner particles with a negative charge. This time, the charge is somewhere between the charges on the drum, averaged for the places where the light touched and where no light touched.

The toner on the toner cylinder is held to one microscopic layer by a *restricting blade*. Rotation moves the charged toner on the cylinder closer to the drum. Where there was no light, the high negative charge repels the negatively charged toner particles. On the other hand, where the light touched the cylinder, there's less of a charge than the toner particles, so they're attracted to the surface of the drum. (A fluctuation mechanism helps ensure that toner particles are more attracted to the drum than the cylinder.)

If you think of the drum surface as a flat plane of equal, negative electricity, wherever the laser beam touches, the surface of the plane sinks downward.

This leaves a hole in the electrostatic surface that you can think of as being clear colored.

A series of holes next to one another is like a furrow in the charged field. Toner particles have an attraction for only the holes and are pushed away from the main surface area. Therefore, developing is the process of shoveling toner particles into the holes and furrows until their surface matches the surface of the original plane. An image begins to develop where the black toner particles fill in the electrostatic holes and furrows on the drum.

 Remember that you can't develop an image unless you first write it to the EP drum. The process is very much like taking a photograph, and you can't develop an image unless you first "snap" the picture (write the image).

Transferring

The surface of the drum now has a layer of toner powder in the pattern of the image that was sent to the printer. The powder must be precisely laid down on a piece of paper; that is, it must be *transferred* to the paper. The problem is that the toner was attracted to the drum by feelings of electromagnetic love and now must be pried away from the drum.

Again, a corona wire, called the *transfer corona wire,* charges the paper in a way similar to the way the drum was charged. This time, the corona charges the paper with a very high *positive* charge. If you've ever rubbed a comb against cloth and then held it over a piece of tissue paper, you saw how the comb attracted the tissue. This is a problem with laser printers: The paper must be charged enough to pull the toner particles off the drum, but not so charged that it will wrap itself around the drum.

The size and stiffness of the paper, along with the relatively small size of the drum, work to prevent the wrapping problem. Additionally, a static charge eliminator called an *eliminator comb* works to counteract the attraction between the paper and the drum. *Everything* is attracted to the drum.

Fusing

The toner particles on the paper are held there only by a combination of gravity and a residual electrostatic charge in the paper and the toner. If you've ever had a printer jam and pulled a piece of paper from inside the laser printer before it was fused, you've seen how easily the toner rubs off onto anything it comes in contact with. Toner must be bonded to the paper before the print process is complete. This bonding process is called *fusing.*

The fusing assembly is a quartz heating lamp inside a roller tube positioned above a rubber pressure roller. The heating roller is made of high-quality, non-stick material. As the paper with the toner on it is drawn between the heated upper roller and the rubber lower roller, the toner is subjected to enough heat to melt it (180 degrees Celsius) and then pressed into the paper by the bottom roller. The combination of fusing roller and pressure roller is called the *fusing rollers,* although only the upper roller produces the heat.

Finally, a fabric cleaning pad located on the opposite side of the heated, upper roller rubs off any residual, melted toner. The temperature of the heating lamp must be highly controlled to prevent fires and internal damage to the printer.

 There could be an exam question having to do with the temperature sensor on the heated fuser roller. This sensor is designed to shut down the system in the event that the temperatures get high enough inside the printer to cause a fire.

End Of Cycle

The paper with its fused image is rolled out of the printer and deposited in the output tray. At this point, the drum is in the process of being cleaned and erased, as we saw at the beginning of the process. An even distribution of light is passed over the entire surface of the drum, causing the entire drum to bleed away all electrostatic charges. The drum is then ready to be conditioned and the next page printed.

 We saw some questions that differentiated between the primary corona and the secondary corona wires. The primary wire charges the EP drum so it can attract toner. The secondary wire charges the paper so it can pull toner away from the EP drum. First comes the drum, then comes the paper. There's no logical sense in running the paper under a blank drum.

The Paper Feed Process

When you send a **PRINT** command to the laser printer, the main motor begins to turn, causing the EP drum, the fusing rollers, and the feed rollers that move the paper along to turn. However, there are two mechanical rollers that aren't part of this process and which don't begin to turn. The paper pick-up roller and the registration rollers are controlled by a separate clutch mechanism.

Figure 7.4 is a representation of the outside of a typical laser printer. The larger pick-up roller, and the two registration rollers are darker. Once the printing cycle is under way, a clutch engages the pick-up roller and drops the roller down on the surface of the top piece of paper in the paper tray. The pick-up

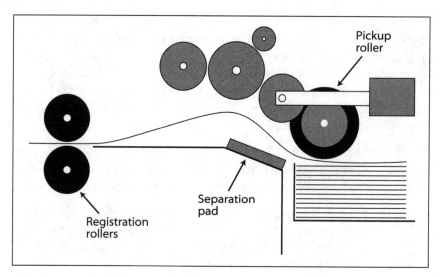

Figure 7.4 The laser printer's paper feed process.

roller is notched and only makes one turn—just enough to pull the edge of the paper in between the registration rollers.

Just as the paper leaves the paper tray, a small rubber separation pad, just below the pickup roller, tries to make sure that only one piece of paper is pulled into the printer. One of the most common causes of paper jams in laser printers is when more than one piece of paper moves between the registration rollers and tries to go through the printer. The registration rollers continue to turn until the entire sheet of paper has passed between them.

When a paper jam occurs and there is paper in the paper tray, the most common cause of the jam is the paper separation pad or more than one page entering the system. Typically, this is due to the wrong type of paper being used, and the pick-up roller can't move the first page. If the pick-up roller can move the paper, then the other most likely problem is that the separator pad can't separate two sheets.

Exam Prep Questions

Question 1

> A black band around the screen image of an LCD panel can indicate what type of problem?
>
> ○ a. Resolution has been set lower than panel maximum.
>
> ○ b. There is a device driver mismatch.
>
> ○ c. More colors have been selected than the panel can display.
>
> ○ d. The scan rate is too slow for the resolution

Answer a is correct. On an LCD panel, an image resolution change can potentially cause a black band to appear around the edge of the panel. Since the display is designed to match the number of pixels in an image, the LCD process turns on crystals based on usage, and if the resolution is set too low for the panel, the images would be too small to go all the way to the edges of the panel.

Question 2

> What is the standard resolution for a VGA monitor pixels?
>
> ○ a. 480 horizontal x 640 vertical
>
> ○ b. 800 horizontal x 600 vertical
>
> ○ c. 640 horizontal x 480 vertical
>
> ○ d. 600 horizontal x 400 vertical

Answer c is correct. A standard VGA monitor has a resolution of 640 pixels horizontally and 480 pixels vertically. We use the "×" to mean the word "by" so the measurement is commonly written as 640×480.

Question 3

> What is the lowest monitor refresh rate that can be used and still avoid perceived flicker?
>
> ○ a. 70 Hz
>
> ○ b. 60 Hz
>
> ○ c. 40 Hz
>
> ○ d. 75 Hz

Answer a is correct. Refresh rate is the rate (cycle of time) at which each line is drawn across the screen from top to bottom. The refresh rate affects what the human eye sees as flickering on the monitor. To avoid flickering, the refresh rate must be at least 70 Hz.

Question 4

> How many times does the electron beam sweep from top to bottom to fully refresh an interlaced monitor's screen?
>
> ○ a. Two
>
> ○ b. One
>
> ○ c. Four
>
> ○ d. None of the above

Answer a is correct. Interlaced mode means that the electron beam sweeps from top to bottom, but that it takes *two* passes to do so. First it refreshes the odd lines, then the even lines. Interlaced mode draws half the screen (every other line) in half the noninterlaced time, then goes back and draws the other half of the screen.

Question 5

> What is the purpose of the erase lamp in a laser printer?
>
> ○ a. The erase lamp places spaces between dots.
>
> ○ b. The erase lamp maintains proper page margins.
>
> ○ c. The erase lamp allows printing of special fonts.
>
> ○ d. The erase lamp resets the photosensitive drum to clear.

Answer d is correct. The laser beam writes a preliminary, or *latent*, image to the photosensitive drum before transferring the image to paper. To clear the latent image, an erase lamp resets the drum to clear.

Question 6

What is the purpose of the rubber cleaning blade in a laser printer?

- ○ a. It is used to clean residual toner from the drum prior to erasure.
- ○ b. It removes foreign matter from the corona wire prior to fusing.
- ○ c. It is used periodically to clean the paper path.
- ○ d. There is no rubber cleaning blade in a laser printer.

Answer a is correct. A rubber cleaning blade is used to gently scrape the drum clean of any residual toner that drops into the debris cavity to the side of the cartridge and below the cleaning blade. Some cartridges allow the residual toner to be returned to the main toner supply.

Need To Know More?

 Bigelow, Stephen: *Troubleshooting, Maintaining, and Repairing Personal Computers: A Technical Guide.* TAB Books, New York, NY, 1995. ISBN 0-07-912099-7. Detailed information from a break-fix standpoint can be found on the following pages: displays (810–823), LCD displays (530–537), matrix printers (276–292), ink jet printers (372–382), and laser printers (501–512),

 Bigelow, Stephen: *Easy Laser Printer Maintenance and Repair.* McGraw-Hill, New York, NY, 1995. ISBN 0-07-035976-8. More information is provided than you need for the exam, but this is a great reference for technicians.

 Messmer, Hans-Peter: *The Indispensable PC Hardware Book.* Addison-Wesley, Reading, MA, 1995. ISBN 0-201-87697-3. More information is provided than you need for the exam, but this reference goes into great detail. Displays are covered on pages 954 through 1011.

 Minasi, Mark: *The Complete PC Upgrade and Maintenance Guide.* Sybex Network Press, San Francisco, CA, 1996. ISBN 0-7821-1956-5. Here is your source for information on peripherals from a repair standpoint: printers are covered on pages 835–893, and displays are covered on pages 939–956

 Rosch, Winn: *Hardware Bible.* Sams Publishing, Indianapolis, IN, 1994. ISBN 0-672-30954-8. Again, far more information is provided here than you need for the exam. Printers are covered specifically on pages 939–968.

DOS

Terms you'll need to understand:

√ Program, application

√ Partitions

√ Formatting

√ Boot, DOS kernel

√ Sectors and clusters

√ Command, command interpreter

√ Wild cards

√ Operating system (OS)

√ File Allocation Table, FAT

√ Conventional, expanded, and extended memory

√ Pointers and vectors

Concepts you'll need to master:

√ The startup sequence (boot process) and files used

√ The DOS command line

√ Internal and external commands

√ How programs use memory

√ Formatting logical drives

√ The bare essential files DOS uses

√ Directory trees and files

√ Working on the DOS command line

√ Simple batch files

√ Working with AUTOEXEC.BAT, CONFIG.SYS files

√ Conventional and extended memory

Hardware is something that you can hold in your hand, drop on your foot, or throw out the window. Software is abstract. You can't see it, smell it, or taste it. In this context, your skull, brain, vocal cords, and lungs are hardware, and the thoughts you think and the words you speak are software.

Software is compiled into *files*, but the disks or modems that transfer the files are the hardware. A computer without software is simply a bunch of metal, gears, silicon, glass, and wires in a box. The CPU is a calculating device, but without software it's only a lump of stuff—a complicated lump of stuff, but still just a lump.

The 1998 A+ exam devotes most of the DOS/Windows component to startup processes and the files the PC uses during the boot sequence. In order to make sense of what happens from the time the power is turned on and the time you can begin working with the computer, you will need a framework to hold the details. Where we discuss an important part of the overall framework, we use notes to focus on important steps. Where we've seen questions on the exam, we use study alerts to direct you to store information in memory. We think the notes may help you to remember the specific points you may be tested on later.

Operating System Programs

A software program is a set of instructions put together in an organized way that tells a microprocessor what to do. When a program is written in English, a human being can understand it. A *computer language* is a special way of using human language so that the instructions written by the *developer (programmer)* can later be turned into machine language. COBOL, BASIC, FORTRAN, and Assembler are all examples of computer languages. Machine language is a binary language of ones and zeros, and the microprocessor can only under-stand instructions presented to it this way.

We usually divide software programs into two categories: *operating systems* and *applications*. Applications are program files that make up a computer tool of some kind. Human beings use applications to produce documents, spread-sheets, databases, mailing lists, new airplane designs, virtual realities, and test scenarios for complex operations on the body, to name a few. Even America Online is an application.

An *operating system* (OS) includes a set of programs that tells a computer how to work with all its parts. The operating system makes all the computer hardware work, whereas applications are designed for human beings to use the com-puter. An operating system uses its program files to gather computer-related instructions and work with the components making up the system. These pro-grams are often called *commands*.

Program Files

A command is somewhat different than a program in that the command is a program designed to affect the underlying computer system in a very specific way. A program usually doesn't work at such a low level and is mostly used to work with data. FORMAT.COM and COPY are commands (programs), whereas REGEDIT.EXE is more of a program designed for the specific purpose of editing a Windows registry. WP.EXE is a program that's more of an application in that it runs a word processor and borrows part of the operating system whenever it copies a file from one place to another.

Command Interpreter

Another part of the operating system is the *command interpreter* (also a program). With so many separate files making up the programs in an operating system, there must be an overseeing manager of some kind that distinguishes between a newsletter you're typing to your mother and characters you're typing in order to make the computer do something. COMMAND.COM is the DOS command interpreter, and both Windows (16-bit) and Windows 95/98 work with COMMAND.COM to control the computer.

The command interpreter is a program containing instructions about how to manage other programs. Within COMMAND.COM are a number of *internal commands* and instructions on how to use batch files. The command interpreter literally interprets keyboard or mouse input and makes decisions as to whether to change the computer or pass the input on to an application program.

User Interface

The third part of an operating system that the exam covers is the *user interface*. We know that monitors can work in text or graphics mode and that we use a monitor as part of the basic input/output process. The underlying decision about how a human being will work with the command interpreter results in either a text environment or a graphical environment. DOS is a text-based user interface, and the DOS command line uses character lines to send commands to COMMAND.COM (the command interpreter).

Windows is a graphical user interface (GUI) and uses objects to provide a way for human beings to work with the command interpreter. Even though Windows provides dialog boxes where text entry occurs, the additional use of buttons, slide controls, drag and drop, and pull-down menus is far more graphical. We tend to say that Windows is a graphical operating system, but the discussion in Chapter 9 points out how Windows is really only an interface.

An operating system (software) is made up of a series of program files: a command interpreter that works with those files and a user interface that allows a human being to instruct the command interpreter what to do.

In our opinion, an operating system requires a file system and several other critical components, but we'll focus your attention on what the exam calls an operating system.

An operating system places its instructions into memory, but the files containing those instructions reside on a disk. Computers use an operating system to "know" how to store information on hard disks, show letters on screens, connect themselves to other computers, and send output to printers. The way that you (the operator) tell the computer how to do this "knowing" of *anything* is through the user interface.

> *Note: A computer can only do exactly what it's told to do. A human being creates every single detail of what a computer "knows" how to do. The human being using a computer is either a programmer or an operator. An operator relies on what the programmer told the computer to do by using special instructions built into a program. Those special instructions are the commands.*

Memory And Programs: Loading And Running

One of the fundamental (and often confusing) principles of using a computer is the idea that a program "loads" into memory in order to "run." Program *files* are a way to store instructions on a computer without needing a constant supply of power. We've seen how RAM loses any data once the power is turned off, and we've also seen how disks store data over the long term.

When a program is executed, the instructions the computer needs at any given moment are *copied* into memory from the program file. The original file remains stored on the disk, untouched and unchanged unless certain instructions are designed to change the stored file. Viruses often copy themselves into RAM and use programming instructions to change the original file on the disk. Understand that the file itself doesn't go into memory, but that a copy of the instructions goes into memory.

The entire process of saving data on a computer revolves around the basic fact that data is always *changed* in memory, but the *changes are only retained if they data is stored back to a storage media* of some kind (i.e., a disk). Memory is not the same thing as storage, even though many novices use the terms interchangeably.

Error Messages

People sometimes forget that a computer doesn't have a conceptual mind, and it can't actually harbor a grudge or get angry, at least not yet. Everything that happens on a computer is created by a human being. When something goes wrong, a message of some kind might show on the screen. That message isn't simply a casual expletive that the computer dreamt up on the spur of the moment.

The actual text of the error messages not only must be written into a program but also must have a connection to an event. Connecting an error message to an event is sometimes called *trapping* an error in a program. The programmer uses what's called an "IF…THEN" logic statement to display an error message on the screen.

For instance, the following statement might be used to trap for a missing file error: IF *filename* X on the command line doesn't match *filename* X in the directory allocation table (DAT), THEN type the message "File not found" on the screen.

Error message text on the screen can also be either misleading or completely wrong in terms of the error being reported. The text itself is not the computer scratching its head and dreaming up a statement, but rather a specific line of text that's written to the screen when an explicit set of circumstances occur. A proposed error message we've seen recently as a candidate to be written into the Windows interface is "Closing current Windows session. Would you like to begin another game?"

The Any Key

The most common way to allow time for a user to read an error message entered on the screen is to temporarily pause the screen until the user provides further input. Remember that the keyboard processor is constantly scanning the keyboard for status changes and keypress activity. When the error message reads, "Press any key to continue," it literally means that you can press any key on the keyboard. The most common key to press is the spacebar.

In order for you to understand computers and DOS, someone had to explain it to you by making information that they already knew easy to understand. Customer service includes the recognition that just because *you* find something to be totally self-evident doesn't mean that you could have discovered that thing without help from another person.

DOS

The exam won't test you on the historical names, dates, or model numbers of DOS (disk operating system), but you'll find it easier to remember some of the details of DOS if you have a mental picture of how it came into existence. The history of DOS is somewhat hazy because of the amounts of money and the various egos that have been involved, but the following section should give you a good idea of how it all came about.

A long time ago, in a place far away, a young girl suggested to her father that a new toy for electronics hobbyists should be called the Altair, after a star system named in a *Star Trek* episode. The Altair, released in 1970, was based on the Intel 8080 chip and was the first computer a person could take home. It had 256 bytes of memory, could hold about four lines of text instructions, and was operated by flipping switches on and off. Even with no keyboard, Bill Gates and Paul Allen were fascinated with it and spent long nights writing a version of BASIC (beginner's all-purpose symbolic instruction code), a computer language that would work with the Altair. They called it Altair BASIC.

> *Note: When a switch was flipped to either on or off, the computer circuitry could use that information in some way. A series of switches taken together, could form a binary number. When a number of switches were looked at by the computer in order to find a number, they were the first "registers." Registers have now become the very small areas on a microprocessor that store binary numbers.*

Gates decided that Altair BASIC should have some sort of file management and disk storage capability, so he upgraded the original system. Their interest in operating languages and their belief that microprocessors would change the world led Gates and Allen to incorporate Microsoft in 1975 (to market a traffic counting machine) and, as soon as 1976, to start complaining about software piracy. At the time, software was stored on cards by punching holes in them.

CP/M

The Intel 8080 processor found its way into another computer called the IMSAI 8080, which came with a floppy drive and was targeted at small businesses. The floppy drive circuitry was controlled by an operating system called CP/M (control program for microcomputers), designed by Gary Kildall.

Kildall was working for a company called Intergalactic Digital Research and wanted a scaled-down language that would work with microprocessors rather than mainframe computers. Perhaps because of a government coverup or something else, the company eventually dropped "Intergalactic," leaving only the name Digital Research. Intel didn't think there was much use for CP/M, so it granted Kildall full rights to it. Features of the CP/M included the following:

➤ Used only 4K of memory space

➤ Introduced a 64K command file and used a three-letter (.COM) extension, to signify the type of file (COM files still have a maximum size of 64K)

➤ Used a command interpreter, or *command processor* program, called CCP (console command processor)

➤ Used two fundamental files, called BDOS and BIOS, to handle files and I/O processing

PCs using IBM's PC-DOS still use COMMAND.COM (the command interpreter), along with IBMDOS.COM and IBMBIO.COM. PCs using Microsoft's MS DOS also continue to use the COMMAND.COM interpreter, and changed the two other *system files* to IO.SYS and MSDOS.SYS.

Apple

In 1976, Steve Wozniak and Steve Jobs took some MOS 6502 chips and built the first Apple computers—the Apple I. Back in 1974, the most popular microprocessors were the Intel 8080 and the Motorola 6800. One of the 6800's inventors, Chuck Peddle, quit Motorola in 1975 and started a new company called MOS Technology. MOS began manufacturing the 6501 microprocessor, which resembled Motorola's 6800.

At the time, Charles Tandy, who had been unsuccessful buying IMSAI computers, had also created his own Tandy TRS-80 product line based on another chip—the Zilog Z-80. Both the TRS-80 and the Apple I computers came fully assembled and, to help keep costs down, used only uppercase letters. Neither Radio Shack nor Apple could keep the computers in stock. An immediate problem that began to crop up between the Apple and the CP/M systems was that:

➤ Operating systems don't necessarily work on all microchips.

➤ The Apple MOS-6502 was an eight-bit processor and couldn't run CP/M.

The Apple II model upgrade added an optional floppy drive and ran a program called VisiCalc—the first real spreadsheet application—created by Dan Bricklin, Dan Fylstra, and Bob Frankston. Businesses could use small PCs to create spreadsheets, and suddenly the PC market came alive. Meanwhile, Gates and Allen were writing BASIC and other programming languages that worked on Intel and Zilog chips. Eventually, Apple turned away from the MOS chips to Motorola chips.

CP/M was a hot programming language, and some very exciting software applications based on the language were arriving on the market. However, these programs would run only on Intel and Zilog chips. Therefore, rather than spend the long hours necessary to translate BASIC into a form that would work with the Apple computers, Gates and Allen chose to license CP/M from Kildall. They sold CP/M, along with an add-on board that had a Zilog chip, so that Apple customers could put the Microsoft card into their computers and run CP/M-based programs.

86-DOS

Meanwhile, in Seattle, Tim Patterson was making motherboards for a company called Seattle Computer Products. Intel had just produced their first 16-bit 8086 chip, and Patterson needed a 16-bit operating system to go with the 8086. Kildall was saying that he would soon be finished with the CP/M-86 (the first vaporware), but Patterson decided that he couldn't wait, so he wrote his own operating system.

In 1980, Patterson created QDOS (quick and dirty operating system). QDOS soon became 86-DOS (for the 8086 processor), then SCP-DOS (after the company), and then simply DOS. In polite company, though, we refer to the "D" in DOS as standing for *disk*.

To simplify matters for the growing number of programmers who were writing for the CP/M operating system, Patterson kept the basic CP/M file management structure, the way CP/M looked, and the way it loaded itself and programs into memory. Along the way, he added something called a file allocation table (FAT), which he found in Gates's Altair BASIC.

PC-DOS

At about the same time, in 1980, IBM approached Microsoft about a possible eight-bit PC that IBM was considering manufacturing. IBM was making mainframes for the most part and looked to young Microsoft as one of the leading (if not only) businesses making computer languages for microcomputers. IBM thought that PCs were mainly a passing hobby, but Gates and Allen were convinced that the microprocessor and personal computer would change the world, and they convinced IBM to change its design to a 16-bit processor. When IBM asked who had a 16-bit operating system, Gates is said to have replied "Gary Kildall." At that point, history gets a bit fuzzy, but somehow Kildall either wasn't available or chose not to sell IBM the rights to CP/M.

Gates and Allen purchased Patterson's 86-DOS for around $50,000 and suggested to IBM that Microsoft become the vendor for BASIC, FORTRAN, Pascal, COBOL, the 8086 Assembly language, and the 86-DOS operating system, which would go into IBM's new PC. IBM agreed in 1980, and in 1981 it released the first PC with Microsoft's DOS 1, which IBM called PC-DOS. (Patterson became successful in his own right and eventually went to work for

Microsoft.) It wasn't until the release of DOS 5 that Microsoft finally started selling its own generic version of MS DOS on the open market.

CP/M Into DOS

Without applications, not many people would be interested in computers. At the time of the first IBM PC, the most popular applications were dBase II and WordStar, both of which ran on CP/M. Because IBM didn't have much in the way of interesting software, it pushed very strongly to make DOS similar enough to CP/M that it could run those other applications. Among the changes that DOS brought to CP/M were the following:

➤ Variable record lengths

➤ Large EXE-format files along with smaller, 64K CP/M-style COM files

➤ Programs called TSRs (terminate-and-stay-resident) that could terminate, but stay resident in memory and snap back onto the screen without reloading

➤ A file allocation table (FAT), which could keep track of all the pieces of files on a disk

➤ The ability to perform I/O operations on peripheral devices (e.g., screens and printers) the same way as it worked with files.

Note: Even today we can use the DOS COPY command to copy a file to the screen and show the results on the monitor (COPY CON FILENAME.TXT). Likewise, we can copy a file to a printer and have the hardware device produce a printed output (COPY FILENAME.TXT PRN).

From the original release of PC-DOS 1 to the release of DOS 6.x, an IBM-compatible PC relied completely on DOS to work. DOS is primarily a text interface, presenting itself to the user in letters on the screen. DOS uses a series of letters entered in a row (a *string* of characters) as commands. These character strings contain *reserved words*, which are the starting points for a set of instructions that command the computer to do something. An example of a reserved word is "copy."

Reserved words contained within COMMAND.COM are referred to as "internal commands" when these internal commands can produce an action without calling on a program other than COMMAND.COM. Internal and external commands are discussed in this chapter in the DOS Commands section.

The text that you enter to spell out commands is called a *command line*. The A> or the C> next to a blinking cursor is called the *prompt*, or *DOS prompt*. A blinking cursor that shows you where the next character you enter will appear on the monitor is the *command prompt*. You type out a character string at the command prompt and press the Enter key. The command interpreter looks at the string you typed and decides what to do about it.

DOS Kept Parts Of CP/M

DOS kept the CP/M-style file names of eight characters, followed by a period, followed by a three-character *extension*. DOS also kept the C> prompt format at the command line. Compatibility also meant keeping the CP/M-style file control blocks (FCBs), program segment prefixes (PSPs), and the way in which CP/M used memory addresses for loading.

DOS also kept the CP/M representation of a directory as a *dot* and the parent directory (the directory one step above) as two dots, or *dot-dot*. We discuss the two dots in more detail later in this chapter when we look at directories and subdirectories.

DOS also gave programmers the ability to write their own versions of the command interpreter—COMMAND.COM—although this hasn't been very successful. DOS also introduced the ability to use a specially reserved extension for files that contained plain-English scripts that a user could write. These special *batch* files, with the .BAT extension, use rudimentary reserved words and need not be *compiled* into machine language.

Compilers And Machine Language

What are compilers? Programs must spell out, in excruciating detail, every single instruction to the microprocessor. No matter how short a speech-based language might be, it still takes far too much space to write even a simple program. Therefore, computer languages use shorthand words to cram as much information as possible into the smallest amount of space. Delete or erase becomes DEL, remove directory becomes RD, list a directory of files becomes DIR, and so on.

Once a program has been written so that a human being can understand it, the result can be reduced even further into something that a machine can understand—machine language. Machine language is composed entirely of ones and zeros. The process of final reduction is called *compiling* the program. Once the program has been compiled (using a separate application called a compiler), the instructions are run as fast as possible.

➤ Compiled programs in DOS have one of either two extensions: .COM (command program) or .EXE (executable program).

➤ *Batch programs*, with .BAT extensions, are not compiled and are entered as plain-English lists of commands. AUTOEXEC.BAT is a batch file, and the name is a reserved name used from within COMMAND.COM.

MS DOS And PC-DOS

Bill Gates and Paul Allen, in one of the shrewdest decisions of modern history, decided to license the use of DOS on IBM PCs rather than sell the operating system outright. Although IBM has the right to make certain changes in the system, it still must pay Microsoft some amount of money for every copy of DOS sold or preinstalled on a PC. When the clone makers began building IBM-compatible PCs, the same licensing process applied to them.

Beginning with the release of DOS 5 there have been two versions of DOS sold in the consumer market: the IBM version and the Microsoft version— PC-DOS and MS DOS, respectively. A few minor differences exist in the two versions, but the exam will use the MS DOS version. Prior to DOS 5, clone computers came from their vendors with MS DOS, and Compaq created its own modification called Compaq DOS (which led to a number of obscure incompatibility problems).

The VER command (internal) is used to discover which version of DOS is running on a PC. At the command prompt, type "VER" and press Enter. The screen will return the version number and tell you whether the computer is using PC-DOS or MS DOS (or some other variation).

A fundamental difference between the IBM and the Microsoft versions of DOS is that they use two system files with different names. MS DOS uses IO.SYS and MSDOS.SYS, and PC-DOS uses IBMBIO.COM and IBMDOS.COM.

IO.SYS and MSDOS.SYS are the two hidden system files that combine with COMMAND.COM (not hidden) to form the most basic DOS operating system.

From DOS To Windows 95

Windows 3.0, 3.1, and 3.11 and Windows For Workgroups are *not* operating systems. Windows 3.x is a GUI (graphical user interface), which, theoretically, makes the daily operation of an IBM-compatible computer somewhat easier than using the DOS command line. However, Windows 3.x and Windows 95/98 still require DOS to run.

The release of Windows 95 included DOS 7, which made a real break from all prior DOS versions. Windows 95 isn't a true operating system, either, but more of an intermediate step between DOS and a new operating system (Windows NT). Nevertheless, many people have accepted Microsoft's claim that Windows 95 is an operating system. In this chapter, we present the workings of DOS from versions 1 through 6 and make specific references to DOS 7.x when necessary.

The Hard Drive

We saw in Chapter 6 that disk manufacturers perform a low-level format on brand-new hard drives whereby they divide the disks into *tracks* and *sectors*. Almost always, sectors are pieces of tracks that can contain 512K of data. The next step in the process is to prepare the disk for an operating system of some kind. In this case, we'll discuss and work with DOS. Other operating systems are Unix, Windows NT (New Technology), and Novell Netware, to name a few.

The manufacturer's physical formatting creates circular bands of magnetic strips on the platters of the disk. These bands are the tracks, and each platter has a set of concentric tracks circling outward from the center. Each platter is vertically aligned, so each track is aligned.

 A vertical stack of tracks, all the same distance from the center, is called a *cylinder*. Even a floppy disk has tracks and sectors, although it's only a single, Mylar platter.

Track 0 on the first platter (holding the boot sector) is sometimes referred to as "head 0," since each platter of a hard drive has its own set of read/write heads.

In Figure 8.1 we've taken the top platter of a typical hard drive and outlined the tracks, sectors, and clusters. Figure 6.1 in Chapter 6 showed a hard drive made up of a number of platters stacked on top of each other.

Observe that in the center of this platter is the spindle motor. The very first track next to the motor is track 0. The next track out from 0 is track 1 and so

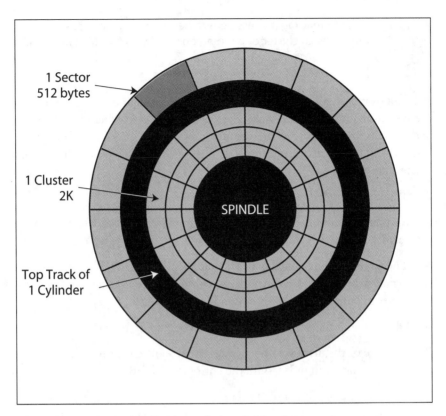

Figure 8.1   The basic division of a hard drive into tracks, sectors, and clusters.

on. Each platter has its own set of tracks beginning with track 0. During the FORMAT process, all the tracks of a given number are formatted at once and the screen will show you which cylinder is being worked on. Moving down from (read/write) head 0, the next platter would have head 1, then head 2, and so on. Head 2 would be the third set of read/write heads down, working on the third platter of the hard disk.

Logical Formatting

A *logical* (as opposed to a physical, or low-level) formatting process creates a FAT (discussed shortly) and defines the minimum number of sectors in the clusters used to store data on that drive volume. The groups of sectors that contain data are called *clusters*, which are units (groups) of sectors that have been allocated (reserved and set aside) for use by file data.

> The formatting process determines how many sectors will be inside each cluster, depending on the size of the drive (not disk).

All data stored on a DOS-formatted, FAT16 file system disk is contained in file allocation units called clusters. Clusters consist of a fixed number of sectors and contain more sectors as the volume grows larger. In FAT16 formatting, DOS controls the variable cluster size. Other features of tracks, sectors, and clusters are as follows:

➤ Tracks are divided into sectors of 512 bytes.

➤ Sectors are combined into clusters, starting at 2K (2,048 bytes), or four sectors.

➤ The largest cluster available to DOS is 64K, making 2GB the largest logical drive that DOS can address with FAT16 (even though many drives as large as 8GB are now coming to market).

➤ Clusters *must* fill the entire volume from beginning to end.

➤ The size of the drive volume dictates the size of the clusters. Clusters will grow larger in order to fill the entire logical drive.

➤ The maximum number of clusters is 65,525.

> *Sectors* are the basic storage unit on tracks—they are not clusters. Sectors can hold 512 bytes (not kilobytes) of information. Tracks are divided into sectors, and drives are divided into clusters.

File Systems

An operating system (like DOS) must include a file system for making sense of bits of magnetized coating on a disk. The file system keeps track of:

➤ Where all the parts of files are located on the disk

➤ Directories and file names

➤ The used and unused space on a disk, that is, allocated space and free space, respectively

➤ Continually updates the cluster locations of all the parts of a file

Note: The Windows 95 long file names feature uses the DOS file system to actually store the data on the physical disk. However, Windows 95 controls how the FAT is used (discussed in Chapter 10).

16-Bit FAT (FAT16)

The original disks were able to store only 160K of information and programs and PCs were using only 64K of RAM at that time. Engineers had to make a decision regarding how much space to set aside on a disk to hold all the information in a file structure (the FAT) as well as the DAT for the directory structure. They needed to strike a compromise between the expected size of future disks and the amount of space to take away from programs and data files.

The original DOS file system was set to work with 16 bits worth of addresses, allowing for 65,525 clusters. Until Compaq DOS 3.31 and IBM DOS 4, DOS disk management capabilities were limited to a 32MB maximum drive size. Back then, no one ever imagined that PCs would be important or useful enough to need more than this amount of space. The original 16-bit FAT continues to this day, and Windows 95 still relies on it. (The so-called FAT32 system is actually a virtual FAT add-on to the basic 16-bit FAT. FAT32 VFAT and IFS are discussed in Chapter 10.)

Save To Disk

Arguably, the aspect of DOS that end users deal with the most is the file-naming process. When you create something in an application, you're creating a temporary version in RAM. If the power goes off and there's no backup UPS (uninterruptible power supply) to provide battery power, what you have created will disappear totally and permanently. Keep in mind that creating and changing data on a computer happens in memory, and the application you're using is working with a copy of itself in memory.

We should mention here (for customer service reasons) that one of the most common errors in semantics made by untrained computer users is to confuse RAM memory with disk storage. If you ask someone how much memory they have, and they respond with something like "one gigabyte," try to cut them some slack and take the opportunity to provide some helpful training information. You'll be greatly appreciated if you do this in a friendly, non-patronizing way, and you'll develop a good working relationship with the person coming to you for help.

Getting back to the point: How often should you save information? The simplest answer is that you should save as soon as you've created enough new information to make re-creating it aggravating. This amount of time will vary, depending on the reliability of the power supply and the complexity of the data being created.

Autosave Features

Most of today's word processors include a configuration feature whereby any data is periodically saved to disk. By default, this time period is usually every 15 or 30 minutes.

Consider an executive secretary who types 80 words per minute non-stop. A typical business page contains around 350 to 400 words. In 5 minutes, the secretary will have typed 400 words—about one full page in a report. In 30 minutes, that secretary will have typed anywhere from 6 to 10 pages of information.

Depending on the speed at which the data is input, the complexity of the creation process, and the difficulty of formatting the data, the Save process can occur anywhere from every single line of data entry to once every hour. We've known people who saved everything for the first time at the end of the business day, just before going home.

FAT (File Allocation Table)

The formatting process creates a root directory that must be at a specific, physical location on a drive. The FAT is designed for a maximum number of allowable entries in that root directory and allows a maximum of 65,525 clusters (not sectors). The DAT (directory allocation table), along with the FAT, keeps track of the directory structure. DOS uses a particular format for making directories on a disk. Sectors are low-level formatted, whereas clusters are decided by the file system during formatting.

The file allocation table is literally a table with bits of information about files. The first piece of data is the name (address) of the cluster that holds the beginning 2K of a file—about one page of typing.

The FAT is absolutely critical to the maintenance of all the data on a given disk. Without a FAT, there's no way to know where anything is on that disk. For this reason, DOS maintains two copies of the FAT in case one of the copies becomes corrupted. Some third-party software tools can recover a disk through the use of the second copy of the FAT. However, this assumes that the second copy isn't corrupted, which usually is not the case.

Time and wear and tear eventually affect the magnetic layers used to store data on disks. Even if no outside interference (e.g., speaker magnets and frigid cold) wipe out data, physical properties of magnetism can cause a loss of data. When this happens and the drive heads can't read or write data to the sector, the DOS format command marks the sector as bad and, from that point, as unavailable.

If the boot sector goes bad, the disk is no longer usable. If the FAT becomes corrupted, most often it's because the entire area where both copies of the FAT are stored has failed.

CHKDSK Vs. SCANDISK

From the beginning (DOS 1), there had to be a way to reconcile the FAT with what was actually on the disk. One of the external programs that came with DOS was the program CHKDSK (Check Disk) that checked the disk.

Running CHKDSK means that you type the characters at the command prompt and press Enter. Running a program means that you type the name of the program file (in this case CHKDSK.EXE) and press Enter. Because the program file has an .EXE, a .COM, or a .BAT extension, DOS assumes you mean to run a program if you don't include the extension. If you have a file called NAME1.DOC and type NAME1 at the command prompt and press Enter, DOS will look for a program called NAME1.EXE, NAME1.COM, or NAME1.BAT.

CHKDSK looks at the FAT for a beginning and ending cluster address for a file. Then DOS goes to that address on the disk (the cylinder, track, and sector) and checks to see whether any readable information is in the cluster. DOS doesn't read the file for news about how Granny is doing in Oshkosh; rather, it uses the drive's read-write heads to copy the information into RAM and write it back again. Then it checks the directory listing and name against the records in the FAT. If all goes well, CHKDSK goes to the next entry in the FAT and does it all over again.

If DOS finds a cluster address in the FAT that does not match the data on the disk, it returns a message to the user that there are *lost clusters* or *cross-linked files.* Lost clusters are areas of the disk that have been allocated to a specific file when the file itself wasn't closed correctly (maybe because of a crash or a lockup). Cross-linked files are more scary. Cross-linking means that, according to the FAT, two files occupy the same space somewhere in a group of clusters. Possibly, either the FAT or the DAT has been corrupted. This can sometimes happen when the power is turned off or lost while the computer is running an application.

One of the first utilities (programs that provide useful tools not included in an operating system) provided by Norton Utilities was Disk Doctor, which allowed a user to check a disk for sectors that were either bad or becoming bad. If bad sectors were found, Disk Doctor would attempt to move any data within them and mark the sectors as bad. CHKDSK does not check for bad sectors in which the physical disk is damaged or unusable. CHKDSK can't be used on a network drive or under Windows 95/98 either.

SCANDISK.EXE

CHKDSK was the only way (without third-party utilities) to validate the FAT and the DAT prior to DOS 6, when ScanDisk was introduced. Essentially, ScanDisk is a more friendly way of checking the system in that the user runs the program and then has some control over events. It gives the user the option to attempt to fix various errors or to read a report of all the errors that were found.

More important, ScanDisk finally allows a basic way for DOS owners to attempt to fix cross-linking, lost clusters, and bad sectors. ScanDisk can't be used on a network drive, but it can be used under Windows 95/98.

 ScanDisk is a way to scan a disk for problems and then work toward repairing some of those problems. DEFRAG is a way to speed up disk access by combining parts of files from all over a disk into organized, continuous blocks of clusters.

Directories And Subdirectories

A DOS directory (or folder, as it's called in Windows 95) is a special type of file. Directories and their subdirectories are used to keep files together that have a common purpose—to organize a disk. For example, C:\DOS usually contains all the DOS operating system files, and C:\MSOFFICE contains the files that pertain to Microsoft Office.

All files have names. All files also contain data. These are two fundamental principles of files, and DOS uses two different ways to keep track of each idea. The FAT keeps track of where the data is on a disk, and the directory table keeps track of the names of the files. Just like a file contains data, a directory name contains file names.

Directory Tree

A directory and all its subdirectories are an example of a hierarchy. The original designers thought it looked like a tree, and the first part of a tree is the root. A directory tree looks somewhat like a root system, where smaller and smaller roots branch off of a larger root, something like Figure 8.2.

At the top of the root system in Figure 8.2 is the *root directory* with its representative backslash (level 1). The root directory is a file that contains both data files and other directory files. Four of the directory files go into making the level 2 subdirectories. One of the level 2 subdirectory files contains four more level 3 directory files. Finally, one of the level 3 subdirectories contains three level 4 directory files.

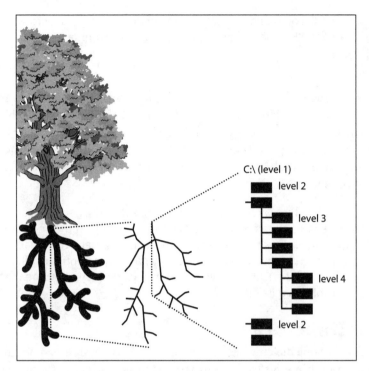

Figure 8.2   The branching subdirectories under the root.

Did you notice how talking about a directory from within another directory changes the first name to a *sub*directory? Directories can contain subdirectories, each of which can contain more subdirectories, each of which can contain more subdirectories, and so on down until the entire name of a subdirectory and file is longer than DOS allows (256 characters). The entire name of a file, including every directory needed to get to that file, and the drive where the file is located is called its *full pathname*.

> *Note: If a directory contains subdirectories, we say that it is the "parent" directory of its "child" directories. Child is another name for "sub" so a parent directory contains (child) subdirectories.*

Subdirectory names are like any DOS name in that they must follow the 8.3 (read "eight dot three") naming convention. Rather than storing specific data from an application, a directory is a file that stores other file names. Each time you make a directory the default directory, you have the option of saving a file in that directory or creating a whole new subdirectory there.

The command to create a directory is MD (make directory). MKDIR is the archaic version of the same command.

The maximum number of characters in the full name of all the directory levels and the file name is 256. If you have a file named C:\level2\level3\4thlevel\ level5\onemore\yikes\toolong\MYFILE.DOC, there are 66 characters in the entire file name (the path). This example contains eight directories—one root directory and seven subdirectories. MYFILE.DOC is a data file in the eighth level down subdirectory.

 Note that each directory is symbolized by the backslash at the end of its name. The root directory is a plain \ at the end of C: showing that it is the root of the C: drive. Level2\ has a backslash showing that level2 is a directory name. This continues all the way to MYFILE.DOC which has *no* backslash, symbolizing that this is a data file.

Root Directory

The FAT uses one directory—the root directory—as the starting point for all the files on a given drive (technically referred to as a *volume*). The root directory can contain only a limited number of files, including both data and program files and subdirectory names. The rules for a root directory are as follows:

➤ Every logical drive (volume) must have its own root directory on track 0, sector 0.

➤ The maximum number of directory entries in the root directory of a volume on a logical hard drive is 512.

➤ To have more than 512 file and directory names, you must use at least one subdirectory.

➤ Subdirectories can have as many directory entries as there is room on the disk.

➤ FAT32 formatting allows the root directory to be located somewhere other than track 0, sector 0.

An interesting problem on some hard drives occurs when DOS prevents the user from creating a new file. An error message referring to insufficient disk space appears, but the user knows that he or she has a 500MB drive available. This might be a case where the user has put all their files into the root directory. With no subdirectories, the FAT directory table has run out of room for a new file name and issues the out-of-space error.

Subdirectories

Subdirectories are symbolized by the name of the *parent* (containing) directory, followed by a backslash (e.g., C:\WINDOWS) In this case, the parent directory is the root directory of the C: drive. The first backslash follows the drive name. Therefore, WINDOWS is a subdirectory of the root directory.

> *Note: Logical drives are always named with a letter of the alphabet. The DOS word for "drive" is the colon (:), hence the C drive is written in DOS as C:.*

C:\WINDOWS\SYSTEM is the name of a subdirectory called SYSTEM. (It could also be the name of a file called System.) The SYSTEM subdirectory is under the WINDOWS directory. WINDOWS is under the root directory. The root directory is the first backslash that follows the drive letter (C:\). WINDOWS is the first subdirectory under the root (C:\WINDOWS).

The next subdirectory is the backslash that follows the parent WINDOWS (C:\WINDOWS\). Finally, the name of the last subdirectory is SYSTEM (C:\WINDOWS\SYSTEM).

Directory File Names

In the name C:\WINDOWS\SYSTEM, "SYSTEM" can be either a file name or a subdirectory name. The last name in a path, or complete file and directory listing, is somewhat ambiguous. You can see this uncertainty when using the XCOPY command to copy a series of files to a different subdirectory. XCOPY will ask you whether you want the destination to be a file or a directory.

Even though subdirectories can have an extension, convention has it that file names use from one- to three-character extensions, whereas subdirectories stay with just the eight main characters of typical file names. This helps keep subdirectories and files separate. Additionally, because subdirectories are files (albeit of a special type), DOS provides angle brackets (< and >) and the DIR abbreviation to indicate that something is a subdirectory: <DIR>.

Because subdirectories are files, they can also have one- to three-character extensions. However, many applications programmers forget to consider this, and those applications can't show the 8.3 type of subdirectory names in their File|Open dialog boxes.

Relative Locations

North, south, east, and west are absolute directions on the planet Earth. It doesn't matter which direction you're facing, north is always in a specific direction. Left and right, on the other hand, are *relative* directions. It depends on who's talking and which way they're facing to determine what absolute direction they're talking about.

If we all are facing the same direction to begin with and someone yells, "Turn left," we'll all end up facing the same way. If we're all facing different directions and someone yells the same thing, we'll still be facing different directions. However, no matter how many of us are facing in different directions, if someone yells "Turn north," then we'll all end up facing one way again (assuming everyone has a compass or we're all homing pigeons).

When you type the full pathname to a file, you're giving DOS an absolute name. If you say, "Change directories (CD) to the C:\WINDOWS\COMMAND directory," DOS knows exactly where that is. On the other hand, you can use the dot-dot to tell DOS, "CD to the next directory up from here."

If you issue the command CD\WINDOWS\SYSTEM, DOS will go to the root directory (the first backslash) and move down through Windows to System. However, if you issue the command CD SYSTEM (using a space after the CD), then DOS will start from wherever you are and try to go down one level to a subdirectory called "System." If you happen to be in the Windows directory, this command will work. If you happen to be in some other directory and there isn't a SYSTEM subfolder in that folder, you'll get a "file(s) not found" error.

> *Note: A space after the CD command is a relative "down" designation. The only warning is that there must be a location to down to. Otherwise, DOS returns an error message. The CD . . command will always move upward to the root. Even at the root, DOS will not return an error message.*

Dot And Dot-Dot

The CD (change directory) command (once known as CHDIR) is used to change the *default directory* to another directory. The default directory is the directory where COMMAND.COM will look first for any referenced program entered on a command line. If you type "CD" (without the quotes) and press Enter, DOS will return the name of the default directory.

> *Note: Throughout the remainder of this book we endeavor to separate actual commands that you might type from the surrounding text by using quotation marks. Since DOS uses quotation marks as a reserved symbol,*

you should never type what you see written here with the included quotes unless you're directed to. If we are using quotation marks as part of a command, we will explicitly tell you that those quotes are included in the line.

If you are logged in to the C:\WINDOWS\SYSTEM directory, you have made that directory the default directory. If you then enter "CD.." (two dots in a row), DOS will change the default to the directory immediately *above* the existing one—the *parent directory.*

From the C:\WINDOWS\SYSTEM directory, you could type the absolute location by issuing the command CD C:\WINDOWS. This would change the default location to one step above where you are, but it means typing a lot more characters.

| Typing two dots after the CD command will move you up one level from where you are, to the parent directory.

The single dot represents "here" to DOS. You can use it as a shortcut with a program such as XCOPY when you want to copy all the files in a single directory of the A: drive (floppy disk) to the current directory. Instead of typing out the whole location, you can enter "XCOPY A: .", using the single dot after the A: so that DOS will know that you want the files to arrive "here." This is handy if you're copying a lot of files from the A: drive to a network location like J:\pdj16\US\station5\1998\edu-work\process\managers\march. In this instance, you can log into the network location and use the single "dot" rather than retyping the entire path.

Creating A Directory

To keep things organized, you can create different subdirectories in which to keep similar types of files together. Batch files are simple to create, can be inspiring to play with, and can make routine tasks easier and faster. A good subdirectory to create is a *batch directory.*

To create a batch directory at the DOS prompt, use the internal MD (make directory) command. (Yes, we know it's easy to use File Manager or Windows Explorer, but what if you can't get them to run?) Make whatever drive and directory that will contain the new subdirectory the default. Suppose we make this batch directory right under the root directory of C:. Type C: and press Enter to log onto the C: drive. Type CD\ and press Enter to make sure we've made the root directory the default location—*logged into* the root directory.

In this case, we want to be at the root of C: and enter "MD\BATCH" and then press Enter. This will create a subdirectory directly under the root directory of C: called BATCH. We would save all batch files (except AUTOEXEC.BAT) in this directory. Once again, by using the absolute path of the first backslash, we tell DOS to make the Batch subdirectory under the root.

If we had been in the C:\WHONOSE directory and typed MD BATCH and pressed Enter, we would have created a BATCH directory under the WHONOSE parent directory. Once again, the space acts like a relative direction.

DOS will also allow you to make directories and change directories from remote drives. If you place a floppy in the A: drive, and type MD A:\JUNK while you're logged onto the C: drive in some subfolder, DOS will create a JUNK directory on the A: drive, the light will spin, and you'll be returned to a command prompt with no indication that anything at all happened.

If you type DIR A: and press Enter, DOS will list the files in the root directory of the floppy. However, if (from the C: drive) you issue the command CD A:\JUNK and press Enter, the floppy drive will spin and you'll be returned to a DOS prompt with no indication again, that anything happened. This time though, if you enter DIR A: you'll see a listing for the A:\JUNK directory.

Note: DOS doesn't allow you to create multiple levels of subdirectories all in one statement. For instance, you can't say MD C:\THIS\THAT and create both the This and the That folders with a single command. You must first create THIS (MD C:\THIS) and then create THAT (MD C:\THIS\THAT).

Removing A Directory

You can't use the RD (remove directory) command if files reside in that directory. RD is also called RMDIR, but nobody uses the longer name now that they can type two letters.. To remove the subdirectory with RD, you must first switch to that directory and process DEL *.* or enter the full pathname (e.g., DEL C:\NOGOOD\THISONE*.*). Once all the data files are removed, then you can go back and delete the directory itself.

Note: If any files exist in a subdirectory, RD won't be successful. Otherwise, once the files are all gone, you enter the RD and the directory name (e.g., RD C:\NOGOOD\THISONE). DOS 6 introduced the external DELTREE command utility, which allows you to remove a directory branch, including all its subdirectories. DOS 7 (Windows 95) includes DELTREE.EXE.

Old Time Commands No One Uses

One of the more bizarre references we saw on the exam was the use of archaic commands left over from DOS version 1. Perhaps this is an attempt to trick you, or it may be some other diabolic forces of confusion at work in the universe. Either way, the following is a list of internal commands with the familiar command alongside its great-grandpa (the old versions are still available in DOS 7):

➤ DEL (delete a file) is also ERASE

➤ CD (change directory) is also CHDIR

➤ MD (make directory) is also MKDIR

➤ REN (rename a file) is also RENAME

➤ RD (remove an empty directory) is also RMDIR

> *Note: You can't ordinarily rename a directory from the DOS command line without using a third-party software utility. However, you can use MOVE (a command that was added to DOS 6) to move an entire directory and all its files to a destination that doesn't exist. DOS will create the new destination and delete the old directory name—effectively renaming the subdirectory.*

The PATH

The path—a file's formal, full name (*pathname*)—is perhaps one of the most common causes of trouble at the software level. PATH= is an internal environment command. The path is also the true name of a file. When we tell someone about a file name, we imply the rest: the drive and the subdirectory chain. When you talk to DOS about a file, you must write out the entire file name, or you can make a specific subdirectory the default location. Some of the important things to know about PATH include the following:

➤ PATH=[*directory*] [;] [*directory*] is the syntax for the path command (syntax is discussed later in this chapter).

➤ Semicolons (traditionally) separate each directory you choose to list in the path.

➤ The user (or an installation routine) *chooses* to enter a path into the environment; that is, a path statement in the environment is not required.

➤ 256 characters is the maximum number of characters allowed in a path, including the word *path* and the space or the equals sign following it.

➤ Typing "SET" and pressing Enter will show you the entire DOS environment, including the current path; typing "PATH" and pressing Enter will show you the current search path.

Search Path

When you enter a word in a command line, COMMAND.COM parses (splits apart) the line and looks for a command file matching that word. Either the command word is found internally or COMMAND.COM looks elsewhere for a file with a .COM, an .EXE, or a .BAT extension. The question is, Where does DOS look? The answer is, in any directory listed in the path.

Suppose that we've made the D:\JUNK directory the default directory by typing D: and then pressing Enter, then typing CD\JUNK and pressing Enter once again. Our current location, then, is D:\JUNK. Now suppose we type FOURMAT A: and then press Enter. What will happen? (Pay attention, and check the spelling.)

COMMAND.COM will parse the line, find A: to be a valid drive location, and expect FOURMAT to be a program file or internal command. DOS will attempt to execute the command through COMMAND.COM in the following order:

1. It will look first inside itself for the character string FOURMAT (which it won't find) and then in the current directory for a program file that begins with FOURMAT. Here, it will look first for FOURMAT.COM, then for FOURMAT.EXE, and finally for FOURMAT.BAT.

    Note: If both FOURMAT.COM and FOURMAT.EXE both exist in the same directory, COMMAND.COM will execute the COM file first and never know that the EXE file exists alongside it. COM files come first, then EXE files, and finally BAT files.

2. If FOURMAT.COM/EXE/BAT does not exist in the current directory, COMMAND.COM will turn to the DOS environment and look for an environment variable named PATH.

3. If PATH= exists, COMMAND.COM will start with the first directory listed and repeat Step 1.

4. If FOURMAT is still not found, COMMAND.COM will start with *each directory after each semicolon* and repeat Step 1.

5. If FOURMAT is not found in any of these places, DOS will write an error message to the screen: "File(s) not found". In this instance, the

odds are DOS wouldn't find FOURMAT.COM since the actual filename is FORMAT.COM, located in the DOS subdirectory.

 PATH is a list of directories that DOS can search to find a program name entered on the command line. The advantage of a PATH is that the command can be entered without being logged into the specific directory containing the program file.

Booting And System Files

We'd like to emphasize that on the exams we've seen, a lot of attention was paid to the startup processes involved in DOS and Windows. Everything about starting a PC revolves around something called the master boot record, and the way DOS works with CONFIG.SYS files and the IO.SYS file. We've tried to focus your attention with Study Alerts, but try to work with a computer and pay attention to everything that goes on when you turn on the power.

The focus of this section is the overall startup process during the boot procedure. We refer to a number of commands that we've left for other areas of this book, because we'd like to maintain a continuity of the process, rather than interrupt to explain each related command. However, we do make reference to where you can find more information about these commands.

When the PC's power switch is turned on, the POST routine in a ROM BIOS chip initializes the system and runs a test of all the components built in to the computer. Therefore, you must physically turn off the computer if you plug in a new peripheral and if you want the POST to access the device at power-up. The POST is run only when power to the CPU is turned off and then turned on again. A *system reset,* or *warm boot,* does not include the POST.

The Three-Fingered Salute

When an irreversible error occurs in memory, the CPU becomes frozen and the computer won't accept input to one degree or another. Sometimes the mouse pointer will move around, but clicking won't do anything. Other times, even keystrokes fail to get recognized. One way or another, if this happens to you, you're experiencing a computer crash.

If the computer's display is frozen, or locked, but the system accepts keyboard input, the universal key combination of pressing and holding the Ctrl key, then pressing and holding the Alt key, and then pressing and holding the Delete key—keeping all three keys pressed simultaneously—will generate a restart, or system reset command, from ROM BIOS. This three-key combination—a warm boot, or system reset—is abbreviated Ctrl+Alt+Delete.

If the computer is so locked up that even the keyboard can't access the system, the only way to restart the computer is either to turn the power off and then back on or to use the Reset button on the face of the casing. This type of lockup is called a *hard crash*, and it requires a *cold boot* to restart the computer.

> *Note: The cold boot will call the POST, not a warm boot or reset, although some third-party software utilities can call the cold boot instruction set from ROM BIOS.*

Following the test for what's connected, the POST looks to the ROM BIOS on the motherboard and begins another program (a parity-checking program) to test the main DRAM memory chips. The parity program writes information to each chip and then reads the information and compares it. Sometimes you can see this parity-checking process take place by the rapidly incrementing numbers at the top of a black startup screen.

Each version of DOS and BIOS contains *fixes,* or *patches,* for problems, and ROM moves some of these patches to lower memory so they won't have to be constantly read from the ROM chip. This is the reserved motherboard BIOS area of memory (how DOS uses memory is discussed later in this chapter). Patches routinely overwrite instructions in the ROM chip.

Finally, the BIOS looks for the first sector (track 0, sector 0) of a floppy disk in the A: drive for a bootstrap loader built in to the operating system. If it finds the bootstrap loader there, it transfers control to the operating system. Otherwise depending on the CMOS settings (in newer computers), BIOS looks at the first sector on the C: drive for the bootstrap loader.

 The boot sector (sometimes improperly called the master boot record) is found on cylinder 0, (head 0,) track 0, sector 0. The boot sector is the absolute first sector on a disk. Whether a disk is bootable or not, all disks have a boot sector.

There's an old saying that relates to pulling oneself up by one's own bootstraps. The saying refers to bettering one's position in life by relying completely on one's own talents and capabilities, not waiting for someone else to lend a hand. Because DOS loads itself (sort of by its own bootstraps), the startup process has come to be known as the *boot* process, or *booting up* the computer.

ROM BIOS Looks At The Boot Sector

Formatting divides the disk into two specific areas: a system area for DOS system files and a files area for data and programs. The system area is called the *boot sector*. Formatting also sets up the two copies of the FAT and creates the root directory. If the disk is to be made bootable (able to start the operating system running), COMMAND.COM and the two system files must be in the root directory of that disk. The boot sector is:

➤ Always the first sector (sector 0) of the first track (track 0) of the first cylinder (cylinder 0) disk

➤ 512K long, just like any other sector

➤ Contained on all disks, regardless of whether they are bootable

The FAT (and directory table) comes directly after the boot sector and takes up different amounts of room, depending on how large the drive is. There are two copies of the FAT to protect against one being corrupted. A *boot-sector virus* is where the boot sector of the disk has become infected (corrupted). We discuss viruses in Chapter 11.

The root directory comes after the FAT and, in FAT16 systems, is 16 kilobytes. The 16K limit on a FAT16 file system format is what makes the 512-name limit in the root directory.

The general file storage area comes after the space set aside for the root directory. FAT32 is a modification that works alongside and with the FAT (the 32-bit VFAT and IFS file system are discussed in Chapter 10). Make a note that VFAT uses the FAT as a *vector* table. (Vectors are discussed later in this chapter.)

Boot Sector Contains Bootstrap Loader

If the disk has been formatted to be a bootable disk, the system area must contain the DOS *system files*. These files can be installed during formatting by using the command FORMAT A: /S or can be copied over using a special DOS external command: SYS A: or SYS C:. (The SYS command is discussed in Chapter 11, along with the FORMAT command.)

> *Note: For SYS.COM to work, the disk must first be formatted as bootable and then lose the two system files to corruption. Space for the system files must be created during formatting.*

The boot sector also contains a very small program called the *bootstrap loader,* which either copies (loads) the DOS *kernel* into memory at startup or writes to the screen the message "Non-system disk or disk error. Replace and press any key when ready". The MS DOS system files IO.SYS and MSDOS.SYS (or PC-DOS files IBMBIO.COM and IBMDOS.COM) must be in a root directory for the DOS kernel to be loaded.

Note: The bootstrap loader is part of the system files and must be in the boot sector. Simply copying COMMAND.COM and the two hidden system files to a floppy disk won't extract the bootstrap loader. The only way to install the bootstrap loader into the boot sector is with FORMAT.COM or SYS.COM

The bootstrap loader contains a *BIOS parameter block* (BPB), which contains information about the physical structure of the disk. If it's a hard disk, the BPB is read only once because the disk won't be removed. If it's a floppy disk, every time the disk is accessed, DOS works with the change-line process to read the BPB if a new disk is in the drive.

If the boot disk is a hard drive, the boot sector also has a small *partition loader* program with 16 bytes of information per partition, identifying the operating system, the starting and ending sector of the partition, and which partition is bootable.

The BPB and partition loader is properly called the *master boot record* (MBR). An undocumented switch for FDISK can sometimes re-create the MBR. In some cases, this may be a way to eliminate a boot-sector virus if a virus protection program isn't available. To use the switch, enter "FDISK /MBR" from a DOS screen (not from a DOS window running within the Windows shell).

 The boot sector is sometimes referred to as the master boot record (MBR). Technically, the master boot record is the BPB and partition loader. On the exam, though, the master boot record probably refers to the entire boot sector.

FDISK /MBR is an undocumented feature. FDISK is used to work with partitions, and we discuss it later in this chapter and in Chapter 11. You should be extremely careful using the /MBR switch with a suspected virus, since certain viral infections can cause the total loss of an entire partition and all its data.

Bootstrap Loads IO.SYS

ROM BIOS runs the bootstrap loader, which loads the I/O device management system IO.SYS (or IBMBIO.COM) and the *operating system kernel* MSDOS.SYS (or IBMDOS.COM). A kernel is just like a kernel of popcorn, in that it's like a seed. The kernel is the starting point where all other related programming gathers around and begins to grow.

 Once again, the technical DOS kernel is MSDOS.SYS, but you may find references to both IO.SYS and MSDOS.SYS as being the kernel. When in doubt, accept the incorrect description if it's the only response that contains any reference to MSDOS.SYS.

The DOS kernel manages system-level functions such as file management and memory management. For the computer to understand itself and for the kernel to be loaded, the two DOS system files must be present in the root directory of the boot disk, either A: or C: (primary, active partition), for a FAT16 formatted drive. We discuss primary, active partitions later in this chapter and in Chapter 11.

 The DOS kernel is MSDOS.SYS. This is different than the Windows kernel (discussed in Chapter 9).

The two system files have their attributes set to Hidden, Read-Only, System. ATTRIB.EXE is the DOS program used to change file attributes: Archive (A), Hidden (H), Read-Only (R), and System (S). In DOS 7, Windows 95 uses MSDOS.SYS and IO.SYS differently.

IO.SYS Checks CONFIG.SYS

Following the bootstrap loader, IO.SYS (or IBMBIO.COM) loads first. IO.SYS contains generic device drivers for the basic peripherals expected to be used on the computer, such as the monitor, disk drives, keyboard, and printer I/O ports. It also contains a module called SYSINIT, which runs through a startup procedure and device driver initialization (device drivers are discussed at length in Chapter 11). SYSINIT (inside IO.SYS) calls the CONFIG.SYS file (if it exists) to initialize modified or new devices.

 IO.SYS always loads first, *no matter what!* Whether it's DOS, Windows, or Windows 95, IO.SYS is always the first program file that loads following the POST and bootstrap routines.

SYSINIT Calls CONFIG.SYS

We just said that IO.SYS takes care of the basic instructions involving hardware devices. Once IO.SYS is loaded into memory, the computer begins to wake up a bit and discover what it is. Until this point, the motherboard and ROM BIOS have for the most part controlled the startup process. This is like when you first realize you're starting to wake up in the morning, but haven't opened your eyes yet. All you know is that you're alive—you're not sure yet who you are (depending on what kind of night you had!).

IO.SYS contains a small segment of programming called the SYSINIT module. Part of the SYSINIT module is a set of instructions that looks for a file named \CONFIG.SYS. This name, which is explicitly written into the program, is spelled exactly that way and contains a specific reference to the root directory of the boot disk. CONFIG.SYS:

➤ Is *not* a required file for booting up

➤ Contains references to the location and configuration of software programs that contain additional instructions on how to run hardware devices (such programs are called software *device driver files,* or *drivers*)

➤ Is a plain ASCII text file created by the user or sometimes by an installation routine

Many people have discovered that CONFIG.SYS is not necessary with Windows 95 Plug 'n' Play. To this extent, CONFIG.SYS is not required by Windows 95. However, the implication for people learning about operating systems, beginning with Windows 95, is that CONFIG.SYS is required by earlier versions of DOS and 16-bit Windows. This is not true. A computer without a CONFIG.SYS and an AUTOEXEC.BAT file can be started. If there are CD-ROM drivers or sound card drivers in the file, those devices won't operate, but the basic computer will start and run. Read any exam questions about CONFIG.SYS very carefully!

 The only files absolutely required to boot a computer into DOS are IO.SYS, MSDOS.SYS, and COMMAND.COM. (IBMBIO.COM and IBMDOS.COM are used by the IBM version of DOS, but we didn't see them referenced on the exam.)

If CONFIG.SYS exists, the IO.SYS/IBMBIO.COM reads the file line by line. DOS specifies the way in which each line of the CONFIG.SYS file is written. The file is much like a batch file in that DOS has the capability to examine each line as a line of instructions. Because this is a SYS file and not a program, we use the term *directives* rather than *commands* to refer to the reserved words used in the CONFIG.SYS file. The CONFIG.SYS file is discussed throughout this chapter and in depth in Chapter 11.

The DOS F5 Key

Beginning with DOS 5, the boot process can be interrupted by pressing the F5 function key at the point where the message, "Starting MS DOS..." appears on the screen. This interruption allows the user to choose from a menu on the monitor's screen. The menu provides choices such as:

➤ Bypass the CONFIG.SYS and AUTOEXEC.BAT files completely

➤ Pause at each line of the CONFIG.SYS and AUTOEXEC.BAT files and choose whether to execute the program line

➤ Choose different types of configurations on the basis of specific formatting within the CONFIG.SYS text file

 In Chapter 10 (Windows 95) we discuss the F8 and F5 keys, along with Safe mode. For those of you who are familiar with the DOS F5 key, the exam room can be a confusing place to try to remember which key does what across all three environments of DOS, Windows 3.x, and Windows 95. As far as we could determine, the main interest was how to arrive at the Safe mode text menu in Windows 95.

CONFIG.SYS Passes To MSDOS.SYS

The DOS system files attempt to find each device driver listed in CONFIG.SYS and to execute the instructions in that driver. Remember that a software driver is a special file that contains instructions from a manufacturer regarding how to operate its piece of hardware.

 CONFIG.SYS is examined before the full operating system has loaded. There has been no opportunity to issue a PATH statement, so each device must be listed by its full pathname.

Once all the device drivers have worked out their differences, found one another, and settled down into RAM, control passes to MSDOS.SYS (or IBMDOS.COM)—the DOS kernel. MSDOS.SYS (IBMDOS.COM) contains all the support functions necessary to run programs and to allow program development. The kernel is where the listing of interrupts is held, as are various patches, fixes, and updates to DOS.

MSDOS.SYS loads into a lower area of DOS memory so that there need not be a constant access to the slower disk drives. An interesting problem occurred when DOS was loaded from a floppy disk in dual-floppy computers. COMMAND.COM would partially load into RAM and keep track of where the rest of itself was stored (the COMSPEC environment variable). A user would replace the COMMAND.COM disk with a word processor or other application disk and use the computer. At the end of the application session, the user would exit the application and discover an error message: "Missing or bad system files". COMMAND.COM was trying to find itself on the now-removed boot disk.

MSDOS.SYS Loads COMMAND.COM

As DOS runs through the lines in the CONFIG.SYS file, the files referred to either exist or don't exist. Chapter 11 explores the kinds of problems associated with the CONFIG.SYS file. At the end of this chapter, we talk specifically about device drivers. Meanwhile, assuming that all the device drivers are found and loaded into memory, the CONFIG.SYS file eventually ends, and control returns to the system files (IO.SYS).

 IO.SYS steps out and looks into any existing CONFIG.SYS file, then regains control of the system long enough to hand off to MSDOS.SYS. Technically, IO.SYS makes this little return engagement, but in a general sense, CONFIG.SYS hands off to MSDOS.SYS.

If no CONFIG.SYS file can be found, MSDOS.SYS looks for COMMAND.COM in the root directory of the boot disk. COMMAND.COM must be from the same version of DOS as the system files are, or the process comes to a screeching halt with the message "Incorrect DOS version". The DOS kernel (MSDOS.SYS) loads COMMAND.COM into memory following any device drives from IO.SYS and CONFIG.SYS.

Note: IO.SYS only began loading device drivers with Windows 95. The initial programming for HIMEM.SYS can be seen in IO.SYS all the way back in DOS 6, but it wasn't activated until Windows 95.

Beginning with DOS 5, COMMAND.COM could be loaded into conventional memory or upper memory, depending on whether a memory device manager (HIMEM.SYS) was run from CONFIG.SYS. However, regardless of the area of memory, COMMAND.COM is run and installs into some part of the first 1MB of RAM (conventional memory).

Summarizing The Boot Sequence

The process that began with DOS, has continued through Windows 3.11, and works the same way with Windows 95/98. For a quick review, here are the steps once again:

1. POST

2. Bootstrap loader

3. IO.SYS

4. CONFIG.SYS

5. MSDOS.SYS

6. AUTOEXEC.BAT

Keep in mind that neither the CONFIG.SYS nor AUTOEXEC.BAT are required, but if they exist, they run at the points just listed. Windows 95 still uses the same steps, and though most of what used to be in the CONFIG.SYS file has now been coded into IO.SYS, the process still follows this same set of steps. Chapter 11 has a deeper view of the CONFIG.SYS file and the main directives it uses.

AUTOEXEC.BAT

If you ever look inside COMMAND.COM, you'll find a reference to a file with a specific name: AUTOEXEC.BAT. This is a batch file and is just like any other batch file that can be created using a text editor. If the file has this name, spelled this way, and it resides in the root directory, DOS will process any instructions as the final step in the boot process. Like CONFIG.SYS, AUTOEXEC.BAT is not required to boot the computer. If AUOTEXEC.BAT does exist, COMMAND.COM will process it as the last step in the boot process.

The AUTOEXEC.BAT file is used to run commands that you want to have processed every time you start the computer. Typically, you will want to set a path each time and tell DOS and Windows to use TEMP directory for various over-flow files. Other things that end up in the AUTOEXEC.BAT file include:

➤ Configuration switches for CD-ROM drives and sound cards. These characters, following a command name, can be exceptionally complicated and arcane. A batch file is a good way to store this kind of complexity within a file with a simple one-word name to enter.

➤ Running network connection files.

➤ Loading certain TSR programs.

➤ Automatically starting Windows 3.x or some other menu program.

Once the last command line in the AUTOEXEC.BAT file has been pro-cessed, control returns to COMMAND.COM, and the computer is ready to begin a working session. If an application's startup program file is the last com-mand, the last thing AUTOEXEC.BAT will do is start the application, placing the user at whatever startup location that application normally provides.

A Sample Batch File

A batch file is a plain-text file composed of command lines and saved with the .BAT extension. Using DOS's Edit or the Windows Notepad, you can create a new file with the following lines:

➤ DIR C:\ /P

➤ ECHO This is a test line

➤ PAUSE

➤ REM I don't want this line to show

➤ DIR C:\ /W

When you are finished entering these lines, with a carriage return (pressing Enter) at the end of each line, you save it as some file name with the .BAT extension, for example, C:\BATCH\TRYTHIS.BAT.

When you type "TRYTHIS" and press Enter, this batch file gives a directory listing of the C: root directory, pausing every 23 lines for a keypress (DIR C:\ /p). When the DIR is finished, it will display on the screen the message "This is a test line" (only without the quotes).

> *Note: The ECHO command is a batch file command that tells DOS to type to the screen whatever follows ECHO and a space.*

The PAUSE command (internal to COMMAND.COM) pauses the process and places the generic message "Press any key to continue" at the next line below the test-line row. When you press a key, the batch file skips over the following line: REM I don't want this line to show

REM (short for *remark*) is an internal DOS batch file command that must begin in the first column of a new line. REM, followed by a space, causes COMMAND.COM to bypass the line and move processing to the next line. An interesting exam question implies that you already know what REM looks like, and then asks you to choose which response will remove SMARTDRV from a CONFIG.SYS file.

REM is often used to *remark out* a line in the AUTOEXEC.BAT or CONFIG.SYS file in a test situation where you might want to keep the commands in the line but bypass them for a number of sessions.

Windows allows this type of "commenting out" in the WIN.INI and SYSTEM.INI files by using a semicolon (;), followed by a space in the first column of the line. REM won't work in a Windows INI file, and a semicolon won't work in a DOS batch file.

Because the line following the PAUSE command has been commented out and won't be processed, you won't see "I don't want this line to show" on the screen. The next thing you *will* see is another DIR listing of the root directory, this time in wide format and without the pause (DIR C:\ /w). When the DIR is finished listing, the batch file turns control back over to COMMAND.COM and returns the DOS prompt.

This is exactly how the AUTOEXEC.BAT file works, and you can edit the file with DOS's Edit, the Windows Notepad, or any other word processor. However, be sure that you save the file in plain ASCII, as it's not unusual for someone to edit the CONFIG.SYS file or AUTOEXEC.BAT file with Microsoft Word and then save it as a DOC file, which contains all kinds of extended, non-ASCII characters. When this happens, the computer either throws up and dies when it hits the non-ASCII file or bypasses the file completely. If the AUTOEXEC.BAT file contains network login commands, the user can end up mystified as to why he or she can't log on to the network.

Note: Always make a backup copy of the latest working CONFIG.SYS and AUTOEXEC.BAT files before editing them so that you have a current, uncorrupted version in case of emergencies.

COMMAND.COM

DOS is really a package of many programs and utilities that take up a lot of space in a default directory called C:\DOS (C:\WINDOWS\COMMAND in Windows 95). When we talk about DOS, we're referring to the whole package and all the various subprograms. However, the essence of the operating system is the *command interpreter* (COMMAND.COM) and the two hidden system files that handle basic I/O.

COMMAND.COM contains many of the instructions for the basic things that a computer is used for. The internal commands are used for file management (e.g., copying, deleting, renaming, and, in DOS 6, moving files). Other internal commands are used for directory management (e.g., changing, removing, and making directories).

DOS Commands

COMMAND.COM contains a number of built-in command instructions. Any commands that have their names within the code for COMMAND.COM are called *internal commands*. Program files that have a separate .EXE or .COM extension and that come with the DOS operating system disks are called *external commands*.

COMMAND.COM is usually loaded into RAM when a computer boots up, and it stays in RAM during the session (the time during which the computer is turned on). COMMAND.COM stays in RAM all the time mainly because DOS almost constantly uses a number of commands that can be accessed faster by staying there.

Some of the *internal*, always-needed commands found in COMMAND.COM are CLS (clear the screen), DIR (directory listing), COPY, DEL, CD, RD, MD, VER (show DOS version), TIME (set/show the time), DATE (set/show the date), and VOL (list the volume name).

Additional internal commands deal with batch files and the DOS environment. The environment commands include PATH, SET, and PROMPT. Batch commands include IF, ECHO, @, FOR, GOTO, and a few other useful and interesting commands.

> *Note: We didn't see any real mention of batch files on the exam other than the AUTOEXEC.BAT file. Batch files are a fascinating way to get involved in simple programming, though the trend away from the DOS text environment has made books about batch files hard to find. There are software applications available (e.g., WinBatch) that allow you to create batch files for the Windows environment in a similar way to the old DOS batch files.*

External DOS Commands

COMMAND.COM is limited to 64K because it's a COM file. However, DOS also allows EXE programs that can be larger than 64K. By using ingenuity and logic, the people who built DOS were able to combine this capability and include a set of instructions in COMMAND.COM for looking somewhere else for help.

When you type a string of characters as an instruction at the command prompt and press Enter, COMMAND.COM reviews what you entered and compares that to its own instructions. If it finds something, it passes those instructions on to the computer. An example is typing "CD\" (without the quotes) at the DOS prompt. Because the instruction "CD" and the "backslash" are built in, COMMAND.COM can work with you.

However, if what you've entered is not found inside COMMAND.COM, it is instructed to check a predetermined list of other subdirectories to find a program that matches what you entered. This list, once again, is the *environment path*, or *search path*.

Today, most systems that install DOS first are set up with a path to C:\DOS. Windows 95 is different, putting the DOS 7.x programs in C:\WINDOWS\COMMAND. Either way, an entire set of additional, necessary DOS subprograms is included with the operating system's installation disks. Any of these programs that COMMAND.COM must search for on the hard disk is an external command.

Some examples of external DOS commands are FORMAT.COM, FDISK.EXE, SCANDISK.EXE, XCOPY.EXE, and MODE.COM.

 SYS.COM is an external command program designed to transfer the three fundamental system files to a preexisting boot sector that used to hold system files.

DOS Command Line

As we've seen, a fundamental part of COMMAND.COM is its ability to read a command line and pass the information contained in the characters back to MSDOS.SYS for processing. If the command line fails to match exact patterns, COMMAND.COM contains a number of error messages that it sends to the screen.

The DOS command line is the single line of characters—a character string—that you enter at the DOS prompt. The DOS prompt is the combination of the symbols at the leftmost column of a plain screen and the blinking cursor, or insertion point. The default prompt is the A> or the C> symbol from CP/M, though you can change the way the prompt looks.

When you enter a string of characters at the command line, DOS breaks up the letters, symbols, and numbers into units that match internal patterns of characters. When you break apart a line of characters into a particular pattern, you parse the line. The patterns of characters are commands, and the commands are part of either the DOS system files (e.g., PROMPT, COPY, RD, and DEL) or a program file.

PROMPT

PROMPT is a reserved word for an internal DOS command. Internal means that the command is built in to COMMAND.COM—one of the main system files. We discuss COMMAND.COM at length shortly, but for now you need to know how a command line works. PROMPT is known as an *environment command* in that it affects the DOS that you see when you're not doing anything. For example, the prompt before the blinking cursor simply exists, waiting for you to do something.

The environment is an area of memory that DOS keeps aside to store system settings. PROMPT, PATH, and COMSPEC are environment commands. SET is the command that controls the environment. On its own, SET, with Enter, shows you the existing DOS environment. SET=[something] changes the environment.

PROMPT uses special symbols called *metastrings* in conjunction with the word *prompt*. When you enter "PROMPT" with a dollar sign ($) and a metastring, DOS sends the information you entered to ANSI.SYS (an auxiliary file that comes with DOS) and changes the environment. The PROMPT command uses metastrings preceded by "$" to make changes. The PROMPT command and switches are case insensitive, meaning that you can enter them in uppercase, lowercase, or any combination of the two.

Some of the metastrings are T (time), D (date), P (default drive letter and directory), G (the > character), L (the < character) and _ (the underscore character, which produces a carriage return, line feed, and a new line). Remember that you must precede the symbols with "$" and enter "PROMPT", starting at the first place in the command line. You must also have ANSI.SYS available on the system for the more interesting prompt experiments.

The command PROMPT=PG (case insensitive) makes the prompt show the default drive, directory, and the > character: C:\DOS>_. The command PROMPT=Type "EXIT" to$_return to Windows$_pg (no spaces in Windows$_$p$g) produces a three-line prompt at a DOS screen as follows:

```
Type "EXIT" to
return to Windows
C:\DOS>_
```

The = character is used by DOS to signify a space. Therefore, you need not enter it, but it's good practice to use it so that you don't accidentally omit a space. The command PROMPT=pg works the same as the command prompt Pg because these commands are not case-sensitive.

Switches

A command line uses words, numbers, and symbols to produce specific results. The words represent program files that DOS can find along the path (internal command words) that DOS holds in COMMAND.COM. Usually, the numbers are variables designed to produce different results, depending on the number. *Switches* are certain symbols that call on variations of the specific command. The important things to remember about switches include the following:

➤ Switches almost always start with a forward slash (/) and are immediately followed by a letter or a character.

➤ Some programmers use the dash (-) as a switch indicator.

➤ A space separates the command word from the switch.

When you use the DIR command to list the directory on the screen, you will see the entire directory. However, a 512-file directory will zoom right up off the top of the screen. To make it stop, use one of the following switches:.

➤ **DIR /p** Tells DOS to stop the list every 23 lines, which make up a *screen page*. ("P" is short for "by the page.")

➤ **DIR /w** Tells DOS to show the files in a wide format, that is, across the screen.

➤ **DIR /s** Tells DOS to show not only the current directory's files but also all the files in every subdirectory below the current one.

Switches can often be combined (e.g., DIR /s /p) to provide combined variations of any command that supports multiple switches. In this case, you're asking DOS to show you all the files in this directory and any subdirectories and to stop the display every 23 lines until you press any key.

The /? Switch

DOS versions 5 and later include a rudimentary built-in Help feature that acts as a quick reminder of how a command can be used. As far back as version 3, MS DOS provided a complete HELP file with an expanded Help feature on how to use commands. PC-DOS didn't include the expanded Help feature until later versions.

At a DOS prompt, you can almost always enter "[command] /?" to obtain a cheat sheet on how to use that command. For example, DIR /? will give you all the switches and a brief explanation of what each does.

Syntax

The dictionary defines *syntax* as follows: "The way words are put together in order to form sentences, clauses, or phrases." A DOS command line is an instruction to DOS to do something, and DOS reads it much like you or I read a sentence. It might help, during the learning process, to try to convert the cryptic DOS symbols and shorthand into sentences. For example, /W could be read as "by the wide," whereas /P could be read as "by the page." This way, DIR /w /p would sound like, "Give me a directory listing of this directory, by its width, and by the page." (You don't need to say "please" because, after all, this is a computer!)

The conventional standard for listing the syntax of a command is to begin with the command followed by square brackets ([ ]), which enclose each and every possible switch. Italicized words that come after the command usually refer to some additional characters that you're supposed to enter to replace the word. For example, DIR [d:] [*path*] [*file name* [.*ext*]] [/P] [/W] [/S] means that the DIR command can (but need not) be followed by any of the items listed in square brackets.

Etiquette suggests that whoever is writing the command syntax description give at least a minimal explanation of anything in the square brackets. In the case above, the writer should include "Where [d:] represents a drive letter, [*path*] represents a directory path, and [*file name*] can be any specific file name being listed or searched for."

About Variables

A mathematical or computer variable is an interesting device and one that you already know how to use—you just don't know that you know it. As is often the case, confusion can arise when someone uses a formal word to describe a common event.

Variables are *placeholders* that are written down somewhere and that act as stand-ins for something real that will happen later. You probably took algebra in high school and used the symbol "X" in equations as a variable that stands for "whatever I'm supposed to find to get the right answer on the test, later."

A classroom containing a number of desks is a variable situation. Suppose that 15 desks are in the room. Each semester, those 15 desks sit in the same place. If you were asked what those were, you would say, "Those are desks." However, each semester 15 students enroll in the class and sit at the desks. The desks are the *variables,* and the students are the *data being held by the variable.*

Depending on which semester it was, if you were asked what those desks were, you would say, "That's Bill's desk" or "That's Sharon's desk." Bill and Sharon are the data being assigned to the variables (desks) at a particular moment in time. The next semester you would point to the same desks and say, "That's Donna's desk" or "That's Phillip's desk."

If you number each desk 1 through 15, you're *naming* the variables. Therefore, a computer program could say, "GO GET THE DATA IN '12.' IF '12' IS EMPTY, THEN 'ANSWER' = 0. IF '12' IS NOT EMPTY, THEN 'STUDENT' = '12.'" The number 12 is a variable representing desk number 12, which either is empty or contains a student. ANSWER and STUDENT are other variables that will also hold information that changes.

By providing the computer with a list of student names with their desk numbers each semester, the computer can tell you whether the desk is empty, whether the student is present, and the student's name.

The DIR Command

One of the commands used almost routinely in DOS and Windows is the DIR command, to show a directory listing. You may think that Windows doesn't use this command, but every time you call up the File Manager or Explorer, Windows is using the DIR command properties to get a listing of the files you're seeing.

If you try to find a file using the "Search" or "Find" options in Windows, you'll be presented with a field in their dialog boxes where you enter some parts of a file name, and something having to do with asterisks (also called the "star"). In a moment, we'll look at the DOS wild cards, but for the moment just make a note that the DIR command does two things:

➤ DIR shows a listing of files on a drive or in a directory.

➤ DIR is used to search for files on a drive or in a directory.

The full syntax for the DIR command is more than a screen full of information and can be called up using the /? switch. Generally, the most common switches used are the /P, /S, and /W as mentioned above.

Wild Cards

If you've ever played poker, then you know that in certain games the dealer can make a card "wild." The wild card can represent any other card. The wild card becomes a variable just like the blank tile in a Scrabble game. You can use the card, and it can represent whatever you'd like it to. DOS has two reserved symbols that represent this sort of variable.

The asterisk (*) and the question mark (?) are the same thing as the wild card in poker, or the blank tile in Scrabble. They each have a slightly different way of working, though, which works out in the following manner:

➤ The asterisk symbol represents one or more characters to the right of the point where the asterisk is used.

➤ The asterisk can be limited to the first eight characters in a file name by placing a dot (period) after the asterisk (i.e., *.)

➤ The question mark symbol can only represent a single character. If more than one character is needed, more than one question mark must be used.

➤ When the question mark is used, then it means there must be one character available for every question mark typed.

Perhaps the easiest way to demonstrate wild cards is to show various ways they would be used with the DIR command. Let's suppose we have a number of files in a directory that have a .WKS extension, and another number of files that have a .XLS extension. The main part of the file name can be anywhere from one to eight characters, though a number of the files start with REP for report, followed by a date (e.g., REP996, REP1096, REP1196).

Let's further suppose that this directory has a number of files with many different extensions. There might be a THISONE.TXT, THATONE.MIS, NEWFILE.DLL, OLD.BAK, REAL.DOC, RUSS.DOC, and MY.WRK.

If we were to try and find every file that was an Excel spreadsheet (.XLS extension), we would have to use one of the wild cards. The way we look specifically for every file with the .XLS extension is to use DIR *.XLS as the command.

If you were to use DIR ????????.XLS under the assumption that you would find anything in the main name, it wouldn't work. The reason is that the question mark doesn't just represent any single character, but it means some character *must* exist as well. In this instance, you would be telling DOS to look for a file that must have eight characters, a period, and the XLS extension. While there may be a few files with eight-letter names, there may also be many files with seven, five, or four characters to the left of the dot.

If you were to use DIR ?.*, then you would have to have a file with at least one character along with an extension. There might be 200 files in a directory, but none of them would only be one character and an extension. DOS would return the "file(s) not found" message, if there were no one-character filenames.

Now suppose you want to find every file that ends with the letter "S" in the extension. If you type DIR *.*S it won't work. The reason is that once you place an asterisk at any point in either the main part or the extension of the file name, DOS takes out any characters to the right of the asterisk. The only way to limit this removal is to place a dot to the right of the asterisk.

In the famous DIR *.* command, you're asking DOS to find any number of characters to the left of the dot and any number of characters to the right of the dot. DIR *.*S is the same thing. However, you could use DIR *.??S. The problem is that the two question marks make an assumption that every file where the extension ends with "S" has three characters in the extension. Unfortunately, the only way to guarantee that you have every file that ends in "S" would be to run the DIR command two times: DIR *.?S, and DIR *.??S

If you wanted to find every file that was a "report" file you would use DIR REP*.* because all these files begin with the letters REP and the company's naming standards require that all reports begin with the letters REP.

Note: Developing a consistent way to name your files allows you to use the DOS wild cards to search for those files in a logical manner.

When you open the Search and Find dialog boxes in Windows, you're expected to use the DOS wild cards in order to find the files you want. Rather than using the /S switch (DIR *.* /S), there's a checkbox asking you if you want to search all subdirectories or subfolders.

To find all the temp files on a C: drive, you would have to know that almost all Windows temp files end with .TMP. Another form of temporary file has the ~ (tilde, pronounced "till-dee") as the first character. You can't use the DIR command to find two different types of files. For instance, you can't use DIR ~*.* ; *.TMP. The semicolon isn't allowed on the command line.

In the above case you would have to issue two DIR sequences. The first would be DIR C:\~*.* /S to find any file that began with a tilde, starting from the C: drive root directory, and looking in every subdirectory on the drive. The second would be to use DIR C:*.TMP /S to find any file in any subdirectory on the C: drive, with a .TMP extension.

Saving Search Results

There is another use for the ">" symbol (without quotes). This is called a redirector and means that whatever results from a DOS command is redirected to someplace other than the standard output device—the screen. Whenever you issue a command, that command performs an action. Many times the command also outputs some type of result. The result can be in the form of messages or, in the case of the DIR command, the listing of your directory.

If you use the > redirector, you can send the output results from DIR to either a printer or another file. For instance, using DIR C:*.TMP /S > PRN will redirect the results of searching for every TMP file on the entire C: drive to the printer, where you can go over the list at your leisure. Another way would be to use DIR C:*.TMP /S > C:\SOMEFILE.TXT. This would create a file called SOMEFILE.TXT in the root directory of the C: drive, that would contain all the files listed in the search result. Later, you could open C:\SOMEFILE.TXT with MS Word, Notepad, EDIT, or any other application that can read a plain, ASCII text file.

Vanilla ASCII (Plain Text)

Batch files, AUTOEXEC.BAT, CONFIG.SYS, and many generic reference files require that only characters from ASCII 0032 through 0126 be in the file. These basic characters are called *plain*, or *vanilla*, ASCII characters (from plain, good ol' vanilla ice cream). You'll often see a reference in books about creating batch files, to using a text editor or your favorite word processor to create these files.

A text editor is a word processing program that allows only plain ASCII characters and no formatting whatsoever. A text editor might allow you to use the Tab key, but when you save the file, the tabs are converted to a number of spaces. The original text editor that came with DOS was called EDLIN.COM (for "edit lines") and drove most early DOS users insane.

Most upscale word processors allow you to choose the File|Save As feature and pick a TXT file type. This combination gives you all the search-and-replace, copying, moving, macros, formatting, and other features of a powerful word processor to create a document; a plain ASCII TXT file is the result.

Common text editors include:

➤ **EDIT.COM** Introduced with DOS 5 and higher; requires QBASIC.EXE, which contains the editor's code. (With the release of DOS 7 and Windows 95, EDIT.COM no longer requires QBASIC.)

➤ **NOTEPAD.EXE** The Windows 3.x text-editing utility (also in Windows 95).

➤ **WORDPAD.EXE** The Windows 95 replacement for Notepad.

File Names

Information can't be saved to any media without a name. Most people think of a file name as being of the 8.3 type. The fact is, a file name is the entire unique string of characters that describes the exact location of the file—the pathname.

Certain file-naming conventions have come to be known in the DOS world, and computer people are often judged on the elegance of their procedures. You *can* create an archive file with something like WinZip or PKZip and call it

ARCHIVE.698 (instead of ARCHIVE.ZIP). However; if another technician needs to conduct research into which type of file it is, you'll probably be considered ignorant (at best!).

Some file names are absolute in their names (e.g., AUTOEXEC.BAT, CONFIG.SYS, SYSTEM.DAT, and USER.DAT). If you spell these in any way other than the required way, they won't work the way you expected them to work. The best policy is to learn the common extensions and stick with the program. Computers are hard enough to deal with, and you don't need to spend extra time decoding someone else's surrealistic file-naming ideas.

Most applications in the past, and many applications today, expect a specific extension to be used. DOS inserts a period even if the user doesn't include one. Common applications that do this are Lotus 1-2-3 (.WKS, .WK3), dBase (.DBF, .IDX), MS Access (.MDB), MS Word (.DOC, .DOT), MS Excel (.XLS), and MS PowerPoint (.PPT, .POT).

Nondisplayed Periods

One confusing aspect of DOS is that when a DIR listing of files in a directory is sent to the screen or printed, no periods appear. It looks like the file names are split into one to eight characters, a big empty space, and then one to three characters, or the <DIR> notation.

Although the screen or printer doesn't print the periods in the file names, DOS needs those periods. If you try to find a file name without using the period, you will receive a "File Not Found" response.

WordPerfect was the first application with a widespread customer base that allowed for an optional extension or no extension and for naming the extension anything the user chose. An interesting problem would arise when a user typed a long document (forgetting to save it every few minutes) and then had to come up with a name at the first save. If the document involved something about, say, a certificate of needs, the user might choose to name it the acronym "CON" and omit the extension. When the user pressed Enter, the document disappeared! Can you guess why?

Going back to the original device names that DOS used for basic hardware peripherals, we're reminded of COM1, COM2, COM3, COM4, AUX (serial ports), LPT1, LPT2 (line printers), PRN (generic printer) and CON (the screen console). A hapless user attempting to save the document with the name CON would inadvertently save it to the screen device. This has the effect of clearing the screen and probably crash-exiting from the application.

Keeping Files Together

If you write a two-page letter and save it as NAME1.DOC, the file system notes the name of the file and puts the two pages onto the hard drive in a set of clusters. Suppose that you then write another two-page letter and save it as NAME2.DOC. Again, the file system keeps track of the name and the clusters containing the second file. How does the file system know which clusters have which data in them?

Keep the picture of your two letters in mind. Suppose that you decide to make some additions to the first letter. You open your application (say, a word processor) and load (from File|Open) NAME1.DOC into memory. You add another two pages of text and then resave (from File|Save) the letter. It still has the same name, but now you have two additional pages of data.

If the file system tries to store the added two new pages next to the original two pages, there isn't any room. NAME2.DOC has taken the neighboring set of clusters. Therefore, the file system skips the two pages of NAME2.DOC and puts the additional pages of NAME1.DOC after the end of NAME2.DOC. If you look at Figure 8.3, you can see how your files can eventually end up in pieces and scattered all over the hard drive.

DEFRAG.EXE And Contiguous Clusters

DEFRAG.EXE was added to DOS 6 (in the C:\DOS subdirectory) as a way to put all the parts of files into one continuous group of clusters. Prior to DOS 6.x, the only way to defragment (DEFRAG.EXE) a file was to use a third-party software utility tool. Because DOS originally included almost no utilities, an entire industry of utility companies sprang up around this void.

The revenues from the utilities eventually reached high enough numbers that, for DOS 5, Microsoft contracted with some of the largest companies to add scaled-down versions of a few of its utilities into DOS itself. For example, MEMMAKER.EXE is a subset of Helix Corporation's memory manager.

DEFRAG.EXE is run from the DOS command line. DOS 7 (Windows 95) includes DEFRAG.EXE in the C:\WINDOWS subdirectory, but it can be run only from within a graphics window. Prior to DOS 6, most people either used the Norton SPEEDISK.EXE utility to defragment a disk, or they didn't know that it should be done periodically.

 Defragmenting a disk means that parts of files are brought together into contiguous sectors. CheckDisk (CHKDSK.EXE) and ScanDisk (SCANDISK.EXE) are used to check the validity of the FAT and the integrity of the sectors. DEFRAG uses the valid FAT to find all the parts of a file and bring them together.

> The DEFRAG process is automatic and requires a perfect FAT and perfect disk. If, at the beginning of the process, DEFRAG finds an error in the FAT, the program halts, and the user is given a message to run ScanDisk.

Wasted Space

Let's say that NAME1.DOC is around three pages long, or about 6K in size. On a 100MB hard drive, the smallest cluster is 2K, so the letter would nearly fill all three clusters (2K × 3 clusters = 6K file size).

Now say that we have a 1GB hard drive partitioned as one logical drive from beginning to end. The smallest cluster size is now 32K, and the whole letter is only 6K. Because DOS can't break up clusters, the entire 32K is used to store only 6K, leaving 26K empty. This space is completely wasted because it can't be used by another file, and the letter is far too small for the cluster. This is one reason for partitioning a large physical disk into relatively small logical drives.

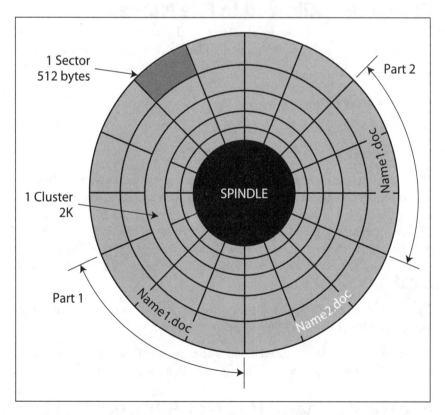

Figure 8.3 Stylized disk showing a file splitting up another file.

Table 8.1 Minimum cluster size in relation to volume size.

Volume Size	Minimum Cluster Size
16MB to 127MB	2K
128MB to 255MB	4K
256MB to 511MB	8K
512GB to 1.023GB	16K
1.024GB 2.047GB	32K
2.048GB to 4.096GB	64K

Table 8.1 shows how the different sizes of a logical drive can change the minimum amount of space a file will take up. Observe that on a 2GB drive, even if you only create a 75 byte file, it would take up 64,000 bytes of space on the drive.

Characters Allowed In File Names

DOS will allow you to use any character on the keyboard other than those reserved for commands and instructions. These characters are the following:

➤ The letters A through Z

➤ The numbers 0 through 9

➤ ', ~, ", !, @, #, $, %, ^, &, (,), -, _, {, }

➤ High-bit characters from 127 through 255

The lower the scan code number of a character, the higher the file name will be on a directory listing sorted by name. This is confusing to some people who expect a list sorted by name to have all names beginning with "A" at the top and all names beginning with "Z" at the bottom. Because one is a lower number than two, all files beginning with one will move to the top of a directory listing. For example, 11NOV98.DOC will appear directly below 1JAN98.DOC, and 2FEB98.DOC will be third.

To force a file name to the top of a directory listing, begin the name with something like !, @, or #, as these have very low scan codes.

By convention, temporary, deletable files often start with a tilde (~), an underscore (_), a percent sign (%), a dollar sign ($), or an ampersand (&).

File Name Characters Not Allowed

We've spoken about the 8.3 file name format. Which characters, then, can you use for file names? Remember the ASCII character set? The original set was

126 characters until IBM added another 126 characters (high-bit) for the extended ASCII character set. DOS allows any character between ASCII decimal number 33 and 255. The following characters are not allowed:

➤ ASCII 0032 is the space created by pressing the space bar (not allowed). DOS does not allow spaces created by 0032, but a power-user secret is to use the 0255 hard space in a file name.

➤ ASCII 0001 through 0031 are control characters (not allowed).

➤ Reserved symbols used by DOS (not allowed).

Reserved, nonallowed characters in DOS 1 through 6.x are:

➤ Control characters less than 0033

➤ Spacebar (32)

➤ Characters that act as spaces: equals signs, commas, semicolons, and the Tab key

➤ Characters used as instructions: periods, colons, backslashes, forward slashes, greater-than and less-than signs, plus signs, and square brackets

➤ Lowercase letters (DOS automatically converts them to uppercase)

A Word About Windows 95 Long File Names

Windows 95 allows the use of long file names from within the graphic environment. These names can include spaces (e.g., "ASCII 32"). Windows Explorer and Windows 95 applications accept such file names. However, the underlying DOS 7 FAT, which does the grunt work of storing the files on the drive, does not allow long file names. Chapter 10 discusses the VFAT and long file names. Some of the ways that long file names interact with DOS include the following:

➤ Windows 95 long file names are not stored in the FAT but in the VFAT.

➤ DOS 7 uses a tilde (~) and consecutive numbers to truncate the long file name into its first eight characters (i.e., prior to the extension). Table 8.2 shows common file name extensions in DOS.

➤ The use of the tilde (~) is a configuration option in Windows 95 setup.

Logical Formatting And Partitions

Logical formatting means that an amount of space—a partition—on the physical hard drive is set aside as a discrete area to store data and program files. A physical disk can contain a number of partitions that DOS recognizes as *logical* drives. Almost all PCs have a physical drive and at least one logical drive. (An

Table 8.2 Common DOS file name extensions.

Extension	Type Of File
.COM	64K compiled command file
.EXE	Large, compiled executable file
.BAT	ASCII plain-text batch file
.SYS	System driver software/instruction file
.GRP	Windows program group file
.BAK, .OLD	Backup file
.TMP	Temporary file (usually deletable)
.INI	Initialization file (DOS and Windows)
.DLL	Windows Dynamic Link Library
.INF	Windows 95 autoscript setup program
.REG	Windows 95 Registry data files
.VXD	Windows 95 and DOS 7.x virtual device driver file
.DRV	Driver software file
.TXT	Plain ASCII file created by text editor
.HLP	Windows HELP hypertext file
.DOC	Document file (full character sets, formatting)
.WRI	Windows 3.x MS Write file
.HTM	Internet HTML (Hypertext Markup Language)
.BMP	Windows bitmap graphics file
.WMF	Windows metafile graphics file
.PCX	MS Paint raster image
.ICO	Windows icon file
.TTF	TrueType font file
.OVL	Program overlay file
.BAS	BASIC program file
.SCR	Script file or screen-saver file
.DAT	Data file
.ZIP	Archive file
.EX_, .CO_	Microsoft expand/extract archive
.DIZ	Internet shareware description text

(continued)

Table 8.2 Common DOS file name extensions *(continued).*	
Extension	**Type Of File**
.WAV	Waveform sound file
.MID	MIDI sound file
.CB	Windows 95 cabinet file

exception is a diskless network terminal, from which the hard disk is removed and the terminal booted up with a floppy disk.)

The maximum number of logical drives is 23. Drive letters are always alphabet letters. A: and B: are built into all computers, and the C: drive is considered the first bootable DOS drive. Twenty-six letters minus 3 letters = 23—the remaining limit.

Formatting a disk means that the DOS file system is used to create the FAT, the DAT, and the root directory and to define the number and size of clusters on the volume.

Because the logical volume or logical drive might be smaller than the physical disk, the names *volume* and *drive* are not interchangeable with *disk*.

You can partition a disk into logical drives or volumes, but you can't partition a drive into logical disks.

Today, when you buy a computer from a store, the low-level formatting has been done by the drive OEM. Typically, the logical formatting has also been done by the dealer. Most dealers format a hard disk as one logical drive—a single partition. Make a note that the larger the partition (also known as the logical drive or volume), the larger the clusters needed to fill that space.

Drive Storage Support

When DOS 1 was released, the hard drive wasn't available for PCs. Version 2 was released partly to support the introduction of the newly released 10MB and 20MB hard drives. Through version 3.3, the maximum amount of space that DOS could handle was 32MB. Although larger hard disks were available, the only way to use them with DOS was to partition them into logical partitions of 32MB or less.

DOS 4.0.1 broke the 32MB barrier, allowing for a maximum 256MB extended partition. Hard disks were beginning to enter the range of gigabyte capacity and could now be broken up into larger logical drives.

When DOS 5 finally arrived, it included support for 2GB logical drive partitions. However, the BIOS for the drive controllers in many computers (e.g., the 80486 chip) couldn't always support the large drives.

LBA

The IDE specification handles drive space up to 512MB (this is logical drive space, not physical hard disk size). *Logical block addressing* (LBA) allows an older PC with IDE controllers to access logical drives larger than 512MB. The IDE controller-addressing model doesn't allow the use of addresses that are large enough to work with larger drives. The 512MB limit was set because of the way in which IBM originally designed disk access on its old AT.

Because of the limited specification, IDE is gradually being superseded by EIDE. LBA, a feature of EIDE, allows the drive controller to perform an address conversion and bypass the controller bottleneck. The LBA allows for drives up to 8.4GB. To support logical drives and primary partitions over 512MB, the computer's ROM BIOS must have LBA capability.

If an older computer can't support the larger drives, a number of larger drives (e.g., Maxtor) come with a proprietary software program that can provide this capability. Each drive has its own way to do this, so consult the drive's reference manual for details.

> *Note: The16-bit File Allocation Table (FAT16) addressing structure has a maximum of 65,525 clusters, each limited to a maximum size of 64K. Therefore, the largest drive using a FAT16 partitioning and formatting scheme is 2GB. LBA provides a way to work with newer ROM BIOS to support up to 8GB of physical disk space. Using today's technology, the combination of FAT16, partitioning, formatting, and DOS/Windows/ Windows 95 allows the largest physical disk to be 8GB, but the largest logical drive is still 2GB.*

Partitioning

By now, you might have heard the word *partition* enough to guess that a partition's size is something that *you* determine. The logical size of a partition is a customer-based decision that is made at the time the disk is formatted by the operating system. Some third-party software utilities allow repartitioning of a disk after the format process while not losing any data. The DOS partition process automatically removes all data from the disk and requires a new format.

The external DOS program used to partition a *disk* is FDISK.EXE. The external DOS program used to format a logical *drive* is FORMAT.COM. Chapter 11 examines FDISK in some detail, but for now keep in mind that:

➤ Partitioning a disk through DOS completely destroys all data and formatting on that disk.

➤ The maximum number of logical drives is 23. Drive letters are alphabet letters. A: and B: are built into all computers, and the C: drive is considered the first bootable DOS drive. Twenty-six letters, minus 3 = 23—the remaining limit.

FORMAT.COM

Partitioning a disk only tells the operating system how the disk is divided into drive space, or logical drives. No matter which operating system (e.g., DOS, OS/2, or Unix) you choose to install on any given partition, you'll need to set up the partition as a logical drive with some kind of file system. FORMAT is the external program in DOS, OS/2, and Windows 95 and NT that prepares the drive's file system. FORMAT will do the following:

➤ Create a boot sector, two copies of the FAT, and the root directory

➤ Perform a low-level check for bad sectors, marking any that it finds as unusable

➤ Provide a single-step systems file transfer option to make a disk bootable

At the end of the FORMAT process, the routine allows the user to label a disk with a volume name.

When a working hard drive suddenly produces an error at boot up that reads "Non-system disk or disk error. Replace and press any key when ready," it may mean that the system files have become corrupted. It could also mean there's a data floppy in drive A: that someone forgot to take out when they shut down the system the last time. SYS.COM is the first step to try to fix the problem.

During a quick format, the program changes only the FAT on the disk and tells DOS that every sector on the drive is now available for data. The data still resides on the disk, but DOS has been told that it can write over anything and put a new entry into the FAT. Unconditional formatting erases data from the entire disk. Safe formatting places a hidden file on a floppy disk, reducing the entire storage area of the disk.

Note: To completely format a disk and have FORMAT.COM examine the entire disk, use the FORMAT [d:] /U switch (for Unconditional).

LABEL.EXE

Oddly enough, a DIR listing (since the time of DOS 1) includes a line that states "Volume in Drive X:" and possibly a label of up to 11 characters. However, there was no way to label a disk other than running a format on it and putting the label on at the end. DOS 3 introduced the LABEL command, which allowed a volume label to be put on a disk without formatting it.

Formatting A Disk

➤ To format a floppy in drive A: the first time, enter "FORMAT A:".

➤ To reformat (quick format) a floppy in drive A:., enter "FORMAT A: /Q".

➤ To format a 720K floppy in drive B:, enter "FORMAT B: /F:720".

➤ To format a bootable floppy in drive A:, enter "FORMAT A: /S".

➤ To format the second logical drive on a hard disk, enter "FORMAT D: /U".

➤ To format a primary, active partition, enter "FORMAT C: /S /U".

Memory

DOS is software and as such loads into memory. It is important to understand the environment of memory—the world that exists within a memory chip—and how DOS, Windows, and any other software lives in that environment. The three main types of memory are:

1. Conventional memory

2. Expanded memory (XMS)

3. Extended memory (EMS)

The 80286 chip was the first real break from the original chipsets and PCs. Another fundamental change came when the 80386 and the 486 family of chips consolidated a number of features. The latest in chips is the Pentium.

Memory has always been a driving force in the advancement of PCs. There never seemed to be enough memory, and the memory that existed was hard to use in stable ways. Each of these chips brought about a major shift in how a computer used memory.

Basic Memory Divisions

You can think of memory as divided into two basic worlds: the world of what used to come with 8088/8086 PCs and the world of everything that was invented later. Remember that modern computers still face day-to-day limitations that are based on the way in which the first XT worked. These limitations have been forced on the manufacturers by the entire concept of *backward compatibility*.

Compatibility refers to new versions of something being workable, in some way, on earlier computers. In other words, if a company is running 30,000 PCs, and every one of those uses DOS 5, that company simply won't buy a new product if it won't run on DOS 5.

The Costs Of Doing Business

Technical people sometimes forget that a computer is a tool that often is used in business to earn profits. A fundamental principle of business is that everything must pay for itself and that whatever remains is profit. Imagine a company using 30,000 computers with DOS 5 as the operating system.

Say that the price of a single copy of DOS 6 is $50 (taking into consideration volume discounts, upgrade discounts, and so on), then multiply $50 by the 30,000 computers. Simply purchasing the software would cost $1.5 million, which doesn't include shipping, taxes, and other incidental charges.

This company has an entire information systems (IS) staff and can assign five full-time employees the task of installing DOS on every computer. The rest of the staff must handle day-to-day problems and questions. Suppose that these five employees each make a salary of $16 per hour.

If it only took 30 minutes per computer to back up the original DOS 5 and install DOS 6, each computer would cost $8 in labor for one IS employee and possibly an additional half-hour of the person whose desk had the computer. Considering only the IS staff, 30,000 machines at $8 each would cost $240,000 in time and labor. With no problems, no errors, and a perfect, first-time installation, it's already costing the company $1.74 million. We haven't even looked at the downtime of every salaried employee whose computer is unusable during the upgrade, from the $8-per-hour clerk to the $175,000-per-year executive (assuming $84 per hour with a loss of $42 of their computer time). Nor have we looked at the time costs that the mail room uses to process all those incoming copies of DOS.

Those 30-minute-per-machine upgrades mean 15,000 work hours divided by the 5 employees, or 3,000 hours per person. Assuming an 8-hour day, it would take each IS employee 375 days to accomplish the upgrade. Naturally, with time off for weekends and sleep, you can see that it would take more than a year simply to change the company from DOS 5 to 6. Think what this would mean if the main spreadsheet program didn't work on the DOS upgrade!

Microprocessors have many switches on their silicon layer and something called *microcode,* which is an extremely small machine language that is designed to process basic logic, arithmetic, and control signals. In addition to the switches, there are *data banks* that keep track of calculations in progress and *registers* that keep track of control data. The registers have a tiny amount of memory capability, only allowing them to store two bytes of information at a time.

If you recall that a byte is 8 bits, naturally, then, 2 bytes would be 16 bits. A byte is something like the letter "G" or the number "5," and a register can contain 2 bytes. When the two bytes are put together, the combination is called a *word.*

A CPU has 14 registers, each of which is 2 bytes long, or 16 bits. The largest number that all these registers can hold (if every one of them had a hexadecimal F) would be 65,536. If you divide 1,048,576 (1MB) by 65,536, you get 16. Coincidentally, the first megabyte of RAM, as we'll see shortly, is divided into 16 segments.

ROM And RAM

PCs are equipped with two kinds of physical memory: RAM and ROM. ROM is stored in small chips and acts to preserve basic information about the computer and its workings. When the power is turned off at the switch, ROM chips continue to "remember" their information. ROM chips have simple instructions coded into them so that they require no electrical power.

RAM, being *volatile* memory, doesn't remember anything when the power supply stops. ROM, being *nonvolatile,* remembers data even without a power supply.

If hardware is what you can drop on your foot, but isn't a set of instructions, and if software is instructions that you can't physically touch, instructions permanently coded into ROM are *firmware* (ROM BIOS can come in this format). The BIOS contains tables of interrupts, copyright information, testing routines, error messages, and some instructions to put characters on the screen in color.

ROM chips also hold a scaled-down version of BASIC that the chip can use to execute instructions on how to move all the stored information into lower memory. Because DOS doesn't start running until after startup, this BASIC code in the ROM chips controls the lights and beeps and initializes the printer and the keyboard.

Conventional Memory

ROM BIOS assigns and keeps track of specific locations in memory. These memory addresses are constantly being attached to bits of data and shuttled across buses and through the system. If the CPU can move 16 bits of information around in its own registers (internal bus), it stands to reason that it should be able to pass 16 bits of information to everything around it (external). Reason, however, has never been a strong point in the computer world. Until the 80386, chips had a 16-bit-wide internal bus to move data but often only an 8-bit-wide bus to send that data to the outside world, causing bottlenecks and slowdowns.

The 8088 could keep track of a bit more (no pun intended) than a million separate addresses in memory, or 1MB (1,048,576 bits). Almost everything involved with moving data around a computer is done by its address. This is like mailing a picture of your new car to a friend: The post office has no interest in the picture, only in the address on the envelope. Imagine that you were a single mail carrier and had a million addresses to work with every day!

To make it easier to keep track of the first megabyte of memory, the 8088/86 CPU used 16 "regional ZIP codes," called *segments*. Each segment of memory is 64K long. Because the 8088/86 could address only 1MB of memory, this was fine. Newer chips have the capability to address far more than 1MB of memory and to do so more directly.

Memory segments are numbered, and the smaller numbers are said to be lower than the larger, higher numbers. For this reason, data stored in the first segments of RAM is said to be in *low memory*.

 The original addressing scheme of the 8088/86 chips, using 16 segments of 64K of memory, is the foundation of all later memory organization. This 1MB of RAM, divided into segments, is referred to as conventional memory. Memory addresses are expressed in hexadecimal numbers.

If you use binary math to calculate the number of addresses available to a 16-bit processor, you'll see that the number is less than the actual number available. Binary math alone won't go the whole distance (it would take 20 bits) because of the two-part address involving the segment and the section. Without going into the details, you should know that memory error messages are reported using both parts of the address.

The *segment address* is one of the 16 "regional" segments of the 1MB. The *offset address* is the specific address within the 64K length of the segment. The combination of segment and offset addresses is how a 16-bit processor can address 20 bits of addresses, or 1MB.

Although you might not be tested on this low level of detail, if you plan to work on computers, you should at least know what a segment address and an offset address look like. The typical presentation to the screen is SEGMENT:OFFSET and appears as 30F9:0102.

80286 And Real Mode

The 8088/86 chips used single addresses for each segment:offset location in memory. The registers in the chip hold the actual hex number of the address as it directly relates to a *real address* in 1MB of memory. This direct, real, one-to-one relationship is known today as the Real mode use of memory. The need for compatibility has kept Real mode, along with the original 1MB of directly addressable memory, alive to this day. The 286 chip changed from segment:offset addressing to something called *selector:offset addressing*. Instead of using a real segment, the registers held a pointer, or *vector*, to some other segment. Because the selector pointer is a smaller number than the full segment address, more selectors can fit into the same number of registers. This concept of using one address to refer to another address is used throughout the computer world. The words that describe this process are *mapping* and *aliasing*.

Aliasing And Mapping

When you rent a box at the post office, you're telling the post office that instead of putting an address on your big house, you want one put on a small box that will *refer* mail to your house. Instead of having to walk all the way to your house, the postal service can immediately move an envelope into your box, and then *you* can come pick it up. The box is vastly smaller than your house, and the distance from the incoming mail dock far shorter.

A cooperative venture between the post office (the CPU), which *could* deliver all the way to your house, and you (the hardware), who walks to the post office, results in faster processing and access to a larger storage area—the whole post office. In a nutshell, this is how expanded memory works.

The external DOS SUBST command (for *substitute*) is a way to shrink a long path of many subdirectories (with many characters) into the two characters of a drive letter. If you substitute C:\WINDOWS\SYSTEM\VBRUNS\100 with G:, instead of entering the full path you can refer to it by using the aliased drive letter, G:. This is called *drive mapping*.

The 286 chip used part of its register group to provide an indicator to a real segment in additional sets of 1MB of memory. In other words, instead of a real address in a single megabyte of real memory, the register holds a sort of PO box number that refers to a whole new megabyte of memory. When the address is called, the CPU is pointed to this new megabyte and gets the segment:offset address of that new megabyte. Using this scheme, the 286 could address up to 16MB of memory.

Aliasing and mapping are used in expanded memory, interrupt vector tables, and, most importantly, in the pseudo-32-bit FAT of Windows 95's IFS (installable file system) and VFAT. It is also used in networking, where very long path names (which include volumes and drives) are mapped to single drive letters.

If you think of air-traffic control as assigning a vector to an airplane, the controller is essentially pointing the pilot in a certain direction. The interrupt vector tables tell DOS where to look to find a particular set of interrupts. An undocumented command in DOS is the TRUENAME command, which returns the formal name of a subdirectory, regardless of how it may masquerade as a mapped or substituted drive letter.

Mapping is commonly used to create network drive letters out of specific subdirectories. Aliases are commonly used in Windows 95 shortcuts (LNK files), which are iconic representations of pointers to executable files somewhere on the drive.

Low Memory (Segment 1)

When DOS begins to load, even before the kernel is hauled up by its bootstraps, DOS BIOS installs its main I/O tools, tables, and instructions in the area of conventional memory that IBM originally reserved for it. The DOS kernel (from the system files) is also put into low memory—the first segment of the conventional 1MB of RAM (0000 to 9000)

DOS uses a low-memory control process to map out the first megabyte of memory and stores this map in a location within the first segment of RAM. This first megabyte is called *conventional memory* and is addressed in the old, 8088/86, *real* way. The 8088/86 could only work directly with memory addresses, and the idea of other modes of computing hadn't been invented at the time. This was the way a real chip worked with real memory addresses, and eventually became known as Real mode. The first segment can easily be very crowded, containing device drivers, parts of COMMAND.COM, pieces of TSRs, disk buffers, and environment and file controls. The first segment of memory goes to:

➤ The interrupt vector table and DOS BIOS low-memory control

➤ IBMBIO.COM (or IO.SYS) and IBMDOS.COM (or MSDOS.SYS), which install to low memory

➤ Device drivers such as MOUSE.SYS and ANSI.SYS

➤ Disk buffers

➤ Stacks (the way the CPU prioritizes and keeps track of tasks that were interrupted by more important tasks)

➤ Environment and FCBs

➤ The *resident* part of COMMAND.COM, which is always in memory and produces the message "Abort, Retry, Ignore, Fail?"

➤ Pieces of the *transient* part of COMMAND.COM, which periodically drops out of memory to disk and then returns when it's needed

➤ The stack and data parts of programs, which are running but lurking in the background waiting to be called on (e.g., the MODE or PRINT commands from DOS or Borland's Sidekick), these are called terminate/stay resident (TSR) programs

When an event needs to interrupt the CPU, whatever generated the interrupt first checks the *interrupt vector table* for directions on where to look for the actual interrupt instructions. This table is in the first segment (low memory) from 0000 to 1000. The interrupt vector table is used by BIOS, DOS, the interrupt controller chip, the main CPU, and any software programs that are running.

COMMAND.COM is a fairly large file, and for efficiency's sake, it doesn't load completely into RAM and remain there using up space. You need some parts of COMMAND.COM only rarely, whereas other parts must be available constantly. For example, the part that watches for a missing disk must be in memory all the time because the event causing the missing disk can happen at any time. This part of COMMAND.COM is resident because it's always resident in memory.

The resident part of COMMAND.COM is like a sentry. It keeps an eye out for a commanding officer while the rest of the command is taking a break. When you exit an application and go to a DOS command line, the resident part calls the transient part of COMMAND.COM, which hurries back from the disk and jumps into memory just in time to produce the C:\> prompt and begin parsing the command line.

You likely won't need to know which parts of COMMAND.COM are resident or transient, but you should know that the command processor isn't held completely in memory all the time.

Upper Memory (Segments 10–16)

Passing over the 640K of applications memory (discussed shortly), the very top segment of memory, from F000 to FFFF, is also grabbed at the beginning of the startup process. The motherboard's system BIOS installs to this segment to run the self-tests generated at the time the power is turned on (the POST). This is also where the ROM-level BIOS instructions are stored for drive controllers, keyboard polling, the system clock, I/O ports (serial and LPT), and a map of the addresses of the memory itself. System ROM (motherboard) and BASIC go to segment 16.

IBM originally left a small 64K gap directly above the area set aside for running programs. This area occurs at segment A000 and was quickly grabbed by enterprising memory management software utilities or was sometimes configurable by DIP switches. Instead of 640K of user memory, this allowed for an additional 64K, making 704K available. In DOS, every little bit counts! Because this extra segment has always been there and has always been unclaimed, OS/2 routinely provides 704K of usable memory for a virtual PC running in a DOS window.

Video RAM (B000)

The 64K block after A000 was intended for EGA and VGA video extensions. IBM's common monochrome adapter (CMA, also known as MDA) also laid claim to this area. However, as soon as CGA and color monitors arrived on the market, B000 to B800 became available to be stolen. DOS steps in with a specific address need only in the B800 CGA adapter area of RAM. Early memory managers could grab the 32K between B000 and B800 for extra RAM on top of the previous 64K.

CGA stakes a claim on the B800 block of memory real estate. Working with a CGA monitor was like looking without glasses on through a screen door through silk underwear at a pine tree blowing in the wind. Not that it was a badly crafted monitor—it just turned the user's eyes into coffee cups. Aside from a lower resolution problem, the adapter card didn't have enough memory, and any scrolling would cause the screen to go black before it redrew itself. CGA vanished as soon as it could, leaving its IBM-reserved memory area free for memory management software.

The most commonly used DOS command with a CGA monitor was the CLS (clear screen) command. This command not only clears all text from the screen but also converts any residual color back to black and white. CLS is an internal DOS command that is built in to COMMAND.COM.

Shortly after the failed CGA attempt, IBM introduced EGA, VGA, and the 8514/A color monitors. EGA and VGA demanded memory and went back to the A000 block to start high-resolution memory processing.

TSRs

Originally, programmers worked with Assembler, a language that created very small, very fast COM programs and didn't require compiling. COM programs are limited to 64K, and memory wasn't really an issue. After all, 640K was available to these programs. To sell software in a market that was beginning to heat up, programmers had to offer more and more features. The only way to do this was to go beyond the 64K limit of COM programs and start using compilers to create EXE programs. EXE programs can grow vastly larger than 64K, as you can see if you look at the 3.4MB of WINWORD.EXE.

Aside from the size of EXE files, a compiled program can off-load parts of itself that aren't used on a regular basis. This generates required, ancillary files such as OVL (overlay) files or, in Windows, DLL files. When the EXE file loads, it might require code from one of these other files and then call that file into memory as well. Memory was becoming very constricted.

Along with the need for more features, people were starting to use PCs for all kinds of important tasks, and the data files were starting to get larger. Larger data files required more RAM to hold them, and the market was demanding this increased memory. To use the application, the program had to create a data file that had to be in RAM at the same time as the application file. At this time, a new software toy arrived on the market: TSRs.

We've seen that RAM is very fast (nanoseconds), whereas disk access is much slower (milliseconds). When you enter the file name for an executable program, COMMAND.COM must parse what you entered, find the file, and load the file into memory before you can begin running the program. If there were a way for the program to stay in memory all the time, it would always be available, and you could bypass all the time involved in searching the disk. On the other hand, if the program is always in memory, there is less room for other programs.

A TSR program uses an ingenious scheme whereby it keeps a part of itself in memory all the time and drops most of itself back to the disk. The part that stays resident in memory is the initial part that the user needs to work with the program. Whereas the user is involved with the first steps of actual work, the program very quickly grabs the rest of itself in preparation for the next thing the user will want to do. This is similar to COMMAND.COM, where the resident part is keeping an eye out for the user while the rest of the program is slacking off on the disk. When the quick task (like looking up a phone number) is finished, the program terminates and sends most of itself back to disk, keeping that little resident stub down there in low memory.

The concept of loading a partial stub for a program that calls the full program only when needed, has permeated throughout the programming world. Many device drivers use this scheme and have the loading stub in memory but also reserve an area of memory for the rest of the program.

The 640K Barrier

DOS functions take up the first 64K segment of the basic 1MB of conventional memory. ROM BIOS, the motherboard, COMMAND.COM, and other parts of DOS take an additional set of segments at the top of the conventional memory. Below these upper functions, video adapters, network cards, and certain drive controllers take up even more space. Because the top and the bottom of the 640K user area is locked in by these other memory tenants, with most of the space taken at the top, people refer to the 640K limit as the *640K barrier* or as *hitting the 640K wall*.

➤ Users were originally given 640K of memory within the first 1MB of conventional memory to run programs and hold data files.

➤ DOS and system functions take up the another 296K of space.

➤ Memory management software grabs any memory blocks that aren't specifically required in a particular DOS session.

➤ Part of the 640K is used by even more slices of COMMAND.COM, DOS, and BIOS.

➤ Network connection files, TSRs, and additional device drivers also take part of the 640K.

 Whatever memory from the 640K of user memory that is left to the user after everything has loaded and all drivers and TSRs are in place, is called the *base memory*. DOS 6.2 included a memory optimization software utility (MEMMAKER.EXE) that could provide close to 600K of base memory. This optimization process takes advantage of every unused piece of memory in the 1MB of conventional memory.

By the time the AT-class computers were arriving on the market and the 80286 chip was getting organized, the hottest application driving the sale of PCs was the Lotus 1-2-3 spreadsheet. Lotus was getting tired of hearing complaints from its customers about running out of memory with big spreadsheets, so it decided to do something about it.

LIM 4 Expanded Memory

Lotus got together with Intel and worked out a process (bank switching) that they decided to call EMS (expanded memory specification) 3. No one knows what happened to specification 1 or 2, but eventually Lotus and Intel brought pressure to bear on Microsoft to join with them and release LIM (Lotus-Intel-Microsoft) EMS 3.2 memory.

➤ LIM 3.2 *expanded memory* introduced access to 8MB of additional memory.

➤ The 80286 could address up to 16MB of additional memory.

➤ LIM expanded memory requires a hardware expansion card.

➤ Software must be written to specifically work with EMS memory and cards.

Not long after the release of the EMS LIM specification, AST (a large motherboard manufacturer) got together with Ashton-Tate, one of the largest software companies and the maker of dBase. Together, these two companies released a far more flexible version of expanded memory specifications called EEMS (enhanced EMS). Lotus, Intel, and Microsoft then one-upped the AST-Ashton-Tate group and enhanced their specification to 4. LIM 4 EMS provided 32MB of addressable memory

EMS and EEMS expanded memory required the user to purchase a hardware expansion card, and software had to be written explicitly to be able to work with the cards. Following the by-now standard process of having no standards, software written for EMS boards might run with an EEMS card, and vice versa, but they weren't routinely compatible. Rather than being a unified set of standards, the two specifications continued to make configuration a general nightmare, ultimately paving the way for XMS (extended) memory. Once extended memory entered the market, the days of the LIM expanded memory card were doomed.

XMS

Properly speaking, any memory beyond the first 1MB of conventional memory is extended memory. However, because there was no way to use this memory until the LIM specifications and hardware cards arrived on the market, the residue of expanded memory still exists. Even under Windows 95, extended memory can be configured so that a part of it is used as expanded memory.

For any kind of memory beyond the conventional 1MB to be accessible by DOS, a memory manager device driver must be loaded from the CONFIG.SYS file. Originally, the device was only an expanded memory manager. With DOS 5, Microsoft began selling DOS directly to the customer. This generic DOS used HIMEM.SYS as a doorway manager to extended memory.

HIMEM.SYS

Third-party software companies have been marketing utilities to access extended memory from the beginning. Quarterdeck's QEMM became famous, and Microsoft wanted a part of the money being generated. When Microsoft decided to sell its own version of DOS, it included HIMEM.SYS with DOS 5. Part of HIMEM.SYS is its ability to access unused parts of the conventional 1MB, which it calls *upper memory blocks* (UMBs). HIMEM.SYS features the following:

➤ Loads from the CONFIG.SYS in DOS versions 5 through 6.2

➤ Loads from IO.SYS in Windows 95

➤ Provides access to any memory beyond the conventional 1MB

➤ Provides access to UMBs, where COMMAND.COM can be moved out of base memory

If HIMEM.SYS is loaded, DOS=HIGH,UMB will move COMMAND.COM into UMBs. HIMEM.SYS does not provide configuration of memory to expanded memory. EMM386.EXE is the expanded memory device drive and will not run unless HIMEM.SYS has been loaded first in the CONFIG.SYS file.

64K Expanded Memory Page Frame

The original LIM bank-switching process used memory that was beyond the 1MB of conventional memory. To do this, an expansion card had to be inserted into a bus slot, a device driver had to be loaded by CONFIG.SYS, and software had to know how to access all that extra memory for data files. Program files, on the other hand, couldn't use the expanded memory.

An original DOS program that could use expanded memory was VDISK.SYS—a device driver that could create a virtual disk in RAM. A RAM disk (later the driver was changed to RAMDRIVE.SYS) holds data only as long as the power is on but runs as fast as RAM because there are no mechanical spindles, heads, or arms.

Think about it: Starting with the 80286, processors could address 2MB or more of memory, but DOS could address only the 1MB of real memory. There had to be a special way to work around that limitation. The workaround, once again, had to do with the selector:offset mapping process. One last segment of real memory was set aside and configured as the EMS page frame segment, which is a 64K block that is set aside somewhere between C000 and E000 (above 640K base memory, but below video RAM).

The 64K page frame is divided into four 16K blocks called *pages*. When a program wants to put data into expanded memory, it assigns an address to the data and assigns a pointer vector to that address, kind of like renting warehouse space. The program puts the data in the warehouse and makes a note of the warehouse's location in the EMS page frame segment.

When the application calls the data, it looks up the storage bin's address (the page of memory) in conventional memory, then switches DOS into thinking that the 1MB of memory it's looking at is one of the extended megabytes. DOS uses the data while thinking that it's in the original 1MB. When the data is sent back to memory, EMM386.EXE drives it back to its remote storage bin in extended memory.

Exam Prep Questions

Question 1

When a PC is first powered up, COMMAND.COM, AUTOEXEC.BAT, and CONFIG.SYS files load in which order?

- a. AUTOEXEC.BAT, CONFIG,SYS, COMMAND.COM
- b. COMMAND.COM, CONFIG.SYS, AUTOEXEC.BAT
- c. CONFIG.SYS, COMMAND.COM, AUTOEXEC.BAT
- d. COMMAND.COM, AUTOEXEC.BAT, CONFIG.SYS

Answer c is correct. CONFIG.SYS sets the environment, the command interpreter COMMAND.COM loads, and finally commands contained in the batch file AUTOEXEC.BAT are processed.

Question 2

Which files does MS DOS require to be present on a disk in order for it to boot? Check all correct answers.

- a. IBMBIO.COM
- b. IO.SYS
- c. COMMAND.COM
- d. MSDOS.SYS

Answers b and d are correct. PC-DOS requires IBMBIO.COM and IBMDOS.COM. MS DOS requires MSDOS.COM and IOSYS.COM. COMMAND.COM is loaded after CONFIG.SYS following the boot process.

Question 3

Files with which of the following extensions can be executed from the DOS command prompt? Check all correct answers.

- a. .TXT
- b. .EXE
- c. .COM
- d. .BAT

Answers b, c, and d are correct. Executable (EXE), command (COM), and batch (BAT) files can be executed from the command prompt. Text (TXT) files contain text data and must be accessed by another application.

Question 4

Inputs entered at the DOS prompt must be interpreted by which file(s)?

O a. COMMAND.COM

O b. CONFIG.SYS

O c. IO.SYS

O d. IBMBIO.COM

Answer a is correct. COMMAND.COM is a command interpreter.

Question 5

The RD (Remove Directory) command immediately removes the specified directory, all files in the directory, and any subdirectories contained in the specified directory.

O a. True

O b. False

The answer is false. Generally, DOS is set up to failsafe with commands such as this one, which can have disastrous effects. In this case, you would need to delete all files (even hidden ones) and remove all subdirectories prior to being allowed to remove a parent directory.

Question 6

Which command allows you to identify the active DOS version?

O a. SETVER

O b. DOS?

O c. VER

O d. OPER

Answer c is correct. Many DOS commands are shortened to forms of the command name. VER stands for *version.*

Question 7

What does the FILES command specify?

- ○ a. The maximum number of files allowed on a disk
- ○ b. The type of files that can be used in an application
- ○ c. The number of files that can be open at one time
- ○ d. None of the above

Answer c is correct. Open files are tracked in memory and require resources. Therefore, for efficiency, DOS limits the number of files that can be open at one time. Large applications often require more files to be open than DOS allows, so the FILES command provides a way to increase the number of open files that DOS will track.

Question 8

What happens when you enter two dots following the CD (Change Directory) command?

- ○ a. DOS reports a syntax error
- ○ b. You are moved up one level in the directory tree
- ○ c. Nothing
- ○ d. You are moved down one level in the directory tree

Answer b is correct. Typing "CD.." and pressing Enter, will move you up one level in the directory tree to the parent directory. The first dot is shorthand for "here," while the second dot specifies one directory up.

Question 9

In which file is the "LASTDRIVE=" command placed?

- ○ a. AUTOEXEC.BAT
- ○ b. DOS.SYS
- ○ c. CONFIG.SYS
- ○ d. DRIVES.BAT

Answer c is correct. LASTDRIVE= configures DOS to hold places in memory for drives (whether you have them or not). More drives require more memory dedicated to placeholders. Because of this, many users set LASTDRIVE= to equal their number of physical drives (e.g., LASTDRIVE=C). If you used this command in your CONFIG.SYS file, you wouldn't be able to add a D:, E:, or F: drive until you changed LASTDRIVE= to include these drives.

Question 10

What does the BUFFERS command in the CONFIG.SYS file affect?

- O a. The space set aside on the primary hard drive for data caching
- O b. The memory allocated to increase the efficiency of data transfer
- O c. The sensitivity of the keyboard
- O d. The number of peripheral devices that can be attached to a system

Answer b is correct. The BUFFERS command allocates space in memory to be used for file and data transfer. All devices within a PC don't operate at the same speed, so the ability to store transfer data for a short period of time while a required device becomes available can greatly increase overall efficiency.

Question 11

PC operation requires the AUTOEXEC.BAT file.

- O a. True
- O b. False

The correct answer is false. The AUTOEXEC.BAT file contains a list of commands that the user wants to execute at startup. The file is not required for basic operation and can be bypassed if needed. *Basic,* in this context, means only those operations where no further configuration of devices or peripherals may be needed beyond loading a device driver. Some peripheral devices (e.g., a CD drive or sound card) may require entries in the AUTOEXEC.BAT file, though the failure to configure these devices won't affect the basic operation of the PC.

Question 12

Which function does the MS DOS ScanDisk utility perform?

○ a. Reorganizes files into contiguous blocks on the disk

○ b. Checks disk integrity and provides a way to review or discard lost memory allocation units

○ c. Ensures that volume labels and data file types are compatible

○ d. Checks rotational speed and head accuracy for a specified disk

Answer b is correct. ScanDisk allows you to locate lost memory allocation units on a disk and to review or discard them.

Question 13

DOS system files must be located in the _____ partition and that partition set to _____ for the computer to start DOS.

○ a. first, primary

○ b. current, initialize

○ c. primary, active

○ d. extended, DOS

Answer c is correct. The DOS system files must reside in the primary partition, and that partition must be active.

Question 14

When using the FORMAT command, what does adding the /S switch do?

○ a. Sets the format to be compatible with single-sided disks

○ b. Specifies a slow format speed be used for accuracy

○ c. Saves the format information for later recovery

○ d. Transfers system files so that the disk will be bootable

Answer d is correct. The /S switch indicates that, in addition to formatting the disk, system files should be copied into the boot sector so that the disk will be bootable.

Question 15

Which command allows you to specify a drive letter for an additional hard drive?

○ a. LASTDRIVE=

○ b. NEWDRIVE=

○ c. DRVNM=

○ d. None of the above

Answer d is correct. With the exception of CD drives, DOS determines logical drive letter assignments.

Question 16

What is the DOS FDISK command used to do?

○ a. Partition a hard drive

○ b. Find the letter assigned to a given logical drive

○ c. Low-level erase all information on a hard drive

○ d. None of the above

Answer a is correct. FDISK allows you to partition a hard drive prior to formatting.

Question 17

What is virtual memory?

○ a. RAM above 640K

○ b. RAM that exceeds the processors addressable limit

○ c. A space on the hard drive set up to emulate RAM

○ d. Memory allocated to TSR programs

Answer c is correct. Virtual memory is a file set up on the hard drive to emulate RAM. It is much slower than actual RAM, but can provide resources when all the system RAM is in use or is allocated.

Question 18

> The first 640K of system memory is most commonly referred to as what?
>
> ○ a. Conventional memory
>
> ○ b. System memory
>
> ○ c. High memory
>
> ○ d. Expanded memory

Answer a is correct. Conventional memory is the term most often used to describe the first 640K of RAM.

Question 19

> Which file would you use to load a memory manager?
>
> ○ a. AUTOEXEC.BAT
>
> ○ b. IO.SYS
>
> ○ c. COMMAND.COM
>
> ○ d. CONFIG.SYS

Answer d is correct. You load a memory manager from the CONFIG.SYS file.

Question 20

> MEMMAKER in MS DOS will change the CONFIG.SYS file to optimize memory.
>
> ○ a. True
>
> ○ b. False

The correct answer is false. MEMMAKER in MS DOS and RAMBOOST in PC-DOS optimize the memory configuration and will change the CONFIG.SYS file.

Need To Know More?

There are a tremendous number of DOS books available, and they all cover this operating system in far more depth than required by the A+ exam. However if you really want to get into it, here are three we like in particular:

Gookin, Dan: *Batch Files and Beyond: Your Path to PC Power*, Windcrest, Blue Ridge Summit, PA, 1993. ISBN: 0830643850.

Minasi, Mark: *DOS 6.2*. Sybex Network Press, San Francisco, CA. ISBN 1-56205-289-6.

Norton, Peter: *Peter Norton's Complete Guide to DOS 6.22*. Sam's Publishing, Indianapolis, IN, 1994. ISBN 0-67230-614-X

9

16-Bit Windows

Terms you'll need to understand:

√ INI file

√ GUI

√ Multitasking and task switching

Concepts you'll need to master:

√ The Windows startup sequence

√ Windows kernel files

√ How Windows creates virtual memory

√ The difference between permanent and temporary swap files

√ The SYSTEM.INI and WIN.INI files, their uses, and their differences

√ How Windows works with DOS

Windows was once a single term that everyone understood. Microsoft brought Windows 2.1, and 2.1a through 2.1d to the market without making any announcement that these versions were different. Windows was still Windows regardless of the minor changes because Microsoft wanted the inner workings of a PC to be transparent to the user. *Transparency* refers to an operation being hidden or invisible from the user. Computer repair technicians weren't talked about in the open market of publicity and advertising. Computer makers began promoting the idea that computer users shouldn't need to know any more about a computer than a driver should need to know about a car.

By 1990, the 80386 processor technology and the number of PCs on the market had reached a point where a GUI (graphical user interface) was finally practical. Windows 3.0, a major update, arrived on the market with much fanfare (not as much as when Windows 95 hit the market though), irrevocably changing the way people saw their computer screens. IBM and Microsoft broke apart a long-standing relationship as Bill Gates decided to bring the graphical front end (what the customer sees when running a computer) of the new OS/2 to market ahead of schedule and without the underlying operating system.

In 1992, Microsoft released Windows 3.1, which fundamentally changed how Windows worked. Windows 3.1 and 3.11 and Windows for Workgroups 3.1 and 3.11 were the final releases of the Windows 3.x systems prior to Windows 95.

To avoid confusion with release numbers, we will refer to Windows 95 and Windows NT by name, and all prior releases of Windows as 16-bit Windows or Windows 3.x. The bulk of the A+ exam questions refer to Windows 3.x and Windows 95. OS/2 and Windows NT are 32-bit operating systems and have no underlying reliance on DOS.

The distinction between 16-bit Windows and Windows 95 can be seen in the changes made between DOS 6.0 to 7.0 whereby the FAT was restructured to handle files and disks in a different way. Chapter 10 discusses these difference in greater detail. The 16-bit FAT continues under Windows 95/98 but has become a sort of subsystem to the installable file system (IFS) and something called FAT32—a *virtual* file allocation table.

Operating Systems Vs. Shells

Recall from Chapter 8 that an operating system includes a file management system and a command processor. File management involves controlling file names and keeping track of the files on a hard disk. The file management system must have a way to write to, read from, and locate tracks, sectors, and clusters. DOS uses the FAT and the root directory as part of its file management system.

What many people think of as day-to-day file management consists of saving, copying, deleting, moving, and modifying files. For clarity, we use the term *management* to mean fundamental operating system processes and the term *maintenance* to mean what a user does with files in terms of saving, opening, running, and choosing locations on various storage devices. Therefore:

➤ File management is what an operating system does.

➤ File maintenance is what a user does.

 For the exam, remember that an operating system can be referred to as three components: system files, a command interpreter, and a user interface.

To further the cause of a transparent interface with the computer, Microsoft introduced a Windows *applet*—a part of Windows—called File Manager (WINFILE.EXE). An applet is a self-contained program application that works from within an overseeing parent application. For instance, in the overall "application" of your kitchen, a can opener would be analogous to an applet. Over time, the underlying processes of the operating system have become blurred as users work with File Manager and Windows Explorer almost exclusively. Likewise, the distinction between an application and an applet has become blurred.

Windows File Manager (WINFILE.EXE) is a graphical interface program that passes a user's intentions to the underlying DOS command processor (COMMAND.COM). It places a *layer* between the user's actions and the underlying operating system. WINFILE.EXE is an applet under the PROGMAN.EXE domain—its companion interface program. PROGMAN.EXE (Program Manager) runs first and then offers the opportunity to run WINFILE.EXE (File Manager) from within it.

SYSTEM.INI And SHELL=

The SHELL= line in the SYSTEM.INI file defines the interface program that Windows will present to the user at startup. In Windows 3.x, the two shells are Program Manager and File Manager. By default, the line reads SHELL=PROGMAN.EXE, which loads Program Manager as the user interface for Windows 3.x.

By editing the SYSTEM.INI file and changing the line to SHELL= WINFILE.EXE, Windows 3.x starts with File Manager as the primary interface. However, File Manager doesn't include a desktop area for creating program groups and icons. The Microsoft Web site still offers MSDOS.EXE (the old MS-DOS Executive from Windows 2.x) for use as a shell interface.

Windows 95 extends File Manager's capabilities to include the desktop, icons, and program groups (folders). EXPLORER.EXE is discussed in Chapter 10.

Menus

For many years, people were marketing menu programs and shells for the text-based DOS, hoping to make *using* computers one thing and *configuring* them another. A computer *menu* is a list of options written to the screen. The user selects one of the options and presses keys or clicks the mouse to pick one of the options.

The underlying programming and operations of a menu control how an option is executed. Some menus include the ability to combine the selection and key-press process into a single event. Simple menus can be created by using batch files (discussed in Chapter 8). Menus reduce the number of keystrokes necessary to run a program and store complicated configurations used in running certain programs.

We've seen that a batch file is a file containing a list of commands, one on each line of the file. Naming the file with the .BAT extension tells DOS that this file is an executable program file. DOS then reads each line of the file as though a user were entering that line. DOS menus use file names such as 1.BAT, 2.BAT, A.BAT, B.BAT, WP.BAT, and LOTUS.BAT, and the files are usually saved to a subdirectory in the search PATH. When the user turns on the computer, the last command in the AUTOEXEC.BAT file might call, for example, MENU.BAT, which draws a menu on the screen.

For the exam, remember that when statements are put into a text file that can be interpreted by COMMAND.COM (a command processor) we refer to that file as a batch file. AUTOEXEC.BAT is a *batch* file. CONFIG.SYS is a configuration file.

By storing complex configuration switches, batch files are used to automate the process of running a program. Some programs require configuration switches to be entered at a command line. Other programs can only be configured from within a CONFIG.SYS file.

Creative ingenuity and high-bit ASCII characters can create many interesting and useful ASCII menu screens. Menu options might appear as A - Word Processor, B - Spreadsheet. The menu screen might include an instruction such as "Type the letter of your choice and press Enter." When the user types "A" (without quotes) and presses Enter, the commands that are included in the A.BAT file are executed. These commands would switch to a word-processing program's subdirectory and run the EXE file (usually WP.EXE) as the last line.

If the underlying batch file isn't located in the correct directory (along the search PATH), a menu choice calling that batch file will leave the user staring at a DOS screen and a message declaring "File(s) not found." Menus require that each choice on the menu have an underlying executable file in a location where the operating system can find it.

Menu choices are essentially the same as *program items* in 16-bit Windows and *shortcuts* in Windows 95. The defining characteristics of a text-based menu choice are:

➤ A program file name

➤ The location of that program file

➤ A description of the program, or descriptive name for the choice

➤ A place to store and start up switches for the program

DOS menus created from batch files typically use the PATH environment variable (e.g., PATH=C:\;C:\DOS;C:\BATCH) to tell the command processor where the executable batch file exists. As more sophisticated menus were created, the setup for *compiled* menu program (menus that are themselves executable programs) included a way to enter program location information in a particular, configuration area of the menu program.

Over time, menu programs became more sophisticated. Some companies included security features in their menu programs whereby a user could access the command processor only through the menu. By controlling how the menu program passed commands to the command processor (the file's properties), menu programs began to become more and more like *shells* (discussed in a moment).

These days, the defining characteristics of a menu choice are often included in what we call "properties." Borland's *Quattro Pro* spreadsheet introduced the idea of using the mouse's right button to call up a menu for changing the properties of whatever the mouse was pointing to. The idea quickly caught on, and now most Windows-based applications access a properties menu from the right mouse button.

File/Properties

Windows 3.x lists the essential properties of a program in the Properties option of the File|Properties choice on the main Program Manager menu bar. Windows 95 incorporates the right-click of the mouse (alternative mouse click) to create a floating properties menu box. Throughout Windows 95, right-clicking (alternative clicking) brings up file properties or the properties options for anything else that can have descriptive information associated with it. Properties and right-clicking are part of what make a program "Windows 95 compatible" (a Microsoft specification).

The Windows 95 Desktop

Windows Explorer (EXPLORER.EXE) creates the Windows 95 desktop and runs constantly during a Windows 95 session. On the other hand, File Manager (WINFILE.EXE) must be explicitly run and closed from within PROGMAN.EXE. To see this, press Ctrl+Alt+Delete in a Windows 95 session from a plain desktop. Task Manager (TASKMAN.EXE) will run, and Windows Explorer will be one of the tasks. Both 16-bit and 32-bit Windows have Task Manager, which installs by default in Windows 3.x, but must be manually installed in Windows 95.

Shells

A *shell* is where the command processor (COMMAND.COM) loads another instance of itself, resulting in two or more separate command processors residing in RAM. In a DOS session, COMMAND.COM is sitting in conventional memory and intercepting keystrokes from the keyboard, then passing them on to the CPU. Strictly speaking, COMMAND.COM is creating a shell around the operating environment whereby any instruction that enters the environment is tracked by COMMAND.COM before the instruction can move out of the environment.

Another way to think of a shell is that it acts like an executive secretary screening calls to the boss. Anyone (program instruction) who wants to contact the executive, must first go through the secretary. The secretary has a list of high-priority people who get passed through immediately. Other people are directed to someone else, depending on their business. Network operating systems often use a shell that works alongside the COMMAND.COM interpreter. Both shells look at incoming program instructions to see which operating system should take the call.

CONFIG.SYS uses an optional directive (statement) called SHELL= to tell COMMAND.COM to increase the size of the environment space in memory (e.g., SHELL=C:\COMMAND.COM /E:1024 /P). This increases the environment to 1,024 bytes and keeps it permanent. The SHELL= directive also sets an environment variable that tells the operating system where to find its command processor. In this case, DOS will always know that COMMAND.COM is in the root directory of the C: drive.

The word *shell*, like many words in the language of computers and operating systems, has been modified to include menus. Remember that making computers more user friendly can be done in two ways:

➤ By changing the way operating systems work

➤ By changing the words used to describe the computer

It's a lot cheaper to change a word than it is to change a basic operating system installed on more than 100 million computers!

DOSSHELL

MS-DOS 4.0 introduced something Microsoft called the DOS shell, which was really a rudimentary graphic file maintenance and menu program. This complicated menu system was run from DOSSHELL.BAT, which used a very small *stub program loader* (SHELLB) to push the main program (SHELLC) into memory. SHELLB was about 3.5K, whereas SHELLC was 150K. This began the process of using a *loader program*, such as WIN.COM, to pull a larger program into memory. DOSSHELL also introduced a way to rename a subdirectory from within a graphically drawn square or a window (the only reason many PC technicians ever bothered with the program).

In DOSSHELL, a single window is drawn on the screen either with menu options or with a list of files and directories. Choosing a menu option erases the current window and replaces it with a new one in the same location. Windows 3.x allows for sizable windows that can exist concurrently with previous windows and that can be placed in front of or behind another window.

File Manager is essentially the DOSSHELL with the advanced graphics capabilities of better graphics cards and newer monitors. MS-DOS Executive was between the DOSSHELL and File Manager.

Windows And OS/2

Everyone in the PC world was looking for a better way to network computers, that is, to connect them for file and resource sharing. Unix and the Macintosh systems use a different file structure and were designed from the ground up to be network operating systems (NOS). On the other hand, DOS was never designed for real networking. IBM and Microsoft were urgently trying to create a new version of an operating system (OS) that would handle more files, larger disks, and better networking; OS/2 (the new, "second" OS) was going to be that messiah of the IBM PC world.

We've seen that a 16-bit FAT limits the number of clusters on a single logical drive and that those clusters increase in size, depending on the size of the drive. OS/2 was going to feature a completely redesigned 32-bit file management system and better control over cluster size. Additionally, the new operating system was going to be designed for networking and provide a better way to run more than one program at the same time.

Multitasking

Multitasking is the ability to run multiple programs at the same time. In other words, if you upload a file from AOL and then switch to MS Excel and print a spreadsheet, both tasks should happen simultaneously and have no effect at all on each other.

If the upload crashes in the middle of the process and AOL halts, the spreadsheet shouldn't even notice that anything has happened. AOL should be dropped out of memory with no fuss, and any gaps in RAM should fill in as smoothly as the ocean covers a sinking ship. If you're playing a musical CD at the same time, you should hear the music as smoothly as if you were playing it on a home stereo system. There should be no jerky pauses in the music.

The physics of a microprocessor is such that, until the Pentium, only one instruction could be carried out at once. However, the speed of that process is so high that software and hardware have never been even close to catching up. The idea of running two programs at once began to stress the CPU somewhat. Running three, four, or five programs at once finally had an effect that a user could notice.

Time Slices

If recalculating a spreadsheet is forcing the CPU into full-time work, the CPU can give only a few *time slices* to the CD every other couple of microseconds to play music. If controlling the data passing through a UART chip is also taking up the CPU's time, you begin to see something like a picture of a harried mother trying to control four young children in the middle of a mall at Christmas! The CPU's attention can only rotate among all the tasks in some fraction of time—a time slice.

Task Switching

The 80286 not only increased addressable memory to 16MB but also introduced the concept of Protected mode. In theory, Protected mode keeps a given area of memory isolated from another area of memory. People using plain DOS were already coming up with ways to do more than one thing at a time on computers, and the most popular way for doing so was by *task switching*. Some commercial menu programs even provided a way for the user to do this. This integration of the menu program and the ability to do task switching made PCs easier to use and more versatile.

Task switching means that the loaded parts of a program and its data files are taken out of RAM and stored to the disk as a kind of photographic snapshot. All the program code for a word processor is saved out of RAM onto a special area of the hard drive called a *swap file*. The data or documents being worked on at the moment of the switch are also stored to the swap file. Task switching uses a process similar to that of the STACKS used by the CPU.

Because it takes a certain amount of time to spin the disk, move the read-write heads, and store the information on disk, task switching is relatively slow. Not only must the contents of memory be stored, but a new program must be loaded into RAM and prepared for the user. Each new task being loaded into RAM requires a new snapshot of RAM: a window.

If a way could be found to keep every program in memory and go beyond the 640K barrier of conventional memory, the slowness of disk swapping RAM could be overcome. Then the *page frame* and expanded memory arrived. Now, a program could be saved into expanded or extended memory just as easily as it could be saved to disk, and the 286 Protected mode would (theoretically) keep everything nice and separate.

Task switching is like a lazy susan on a dining room table. Someone who wants an item spins the rotating platter until the choice comes around. However, instead of the other choices becoming available to the other side of the table, the other programs are spun through the page-frame doorway into expanded memory or are saved to the disk. Later in this chapter, we look at the Windows swap file in our discussion of virtual memory.

Page Swapping

The 286 chip's Protected mode and a LIM expanded memory card can give a user access to 16MB of memory for use by programs and data. The idea was that if something could keep track of those snapshots of conventional RAM and shift them up into expanded memory, several programs could be run at once in the same base memory area. The 80286's protection features would make sure (in theory) that each program in memory had its own specially protected area and that, if something went wrong, the program could be shut down only in that area while everything else continued to run.

Task switching to expanded memory was a nice idea, but it didn't work out quite as planned. DOS had a hard time keeping the various balls it was juggling in the air and tracking which parts of memory were supposed to be used for what. Aside from that, the 64K page frame area was becoming a bottleneck as users had to move a 550K process through it during a switch and another 612K process back up into EMS memory.

If you think of expanded memory as a sort of warehouse on the second floor of a building, then you can imagine a loading dock on the first floor. When a program is running, it's like a truck being loaded from the dock. If another truck (program) has to be loaded (run), then in our imaginary warehouse, all the boxes (program code) from the first truck have to be sent back up to the warehouse (expanded memory) on an elevator. New boxes have to be sent down the elevator and the second truck has to change places with the first. The elevator is like the page frame.

The 286 had some internal problems as well. For example, when a program crashed in a so-called protected area, it usually brought the entire system tumbling down with it regardless of how well its area was protected. This would lead to a reboot, which would cancel whatever had been going on with any other programs. The swap file would be erased during the reboot, and any data that hadn't been saved would be lost.

Processes And Threads

As instructions move back and forth between software, hardware, and the CPU, we say that they all have a *process* of some length of time. A program file is a complete set of instructions. When that program runs, we can think of the process as complete: It begins and ends, and it expects not to have any interruptions in memory addresses.

If a user wants to run two or more programs at the same time, a way must be set up to overcome a program's expectation of having the whole world of RAM to work in with no unexpected memory gaps. Putting part of a program in base memory (the 640K of the first 1MB of conventional memory) and another part in expanded memory leads to confusion, lock-ups, and crashes. Memory can become fragmented, just like a disk full of files can be fragmented. Although DOS includes DEFRAG.EXE for disks, it doesn't include a way to defragment memory itself.

Note: There are some third-party software utilities that can defragment the small area of memory used for Windows resources. This can sometimes be helpful when many applications have been opened and closed over a session. Sometimes Windows reports there is enough memory to run an application, but the application returns an "insufficient memory" error. Defragmenting, or "compressing" the Resources area may fix the problem.

We've seen a similar problem when hardware or software runs a process and calls for work from the CPU. In this case, interrupts are sent to the CPU to interrupt whatever it's doing and reorder the priorities of action. If a process in the CPU hasn't finished, a snapshot of the whole process is switched into a STACK and is retrieved when the new process has run its course.

Threads

Threads are a way for an application process to be divided into precise subprocesses that happen at the same time. You can think of a thread as the smallest amount of time required by the CPU to complete a single set of instructions. Threads operate very fast because they're very small pieces of code. Because threads are written into an application, they have full access to the entire program. They also share address space, file access paths, and other system resources associated with the application.

You can also think of a thread as a kind of interrupt written into an application by the programmer. The programmer decides, thread by thread, what the smallest piece of code is. The program can then send only the instructions that are necessary at a given moment. Threads also allow different areas of the same overall application to use only the instructions for those areas (e.g., to recalculate while redrawing the screen).

Threads can be moved into RAM at the same time for different features within a single application. Threads can also carry with them (within the thread), a piece of code that tells the CPU how important that piece of code is in the overall scheme of things. This provides some help to the CPU as it moves processing in and out of the STACK and allows one thread to interrupt (preempt) another thread.

The importance of a given thread is therefore prioritized, allowing one thread to "preempt" the time being called for by another thread from the CPU. This capability is called *preemptive multithreaded multitasking.* True preemptive multitasking requires that software be written with threads and that the operating system be written to understand threads.

Windows Versions

The Microsoft and IBM partners noticed that they were losing customers who wanted task switching. Microsoft was looking at how many customers were buying into the easy-to-use graphical environment of the Macintosh, and they wanted something to lure those customers away from Apple. IBM had promised to provide an operating system for the so-called 286 multitasking chip and, in 1984, released Top View, a text-based task switcher.

IBM was also working on a multitasking environment for the new 80386 chip that Intel was researching. The 386 would correct the protected memory problems in the 286, and both IBM and Microsoft wanted an operating system that could take advantage of this, both for multitasking and for the user-friendly interface of the Mac's graphics. Both companies wanted safe multitasking, network capabilities, large disk- and memory-handling abilities, and a user-friendly graphical interface.

The two companies decided that Microsoft's Windows would be the front-end interface of this new, second-generation operating system (OS/2) that had some memory management functions built into the overall menu interface. IBM would take care of changing the underlying operating system and provide a way for software to use threads for multithreaded preemptive multitasking. The two companies agreed to release individual products, but, for compatibility and cost savings reasons, they also agreed to share their underlying work, research, and code.

Windows 2.x

In 1987, IBM released OS/2 version 1, which included the text-based Presentation Manager front-end interface. IBM designed this version to run hardware-based (chip) multitasking to take advantage of the 80286, but had the much better 80386 in mind. IBM deferred the development of the graphics to Microsoft, and Windows 2.0 arrived on the market with the ability to create so-called virtual 8086 computers out of 640K snapshots of memory.

Windows used MS-DOS Executive as its user interface. Meanwhile, IBM was having serious trouble developing its operating system, and Microsoft was becoming impatient because of Apple's constant increase in computer sales. Windows 2.x offered the ability to create a virtual 8088 memory environment called Real mode. As we've seen, memory addressing in Real mode is done directly, in the same way that original memory addressing was handled by the 8088/86 processors using conventional memory. Windows 2.x also introduced the concept of DDE (dynamic data exchange), whereby applications running together under Windows could communicate with one another.

Microsoft released a 2.01 incremental upgrade shortly after releasing version 2. The main reason for the upgrade seems to have been that Windows took on IBM's SAA (systems application architecture) standard for how a program looks to the user; that is, it describes how windows, menus, and dialog boxes should look for any and all programs running in a graphical environment. The idea was that, as with Macs, users shouldn't be required to relearn the skills they acquire from one program when learning a new one. The SAA standard has become the standard for all IBM-type computers running a graphical, Windows-style interface.

Rudimentary Memory Management

Another important aspect of Windows 2.x was that, once it was loaded, it took on some of the underlying DOS operations. In other words, while Windows was looking like a menu system and acting like a shell, it was also reaching down into the basic operating system to control how memory addressing and management was being done.

Windows uses resources that are called for by a program. The resource instructions to Windows are contained within EXE and DLL files. These resources are the amount of memory a program or screen item will need at any given time while it's active. Rather than leaving the moment-by-moment control of memory to DOS, Windows takes over the management tasks (resources are discussed in more detail later in this chapter).

Windows 3.0 And NT

Microsoft and IBM were working together to improve both OS/2 and the Windows interface. Primarily, IBM was focusing on an operating system that communicated directly with the CPU, taking advantage of protection capabilities built into the 286 and 386 chips. Microsoft was focusing more on the way in which the user was using the computer. IBM has always tended to pay more attention to hardware; historically it seems as if Microsoft has been more interested in how things look to the user.

OS/2 version 1.x was a whole new way of programming, and the API (application programming interface) was difficult to learn. However, even in that version, OS/2 changed the FAT to support much larger drives. In 1989, IBM released OS/2 1.20, which had an improved Presentation Manager. Shortly thereafter, version 1.2 EE introduced something called the HPFS (high performance file system). HPFS is much more efficient and faster than FAT, and it keeps track of data on disks with fewer errors and better security. The HPFS would eventually grow to be a true 32-bit file management system that could be located anywhere on a logical drive, not exclusively in the root directory.

IBM's HPFS is a true 32-bit file management system. Windows 95 IFS (installable file system) is a virtualized 32-bit FAT (VFAT, or virtual FAT) that relies on the DOS 7.0 16-bit FAT for actual file management. Chapter 10 discusses the details of the IFS in greater detail.

IBM had begun work on two new OS/2 products: OS/2 2.0 and 3.0. Version 2.0 was going to be the first 32-bit operating system for PCs. It was designed specifically for the Intel 80386 processor and later models and would no longer be compatible with the 80286 processor. Version 3.0 was going to be a network server version of the operating system. It was also intended to be platform independent, meaning that the same operating system could run on PCs using different types of chips. Version 2.0 would focus on the individual user, whereas version 3.0 would focus on the business world and networks.

Because OS/2 was going to be built on top of something called a *microkernel*, it wouldn't matter what type of hardware it was running on. Therefore, it could run on Intel processors and on other types of chips made by Sun, DEC, and Motorola. Everything was fine, except that IBM was way behind in its work, and Microsoft was ready to go with an interface that looked almost exactly like a Mac screen.

In 1990, Bill Gates decided to release Windows 3.0, without IBM's agreement, in a move to lure customers away from the Macintosh to the Intel-based operating systems. DOS was *the* operating system in this market, and Microsoft wanted the Mac customers. IBM decided to step in to try to keep Microsoft from dominating the entire operating system market, and a great divorce battle ensued.

When the dust settled, an agreement had been made that IBM would continue to develop OS/2 2.0 for personal computers and Microsoft would take over development and funding for OS/2 3.0 (the network server version). Microsoft agreed and renamed the experimental network operating system Windows NT (New Technology).

Program Manager And File Manager

One of the fundamental differences between Windows 2.x and 3.0 was the way it showed itself to the user. MS-DOS Executive was like a 2D version of File Manager; it had no colors, and it looked very similar to the results of a DIR command printed on paper. The difference between the DIR and MS-DOS Executive was that you could double-click on an application file's name, and the program would actually run. Windows 3.0 allowed running a mixture of Windows and DOS programs at the same time. It had its bugs, but it was progressing.

Another basic change in the way in which Windows 3.0a and 3.0b looked was the introduction of *icons* and *program groups*. A program group is much like a subdirectory, but it looks almost exactly like the folders and subfolders of the Mac operating system. Icons incorporate a *program item* properties dialog box, where information is entered about the location of a program and how it starts.

Windows 3.1

Windows 3.0 and OS/2 2.0 included TrueType fonts (another war was being waged over who had the best way to draw letters on a screen and print them to printers). The idea of WYSIWYG (what you see is what you get) became a reality as Windows took on the ability to display characters the way they would actually look on the printed page. Microsoft wanted everything to connect to everything, and their new rallying cry became "Windows everywhere!"

In 1992, Windows 3.1 was released with all the improvements that were needed as a result of the somewhat rushed release of 3.0. Windows 3.1 improved the File Manager shell/applet interface and added internal fonts. Another improvement was the OLE (object linking and embedding) technology for interconnecting data produced by different applications.

> *Note: The instructions and connections used in OLE were moved to a special database called the Registration database (REG.DAT). To prevent unsophisticated users from accidentally breaking links between programs, this database took on a proprietary form and could only be edited with a program call REGEDIT.EXE. The Windows 3.x Registration database became the foundation for the Windows 95 Registry.*

There were many improvements in Windows 3.1 over 3.0, making it more of a full version upgrade than the implied, minor point revision of the number. The stability was significantly improved, and the way in which programs were isolated in memory became much more secure. Windows 3.1 also featured:

➤ The ability to shut down a frozen window without rebooting the entire computer

➤ The common dialog box programming library (COMMDLG.DLL) so that the programmer didn't need to "re-create the wheel" every time they needed a dialog box

➤ The Registration database and Registration Info Editor (REGEDIT.EXE)

It's important to note that these common dialog features are held in certain files that change with Windows 95 but keep the same or similar names. The files are COMMDLG.DLL, VER.DLL, SHELL.DLL, DDEML.DLL, and LZEXPAND.DLL. Although the exam won't test you on these names, you should keep in mind that 32-bit and 16-bit Windows applications might use different versions of these files and therefore aren't interchangeable.

Fonts

The words *font* and *typeface* are used to describe two ways of looking at a letter. A font is the overall way a set of characters looks. A typeface refers to whether the font characters are bolded, italicized, or plain (regular). In the days of hot-metal type, three different character sets had to be created to produce the three changes in the typeface of a single font.

Without going deeply into the process of mathematically creating lines, points, and curves on a computer screen, we can say that software can produce graphics in two different ways: by vector calculations and by pixel points. Remember that a pixel (picture element) is the smallest dot that can be represented on a graphic display.

DOS uses a grid and BASIC to fill in sets of squares created by intersections of columns and rows (a matrix). Windows converts information being sent to the screen to a graphic—the GUI. Rather than working with the fixed character spacing of the DOS rows and columns, Windows uses pixels to draw everything, including letters.

Raster Vs. Bitmap Fonts

Imagine a blue square with black lines making up the outline of the square. You can draw that square in two different ways. One way is called a *vector drawing*. You send a mathematical point coordinate to the computer, which puts the point on the screen and virtually extends a line for a specified length in a specified direction. From the end of that line, the computer can extend the line in a different direction. Each time you click the mouse one time and move in a new direction, you tell the computer to remember the new length and direction.

When it comes time to print, the printer prints the line(s). Because the computer knows where every intersection for each part of the line is located, it can fill in any area enclosed by that line with some color. This fill color is a single color (in this example, blue) that is surrounded by the connecting line points, and it exists virtually until the printer converts it to ink.

In other words, you're telling the computer to keep track of when you click in an area, and how far you moved the mouse pointer before you clicked. The computer only remembers numbers and doesn't care what kind of shape you're drawing. When you use a coloring book to connect numbered dots and make a picture to color, the dots and their numbers are similar to the data the computer stores about a vector graphic.

Another way to draw the square is with dots (pixels). Starting at a certain point, the computer draws small dots to the left or to the right as you move the mouse along. The next line in the drawing begins at a new point, and does the same thing all over again with some number of dots. The dots are pixels when they're created on a monitor, and dots per inch (dpi) when they're created by a printer. These types of images are called *bitmaps*, because every single bit (dot) of the image just created is stored by the computer. If you draw lines and then color them in, every dot used for every line and every part of the coloring is a separate piece of data to be stored.

In summary, raster images are mathematically created by a vector-drawing process. Microsoft calls vector-based fonts *vector fonts*. You might also hear them called *raster fonts*. Bitmap images are grids of pixels; a grid position either has a dot of some color or is blank (containing the background color).

To change the size of a vector image, you simply tell the computer to change the image's stored numbers and recalculate the lengths of the virtual lines. To change the size of a bitmap image, the computer has to change the size of every one of the image's dots and recalculate the overall image.

TrueType Fonts

We've seen that dot matrix and thermal ink technology printers place dots of ink on paper. Because of this ability to reduce anything to a series of dots, an application can create a font in memory, break down each letter to a dot, and send it to the printer as a bitmap graphic image. It takes a lot of time to create a grid for every letter and to determine which squares in the grid will be dots.

Another problem with bitmaps involves the size of the dots. If you create a square using 16 dots, where each dot is one inch in diameter, you would have a nice four-inch square. But suppose you wanted to enlarge that square to 16 inches? The original dots are only one inch wide, so the bigger square would look fuzzy because of the spaces between the one-inch dots.

Adobe's Postscript font description language provides a way to tell a computer how to draw a letter from a mathematical description (vector drawing). The advantage of this is that regardless of how large or small the letter is, the computer sees it only as a series of mathematical line segments. The virtual lines and the places where they change directions can be as long or as short as you choose, making for very little degradation at the edges and therefore a sharper-looking font. The color of the font can be changed on the fly by telling the computer which fill color to use.

Microsoft and Adobe had an argument over how much it would cost Microsoft to license the Adobe process. Eventually, Microsoft figured out a way to make its own raster fonts and named the process TrueType. The original invention wasn't perfect, so Microsoft worked on it and released a second version that fixed the problems in the first version.

TrueType and TrueType II fonts are vector-based raster fonts. TrueType fonts can be *scaled* (enlarged or shrunk), in increments of 1 point, by the computer from the minimum display capabilities of a printer or monitor, to as large as 999 points. A point is $\frac{1}{72}$ of an inch, making a 72-point letter 1 inch tall.

> *Note: Modern laser printers can often allow a font to be scaled in increments of less than 1 point.*

Windows 3.x includes three vector-based fonts stored in files that use a .FON extension as well as a number of TrueType fonts, in a TTF file and a companion FOT file for each typeface. When a laser printer contains the stored calculations for a vector font, those fonts are called internal fonts. Windows added a feature whereby it could work with printers to convert its TrueType fonts to graphics, and the printer would print what Windows was showing on the screen even if there were no matching internal fonts.

Starting 16-Bit Windows

Chapter 8 discussed the basic loading of the operating system, ending with the DOS command prompt that appears after the final line of an AUTOEXEC.BAT file. Typically, on a computer set up to run Windows 3.x, the last line of that AUTOEXEC file is WIN. This means that there must be a program somewhere on the disk called WIN.* (using a DOS wildcard). That loader program, WIN.COM, is found in the C:\WINDOWS directory.

 For the exam, remember that many questions rely on your knowledge of the loading order of DOS files, Windows 3.x files, and Windows 95 files. Pay close attention to which files are critical and which files make up the essential core (kernel) of Windows.

We mentioned the DOSSHELL.BAT program, which ran a small loader stub that called a larger program file into memory. WIN.COM is the next iteration of that loader stub, and it calls into memory USER.EXE, GDI.EXE, and KERNEL.EXE—the core Windows files.

For the exam, remember that the core Windows 3.x files are USER.EXE, GDI.EXE, and KERNEL.EXE.

SETUP.EXE

DOS programs often included a separate installation program (routine) to make sure that every step of the installation is followed correctly. You can usually tell whether you're looking at a DOS- or Windows-based application by the name of its installation program. DOS programs continue to use INSTALL.EXE as the first file to run in setting up the program. Windows programs use SETUP.EXE.

Windows itself uses a SETUP.EXE program, which goes farther than the DOS installation routines in that it not only copies (and expands) files to various locations on the disk, but also examines the hardware and software in the system. The theory behind this examination is that users shouldn't need to know how their computers run. Following the Microsoft lead, most modern installation programs attempt to identify the existing system before installing their application.

Most installation and setup programs make a number of assumptions about the destination computer—the default setup—and offer the computer owner a way to take only some control over the installation. Typically, the installation routine offers a somewhat misleading "express" and "custom" pair of setup options.

You should always choose the custom or advanced option, if the setup routine offers one. In every case we've ever seen, there is a default setting for any steps in the program where you're given a choice. In situations where you don't know what you're looking at, you can choose the default. However, in places where you do know what you're looking at, you may often disagree with what some faraway programmer has decided to do to your system.

SETUP.EXE (located on disk 1 of the Windows disk set) examines the type of hardware and memory available on the computer. It offers some basic configuration options, such as the directory to install Windows in and which kind of display, keyboard, mouse, and network configuration to use.

The key file used by SETUP.EXE and SETUP.INF (information file) contains entries that determine which files will be copied during the installation.

SETUP.EXE also uses EXPAND.EXE to decompress the files on the Windows installation disks. Because the files are stored in a shrunken (compressed) format, the DOS COPY command isn't enough to fully install Windows from original disks.

Note: You can usually tell that a file has been compressed by Microsoft by looking at the last character in the file's extension. Microsoft's proprietary archive process usually makes this last character an underscore (PROGRAM.EX_).

The initial options offered at the beginning of the custom installation can be changed later from within Windows by the Win Setup applet in the Main program group. If the automatic (default) setup is chosen, Microsoft decides which files to install and where to install them. Windows 3.0 didn't offer a choice, providing automatic installation only. Windows 3.x returned to the user some control over the setup process.

DOS, beginning with version 5.0, installs a program in the root directory of the primary, active drive that will tell Windows that the computer can support Enhanced mode. Once SETUP.EXE determines that Windows can be installed on the computer (i.e., that there's enough room), it copies the core files and many of the required files to the hard drive.

SETUP creates a \WINDOWS subdirectory (typically on the C: drive at the root directory). It also creates a \WINDOWS\SYSTEM directory that Windows searches regardless of which other subdirectories are listed in the DOS PATH= environment variable. The DOS file that tells Windows about Enhanced mode capabilities is WINA20.386, which is located in the C:\ root directory (read-only).

During the setup process, SETUP.EXE combines VGALOGO.LGO and VGALOGO.RLE (the Microsoft logo screen) with WIN.CNF and creates WIN.COM, which loads the Windows program into memory and continues forward in graphics mode. Depending on whether automatic or custom installation was chosen, the routine pauses at various points to allow further choices in terms of which applets will be installed.

Note: VGALOGO.* are the two files Windows uses on systems with VGA graphics capabilities. Where the system uses a CGA or EGA monitor, Windows has two files each for CGALOGO.* and EGALOGO.*, which it can compile into WIN.COM.

SETUP.EXE allows various switches at startup. You can always get a quick reminder of the switches by using the SETUP /? switch for DOS online help.

Three of the switches that you might need to know for the exam are:

➤ **/N** Sets up a shared copy of Windows for Workgroups from a network server

➤ **/O:file** Specifies the SETUP.INF file

➤ **/A** Places Windows for Workgroups on a network server (administrative setup)

WIN.COM

Entering "WIN" at the command prompt or having the AUTOEXEC.BAT file enter it for you runs a small COM file (WIN.COM) that does some preliminary checking before it begins to search for the necessary core files for the Windows program. WIN.COM checks to see what type of computer, CPU, and memory are installed. The memory might be real, extended, or expanded.

Next, WIN.COM checks to see which device drivers have been loaded—especially virtual memory devices (HIMEM.SYS)—then makes a decision regarding the mode in which Windows should start. WIN.COM also allows switches on its command line to force certain ways of loading. These different ways of running are called *modes* of operation. Depending on the amount of memory, the type of processor, and whether an extended memory device driver is present, WIN.COM can use:

➤ /R Real mode

➤ /S or /2 Standard mode

➤ /3 Enhanced mode

➤ /B To keep a boot log text file of any problems encountered during startup

Note: Additional switches can be used, but the details of these are beyond the scope of this book. Entering WIN : (a space and colon after WIN) will start Windows 3.x without the Microsoft logo screen (or "splash" screen) during the startup process.

Windows 3.x Core Files

Once WIN.COM has defined a running mode, it transfers control to DOSX.EXE and WIN386.EXE, which then load the Windows core programs into memory. Windows also loads its own device drivers from the SYSTEM.INI file, just as DOS uses the CONFIG.SYS file to load device drivers. We'll discuss the Windows devices shortly, but for now the core Windows files are as follows:

➤ **USER.EXE** Creates and maintains windows on the screen and handles requests to create, move, size, or close windows. Also controls the user interaction with icons and other interface components, including input devices such as the keyboard and mouse.

➤ **GDI.EXE** Controls the graphics device interface, which is responsible for graphics operations that create images on the monitor or other display devices.

➤ **KRNL286.EXE or KRNL386.EXE** Controls memory management, program loading, program code execution, and task scheduling. KRNL286.EXE is specific to the 80286 processor, and KRNL386.EXE applies to all later chips.

Real Mode (WIN /R)

Real mode Windows 3.0 was designed to run on 8086-based computers. Microsoft offered this mode, but those computers were so limited that Windows ran too slowly for all practical purposes. Real mode was a 100 percent compatible mode for running pure DOS. Some games that run under DOS environments have a problem running under Windows 3.0 and vice versa. DOS programs, especially these kinds of games, often write directly to the screen, and with Windows trying to handle device operations, the confusion causes lock-ups and crashes. Real mode required at least an 8088/86 processor and 640K of conventional memory, was used mainly for running Windows 2.x applications that hadn't been converted to Windows 3.0, and was eliminated in Windows 3.1.

Real mode was designed almost exclusively for DOS programs. It allowed DOS programs to be task switched (with Windows swapping itself out of memory) to disk. Real mode required that DOS programs run in full screens and allowed DOS programs to run in Protected mode, if the CPU chip was a 286 or faster.

 For the exam, remember that Windows 3.1, 3.11, and Windows for Workgroups support two operating modes: Standard mode and 386 Enhanced mode. The choice of mode is defined by a combination of the system hardware, the amount of installed (accessible) memory, and any startup switches used with WIN.COM.

Standard Mode (WIN /S)

We saw that Windows grew out of changes in the way in which the processor manages memory. In a way, Windows does send instructions directly to the CPU. Remember that 286 Protected mode is really what started everything. WIN.COM transfers control to other programs that take over management of expanded memory, extended memory, or both.

If WIN.COM finds HIMEM.SYS (extended memory manager) in memory and at least 256K of conventional memory and 192K of extended memory, Windows can start in Standard mode. Windows uses Standard mode when the computer has an 80286 chip with 1MB or more of memory or a 80386 processor with more than 1MB but less than 2MB of memory.

If the computer has more than 2MB of memory and a 386 CPU, Windows uses Enhanced mode by default.

Recall from Chapter 3 that the ability of the chip to switch between Protected mode and Real mode without rebooting was one of the main differences between the 286 and the 386 chip. Although the 286 could switch into Protected mode during a session, it required a system reset to switch back to Real mode. This may be the reason that Bill Gates called the 80286 chip "brain-dead" and tried to push IBM into skipping development efforts to the 80386 rather than waste time with the 286.

The Global Heap (Memory)

The *global heap* in Windows 3.x is the entire amount of memory available at startup. Windows reads the existing environment created by CONFIG.SYS and HIMEM.SYS (if it was loaded). Whatever programs have been installed by DOS prior to running Windows are recognized by Windows, and whatever memory is actually available for programs is taken by Windows.

Essentially, Windows is acting like a program that takes over all available memory after DOS starts. Windows then controls that memory directly, much like a memory management program. Windows also takes control over video processing, using its own functions and controls.

 For the exam, remember that the global heap is all available memory that Windows 3.x can see at startup. The maximum amount of actual memory Windows 3.x can use is 16MB.

Windows divides the global heap (all available memory) into three main areas:

➤ **Conventional memory** This is the same as base memory in DOS real sessions, that is, segments above low memory and below A0000h.

➤ **(HMA) High-memory area** If DOS has set aside areas above the A0000h segment for use by applications, Windows takes control of that area and adds it to the global heap of memory.

➤ **Extended memory** Once Windows starts, it already knows how much memory you have in your system by reading the virtual memory driver (HIMEM.SYS) and takes over control of that memory from DOS and accesses it directly.

 For the exam, remember that while there is a formal distinction between base memory and conventional memory, questions will usually apply the term "conventional" memory to the 640K used for applications, and refer to High Memory by name.

Once Windows has taken over the management of RAM, it makes no difference whether the memory is extended or conventional. Windows sees all memory up to 16MB as part of the global heap. The theoretical limit to extended memory available to Windows 3.x is 15MB: 16MB minus the 1MB of conventional memory.

System Resources

All free memory available from the first DOS prompt is referred to as: base memory (640K), HMA (high-memory area above A000h), and extended memory (beyond 1MB). Once Windows is up and running, it takes control of memory on the system and loads device drivers, program code, and data files into free memory. DOS is out of the loop except for file management at the disk level and hardware management at the interrupt level.

The names used for memory in a DOS session change once Windows is running. All of memory becomes the global heap, or simply the heap. Windows loads program code into the heap by putting it first into lower segments and then into increasingly higher segments. The global heap is divided into two areas: USER.EXE and GDI.EXE. Each smaller area also has a *local* heap of memory.

The local heap is reported as the *system resources* (under Help|About from any Windows menu), some of which is used and some of which is freed up as code moves in and out of memory. Each area is limited to one 64K segment for a total of 128K for the heap.

The amount of global memory that Windows thinks is available on the system can also be read as free memory in the Help|About menu option. The system resources are a fractional part of a PC's memory, used for managing the events taking place on the screen. The following system resources (memory) are a special area set aside by Windows:

➤ The USER and GDI local heaps together make up the Free System Resources percentage seen under the Help|About menu option from any main menu in a Windows-compliant application.

➤ Everything in the Windows environment (both 16-bit and 32-bit) uses a percentage of the system resources, including icons, windows, programs, applications, data, menus, program tools, and screen savers.

➤ The total amount of RAM set aside for the Windows 3.x resources is 128K.

➤ System resources are reported as a percentage available. Typically, there should be between 50 percent and 85 percent resources available at any given time in a Windows 3.x session (taking into account all programs running in that session).

➤ So-called memory doubler software does not double the amount of installed RAM; rather, it doubles the amount of system resources available from the two local heaps.

Programs are supposed to be written in such a way that resources are taken from the free system resources and given up again when the code for that program terminates. Unfortunately, not all programmers follow the rules, and not all programs work the way they were intended to work.

If something takes up resources, but fails to release them back to the heaps at conclusion, those resources never return to the Windows resources memory. This problem is sometimes referred to as a *resource leak*. Windows must be exited and restarted to re-create a new heap and start again with maximum free resources. This problem can occur as easily in Windows 95 as in Windows 3.x, although fewer programs written for Windows 95 steal resources.

An "Out of Memory" error in Windows often refers to the lack of enough free system resources, not to the amount of total free memory on the computer.

 For the exam, remember that GDI.EXE is the program file for the graphics device interface. You can remember that KRNL is the "kernel" and USER should remind you of the person using the computer. The kernel handles code, and USER.EXE works with you while you navigate in Windows. The GUI is managed by the GDI, so all you really need to memorize is that the "D" stands for "Device."

386 Enhanced Mode (WIN /3)

The 386 Enhanced mode is usually referred to simply as Enhanced mode. Its startup sequence is the same as it is for Standard mode, except that Windows switches the 386 chip into 32-bit Protected mode. Instead of calling the 286 kernel, WIN.COM loads KRNL386.EXE, which then loads the rest of Windows. Windows Enhanced mode requires a 386 or faster processor and can, therefore, switch between Protected mode and Real mode without the problem of resetting the computer.

The 80386 processor chip introduced virtual memory by creating an illusion for DOS that 1MB of memory stayed constant. The chip would change the addresses to point to extended memory (vectoring) and report back to DOS that nothing was different—the memory was the same as it was a minute ago. Each new 1MB of memory is placed in front of DOS, page by page, using the page-frame segment of conventional memory.

In the same way that the 386 chip was fooling the old DOS into thinking that only 1MB of RAM was present, it fools Windows into thinking that many virtual 8086 PCs are running in the same place. The 386 Enhanced mode also takes better control of DOS programs that bypass BIOS with video functions and intercepts those function calls (e.g., games). This allows most DOS programs that use a graphics mode to be run under Windows in Enhanced mode.

The 80386 protects both memory areas and hardware process operations by intercepting all memory addressing calls and calls to the hardware. Windows and the CPU get together and intercept *everything* an application tries to do. When two applications try to access the same device at the same time, Windows arbitrates and decides which one gets access first.

Virtual Machine (VM)

As we've seen, 386 Protected mode provides a way for the processor to create protected areas of memory that can be used to emulate a standalone 8088/86 PC and the way in which it addressed memory. These fake machines are called *virtual machines*, or *virtual PCs*. A virtual machine (VM) is an executable task (i.e., a program) that combines application, support software such as ROM BIOS and DOS, memory, and CPU registers.

Windows uses a single virtual machine called the System VM to run the Windows kernel, its other core components and extensions, as well as all Windows-based applications. Each time a DOS application is run, it creates a separate VM that exists for only the length of time that the DOS application is running. The PIF editor (discussed shortly) controls how that session's virtual machine runs.

Virtually Real

Existence can be broadly divided into physical and metaphysical reality. Metaphysical (from *meta*) is literally greater than physical. In physical reality, all things have attributes, or characteristics. When we point to an object and define it, we're taking out and using the single, unique attribute that distinguishes it from any other object in existence. Physical objects are accessible through our senses (perceptions) and can be touched, smelled, heard, seen, or tasted.

A virtual object is a thing that exhibits all the attributes of the same objects in its class (or set) except for one: physical existence. Virtual objects are not "sensible" to physical perceptions (yet). A virtual machine is a machine that works and acts exactly the same way as a physical machine, except that you can't reach over and pick it up with your physical arms.

Virtual reality (VR) can provide you with virtual arms. In this situation, your nonphysical arms work the same way as your physical arms. The difference is that you can use virtual arms to pick up a virtual machine. The end result is then reflected in the virtual reality as having consequences just like in the physical world. For instance, you could end up with a virtual hernia.

INI Files

The so-called Windows operating system environment includes a number of support files, just like DOS does. Windows was designed to succeed DOS and become the main (and only) interface between the computer and the user. As a result, Microsoft tried to gather as many device drivers as possible and pull them together under a single umbrella. Additionally, as program files became larger, some of their supporting code was moved outside the EXE or the COM file to additional files. These files are required to run the application because the main executable file contains internal references to those files. Generally, these support files are located in specific directories called the *working directory*.

For various reasons, PC users found that it was useful to locate the main program files in one place and some of the auxiliary files somewhere else. Not only that, but the data files created by an application are often placed on completely different drives (as in networks). To make some sense out of all this, certain types of configuration files were created to hold information regarding how the main executable file was supposed to run. These particular configuration files are called *initialization files,* and almost always have a .INI extension (read "dot I-N-I").

We've seen that *properties* describe to a *menu* or shell important information about the location of a main executable file and how to run it. Initialization files, on the other hand, describe to an *executable file* important information about how it should run and where to find external support files.

The two fundamental INI files used by Windows 3.x are the WIN.INI file and the SYSTEM.INI file. Both files are plain ASCII text files located by default in the \WINDOWS directory. These two files are discussed shortly.

New sections can be added to INI files either by other program installations or by the user. Sections are enclosed in square brackets (e.g., [restrictions]) with a unique name that can be used for security control over Program Manager.

Windows 3.x Group (GRP) Files

16-bit Windows typically shows the user the Program Manager shell (PROGMAN.EXE). Within the Program Manager, a number of additional windows are installed by default, and can be added by the user. Each of these smaller windows are called *program groups.* Finally, each program group contains graphic symbols (icons) representing individual *program items.* Both program groups and program items can be created with the File|New option of the Program Manager menu.

Program groups contain icons pertaining to related programs, or they act as a sort of bucket to hold programs the user wants easy access to. Either way, Windows stores the information about what icons are in any given program group, along with each icon's properties. The files where this information is stored generally use the first eight letters of a window's title (found on the title bar), and a .GRP extension. Group files are normally stored in the \WINDOWS directory. During the creation process, program groups offer the user an opportunity to name a specific location and file name, but most people don't use this option.

A common problem found on Windows 3.x systems occurs when a user has accidentally highlighted a program group icon and deleted it. While the group file has been deleted, the underlying programs are not affected at all. Create an \INIBACK directory (or some other name) and copy the group files and INI files to it. In the event a GRP file is accidentally deleted, you can restore the program group by simply copying it back to the \WINDOWS directory.

For the exam, remember that before you upgrade a Windows 3.x system to a Windows 95 environment, you should back up all GRP files, along with all INI files. Windows 95 can interpret both types of files and carry the previous configuration through the upgrade.

The DOS command DIR [d:]*.GRP /S and DIR [d:]*.INI /S will find all GRP and INI files on a drive (where [d:] is the drive letter). The *.GRP and *.INI can also be used within File Manager (File|Search) and within MS Explorer (Tools|Find).

SYSEDIT.EXE

SYSEDIT.EXE, located in the \WINDOWS\SYSTEM directory, is a small editing utility applet that opens and cascades the primary configuration files for Windows 3.1x and Windows 95. In 16-bit Windows, the main files are CONFIG.SYS and AUTOEXEC.BAT for DOS, and SYSTEM.INI and WIN.INI for Windows. All four files are opened and arranged (cascade style) and can be viewed and edited. If Windows for Workgroups is installed, SCHDPLUS.INI is included in the editor for Schedule Plus (a workgroup schedule management program). 32-bit Windows includes PROTOCOL.INI (for Windows networking protocols).

Note: SYSEDIT can be set up in any program group window by using the File\New\Program Item dialog box in Program Manager.

PROGMAN.INI

The poorly documented PROGMAN.INI file is a configuration file that controls the way the Program Manager appears to the user. The default INI file contains a list of the program groups and very little other data. However, this file can be used to provide basic security on a system by removing certain options from the shell.

Usually the last line under the [Groups] section is Order=, specifying the order Program Manager loads various groups. An optional section can be added by editing the PROGMAN.INI file and typing in [Restrictions]. The *xxxx*= lines added to this section can tell Program Manager whether or not to allow a user to run a program (NoRun=), change settings (NoSaveSettings=), or even whether they can use the File menu (NoFileMenu=), among other things. Using the [Restrictions] section can prevent someone from accidentally deleting (and/or creating) program groups.

Dynamic Link Libraries (DLL)

Along with the Windows kernel and core files, Microsoft provides the Windows *extensions* that are meant to standardize many Windows functions, including the look and the feel of the interface. We've mentioned that COMMDLG.DLL is a generic way for a programmer to work with Windows to create standardized dialog boxes. DDEML.DLL is a library of management tools for DDE (dynamic data exchange), and MMSYSTEM.DLL is a library of management tools for sound and multimedia.

The Windows extensions are designed to make the Windows environment as flexible as possible. *Dynamic link libraries* (DLLs) are Windows-executable files that allow applications to share program code and necessary resources. A programmer can extend the basic Windows environment by writing a DLL to make it available to other Windows applications. Dynamic link libraries commonly have the .DLL extension, but can also have a .EXE or other extension. KERNEL.EXE, USER.EXE, and GDI.EXE are DLLs that have the .EXE extension.

The SHELL.DLL library provides the drag-and-drop capabilities used with File Manager. Such routines can be used by other applications without needing to rewrite the code. The programmer calls up the routines from the SHELL.DLL file (which installs with Windows by default).

Virtual Device Drivers (VxD)

The lowest area of the global heap (memory) is set aside for Windows to load Windows-based device drivers that handle the interface between Windows, DOS, and hardware devices. We saw that the CONFIG.SYS file in DOS installs device drivers in the first segment of conventional memory prior to loading Windows. The Windows device drivers are loaded into the lowest segment of the global heap, which is usually just above the low-memory area set aside by DOS.

Windows has its own device drivers to handle the keyboard, mouse, printers, video monitors, sound cards, scanners, and anything else that connects to the motherboard. All these device drivers are listed in the SYSTEM.INI file with any additional information they might need during startup.

 For the exam, remember that a virtual device driver (VxD) is a 32-bit Protected mode DLL that manages a system resource (i.e., a hardware device or installed software) such that more than one application can use the resource at the same time. The 32-bit Protected mode comes from the 32-bit 80386 chip architecture and therefore is available only for a 386 or faster CPU.

The VxD abbreviation is used to refer to any (V)irtual *device* (D)river, where *x* is used as a stand-in variable. The specific device driver replaces *x* with a character or characters referring to the specific type of driver. For example, a VDD is a virtual *display* driver, where *D* represents *display*.

VxDs work together with DOS to support multitasking in that more than one application can access the device at the same time in an arbitrated (managed) way. The VxDs work together with Windows to process interrupts and carry out I/O processes for a specific application without interfering in another application's use of the same device. All the hardware devices on a typical computer have a VxD, including the motherboard PIC (programmable interrupt controller), the timer oscillator, DMA access channels, disk controller(s), serial and parallel ports, keyboard and input devices, math coprocessor, and monitor display.

A virtual device driver is generally written to hold code for specific operations of a device that might not be included in the basic Windows installation. However, a VxD is required for any device that can retain settings information from an application that might mess up a request from another application. VxDs can also be written for any driver software that was installed by DOS during the CONFIG.SYS process.

When a VxD is a software driver, it's usually surrounding the existing device (or TSR) and providing a specialized environment coming from Windows. This fools the existing driver into thinking that only one computer running one application is present and that only that application will be using the hardware device controlled by the real driver. Again, the VxD is acting as a liaison between the Windows control management system and the individual device that is looking for a secure set of memory addresses.

 For the exam, remember that VxDs are installed from the SYSTEM.INI file, usually in the [386Enh] section of the file, and begin with DEVICE=, the same as they do in the CONFIG.SYS file. Windows 95 extended this process and tries to substitute a VxD for any device listed in a CONFIG.SYS file.

SYSTEM.INI

Anyone who installs a new piece of hardware or a new software application under Windows 3.x is touching the SYSTEM.INI file. This is the initialization file that Windows looks at after all the necessary and core system files have been installed. The SYSTEM.INI file contains the controls for the interface between Windows and DOS and, as we just saw, is where Windows VxDs are loaded into memory.

What Happens If...?

There may be some peculiar scenarios on the A+ exam, and one of the more unusual ones that you may encounter is a situation in which one or the other of the SYSTEM.INI and WIN.INI files is missing. If the SYSTEM.INI file is missing, Windows simply won't start at all, and it will produce an error message to that effect.

If the WIN.INI file is missing, Windows will start in a default, VGA mode (assuming Enhanced mode is possible). This is the precursor to the Windows 95 Safe mode, where Windows will start with a basic configuration. When Windows can't find a WIN.INI file, it will create one when it starts. Any environmental customization (e.g., colors, icon spacing, or mouse configurations) will be missing, but you will at least be in Windows.

 For the exam, remember that the SYSTEM.INI file is loaded after the core files and before the WIN.INI file. Windows 3.x *requires* a SYSTEM.INI file, but does *not require* a WIN.INI file. If a WIN.INI file doesn't exist, Windows 3.x will create one.

The SYSTEM.INI file is a plain ASCII text file that can be edited by NOTEPAD.EXE (Windows applet), the DOS Editor (EDIT.COM), SYSEDIT.EXE, or any word processor that saves files in plain ASCII low-bit format. The file is divided into *sections*, each of which has a heading enclosed in square brackets ([ ]). The most common areas of user interest are the [386Enh] section for device drivers and the [boot] section, where the SHELL=PROGMAN.EXE line points to the shell file that runs the Program Manager at startup.

Note: Changing SHELL=PROGMAN.EXE to SHELL=WINFILE.EXE will cause Windows to start up with the File Manager as the first window.

The only unusual thing to remember about the SYSTEM.INI and WIN.INI files (or any other Windows INI file) is that REM (Remark) isn't the way to comment out a line in the file. To skip over the line in an INI file, you must use a semicolon (;) in the first column of the specific line, followed by at least one space. REM is used for DOS batch files.

 For the exam, remember that SYSTEM.INI installs device drivers and VxDs. Windows 95 continues to use the SYSTEM.INI file to load certain types of device drivers, so even Win95 often has a SYSTEM.INI file.

WIN.INI

The second, basic initialization file that Windows looks through at startup is WIN.INI. As we've seen, WIN.INI isn't required, but if it doesn't exist, Windows will create a default version. The WIN.INI file is where all the information about the overall user environment for Windows is stored. If SYSTEM.INI is similar to the CONFIG.SYS file in the DOS startup process, WIN.INI is similar to the AUTOEXEC.BAT file at the end of the startup process.

WIN.INI contains the [windows] section, where programs can be set to run automatically without putting them in the Startup group window. LOAD= tells a program to run minimized on Windows startup, and RUN= tells a program to run normally at Windows startup.

> *Note: When you can't find a reference to some program that seems to run from the Startup program group, you'll almost always find it referenced in either the LOAD= or RUN= line at the top of the WIN.INI file. Screen savers and antivirus programs typically use this line, as do mouse configurations.*

The WIN.INI file also contains a listing of all the fonts installed into Windows, along with associated extensions for programs. For example, the [extensions] section of the WIN.INI file might have the line bmp=C:\windows\mspaint.exe ^.bmp, which tells Windows that any time it sees a DOS file with a .BMP extension, it can make an assumption that the program MSPAINT.EXE will be used to open that file.

File Associations

Files are *associated* in the [extensions] section of the WIN.INI file by selecting the Associate option in File Manager's File menu. This used to be a simple process in Windows 3.x and has typically become far more complex under Windows 95. Associating a program means that you can double-click on a file name in either File Manager or MS Explorer, and Windows will run a program that can work with the file.

A common association is where any file ending with a DOC extension will automatically open MS Word. Both Windows 3.x and Windows 95 install with certain pre-defined associations. Typically, INI files, BAT files, and TXT files are associated with Notepad or Wordpad (text editors). Many shareware programs (try before you buy) include a DIZ description file. If you download a lot of shareware, you can easily associate the DIZ extension with Notepad, thereby making it easy to double-click on the description and read it.

Windows 95 Associations

As long as we're talking about associations, we'll mention the process for Windows 95 here rather than later. The files association feature in Win95 is found under the MS Explorer's View|Options|File Types menu.

Once the Options dialog box opens (if anyone ever finds it) it presents two tabs: View and File Types. Under the View tab, one of the check boxes allows you to "Hide MS DOS Extensions…" The other tab is where you associate file extensions. Whether or not you hide the extensions, the associations will produce a description in the Explorer window. The Windows 3.x File Manager shows all file extensions by default, and choosing File|Associate immediately calls up a dialog box. Windows 95, on the other hand, requires that you either do some detective work for find what program is already associated with an extension, or fill out a nearly incomprehensible description form.

Virtual Memory

When Windows runs an application, that application looks at what it *thinks* is DOS and works with various memory addresses. Windows, though, intercepts every addressing call from the program and hands the program an address based on Windows' own memory decisions. If a lot of memory has been used, Windows starts using disk space (*swap files*, discussed shortly) as additional virtual memory.

When Windows puts an application's memory addresses on the disk, it uses 4K chunks and doesn't tell the program that the apparent memory is somewhere on a disk. Often, an application thinks that it's addressing a continuous set of addresses in a RAM segment. When the application calls for memory addresses that aren't in actual RAM, it generates a page fault request, telling Windows to go to the disk and find those addresses. Windows pages (loads) those addresses back into RAM, then hands them to the application as though everything were completely normal.

32-Bit Access

Windows 3.1x introduced the ability for Windows to work directly with a 32-bit processor chip (i.e., the 80386). The method of accessing the chip depends on the type of BIOS installed on the system board. If the Windows kernel is able to access virtual memory directly through the processor, the Virtual Memory dialog box under the Enhanced choice in the Control Panel will show the disk status as "Using 32-Bit Access." If Windows can access 32-bit virtual memory, but not directly with the chip, it will use system BIOS, and the disk status line will show "Using BIOS."

Program Information Files

Windows provides heap memory to a DOS application in the same way that any PC comes with base memory to run programs. The amount of DRAM memory on a real PC is determined by chips and buyer choices. The amount of virtual memory on a virtual PC is determined by the requirements of the application asking for a VM (virtual machine). If no one does anything, the default settings are created by the _DEFAULT.PIF file that comes with Windows 3.x.

A PIF (program information file) file is stored in a proprietary format, and can't be edited using a typical ASCII text editor. Much like the Registration database (and Windows 95 Registry) uses REGEDIT.EXE as a specialized editor, PIFEDIT.EXE is used to edit PIF files. Some of the important things to remember about the PIF Editor, include:

➤ PIFEDIT.EXE, with PIFEDIT.HLP (a Help file), is a Windows applet that lets you define the amount of memory in a virtual PC that a specific program will use.

➤ The PIF editing dialog box asks for information about the program, including its full pathname and command file name, along with any startup switches that you want to use for that program.

➤ The PROGRAMS= line in the WIN.INI file specifies that .EXE, .COM, .BAT, and PIF file extensions are to be considered executable by Windows. Note that a PIF file is an executable file in the Windows 3.x environment.

➤ Rather than pointing the Windows program item properties to the EXE or COM file, the properties can be used to point to the PIF file associated with the actual executable file.

➤ A PIF file can also tell Windows how much time (in time slices) to give to the processes generated by the DOS application.

Tricky Semantics

Because Windows decides (on the basis of PIF time slices) whether and when a DOS application will have access to the CPU, the term *preemptive multitasking* for DOS applications crept its way into the language with the arrival of Windows 3.x. Because DOS applications aren't written in a threaded format, this use of the term isn't really accurate. It's true that Windows is literally preempting the DOS application's access to the CPU, but that doesn't mean that Windows is using preemptive multitasking in the way that it's formally defined.

Microsoft tends to advertise Windows 3.x as having preemptive multitasking capabilities. This is true semantically, but not in the generally accepted meaning of the term. The exam might ask you whether Windows 3.x or Windows 95 offers real multitasking (without reference to its being preemptive). We believe that the politically correct answer would be yes.

Translation Buffers

Windows still requires DOS to handle certain functions, such as reading or writing a file to disk. To do this, Windows switches the CPU back to Real mode so that DOS can run in Real mode and read the conventional memory for instructions. To communicate with DOS, Windows places *translation buffers* in the upper-memory 384K area.

Translation buffers act as a kind of vector table for Windows to hand addresses to DOS. Windows also uses translation buffers to make Real mode networking calls to an NOS (network operating system). Windows allocates two 4K translation buffers for each virtual PC. Running an application creates a virtual PC, so each running application uses 8K (2 × 4) of real memory in the form of translation buffers. Networked physical computers use six 4K translation buffers per virtual PC: 24K per application.

Because every adapter card, including NICs (network interface cards), use some address space in upper memory, a physical computer with a number of adapter cards can eventually take up all the upper memory. In this event, Windows can be told to use base memory for translation buffers. Translation buffers can't be split between upper and base memory, either. If the translation buffers end up in base memory, every virtual PC that Windows creates will inherit the buffers, leaving less memory for the application to run.

 Remember that Windows creates virtual PCs out of the existing environment when it loads. Therefore, when an application runs and Windows creates a virtual PC for it, the VM inherits the DOS environment that was in existence when Windows was started. All TSRs, device drivers, and other programs in memory at Windows startup will be in memory in the VM. If the base memory was 512K at Windows startup, any consequent VM will also start with 512K.

Windows Swap Files

In Enhanced mode, Windows has two ways to set aside space on a hard drive to handle page overflow: *temporary* and *permanent swap files*. Windows 3.x can manage a maximum of 16MB of installed RAM, but it can use far more than that by saving 4K pages (chunks) of memory to the disk as a swap file. The default location of the swap file is the root directory of the drive Windows was installed to, usually the C: drive.

The difference between a permanent and temporary swap file is mostly speed of access, leading to system performance issues. If Windows is going to swap out memory to the disk, it has two options: it can create a file somewhere on the disk and put memory there, or it can go to a preexisting file. If Windows creates the file, then it's a temporary swap file and is deleted when the session ends. Otherwise, you can create a permanent swap file out of contiguous sectors and save some time by not making Windows create the file when it needs it.

Windows creates two files when it sets up the drive's swap file. The first file is a small read-only file in the Windows subdirectory called SPART.PAR. The sole purpose of this file is to tell Windows the location and size of the other file (the swap file). The actual swap file is usually in the root directory of the installation drive, but it can be on another, larger drive.

In Windows 3.1x, the permanent swap file is called 386PART.PAR and can be seen with File Manager if the View (by file type) options are set to show hidden files. The temporary swap file is usually called WIN386.SWP. A disadvantage of the temporary file is that it grows or shrinks depending on Windows' needs. The permanent swap file is fixed and doesn't grow to take over your disk.

 Remember that the Windows permanent swap file is called 386PART.PAR and is located, by default, in the root directory of the C: drive.

A permanent swap file must contain contiguous clusters, so it's better to defragment the disk before loading Windows and then change virtual memory to make the swap file permanent. The virtual memory dialog box is under the Enhanced choice in the Control Panel, under Virtual Memory|Changes.

If Windows is running in Standard mode, a third type of temporary swap file—an *application swap file*—is created whenever a DOS application is started from within Windows.

Windows will recommend a file size. This recommendation can be changed in Windows 3.1x. The file will use the available space on the Windows installation drive and the largest block of contiguous, unfragmented space to recommend a file 2.4 times the size of the physical memory installed on the computer.

Controlling Swap Files

User control over the type and size of the swap file is handled by the Control Panel applet in the Main program group of Program Manager. Control Panel is run by the CONTROL.EXE program in the \WINDOWS directory. Any changes are stored in the CONTROL.INI file and in the \WINDOWS directory.

CONTROL.EXE can be run directly from File Manager or as a separate iconized applet from within Windows. The Control Panel icon opens to the control panel window, which contains icons for the internal subroutines held within CONTROL.EXE. If Windows starts in 386 Enhanced mode, one of the available icons is the Enhanced icon (a graphic picture of a CPU) through which virtual memory settings can be changed. The Enhanced option in the Control Panel is used to change virtual memory settings, swap file size and type, and device contention between I/O ports. The Enhanced option also provides for configuring task scheduling and Windows foreground, background, and exclusive processing.

If SETUP.EXE is run with the express setup option, Windows will automatically install a permanent swap file in the root directory of the \WINDOWS installation directory. The permanent swap file is a bit faster than a temporary swap file because it contains contiguous clusters (DEFRAG.EXE) and need not be created before Windows can use it. A temporary swap file must be created and saved before Windows can transfer the first 4K memory block to the disk.

Windows For Workgroups (WFW)

Windows 3.1x came in two versions: Windows 3.1/3.11 and Windows for Workgroups 3.1/3.11. Windows for Workgroups introduced peer-to-peer networking, in which individual computers could be connected through network interface cards and cables. The Windows for Workgroups program provides network services in an inexpensive, basic way and was Microsoft's preliminary attempt to combine the operating system with networking capabilities. See the end of Chapter 10 for a basic discussion on networking.

OS/2, Unix, and the Macintosh operating system came with networking services nearly from the beginning. Windows NT (beginning with OS/2 3.0) is designed to be Microsoft's full-fledged NOS (network operating system). Between Windows 3.0 and Windows NT, Windows 3.1x and Windows 95/98 have been incremental releases aimed at adding the integrated networking functions.

The certification exam isn't designed to test your thorough knowledge of networking protocols and configurations. However, you should have a basic understanding of two terms: *peer-to-peer networking* and *client/server networking*. Simply put, peer-to-peer networking allows each computer on a network to share files and services with other computers—its peers—depending on how that computer is configured. It might help to remember that the sociological term *peer pressure* means that a person is influenced by his or her friends and other people who he or she considers equal.

Client/server networking means that one computer—a *file server*—is set up with some control over a network of other computers—*clients*—that use services and files from this central file server. Because so many computers can access a single file server, the NOS on the file server must be very fast and able to handle a lot of activity. Windows NT is fundamentally designed to be a client/server network operating system.

Windows for Workgroups 3.1 and 3.11 are capable of peer-to-peer networking. An individual computer in a peer-to-peer network is called a *workstation*. In client/server networking, a user's computer is usually referred to as the *local* computer or workstation. For Windows for Workgroups networking services to be installed, SETUP.EXE must discover and then communicate with a NIC in the expansion bus.

SETUP.EXE looks for a NIC if a Real mode network device driver is loaded from within CONFIG.SYS. A Windows 95 computer can be installed with network services even without a NIC to keep user preferences separate on the same computer. To provide network services, a Real mode network device driver must be installed in the CONFIG.SYS file. Note that even with Windows 95, this is a situation where a CONFIG.SYS file is required.

Remember that while Windows 95 theoretically doesn't make use of a CONFIG.SYS file, many times the only way a device driver can be loaded under Windows 95 is from within a CONFIG.SYS file.

Windows for Workgroups requires an 80286 or faster CPU (according to Microsoft) with slightly more than 2MB of installed RAM. This configuration will run Windows for Workgroups in Standard mode as a network workstation. However, a workstation in Standard mode can't share resources, though it can access network resources from other workstations. It uses the NET LOGON user ID and password.

For the exam remember that sharing resources means sharing something that contains user information that would ordinarily be exchanged through a "sneaker network" (where people run around in sneakers and hand files to someone else). Peer-to-peer networking does not normally provide sharing of things like monitors, pencil sharpeners, mice, scanners, or sound cards.

Peer-to-peer networking is typically used to share hard drives and directories, files, CD-ROM drives, printers, and sometimes modems or fax machines.

To "bind" the NIC found in the CONFIG.SYS file, the command NET START must be issued at the DOS command line prior to starting Windows for Workgroups. This can be done in the AUTOEXEC.BAT file.

To access *full* network functionality and provide resources to other computers on a network, Windows must be running in 386 Enhanced mode. With full functionality, the workstation can allow a remote user on the network to access files located on the local PC. In this case, the workstation is providing server-type functions.

Network server components are written only as VxDs and therefore require that Windows runs in 386 Enhanced mode. WFWNET.DRV, the VxD loaded by the kernel, handles user interaction with the network (e.g., logging on and off and sharing resources). The driver also handles access to shared resources such as printers and files located on another workstation.

80386 Network Boot Sequence

The exam won't test you on the sequence and files needed to launch Windows for Workgroups in a full network mode. However, as a summary of the basic components of Windows, the following sequence can help you visualize everything you've been reading to this point. The 386 Enhanced network mode boots as follows:

1. The user executes WIN.COM at the DOS prompt.

2. WIN.COM runs the DOS Exec function to WIN386.EXE, the 386 Enhanced mode system kernel.

3. WIN383.EXE loads the virtual machine manager (VMM) and all VxDs listed in the SYSTEM.INI file.

4. The VNETSUP.386 network support VxD initializes all the Windows for Workgroups VxDs (e.g., VNB.386 and VNETBIOS.386). VNB.386 and VREDIR.386 are bound together in a WORKGRP.SYS device driver.

5. The network redirector VREDIR.386 starts the network redirector in the same way that a user might type "NET START WORKSTATION" at a DOS prompt and press Enter.

6. WIN386.EXE loads KRNL386.EXE, the 386 Enhanced mode kernel.

7. KRNL386.EXE then loads the Windows drivers files in the SYSTEM.INI, along with the Windows core files, GDI.EXE and USER.EXE. The driver files are the DRV files in the SYSTEM.INI.

8. SYSTEM.INI also tells KRNL386.EXE to load additional Windows support files (e.g., fonts).

9. KRNL386.EXE loads the network driver, WFWNET.DRV.

10. The network server driver VxD (VSERVER.386) starts the server services.

11. WFWNET.DRV loads the network DDE communications application, NETDDE.EXE, and the ClipBook Server background application, CLIPSRV.EXE.

12. WFWNET.DRV prompts the user to log on to the network and restores any connections that were made during the last successful logon session.

13. KRNL386.EXE reads the SHELL= line of the [boot] section at the top of SYSTEM.INI and launches whatever shell (Program Manager or File Manager) is stated there.

Note: An additional switch available to WIN.COM is WIN /n, which loads Windows and bypasses any network initialization. WIN /n is sometimes used to troubleshoot Windows start problems, without completely deactivating the network connections.

Why Windows?

This chapter has attempted to give you the background and concepts you need in migrating from a text-only DOS screen to the GUI of Windows. We want you to understand that Windows 3.x (over DOS 3.x through 6.x) and Windows 4.x (Windows 95 and 98 over DOS 7.x) are pretty much cobbled-together enhancements, utilities, workarounds, and new software ideas designed to make using a PC as far removed as possible from configuring and troubleshooting a PC.

Microsoft's Windows NT and IBM's OS/2 are full-fledged 32-bit operating systems with fundamental design changes that make them incompatible with DOS to varying degrees. Both companies understand that they won't sell a lot of products to the vast, installed base of customers who started out with DOS. Therefore, Windows has been a way to provide a constantly backward-compatible operating system interface while processors and hardware have become more and more powerful. The constant need for backward compatibility has been the underlying cause of the instabilities and configuration problems Windows has had. This need has also been an inducement to customers to move into new ways of using a PC.

The latest generations of Intel, AMD, Cyrix, Motorola, and Digital processors (to name a few) can handle 32-bit and 64-bit processing; internal parallel processing; terabytes of memory; and multiple, simultaneous instructions. DOS with its Windows shell interface is far too slow and simplistic to take full advantage of the new hardware. The historical upgrade path between the 8088/86 and P2 microprocessors has been the world of Windows.

Exam Prep Questions

Question 1

> The SHELL= line of the SYSTEM.INI file is used to load the
> _____ file which is called _____.
>
> ○ a. COMMAND.COM, Command Processor
>
> ○ b. FILEMNGR.EXE, File Manager
>
> ○ c. PROGMAN.INI, Program Manager
>
> ○ d. DOSSHELL.EXE, DOS Shell

Answer c is correct. Both COMMAND.COM and DOSSHELL.EXE are DOS programs, and the SYSTEM.INI file is a Windows initialization file. Although there is a shell called File Manager, the executable file to run it is called WINFILE.EXE.

Question 2

> When you are asked to convert a Windows 3.11 system to a Windows 95 system, which are the most important Windows files to back up?
>
> ○ a. GRP and BAT
>
> ○ b. INI and SYS
>
> ○ c. INI and GRP
>
> ○ d. BAT and SYS

Answer c is correct. Windows 95 can read both program group files (GRP) and Windows initialization files (INI) and use the information from these files to configure the new installation as closely as possible to the old configuration. BAT files are DOS batch files, and SYS files are usually device drivers. While these files are useful to back up, the more important files are the group and initialization files.

Question 3

> SYSTEM.INI and WIN.COM are required in order to begin a Windows 3.11 session.
>
> ○ a. True
>
> ○ b. False

Answer b is correct. While WIN.COM will be created if Windows fails to discover it in the \WINDOWS directory, it is not required to run Windows.

Question 4

> What type of image is created by a vector drawing process?
>
> ○ a. Bitmap
>
> ○ b. Raster
>
> ○ c. Pixel
>
> ○ d. dpi

Answer b is correct. Raster images are mathematically created by a vector-drawing process. Microsoft calls vector-based fonts *vector fonts*. You might also hear them called *raster fonts*. Bitmap images are grids of pixels; a grid position either has a dot of some color or is blank (containing the background color).

Question 5

> The total memory available to Windows 3.x at startup is called —————?
>
> ○ a. The global heap
>
> ○ b. Swap file
>
> ○ c. Extended memory
>
> ○ d. Expanded memory

Answer a is correct. The *global heap* in Windows 3.x is the entire amount of memory available at startup. Windows reads the existing environment created by CONFIG.SYS and HIMEM.SYS (if it was loaded). Whatever programs have been installed by DOS prior to running Windows are recognized by Windows, and whatever memory is actually available for programs is taken by Windows.

Question 6

What type of files are used by Windows 3.x for page overflow?

- ○ a. Temporary data files
- ○ b. Check files located in the root directory
- ○ c. OVL files stored in the windows directory
- ○ d. Permanent and temporary swap files

Answer d is correct. In Enhanced mode, Windows has two ways to set aside space on a hard drive to handle page overflow: *temporary* and *permanent* swap files. Windows 3.x can manage a maximum of 16MB of installed RAM, but it can use far more than that by saving 4K pages (chunks) of memory to the disk as a swap file. The default location of the swap file is the root directory of the drive Windows was installed to, usually the C: drive.

Need To Know More?

 Andrews, Jean: *A+ Exam Prep.* Coriolis. ISBN 1-57610-241-6. Pages 437 through 463 discuss memory utilization within DOS, 16-bit Windows, and Windows 95. Pages 519 through 578 discuss Windows-specific issues.

 Karney, James: *Upgrade and Maintain Your PC.* MIS Press. ISBN 1-55828-460-5. Pages 31 through 57 address operating systems, including 16-bit and 32-bit Windows from the standpoint of selecting the best operating system given a specific set of needs. Although this information is not covered on the exam, it is good material to know.

Windows 95

Terms you'll need to understand:

√ Virtual device drivers (VxDs)

√ PnP (Plug 'n' Play)

√ Log files

√ Safe mode

√ Registry

√ FAT32 and long file names (LFN)

√ Protocols

√ Network

√ Peer-to-peer networks

√ Client-server networks

Concepts you'll need to master:

√ Right mouse click (alternative click)

√ Using the Installation Wizard

√ Running the step-by-step startup sequence

√ Using REGEDIT

√ The Registry

√ Enabling Windows 95 networking

√ Using Windows 95 Explorer

Windows 95 Overview

Operating system development is evolutionary, not revolutionary, and understanding previous versions is often the key to understanding present ones. Although Windows 98 has shipped, its most important change seems to be the integration of the Microsoft Internet Explorer browser with the Desktop. Windows 98 is still too new to be included on the certification exam.

Windows 95 is the latest Microsoft offering in the ever-upward movement toward a fully graphical, 32-bit multitasking operating system. Although the usual description of Windows 95 is that it is an operating system, the technical fact remains that Windows 95 requires DOS 7 and a 16-bit FAT for file management. In fact, many of DOS 7's more powerful commands and utilities remain, being designed to work directly with the graphic component of the operating system. All this is necessary because no one can afford to write off the massive installed base of PCs and existing applications.

Many of the executable programs that were found in DOS 6.x have their same-name counterparts in version 7 but can be run only from within the GUI of Windows 95. Defrag (DEFRAG.EXE) is an important program that can be run only under the GUI, whereas ScanDisk, XCOPY, EDIT, and MSD.EXE still run in either plain DOS or an MS DOS window.

SCANDISK.EXE is a particular example of the transitional aspect of Windows 95. DOS 6.x introduced the utility as a replacement for CHKDSK.EXE. ScanDisk offers more user interaction and combines several different types of disk-checking procedures. Originally, ScanDisk was a plain DOS program. The version offered with DOS 7 can now run as a text-based program, or a Windows-based program, depending on which interface the program starts from.

> *Note: The fact that SCANDISK.EXE runs before Windows 95 is even set up, and that in OSR/2 (version B) a crash and improper close will automatically run ScanDisk, shows you how important DOS continues to be.*

The startup process still opens into DOS before loading Windows, and starting the Windows from the DOS command mode still requires running WIN.COM to load Windows 95. The old QBASIC that supported EDIT disappeared, but the new Windows 95 version of Edit allows full Windows functionality (e.g., scrollbars, mouse pointer, and cut-and-paste) to seamlessly carry into DOS windows (unlike Windows 3.x).

The MS DOS windowed sessions in Windows 95 have taken on the GUI functions of Windows applications, with copy and paste functions, along with resizable text fonts.

It might help to think of the Windows versions as a transitional system moving from DOS to NT. Windows 95 moves farther toward the GUI environment, but is still composed of two intertwined components: the DOS component and the graphic interface component. The GUI component can't work without the DOS component, whereas the DOS component has such limited functionality that it's almost not worth running alone. The important thing to know about the DOS component is that it controls the physical file locations on the disk and is required for disk partitioning.

Windows 95 comes with many of the features found in Windows NT, making it superior in memory management and device control over Windows 3.x. In fact, the improved device handling of new virtual device drivers (VxDs) makes it more efficient to run almost any DOS program (including difficult game software) in a Windows 95 MS DOS window, or *session*—the virtual DOS machine. We've mentioned that the primary shell is an upgraded File Manager (i.e., EXPLORER.EXE), which incorporates the elements of a desktop that once was unusable space sitting behind Program Manager.

The Windows 3.x desktop wasn't completely unusable in that when an icon was minimized, Windows put it on the desktop. However, the Windows 3.x desktop was really only a place to store minimized icons rather than a place to organize work and applications. Windows 95 uses the Desktop as the main metaphor and the Start button, Taskbar, and Tray in place of the old Program Manager.

When you start Windows 95, the new Desktop is nearly empty. The only icons that Setup installs are My Computer, Network Neighborhood, and the Recycle Bin. To provide interactive help to a novice user, the Taskbar is at the bottom of the screen and the Start button is prominently displayed. Rather than having Program Groups with icons sitting inside them, Windows 95 groups the programs in a cascading series of menus, growing from each menu item on a previous list, starting from the main Start menu.

 Windows 95 can read GRP files and INI files from a Windows 3.x installation and convert all Program Groups to cascading menus. For this reason, you should back up the existing set of these files before running an upgrade installation.

Right-Click For Properties

The user is provided with a Properties menu list for every aspect of Windows 95 that is always available by right-clicking the mouse. Microsoft began introducing the expected, future break from backward compatibility with Windows NT. The company launched the "fully Windows 95–compatible" strategy. This meant that in order for new software and hardware to represent itself as conforming to the Windows 95 standards, Microsoft had to be involved in a certification process and authorize the use of its logo on the packaging. Essentially, Microsoft is bringing to a close the instability problems of constant workarounds in the operating system that were brought on by trying to maintain the compatibility and looseness of the old DOS environment.

The right mouse button had been mostly useless in all the previous versions of Windows. A few pioneering companies (e.g., Borland) decided to use the right button to offer a shortcut to the main menu at the top of the screen. This was called a *properties floating menu*. The idea caught on, and Windows 95 compatibility requires that all programs running under Windows 95 use the right-click of the mouse for properties.

 CompTIA refers to clicking the right mouse button as "alternative click(ing)." This alternative click process has nothing to do with pressing the ALT key.

Windows 95 differs from Windows 3.1x primarily by:

➤ Using IO.SYS and MSDOS.SYS as the primary device-loading programs rather than CONFIG.SYS and AUTOEXEC.BAT

➤ Using loadable, dynamic, 32-bit virtual device drivers alongside static, fixed, 16-bit VxDs

➤ Using OLE *shortcut objects*, with links to data and/or the programs that created the data

➤ Using a floating Properties menu accessed by right-clicking the mouse or using a special Windows key on Windows 95 specialty keyboards (not at all unlike the special command key used on Apple keyboards)

➤ Allowing long file names (LFN) through a virtual FAT (VFAT)

➤ Placing most of the system configuration details in the Registry files

➤ Showing the user a Desktop with a Taskbar and Start button rather than Program Manager, Program Groups, and Task Manager

➤ Including a more sophisticated and integrated Installation Wizard and Installation Shield for installing new software

➤ Improving the integration of networking within the Windows environment

➤ Improving system resource control with a larger memory heap

➤ Microsoft's becoming directly involved in controlling the Windows 95–compatible certification and approval of software applications

Installing Windows 95

Windows 95 provides two installation methods and several different versions. The two installation methods are the *upgrade* and *full version*. The upgrade installation materials (disks or CD-ROM) require that the computer already have a copy of DOS and Windows 3.x installed, whereas the full installation disks require that no previous copy of Windows exists on the installation hard drive. Both formats require a logical partition with more than 32MB of free space.

Although the Windows 95 upgrade can be installed in a way that the computer can boot up into either Windows 3.x or Windows 95, the documentation doesn't really explain how to maintain the full integrity of DOS files earlier than version 7 and all the existing Windows 3.x files. All the previous DOS and Windows 3.x files will ordinarily be removed from the hard drive.

Note: Third-party books about Windows 95 often provide far clearer documentation and understanding of how to install an upgrade in such a way as to keep the Windows 3.x system safe and retain older DOS versions.

CD-ROM Device Drivers

Windows 95 often comes preinstalled on a hard drive, the installation being done at the retail point of sale. Usually, disk images are copied to the hard drive, and the user has the option of making floppies from these images. Otherwise, Windows 95 is available on CD-ROM. Disk images are special files that can be used to create an exact copy of a floppy disk, including bootable floppies.

The CD-ROM drive requires a device driver. On a system on which Windows 95 is running smoothly, the CD-ROM device is handled by Windows 95's internal list of device drivers. Many computer vendors don't include any external device driver for the CD-ROM drive, assuming that Windows 95 is a full operating system. If the hard drive becomes irrevocably corrupted and must be reformatted, how will the user use the CD-ROM drive to install Windows 95 from a CD-ROM?

The full installation version of Windows 95 includes a bootable 3½-inch disk for partitioning and formatting, but doesn't include the

CD-ROM device drivers. It is good practice to maintain a separate DOS system disk with the CD-ROM device driver for the installed drive.

Installation Phases

Another feature added to Windows 95 is the *wizards* that are used for walking the user step by step through a process. Applications often use wizards to help with complex tasks in which it might be difficult to remember all the steps involved in completing those tasks. The Windows 95 Installation Wizard works with the Installation Shield, almost like a complicated batch file.

When you double-click the Setup program for any new application, the Installation Wizard starts, then asks the relevant hardware and software questions and produces an event log for the Install/Uninstall applet in the Control Panel. The Installation Wizard makes sure that all the steps are followed in the correct sequence to successfully install the application.

The four phases for installing Windows 95 are as follows:

1. The startup and information-gathering phase

2. The hardware detection phase

3. The copying and expanding files phase

4. The final system configuration phase

Windows 95 takes over more of the decision-making process from the user and provides more direct control over how the software will be installed on a given computer. Again, the idea is to make *using* the computer as far removed from the technical configuration of that computer as possible. Many potential problems that arise in installations can be traced to the fact that the computer is still under the control of the user, and not every computer is set up exactly as the Installation Wizard expects to see it.

Startup And Information-Gathering Phase

When you run SETUP.EXE from a DOS prompt, the program searches all local drives for a previous version of Windows (3.x or 95). If you started from DOS, the program assumes that an existing copy of DOS is on the bootable hard drive. If a previous version of Windows is found, one of two things will happen, depending on whether you have an upgrade or a full installation version of Windows 95 to install. If you're using an upgrade version, Setup pauses, then suggests that you run Setup from within Windows. If you're installing a full installation version, Setup quits, then displays an error message that a previous copy of Windows was found. The suggestion to run Setup from within Windows can be bypassed.

It may come in handy to know that Setup only looks for WIN.COM and WINVER.EXE to determine if a previous version of Windows exists on the drive. If you need to reinstall the upgrade version of Windows 95, it's less messy and you can save a lot of time by just copying these two files to a C:\WINDOWS directory, then running the Windows 95 setup.

If you need to reinstall a Windows 95 system and you only have the full installation version CD, you can just delete or rename WIN.COM and run Setup. The system won't detect the presence of the Windows 95 installation.

As phase 1 continues, Setup runs SCANDISK.EXE (located on the installation disk) and looks at the hard drive to make sure that it's running correctly and that it meets the minimum requirements for installing Windows 95 (e.g., enough memory, modern CPU, and disk space). If any of the setup requirements is missing, the installation quits.

The rest of phase 1 checks for extended memory and runs an XMS memory manager if one isn't running. Setup installs HIMEM.SYS if no other extended memory manager is found. Setup then checks memory for any existing TSRs that are known to cause problems, then pauses to warn you before proceeding.

Windows 95 requires extended memory. If no other memory management program is loaded, Setup installs HIMEM.SYS and IO.SYS loads HIMEM every time the system starts.

From a DOS startup, Setup installs the minimum files required to run Windows 3.1 and starts the kernel using the SHELL=SETUP.EXE in the SYSTEM.INI file. Until this point, Setup is running in Real mode, and nothing is showing on the monitor until the system starts the GUI.

Once the GUI starts, the Installation Wizard begins prompting the user for which components will be installed and various networking options. It asks for user information, registration information, and which directory to install Windows in. When all the questions have been answered, the Installation Wizard moves on to the next phase.

Hardware Detection Phase

At this point, the newer features of Plug 'n' Play (PnP) and the concept of VxDs come into effect. Setup checks the entire system for hardware and peripherals attached to the computer. It also checks the system resources for I/O addresses, IRQs, and DMAs. This is where Windows 95 begins to build the first *Registry*.

The Windows 95 Registry is a set of two files. SYSTEM.DAT is the main file and can become very large. USER.DAT is the second file, containing mostly configuration information. We will be discussing the Registry at length later in this chapter, but the two files have been introduced here so that you don't get lost.

 PnP is a standards specification that attempts to remove IRQ and DMA conflicts among hardware devices. PnP data must be built in to ROM BIOS and a BIOS chip on the device. Finally, the operating system must be able to read the BIOS data and work with it for configuration purposes.

PnP devices communicate to Windows 95 what they are and which resources they need to run. For non-PnP devices, Windows 95 looks at I/O ports and specific memory addresses, compares them against a database of known devices, and makes a best guess. If the computer has PnP BIOS, Windows 95 queries the system board's CMOS for all installed devices and their configurations. This same hardware detection process is used from the Control Panel under the Add New Hardware option when any new hardware device is added to the computer.

 The Windows 95 Registry is built around six master sections called Hkey_[SectionName] where [SectionName] is the name of each specific section. At the top of the Registry tree is Hkey_Classes_Root. The section used for hardware is Hkey_Local_Machine.

Copying And Expanding Files Phase

A number of *archiving programs* have been developed over time to pack as many files as possible onto a relatively small floppy disk. These programs (e.g., PKZip, Extract, and LHArc) change the form of a file to reduce its size (compression). Microsoft uses EXTRACT.EXE to *expand* these stored programs back to their original sizes. The DOS COPY command is insufficient to install either Windows 3.x or Windows 95 because the files are on the installation disks in archived form.

The File Copy phase uses a list of files that has been created during the hardware detection phase, depending on which components should be installed. Windows 95 then copies all necessary files to the installation destination directory and extracts them to their full executable size. While the files are in their compressed format, DOS is unable to read or execute the programs. Various Setup DLL files are run after the files are copied to create directories that might not exist and to install network capabilities.

Creating A Startup Disk

The Installation Wizard offers the user the option to make a startup disk during the files expansion phase of the installation. The disk can be made at this time, or the option can be bypassed. If the option is bypassed, a startup disk can be made at any time by using the Add/Remove Software applet in Control Panel. The startup disk requires a minimum of 1.2MB of storage.

Emergency Startup Disk

The so-called emergency startup disk is designed mainly for troubleshooting the Windows 95 program and system. Many users think that the disk is a way to start their computers in DOS mode and to access the regular features and configuration of their PCs. However, the disk assumes that Windows 95 is available on the hard drive, but is not starting for some reason.

The files on the startup diskette include the bootable system files (COMMAND.COM, IO.SYS, and MSDOS.SYS) along with FDISK, FORMAT, EDIT, SYS.COM, and a few other files for low-level access to partitioning and reformatting. Note that the copies of IO.SYS and MSDOS.SYS are the startup files for Windows 95, not the same files that started DOS 6.x and earlier.

> *Note: If Windows 95 has become corrupted, the startup disk does not contain any device drivers or CONFIG.SYS or AUTOEXEC.BAT files to get the computer up and running. The computer will start, leaving the user at a plain DOS command line and with no device drivers loaded (e.g., CD-ROM drive).*

Final System Configuration Phase

At this point, Setup makes irrevocable changes to any preexisting Windows 3.x files and directories. Setup makes upgrades to files in the C:\WINDOWS and C:\WINDOWS\SYSTEM directories and installs DOS 7 to the C:\WINDOWS\COMMAND directory. DOS 7 replaces COMMAND. COM with a new version of COMMAND.COM.

To protect a previous version of DOS during installation, keep a copy of the three system files in a different directory than the root directory (perhaps C:\OLD_DOS). Unless any files in the C:\DOS directory have been protected, Setup removes them and prepares the computer for Windows 95. To allow booting from a previous version of DOS, Windows 95 must be set up in its own directory, and the older system must remain intact.

Because Windows 95 has a tendency to insist on looking in the WINDOWS and WINDOWS\SYSTEM folders (subdirectories) for files, it's usually best to rename the Windows 3.x \WINDOWS directories to something new (e.g., WIN3_1) and install Windows 95 into the expected WINDOWS folder. Likewise, to protect a previous version of DOS, it's best to transfer copies of everything in the DOS directory to something like DOS6_0 to avoid the high probability of losing them during Windows 95 installation.

Setup prompts the user to restart the computer to continue the installation from within Windows 95. Prior to restarting the computer, Setup:

➤ Modifies the boot sector of the boot drive and replaces the previous version of IO.SYS with the new Windows 95 version

➤ Replaces the old MSDOS.SYS with the Windows 95 version

➤ Renames preexisting versions of the (hidden) DOS system files as IO.DOS and MSDOS.DOS

➤ Updates MSDOS.SYS with device drivers, startup mode notations, and any preexisting CONFIG.SYS settings, along with any new configuration information that Windows 95 will require at startup

First Restart

Windows 95 keeps track of the start and restart events both during installation and with each new session. Following a successful restart of the computer for the first time during an installation, Windows 95 makes further updates to the configuration of the system through the following process:

1. WINIT.EXE processes three sections of the WINIT.INI file (arial.win, user32.tmp, and logo.sys) to create a combined VMM32.VXD with all the VxDs needed by the specific computer.

2. SYSTEM.DAT is renamed SYSTEM.DA0, and SYSTEM.NEW is renamed SYSYTEM.DAT.

3. The Registry flag is set to indicate that this is the first time Windows 95 is being run following a new installation.

4. The Run Once module is run to configure printers, MIDI, and PCMCIA devices (on a new computer), and to run any new hardware manufacturer's custom setup program(s).

5. If the installation was done over a preexisting Windows 3.x system, GRPCONV.EXE converts all Program Groups and Program Items from the previous version of Windows to Windows 95 format and renames the files to use long file names.

Installation Log Files

Windows 95 Setup tracks each phase of an installation and makes success or fail notations in SUWARN.BAT. Setup also makes notations in the AUTOEXEC.BAT prior to a successful complete installation. Much of the moment-by-moment installation process is tracked in SETUPLOG.TXT and DETCRASH.LOG in case the setup crashes. If the installation and setup are successful, DETCRASH.LOG is deleted.

The Windows 95 Setup can fail at three points:

1. When insufficient, incorrect, or unavailable system resources are detected during SETUP.EXE in Real mode

2. When a crash occurs during the hardware detection phase, creating DETCRASH.LOG

3. When a device stops working following hardware detection

Setup uses SETUPLOG.TXT to list information about the steps in the installation, including their sequence and the error information returned at the end of the step (whether it completed successfully or why not). In case of a failed setup, Windows 95 uses SETUPLOG.TXT to bypass the steps that completed successfully and continues only with the steps that failed.

If the installation of Windows 95 fails, the process is designed to continue from a restart of the computer. Rather than reformat the drive and reinstall from the beginning, restart the computer and let Windows 95 Setup pick up where it left off, trying to correct the installation problem itself.

Log Files

Windows 95 uses a number of *log files* for tracking the state of applications and the way in which the applications load. During installation, even with custom choices and settings offered by the Installation Wizard, Windows 95 still fails to install many of the additional utilities that come with Windows 95 on the installation disks or CD-ROM.

The files in the root directory that Windows 95 Setup uses to track installation and successful configuration are:

➤ **SETUPLOG.TXT** Setup sequence and pass/fail

➤ **DETLOG.TXT** Hardware detection log file

➤ **NETLOG.TXT** Networking setup log file

➤ **DETCRASH.LOG** Hardware detection failure/crash log

➤ **BOOTLOG.TXT** Success/fail boot sequence log

DETLOG.TXT keeps track of what hardware devices are found on the system. BOOTLOG.TXT keeps track of the first startup process and the success or failure of each step.

If the F8 Startup Menu key is pressed, BOOTLOG.TXT can be changed to reflect the current startup, and the previous version is overwritten. To keep a copy of the original installation startup sequence, copy BOOTLOG.TXT to another name (e.g., FIRSBOOT.TXT).

Windows 95 includes the SYSEDIT.EXE program that came with Windows 3.11. SysEdit examines initial configuration files, but doesn't open the Windows 95 log files. Log files can be opened with any ASCII text editor (e.g., WordPad) for viewing and printing.

Log files are plain ASCII text files (TXT) that show when a program was last run and that report any problems encountered at the time. If they find no problems, the log file holds an exit-status report. The LOGVIEW.EXE program utility is similar to SYSEDIT, but shows all the log files on the drive.

LOGVIEW.EXE is found in the OTHER\MISC\LOGVIEW folder on the Windows 95 installation CD-ROM and must be copied from the CD-ROM manually to a destination on the hard drive.

BOOTLOG.TXT

The BOOTLOG.TXT file is a hidden ASCII text file located in the root directory of the primary active drive. This file keeps a record of the entire startup process for the first time Windows 95 is installed successfully. The F8 option for an interactive Startup menu (pressed when the "Starting Windows 95" message displays at bootup) allows you to create a new BOOTLOG.TXT file at any time. Additionally, you can create a new file by using the /B switch with WIN.COM (i.e., WIN /B) from a DOS command prompt.

The details in the BOOTLOG.TXT file are written in sequence during the startup and generally break down to about five major sections. Although a line in the BOOTLOG.TXT file might indicate that something has failed, it doesn't necessarily mean that the startup process has aborted. For example, a loadfailed= line entry means that the specified VxD failed to load for some reason, probably because whatever the driver was referring to doesn't exist or couldn't be found.

It's usually wise to make a copy of the file before creating a new one, just to have a copy of a successful installation and startup.

Starting Windows 95

Windows 95 requires a minimum of 3MB of uncompressed space on the bootup partition (i.e., Active, Primary). Under DOS and Windows 3.x, the DOS system files were COMMAND.COM, MSDOS.SYS (IBMDOS.SYS), and IO.SYS (IBMBIO.SYS). The DOS command processor looked to the CONFIG.SYS file to load device drivers, and it also transferred control to AUTOEXEC.BAT to display recurring configuration commands at startup.

Windows 95 changed the basic system files, using the hidden IO.SYS to read configuration and device information from the MSDOS.SYS hidden file, a CONFIG.SYS file (if one is present), or both. IO.SYS must still be in the boot sector of the bootable partition; MSDOS.SYS is placed in the root directory, also hidden. COMMAND.COM is also carried forward in DOS 7, and installed in the WINDOWS directory.

 Technically speaking, IO.SYS reads CONFIG.SYS, then MSDOS.SYS, then passes control to MSDOS.SYS. After MSDOS.SYS, control passes to COMMAND.COM, which reads CONFIG.SYS *again* before passing control to AUTOEXEC.BAT.

While technically, CONFIG.SYS is read twice, we believe the exam expects CONFIG.SYS (if it exists) to process following COMMAND.COM. This is one of those ambiguous, imprecise questions where Microsoft says what happens, but the proper response isn't listed on the exam.

IO.SYS runs first from DOS 7 (just as it did in DOS 6.x) but contains a series of commands for processing device drivers out of both the MSDOS.SYS and the CONFIG.SYS file. CONFIG.SYS and AUTOEXEC.BAT are still required by some applications, which won't start without finding one of these files. The Windows 95 emergency recovery utility (ERU) requires that a CONFIG.SYS and AUTOEXEC.BAT file exist.

POST And Bootstrap

No matter which operating system you use, the motherboard's ROM BIOS runs the POST routine when the computer is first turned on. Everything that applies to a plain DOS computer applies to a Windows 95 computer. The bootstrap loader (discussed in Chapter 8) looks to the boot sector of the Primary, Active (boot) partition for instructions on how to start whatever operating system is installed on that partition.

The boot sector and the master boot record (MBR) are technically two different things. However, the exam tends to confuse the two and may ask you to treat the MBR as though it were another name for boot sector.

Windows 95 looks in the boot sector, where it finds IO.SYS. Windows NT and OS/2 can be booted from the *boot track,* making it possible to boot them from a different partition than the Primary, Active one. In Windows 95, the "Starting Windows 95..." message is displayed on the screen following the initial POST and parity check, and is written into IO.SYS.

Pressing F8 between the "Starting Windows 95..." message and the Windows 95 logo splash screen will interrupt the boot process and allow you to choose various options from a Startup menu (more on this shortly).

Note: A "splash screen" is jargon for anything that appears on the screen prior to the actual program environment. This can often be a corporate logo, a shareware registration screen, or simply a notification screen that the program is still being prepared to run.

DOS

If you remember the DOS boot sequence, you'll recognize IO.SYS as one of the system files in DOS startup trio. IO.SYS is a hidden system file in the root directory of the bootable partition and starts DOS in Real mode. IO.SYS in Windows 95 does the same thing as in DOS. It sets up the segment addressing in conventional memory and loads low-level Real mode device drivers into the first segment of memory (low memory). IO.SYS then reads MSDOS.SYS (or an existing CONFIG.SYS file).

Windows 95 uses a preliminary hardware profile from the hardware detection phase to attempt to start the computer (e.g., interrupts, BIOS serial and parallel ports, and CMOS or BIOS system board identification). Once the computer is started for the first time, the Registry tells Windows 95 which settings to use at startup. IO.SYS reads the MSDOS.SYS file to process specific devices and the Registry (SYSTEM.DAT) for device *settings.*

If a CONFIG.SYS file, an AUTOEXEC.BAT file, or both are supposed to run, IO.SYS loads the COMMAND.COM command interpreter and runs the two configuration files. Depending on which lines are found in these files, DOS runs other Real mode commands and programs. Remember that whatever is loaded into the DOS environment at this point will descend to any DOS sessions run from within Windows.

CONFIG.SYS Confusion

IO.SYS runs once to determine whether a CONFIG.SYS file should be read. Then it drops out to allow the CONFIG.SYS file to load any Real mode device drivers, if any exist. Once an existing CONFIG.SYS file has completed, IO.SYS returns to read MSDOS.SYS again for the rest of the startup process.

As we've said, this quick pass into CONFIG.SYS can lead to some confusion on the exam. Our information comes from the Microsoft technical description of the Windows 95 start process, though we found it to be difficult to find. In our opinion, the exam makes an assumption that this first look at CONFIG.SYS doesn't happen.

 Before loading hardware device drivers from a CONFIG.SYS and an AUTOEXEC.BAT file, try commenting them out to see whether Windows 95's autodetection capabilities can run those devices with VxDs.

MSDOS.SYS

Whether or not CONFIG.SYS, AUTOEXEC.BAT, or both exist, IO.SYS reads the MSDOS.SYS file first and reads it again for VxDs and other configuration settings. MSDOS.SYS is a plain ASCII text file that can be edited by DOS's EDIT.COM or Microsoft's WordPad. The important point is that all attributes are set on the file, making it hidden, system, and read-only. Before you can edit MSDOS.SYS, you're expected to know what you're doing and how to change the file attributes (see Chapter 11).

The MSDOS.SYS file tells Windows 95 about multiple booting options, Startup menus, which mode to start in, and whether the Windows 95 GUI is supposed to start at all following bootup. If you press and hold the Shift key before the Windows splash screen instead of the F8 key, MSDOS.SYS is bypassed and not read at all.

WIN.COM

If MSDOS.SYS is configured to start Windows 95, it runs WIN.COM and loads Windows. Windows then looks for and runs WINSTART.BAT if the file is found. MSDOS.SYS contains path locations for important Windows files, including where to find the Registry. To enable the F4 shortcut key option (discussed shortly) of running a previous version of DOS, the directive BootMulti= must have the value 1 (BootMulti=1) in the [Options] section of MSDOS.SYS.

Start Sequence

Remember that Windows 95/98 is an interim interface that's trying to keep compatible with 16-bit Windows 3.x and DOS 6.x applications. Microsoft is also trying to induce programmers to write programs in the Windows NT 32-bit format. The resulting combination of 16-bit Windows, DOS, Windows NT, and 32-bit Windows 95 is confusing. Files have the same names, but act completely differently, and there's no easy way to remember what's what. Again, we think that understanding Windows 95 from the floor up will help you on the certification exam.

We found a number of questions that tested your understanding of the exact sequence of startup programs. The important files to remember are IO.SYS, MSDOS.SYS, COMMAND.COM, CONFIG.SYS, AUTOEXEC.BAT, and WIN.COM (just like DOS), along with SYSTEM.DAT and USER.DAT (the Registry).

We include a detailed process with many other files to provide a framework and context for visualizing the overall startup sequence.

If IO.SYS determines that a CONFIG.SYS file, an AUTOEXEC.BAT file, or both exist, their listed device drivers and TSRs are run and loaded into memory in Real mode. Following any Real mode device drivers, Windows 95 loads any *static* VxDs required by Windows 3.1x programs.

Virtual device drivers were first introduced in Windows 3.1 by loading into memory and remaining there throughout the session, making them static, that is, not moving. Windows 95 dynamic VxDs can be loaded into memory for use, then unloaded when a program terminates, if the VxD is no longer needed.

Just as in Windows 3.1x, the executable Virtual Machine Manager (VMM) runs, but this time VMM32.VXD includes both a Real mode loader and the VMM as well as common, static VxDs from 16-bit format (in MRCI2.VXD).

VMM32.VXD is a combination file with many common VxD files bound up inside it. Typical VxD files are about 80K, and typical VMM32.VXD files are about 650K. The devices found inside this file were once loaded in the [386Enh] section of the SYSTEM.INI file. Windows 95 first checks the WINDOWS\SYSTEM\VMM32 directory for any 32-bit VXD files, rather than the VxDs bound in VMM32.VXD, and loads any newer files from there.

Assuming Windows 95 finds no later-version virtual device drivers in the VMM32 folder, VMM32.VXD loads static device drivers found in the DEVICE= line of the SYSTEM.INI file (which still comes with Windows 95). The actual devices load from within VMM32 but show in the SYSTEM.INI file for backward compatibility.

The Registry contains entries for every VXD file and, through its processing, controls VMM32.VXD. The Registry also contains entries for every VxD that isn't directly associated with a piece of hardware. If two devices have a conflict at load time, the VxD in the SYSTEM.INI DEVICE= takes precedence over the one specified by the Registry. If the device can't be found, an error occurs.

As Windows 95 starts up, the following three files are run in the sequence listed here (note the continued use of WIN.COM and SYSTEM.INI):

➤ **WIN.COM** Controls the initial environment checks and loads the core Windows 95 components

➤ **VMM32.VXD** Creates the virtual machine (VM) and installs all VxDs

➤ **SYSTEM.INI** Is read for DEVICE= entries, which may differ from the Registry entries

Final Steps To Loading Windows 95

Once device drivers have been loaded into memory and the Virtual Machine is up and running, Windows loads KERNEL32.DLL for the main Windows 95 components and KRNL386.EXE, which loads Windows 3.x device drivers. GDI.EXE and GDI32.EXE load next, followed by USER.EXE and USER32.EXE. Notice the continued path from Windows 3.1x as the same files append a "32" to their names.

In order to ensure backward compatibility, Windows 95 loads in the same way the Windows 3.x loads. One of the primary differences, though, is that Windows 95 runs DOS programming code under a virtual 8086 machine rather than a Real mode machine. The upgrade installation shows some of the results of the overall compatibility path where Windows 95 uses a Real mode driver for a device during installation. Once the installation is complete and Windows 95 starts from the hard disk, Windows 95 goes back and checks to see whether or not it has an internal 32-bit VxD that matches the device driver in memory. If it does, it comments out the original device's line in either CONFIG.SYS or AUTOEXEC.BAT.

When the startup process calls WIN.COM to start Windows 95, the SYSTEM.INI file is read for Real mode device drivers, and the SYSTEM.DAT file is read for the rest of the device configurations. In other words, Windows 95 reads both the Windows 3.x INI files and the Registry DAT files as it loads. Most of the devices and their configuration are installed from the SYSTEM.DAT file, but SYSTEM.INI is read first.

Following the SYSTEM.INI and SYSTEM.DAT processing, WIN.INI is read for associated resources and environment values such as fonts, wallpaper, associated file extensions, and so on. Once WIN.INI has been processed, the USER.DAT file is read.

If networking has been enabled, Windows 95 reads the USER.DAT file after the WIN.INI file, for Desktop configurations. Sometimes USER.DAT and networking are used on standalone machines, in order to maintain consistencies throughout a corporate environment. At home, networking can be enabled in order to allow individual family members their own customized Desktop.

Finally, the SHELL= line in SYSTEM.INI is run, loading EXPLORER.EXE, assuming that no other shell has been specified in a default installation.

You might want to keep in mind that Windows 98 seems to be more of an incremental upgrade/fix to Windows 95 in the same way that Windows 3.11 was a change/fix for Windows 3.1. The main change introduced in Windows 98 (and the subject of so much interest by the U.S. Department of Justice) is a very tight integration between the MS Explorer shell and the MS Internet Explorer Web browser.

A potential problem of this integration is that whereas Windows 95 ran Internet Explorer as a separate application in a separate window, Windows 98 is *always* running the browser as part of the operating system. In the event that the browser should happen to lock up during an Internet session, there's a very high likelihood that the whole system will crash rather than just the isolated window.

Rudimentary security can be configured for the Windows 3.x Program Manager by making changes to the PROGMAN.INI file. These security measures (now called *policies*) have been enhanced with the Windows 95 Policy Editor, allowing for more complete security maintenance.

Note: Policies and the Policy Editor are beyond the scope of this book. For more information on Windows 95 networking and policies, see the Microsoft Windows 95 Resource Kit, *published by Microsoft Press.*

Loading Device Drivers

IO.SYS has always been Microsoft's Real mode DOS system file, and Windows 95 continues to use it to begin the startup process. (If the computer is started using a previous version of DOS, IO.SYS is renamed WINBOOT.SYS.). Even in DOS 6.x, IO.SYS had rudimentary capabilities built into it to handle some of the basic directives of the CONFIG.SYS file. However, the program wasn't ready to assume full control until Windows 95.

The Windows 95 IO.SYS finally takes over from CONFIG.SYS and loads HIMEM.SYS, IFSHLP.SYS, SETVER.EXE, and DBLSPACE.BIN or DRVSPACE.BIN by default, if they exist (see Table 10.1). Additionally, the DOS 7 version includes defaults for all the old CONFIG.SYS directives, such as FILES, BUFFERS, COUNTRY, and SETVER.

Table 10.1	**The common device directives that moved from CONFIG.SYS to IO.SYS.**
DEVICE=	**Description**
DOS=HIGH	IO.SYS does not load EMM386.EXE (If this expanded memory manager is found in an existing CONFIG.SYS file, the UMB line is added.)
HIMEM.SYS	Real mode memory manager to access extended memory; part of IO.SYS by default
IFSHLP.SYS	Installable File System Helper that loads device drivers and allows the system to make file system connections from within Windows to the DOS file management I/O
SETVER.EXE	To maintain backward compatibility with some older TSRs that won't run under newer versions of COMMAND.COM; optional and usually not necessary
FILES=60 (default)	Included for compatibility; specifies how many files can be open at any one time when running an MS DOS session; not required by Windows 95
BUFFERS=30 (default)	Specifies the number of file buffers; used by IO.SYS calls from DOS and Windows 3.x programs
STACKS=9,256 (default)	The number and size of the stack frames that the CPU uses during prioritization of incoming interrupts; used for backward compatibility; not required by Windows 95
SHELL=C:\COMMAND.COM /p	Indicates which command processor to use (e.g., NDOS or DRDOS); not the same as the SHELL= line in SYSTEM.INI (If the directive is used, but the /p switch is not used, AUTOEXEC.BAT is not processed. /p makes the command processor permanent in the environment.)
FCBS=4 (default)	A very old method of controlling open files (file control blocks); necessary only with DOS programs designed for DOS 2.x and earlier

Note: CONFIG.SYS ordinarily doesn't use a SHELL= directive since the default assumption of the system is that COMMAND.COM is used and found on the boot disk. This directive is used primarily to increase the DOS environment space, and in that case, the /p switch must be included, as noted above. We will discuss the DOS environment further in Chapter 11.

Because of market pressures to maintain backward compatibility, IO.SYS still checks for a CONFIG.SYS file just as the older version did. If the CONFIG.SYS file is found and if it contains a DEVICE= line with the same directive as one found within IO.SYS, the one in CONFIG.SYS takes over.

To change a DEVICE setting from the default within IO.SYS, create a CONFIG.SYS file and use the same DEVICE= directive, but with a different setting. For example, FILES=100 would override the default FILES directive in IO.SYS and change the default from 60 to 100 possible open files. Some final thoughts to keep in mind regarding IO.SYS:

➤ IO.SYS cannot be edited (unlike MSDOS.SYS).

➤ Directive values in CONFIG.SYS must be set to the default or higher in IO.SYS to change their settings.

➤ EMM386.EXE can be loaded only in CONFIG.SYS for DOS, 16-bit Windows, and Windows 95.

AUTOEXEC.BAT

Windows 95 changes the process for loading device drivers (as we've seen) and uses IO.SYS along with the Registry (SYSTEM.DAT) and the SYSTEM.INI file to load and set the values associated with each driver. However, to keep the backward compatibility, Windows 95 looks for both the CONFIG.SYS and the AUTOEXEC.BAT file to load older Real mode DOS drivers and TSRs.

Windows 95 specifically disables (with REM) SMARTDRV, DBLBUFF.SYS, and MOUSE.SYS from any existing CONFIG.SYS, and disables any incompatible TSRs in an existing AUTOEXEC.BAT file by using an internal "known conflicts" list. It removes WIN and SHARE commands from an existing AUTOEXEC.BAT file, if they exist, and updates the PATH line.

Note: Before making updates to an existing AUTOEXEC.BAT, Windows 95 copies the file to AUTOEXEC.DOS.

Many of the older device drivers that were needed for DOS and Windows 3.x are handled by the loadable VxDs in Windows 95. Microsoft says (in a technical white paper) that it will use 32-bit code in Windows 95 "wherever it significantly improves performance without sacrificing application compatibility, or where 32-bit code would increase memory requirements without significantly improving performance." To that extent, it's sometimes difficult to tell whether a given device would be better off using the Windows 95 32-bit VxD or the 16-bit device driver loaded from within CONFIG.SYS.

Devices loaded from CONFIG.SYS often require command line-setting switches in the AUTOEXEC.BAT file. An AUTOEXEC.BAT file is usually required to set the path to something other than the Windows 95 default search path (C:\WINDOWS; C:\WINDOWS\COMMAND). Likewise, an AUTOEXEC.BAT file is needed to change the Temporary (TEMP) directory to something other than C:\WINDOWS\TEMP.

Networking usually requires an AUTOEXEC.BAT file to run the command for NET START. However, because Windows 95 is designed to handle many of the networking capabilities from within itself, it's usually better to create a separate batch file for starting the network and then place that file in the Startup folder. Generally, for everything except the most ornery DOS-based Real mode programs, let Windows 95 try to use one of its own VxDs.

SYSTEM.INI And WIN.INI

Windows 3.x used the SYSTEM.INI and WIN.INI files to load various devices and to set the overall Windows environment. We've seen that Windows 95 still uses these two files and that devices in the SYSTEM.INI take precedence over those in the Registry if there's a conflict over two of the same devices. The Windows 95 Control panel allows you to change many of the Registry settings from within a Windows session:

➤ Memory-related options are set in the System option of Control Panel.

➤ Hardware device options or parameters are set in the Device Manager option of Control Panel.

➤ Network and resource-sharing parameters are set in the Network option of Control Panel.

➤ Mouse and Keyboard options and parameters are set from the Mouse and the Keyboard option, respectively, of the Control Panel.

➤ All screen and display options are set either from the Display option of the Control Panel or by right-clicking on the Desktop and selecting Properties.

Useful Additional Components

Oddly enough, Windows 95 doesn't automatically install some of the more useful utilities that come on the installation CD-ROM. Among these extra utilities are the Accessibility options for people with disabilities, the LOGVIEW program mentioned earlier, and the Emergency Recovery Utility (ERU.EXE), which can back up the Registry files. Although the Accessibility options are important for people who need them, they can be useful for just about anyone. (The Accessibility options are routinely installed during an Express setup.)

Not all the extra utilities are listed in the Windows Setup Wizard. For example, the Emergency Recovery Utility is in the OTHER\MISC\ERU folder and must be manually copied to the hard drive. Remember that you can click once on the folder icon and press Ctrl+C to copy, and then Ctrl+V to paste the entire folder into a new location—perhaps a new folder called Registry Backup, rather than the obscure ERU name.

To install additional Windows 95 components from Control Panel:

➤ Insert the installation CD-ROM into the drive bay

➤ Select Add/Remove Software

➤ Select the Windows Setup tab on the dialog box

➤ Check the new component's checkbox (leaving any previously installed check boxes gray). If you uncheck something that already was installed (showing as gray), Setup will assume that you mean to remove it.

The Registry

The Windows 95 Registry is an outgrowth of the Windows 3.1x Registration database (REG.DAT). This original database is a little-known tool that manages OLE and the drag-and-drop features in Windows. OLE is a way to place inside (embed) a document (client), a kind of pointer to data (package) from an outside program's (server's) data. This kind of document is called a *compound document* because you can view or edit the data in the OLE connection (link) without knowing which application created it.

For example, the [Embedding] section in the WIN.INI file might contain the entry PBrush=Paintbrush Picture,Paintbrush Picture,C:\Programs\Access\ MSPAINT.EXE,picture. This would indicate that a certain type of OLE picture object found in, say, an MS Word document should find MSPAINT.EXE in the specified location. Furthermore, the line tells Windows that it should use MS Paint to open the picture, when the picture's OLE object is double-clicked.

When a program can embed a piece of itself in the form of an embedded object, that program is said to be an *OLE server*. It's called a server because it provides functional services to the program trying to open the object—the *OLE client*.

The Registration database maintains information about the pathname and file names of OLE servers, the file names and extensions of data files and their associated programs, the class name of the objects that the OLE servers can edit (e.g., a picture), and protocols used by the objects. The Windows 3.1x Registration database is held in a binary file called REG.DAT, which can be edited only by using a registration information editor called REGEDIT.EXE.

OLE is a relatively new technology that Microsoft claims will increase the amount of interconnectivity among computer applications. Compound documents (they say) will focus users more on the data and documents they're working with rather than worrying about how to open and use a particular program. To some extent, the World Wide Web's HTML (Hypertext Markup Language) is bringing this about, though not necessarily by using OLE. The technology behind OLE and DDE is complex, but you should know what the acronyms stand for: object linking and embedding, and dynamic data exchange, respectively.

SYSTEM.DAT And USER.DAT

Windows 3.1x used a combination of the SYSTEM.INI, WIN.INI, and REG.DAT files to keep track of the device drivers, environmental settings, and *objects* being controlled by Windows. When Windows 95 came along, the decision was made to remove the two INI files and move as much as possible into a greatly expanded Registration database—changing the name to *the Registry*. Since then, the Windows 95 Registry has become one of the most obscure and complicated aspects of low-level work with Windows. Practically no one really understands the Windows Registry, but you should know how to identify some of its parts.

The Registry is composed of two files—SYSTEM.DAT and USER.DAT—both of which are binary and neither of which can be edited with Notepad, Edit, or any other ASCII editor. (The only way to edit the Registry is by using REGEDIT.EXE or a third-party program designed specifically for the purpose.)

Note: The data in SYSTEM.DAT can be exported (copied to another format) in an ASCII format, where it can be changed using an ASCII text editor. Once the changes have been saved, another feature of REGEDIT.EXE is that it can import (reabsorb information from

another format) the ASCII file, thereby changing SYSTEM.DAT.
However, REGEDIT.EXE is still required in order to perform the
export and import process.

REGEDIT.EXE is installed into the WINDOWS folder during setup. The two, final Registry files (DAT) are also stored in the WINDOWS folder, and have all their attributes set as Hidden, System, and Read-only. (ATTRIB.EXE and file attributes are discussed in Chapter 11.)

Although a common procedure for making a copy of SYSTEM.DAT includes turning off all the attributes in order for DOS to see the file, the Explorer or File Manager will happily copy or move hidden files with only a brief dialog box asking for confirmation. Be sure that you check a question about SYSTEM.DAT for any reference to which environment is being used.

SYSTEM.DAT holds the hardware and software configuration information for Windows 95, and USER.DAT contains specific environment configuration (e.g., the Desktop) for the user, that is, the *session user*. If networking is enabled and a computer is configured for multiple users, a separate USER.DAT file is created for each user. This file can be accessed by capturing the User ID and password at the time the user logs into Windows. Typically, the User ID is part of the file's name. For instance, Bob Smith's User ID might be BSmith, which would lead to a BSMITH.DAT file. USER.DAT is the default user configurations file, but all of these user files are part of the Registry.

The Structure Of INI Files Revisited

The Microsoft Windows 95 Resource Kit states that "the Registry simplifies the operating system by eliminating the need for AUTOEXEC.BAT, CONFIG.SYS, and .INI files (except when legacy applications require them)." This is about as true as saying that Congress simplifies the government of the country by eliminating the need for citizens to govern themselves. Initialization files are used routinely in Windows 95, and, as we've seen, both CONFIG.SYS and AUTOEXEC.BAT are alive and well. Yes, it's true that neither of the startup files are as necessary as before, and INI files aren't the *only* way to configure Windows 95, but they still exist and are used regularly.

Most, but not all, of the information that was once in INI files is now stored somewhere in the Registry. In some cases, Windows 95 itself creates new INI files (e.g., TELEPHON.INI) that didn't exist under Windows 3.x. Most INI files are stored in the WINDOWS folder (subdirectory). As a review:

➤ INI files can be edited by any ASCII-capable editor and store information that changes from computer to computer and program to program.

➤ Because every computer can be different, and because software can be different on every computer, INI files store specific settings and parameters for specific computers.

➤ INI files are divided by section headings enclosed by the reserved symbol of square brackets (e.g., [386Enh] or [Boot]).

➤ INI files often contain the name and location of files needed by Windows (e.g., txt=notepad.exe ^.txt), specific values for a particular setting (e.g., WallpaperStyle=0), and hardware or software configuration values (e.g., COM1:=9600,n,8,1,x).

The important INI files used by Windows 3.x and Windows 95 include SYSTEM.INI, WIN.INI, PROGMAN.INI, and CONTROL.INI (Control Panel). PROGMAN.INI contains a listing of the Program Group files (*.GRP) used within Program Manager.

REGEDIT.EXE

Volumes have been written about the Windows 95 Registry, and the certification exam isn't designed to test your full knowledge of configuring the Registry (the Windows 95 certification exam does that). The overview presented here is designed to give you enough of a familiarity with the Registry that you'll be able to keep track of its main parts.

We've said that the REGEDIT.EXE editor is installed to the WINDOWS folder during setup; however, no icon or menu entry is created. Although some entries and *keys* in the Registry are created by the different versions of Windows 95, we're concerned here only with the generic Registry format and entries.

Working with the Registry requires a serious amount of caution, as accidental changes can lead to a total reinstallation of Windows 95. Unlike word processors, changes take place in the Registry as soon as the Enter key is pressed. Some key points to remember about changes in the Registry include the following:

➤ The Registry is changed directly by changes to Control Panel or some other Windows 95 applets.

➤ The Registry is also changed directly by using REGEDIT.EXE or a third-party application specifically designed to edit the DAT files.

➤ Some installation routines use INF files to write changes to the Registry automatically.

➤ Changes to the Registry take place immediately and are written to the SYSTEM.DAT and USER.DAT files without using a typical File|Save option.

➤ The only way to undo a change in the Registry is to either re-edit the line that was changed, or copy a previous version of the DAT file over the newly changed version.

Unless you know exactly what you're doing, you shouldn't edit the Registry. Use the Control Panel interface to make changes to the system. As always, before you install any new software, or any new hardware device, you should make a safe backup of the existing SYSTEM.DAT file and USER.DAT file.

Bizarre and amazing changes to Windows 95 can occur with the installation of any new component. Sometimes, mystical gremlins can knock out a piece of hardware for no apparent reason. Copying SYSTEM.DAT to another directory (e.g., REG_BACK) is simple to do from MS Explorer and can save you hours (if not days) of time recovering from a corrupted Registry.

To copy Registry files from a DOS command line, their hidden, system, and read-only attributes must be turned off. From within Windows Explorer, they can be copied without adjusting the attributes. If you use the Explorer (or File Manager) to copy the SYSTEM.DAT file, you must be sure to set the capabilities to show hidden files. From the main menu bar in the Explorer, choose View|Options|View tab and check the Show All Files button. From the main menu bar in File Manager, choose View|By File Type|Show Hidden|System Files.

HKeys

The HKey is Microsoft's language for a program *handle* to a *key* that contains configuration information. A "key" looks identical to a folder or subdirectory, except that the name applies to levels and sublevels within the Registry. Looking at the various HKeys in REGEDIT is the same as looking at a drive in Windows Explorer. Each key is represented by a folder icon that can be expanded or collapsed just like folders and subfolders.

You may see a question that asks you what the little + sign is to the left of a folder. If you don't know that this is a one-click way to expand the folder, then we suggest that you postpone taking the exam until after you've installed Windows 95 and played around with it for awhile.

The Windows 95 Registry contains six primary HKeys. Each HKey is like a primary folder located in the root directory of a drive and has many levels of subkeys that descend like a directory tree. The root directory is called HKEY_CLASSES_ROOT. The six primary HKeys are:

➤ **HKEY_CLASSES_ROOT** File extensions and applications used for OLE

➤ **HKEY_USERS** Data stored in USER.DAT that keeps network information and user configuration options

➤ **HKEY_CURRENT_USER** User information specific to the Windows 95 user at the moment (if networking is disabled, this is a duplicate of HKEY_USERS)

➤ **HKEY_LOCAL_MACHINE** The hardware and software configurations for a computer (multiple configurations can be stored for the same computer)

➤ **HKEY_CURRENT_CONFIG** Printers and display settings

➤ **HKEY_DYN_DATA** Dynamic data in RAM having to do with how Windows 95 is running (shown by the System Monitor applet)

Note: While we didn't see any questions asking for a list of all the main HKeys, there may be a reference to the Local Machine key as the location for all the device configurations. The odds are high that questions about the Registry keys will provide the correct names in the response or body of the text. You would be asked to choose or identify an HKey in terms of what it does, and we're fairly confident that you'll only have to know the Local Machine.

Most of the Registry is controlled by Windows 95 or is set up during installation. If problems occur during setup and some hardware device refuses to be recognized, editing the Local Machine key might help. However, the main problem generally is that removing software or changing a hardware device doesn't automatically change its entries in the Registry.

Information about hardware and software is stored in *many* places within the Registry, and uninstaller programs have varying degrees of success in finding all occurrences and references.

Note: Always make a backup of the Registry, particularly the SYSTEM. DAT file, before you make any changes to the system. This includes running an uninstaller program, since an incorrect guess on the part of the program can render the system totally inoperable.

Copies Of Registry Files

When Windows 95 is set up for the first time (from installation disks), a SYSTEM.NEW file is created as the first Registry. This file contains the hardware and software configuration information made during the detection phase of Setup. If everything works well and Windows 95 starts successfully without crashing, SYSTEM.NEW is renamed SYSTEM.DAT.

Once Windows 95 is installed and working, the first successful Registry (SYSTEM.DAT) is renamed SYSTEM.DA0 and held as a backup of the original Registry. The very first SYSTEM.DAT used when Windows 95 starts from the hard disk, is also copied to SYSTEM.1ST in the root directory as another backup of the clean, first installation.

SYSTEM.1ST includes everything up to the first reboot of the system. If you replace SYSTEM.DAT with SYSTEM.1ST at any time and reboot the computer, you'll get the "Starting Windows 95 For The First Time" screen and Windows 95 will go through configuring hardware process, initializing the Control Panel, Start menu, and all the other aspects of a first-time start. Windows 95 will then reboot and start up normally.

Every time Windows 95 starts successfully, it backs up SYSTEM.DAT to SYSTEM.DA0 and USER.DAT to USER.DA0 (overwriting any existing DA0 files). If something goes wrong, the DA0 files are used automatically on restart to return the computer to the successful previous startup.

Backing Up The Registry

Don't rely on the DA0 files as a backup of the Registry. If you do, it's easy to start the computer and create a bad SYSTEM.DAT file, which copies to the SYSTEM.DA0 file along with the bad information. If the computer locks up and is rebooted, the bad SYSTEM.DA0 can copy over the bad SYSTEM.DAT and cause the same problem, leaving two copies of the bad Registry file. Then, your only recourse is the SYSTEM.1ST file, which has only original configuration information—no changes that have been made since the original installation.

The Emergency Recovery Utility can be used to back up the Registry, but usually not to a floppy disk. SYSTEM.DAT is often larger than 1MB and, except for the most minimally configured computer, won't fit on a single floppy. However, ERU can copy specified system files to a different drive or directory, so using an Iomega Zip disk or Imation Super Disk will work, as will copying critical Registry files to a different directory on the hard drive and using a disk-spanning archive tool.

If Windows 95 is unable to start correctly, it will try to do so in Safe mode. If the problem is something that Windows 95 can recognize clearly enough to start the session in Safe mode, the Registry files are *not* copied to the DA0 names. By manually copying the previously good DA0 files to DAT names, Windows 95 can start successfully again. However, not all problems are recognized by Windows 95's recovery capabilities.

To be safe and to provide the most convenient and speedy recovery from inadvertent or random corruption of the Registry, keep the following points in mind:

➤ Always keep a backup of the latest successful Registry: SYSTEM.DAT and USER.DAT somewhere other than in the WINDOWS folder.

➤ SYSTEM.1ST is a last-resort backup of the first configuration file created following a successful first-time installation on a given computer. If this file doesn't work, you're probably going to have to reinstall everything on the computer (Windows 95 and all the software that's been added since the last installation).

➤ SYSTEM.1ST is located in the root directory of the bootable partition.

➤ SYSTEM.DAT and USER.DAT are located in the WINDOWS subdirectory.

➤ SYSTEM.DA0 and USER.DA0 are also located in the WINDOWS subdirectory (by default).

Startup Menu (F8) And Safe Mode

If you press the F8 key between the time the POST has ended and the Windows 95 splash screen appears (when you see the "Starting Windows 95..." message), you halt the processing of MSDOS.SYS and call up the Windows 95 Interactive Startup menu. This menu allows you to start in DOS 7 mode, Safe mode, or other options. Each of these choices offers different processes and results. The Startup menu offers the following choices:

➤ Normal

➤ Logged (BOOTLOG.TXT)

➤ Safe mode

➤ Safe mode with network support

➤ Step-by-step confirmation

➤ Command prompt only

➤ Safe mode command prompt only

➤ Previous version of DOS

Without going into detail, we can provide a quick review of the options on the Startup menu that are available with a timely press of the F8 key. The message "Starting Windows 95..." is written into IO.SYS, which means that if you make a bootable system disk and start the computer, you'll still see the message, even though you don't have the files available to start Windows. You can press F8 to bring up the Startup menu (also contained within IO.SYS), although you won't necessarily have access to all the options on the menu. For example, selecting Option 3 will leave you at the command prompt because the floppy disk doesn't contain WIN.COM or a path to the Windows subdirectory.

Normal And Logged

Normal (Option 1) starts Windows 95 normally and brings the user to the Desktop. If any networking configuration data is installed, Windows connects to the network and provides Login or Logon dialog boxes from within Windows (depending on the type of network). Don't confuse *logged* with *logging in* to a network. Normal and Logged (Option 2) are the same thing, except that Logged writes the steps and status of the startup to the BOOTLOG.TXT file in the root directory of the bootable drive. BOOTLOG.TXT is a hidden file in the root directory of the drive from which Windows 95 starts.

 BOOTLOG.TXT is created following the first successful startup of Windows. The file contains lines for each step of the startup process and a notation regarding their successful or failed outcome. A new boot log is only created when you choose the option from the (F8) Startup menu.

Safe Mode (F5)

One of the critical concepts you need to know about Windows 95 is the use of VxDs (those first developed for Windows 3.1). In Safe mode, Windows 95 bypasses all network configurations, bypasses CONFIG.SYS and AUTOEXEC.BAT, and loads with the most generic settings.

Pressing F5 at the "Starting Windows 95..." text screen is the same as selecting Option 3 from the menu to bypass all configuration files and start the session in Safe mode. Safe mode installs the minimum Windows setup, in VGA graphics mode, with no network connections.

Safe mode does not load any device drivers other than a keyboard driver, HIMEM.SYS, and the standard VGA device.

Safe Mode With Network Support (F6)

Windows for Workgroups 3.11 introduced basic peer-to-peer networking services, available from within Windows. Windows 95 has carried that internal networking capacity forward and allows the same peer-to-peer networking. However, Windows 95 also has a full-bodied configuration capability for client-server networking along with connections to Windows NT Server.

Safe mode starts Windows without any network configuration or connections. Safe mode with network support provides whatever networking connections are possible. Safe mode is available in both choices mainly to help troubleshoot when Windows 95 doesn't start correctly. Sometimes Windows 95 will start in Safe mode, but for some reason won't allow the network connection. Safe mode is primarily a diagnostics mode, or the way in which Windows 95 starts when a problem exists.

Step-By-Step Confirmation (Shift+F8)

Beginning with DOS 5, two keystrokes have been available to control the way in which the system starts up. You must be watchful and quick with your fingers, but if you use the keystrokes, you can bypass configurations or choose a line-by-line agreement for every configuration step. The following startup messages appear right after the initial BIOS startup messages:

➤ "Starting MS-DOS..." (DOS 5 and later)

➤ "Starting Windows 95..." (DOS 7 and Windows 95)

Choosing the step-by-step confirmation option from the F8 Startup menu is the same as pressing Shift+F8 at the "Starting Windows 95..." message in Windows 95. This combination of F8 and F5 and their shifted states can be confusing, but you should know the differences for the exam. Table 10.2 lists what happens if you press the keys as soon as you see the "Starting" messages for DOS or Windows 95.

If you press and hold the Shift key from the time you see the first Windows splash screen until you see the Desktop and the Taskbar, Windows 95 will bypass anything in the Startup folder.

Table 10.2 F8 and F5 "Starting" options in DOS and Windows.	
DOS Keystroke	**Result**
F5	Bypasses CONFIG.SYS and AUTOEXEC.BAT configurations
F8	Processes CONFIG.SYS and AUTOEXEC.BAT one line at a time
Windows 95 Keystroke	**Result**
F5	Starts Windows 95 in Safe mode, bypassing CONFIG.SYS and AUTOEXEC.BAT
Shift+F5	Starts in Real (DOS 7) mode
F8	Calls up text-based Startup menu
Shift+F8	Starts Windows 95 and processes configurations line by line

Command Prompt Only (Shift F5)

If you want to start the computer in plain, real DOS 7, you can either modify MSDOS.SYS to always start with the command prompt or choose Option 6 in the Startup menu. Certain commands (e.g., FDISK.EXE) can't be run from within Windows, and this option gives you a plain DOS environment.

To start Windows 95 from the command prompt, type "WIN" and press Enter. When you exit a Windows 95 session after starting from the command prompt, you return to the DOS prompt rather than the "It is now safe to shut off your machine" final exit prompt.

Safe Mode Command Prompt Only

This is like pressing the F5 key in DOS 5 and 6. This option starts DOS with no networking, bypasses the CONFIG.SYS and AUTOEXEC.BAT files, and stops at the command prompt. It probably would've made more sense to call this option "Command Prompt with No Configurations."

Previous Version Of DOS (F4)

This option from the Startup menu can also be run by pressing the F4 key when the "Starting" message appears. The option is a bit misleading because a default installation of Windows 95 deletes any previous version of Windows 3.x and DOS. For this option to work, the convoluted process of moving DOS and Windows 3.x into a backup directory and then installing Windows 95 must be run.

You'll need to remember that F8 and F4 are important Windows 95 startup keys. F8 gets you the text-based Startup menu. F4 (may) get you a previous version of DOS.

FAT32, IFS, And Long File Names

DOS has always had the 8.3 file name structure. Although the creative use of directory and subdirectory names can produce a lot of information about a file, Apple's method of using common English names has been easier for most users. Because of the way the DOS FAT works, the maximum limit for a file name, including all the directory information, is 64 characters. Windows 95 long file names allow up to 255 characters and can include previously illegal characters, such as <space> and the + symbol.

One of the changes in OS/2 is the way the FAT stores file names. Using a 32-bit FAT rather than a 16-bit FAT allows more room for the file name. Because OS/2 and Apple were using these long file names, Microsoft was feeling the heat to have the same ability in DOS and Windows.

Novell's Netware NOS (network operating system) created something called the OS/2 name space feature, which was designed to resolve conflicts between DOS and Apple computers running on the same network. If an Apple user saved a file as "1997 Third Quart Annual Report" and a DOS user opened and saved that file again, the Apple user might see "1997thir.dqa" as the new file name. Netware and the OS/2 name space helped resolve the abrupt cutting off (truncating) of anything after 11 characters.

Windows 95 uses something similar to the OS/2 name space in that IFS Manager (the Installable File System Manager) works to convert long file names to the 8.3 names required by the underlying 16-bit FAT. IFS Manager works the other way as well in that a request for a short file name goes out to retrieve the correct long file name in the directory listing.

File naming conventions are voluntary ways of naming files. File naming rules, on the other hand, are statements of what characters may or may not be used in a file name. The exam may confuse you by using the term "convention" to mean "rule."

Remember that in DOS file names, the <space>, plus, asterisk, question mark, and slashes are not allowed. Even though Windows 95 LFNs will allow some of these illegal characters, our feeling is that the exam will test your knowledge of allowable characters rather than whether a certain file name is possible under the extended capabilities of the long file name feature.

IFS (Installable File System) Manager

We know that Windows 95 is tied to the 16-bit FAT and the DAT (directory allocation table) carried over from DOS through Windows 3.x and into the underlying Windows 95/98 environment. At the same time, Microsoft has been working on Windows NT, which began as the 32-bit OS/2 v3. The concept and capability of the Mac's long file names have been around for a long time, and Windows 95 is where Microsoft pulled it all together. Windows 95 still isn't a 32-bit operating system, but it can connect any number of 32-bit network operating systems and work with long file names.

The Windows 95 IFS is a way to store additional file information about LFNs, while allowing the DOS 16-bit FAT to control the location of the basic file clusters and sectors. Remember that part of a file system's job is to associate human names to a series of numbers that describe the cylinder, track, sectors, and clusters where data is physically stored. This new file system is made up of three parts:

➤ IFS Manager, which works out the problems and differences between different file system components

➤ File system drivers, which provide access to low-level disk devices, CD-ROM file systems, and network devices

➤ The block I/O subsystem, which deals directly with physical disks

People sometimes refer to "FAT32," "32-bit FAT," "VFAT," or even "HPFS" when discussing the Windows 95 IFS. "VFAT" stands for "virtual FAT" and is part of the Installable File System. VFAT was first introduced in Windows for Workgroups 3.11 and was tightened up in Windows 95. The IFSHELP.SYS driver reference in the Windows 3.x startup sequence refers to the prototype version of what went on to become the Windows 95 IFS Manager.

On the other hand, "HPFS" stands for "high performance file system," which was engineered into OS/2. Neither Windows 95 nor Windows NT uses nor currently support the HPFS. NT uses the NTFS (NT file system). For simplicity, we refer to the underlying 16-bit FAT as the *base file system*, the Windows 95 modification as the IFS, and any other file systems by their own names. Windows 95 uses a 32-bit VFAT that works in conjunction with the 16-bit base FAT controlled by DOS 7. The "32" in FAT32 refers to this VFAT.

OS/R2 (Windows 95 version B) and Windows 98 include an option to format a logical partition for a 32-bit FAT. This will allow for multithreaded Protected mode access to the disk through VFAT and a faster, more efficient method of disk caching. However, common acceptance of the Windows 95/98 file system has yet to be determined.

We've seen that the maximum allowable size for a 16-bit FAT formatted logical partition is 2GB. Current systems routinely come installed with huge hard disks of at least 6GB, and often as large as 15GB. How is this possible? The FAT32 feature in Windows 95/98 allows for these single, large partitions. However, once a disk is setup with the FAT32 feature, it can't be changed back to 16-bit FAT. Unfortunately, most new computer buyers haven't the slightest idea (or interest) in the underlying decisions being made for them by their system dealers.

Windows 98 provides a conversion utility to convert an existing FAT16 to FAT32 without data loss, similarly to Windows NT. In Windows 95, a drive can be set up with one or the other, or converted from FAT16 to FAT32 also. Although the conversion utility allows a drive to be converted from FAT16 to FAT32 (or NTFS, in the case of Windows NT), the user is unable to revert back to FAT16 without reformatting the partition.

 NTFS is the Windows NT file system, while WINS is a Windows Internet naming system used for certain type of network protocols. While we don't believe you'll see a question on the WINS, NTFS, or HPFS, you should make note of their names and abbreviations.

Network Redirectors

When you use features like the File|Open, File|Save, and File|Save As menu items in an application, you're asking the program to access the basic file system. When you use DOS commands such as DIR, COPY, DEL, or MOVE, you're also using the file system. When you create shortcuts in Windows 95, you're not only creating an OLE LNK file but also accessing many other files and using the file system as well.

Usually, an application, operating system, or both use Interrupt 21 to access the disk and file system. Networking operating system *redirectors* (TSRs) and CD-ROM drivers keep an eye on Interrupt 21 and determine whether the file system request is for the base file system or for their own 32-bit systems. A redirector grabs a request for the base file system and redirects the request to a different file system. Once again, a redirector is like the executive secretary, watching the phone and directing calls either to the boss or to someone else in the company.

One problem with this idea is that you must load different device drivers for each system watching over that ever popular IRQ 21. Different networks have their own redirector devices, which often argue about who gets to take the file home to Mom and Dad. Aside from that, PCs have a terrible time connecting to more than two different networks at the same time.

The Windows 95 IFS Manager controls all the network redirectors as though they were different file systems. This allows an unlimited number of 32-bit redirectors to be used at the same time and for connecting with any number of different networks. The DOS file system is used as though it were just another network file system.

The IFS manager takes over management of multiple file systems in the following manner:

➤ IFS Manager controls how Windows 95 connects to other NOSs.

➤ FS Manager calls different file system drivers depending on the format of the file that the application is sending.

➤ IFS Manager takes all calls to the file system and controls how they're implemented.

Disk Device Drivers

For any software to work with any hardware, instructions must be stored somewhere, either in a ROM BIOS chip on an expansion card or in a software program—a device driver. One way or another, the device driver must end up in memory somewhere. DOS (IO.SYS and MSDOS.SYS) contains some generic device drivers for the basic I/O interface components found on almost every computer (e.g., COM and LPT ports).

Although memory isn't a hardware device per se, extended memory still requires an XMS device driver (e.g., HIMEM.SYS). Likewise, expanded memory requires an EMS device driver (e.g., EMM386.EXE) in conjunction with and following the extended memory driver.

Over the years, a number of hard drives and CD-ROM drives have become popular, and Windows 95 contains many of the VxDs that support these drives. The limitations of the FAT and the large storage capacity of new hard drives and CDs are putting an increasing strain on the capabilities of the old 16-bit FAT to keep up. If only DOS could be magically turned into a network operating system, many of those problems would just go away!

The IFS Manager is that interim magic wand and acts somewhat like a network redirector by grabbing all the Interrupt 21 requests from applications that want to access the DOS file system. The DOS file system is still laying down bits of information in clusters, on sectors, in tracks, and on cylinders. However, instead of DOS making the decisions about names, IFS Manager is now doing that.

SMARTDRV.EXE

In the section on SRAM chips back in Chapter 4, we saw how a cache works. To quickly review, a cache is a set of algorithms that attempt to predict what will happen next. If you open a document and view the top half of page one, the probability is high that the next thing you'll do is read the bottom half of the same page.

A disk cache contains the instructions to read the bottom half of page one into cache memory and hold that information until (presumably) you ask for it. If you do ask for it, the time it takes to spin the disk and move the read-write heads is already done. The system need only move the data from one area of memory to another, and that's much faster than the mechanical movements of hardware.

SMARTDRV.SYS is a 16-bit cache device driver that became available in DOS 5. It became SMARTDRV.EXE in DOS 6.x. Windows 3.x, limited to 16MB of RAM, introduced virtual memory, where overflow cache memory could be stored to a disk file. The Windows 95 File System uses VCACHE in conjunction with IFS Manager to increase the efficiency to 32-bit processing rather than the older 16-bit code of SmartDrive.

VFAT

The DOS file system has always been the 16-bit Real mode system inherited from CP/M. Probably the only reason it remains in existence is the fact that there are millions and millions of copies of DOS running on PCs all over the world. However, most of the other operating systems designed for PCs were designed *after* the PC became such an astounding success.

The 16-bit FAT is the main limiting factor in the number of files that can be stored on a disk, and some very large storage devices have arrived on the market since the old 10MB hard drive was invented. CD-ROMs and network file servers store huge numbers of files and run mostly on specifically designed 32-bit file systems.

Using long file names and improving disk caching required a way to connect these newer network operating systems to the old DOS file system on the same computer. Because the required FAT couldn't be eliminated, a second FAT had to be developed—a *virtual FAT*. This new VFAT had to live side by side with the original, and that could work only if one of them was the boss. IFS Manager makes sure that VFAT is in charge.

When Windows 95 starts up, the IFS waits for the system files to run all the Real mode device drivers and for the drivers to connect to the file system and hardware devices. Once DOS has the computer functioning, Windows steps in and takes control with VMM32. As we saw earlier, VMM32 uses its compiled library of internal VxDs to replace whatever Real mode drivers it finds in memory.

The VxDs in VMM32 are designed specifically to communicate with the IFS Manager, so the DOS file system is mounted (connected) in the same sense that a network volume is mounted and recognized by a network operating system. This ability to communicate with the IFS is part of what it means to write a 32-bit application that's 100 percent Windows 95 compatible.

Short File Names

Windows 95 has an internal list of all the interrupts that DOS can use (a maximum of 71) and adds a few more. Among the extra interrupts is the way in which long file names can be recognized by the operating system. Because DOS itself can't recognize the long name, IFS Manager uses one of the extra interrupts, stores the file name with an *alias* pointer (similar to a vector), and returns to tell DOS what to do with the file.

IFS Manager also takes what you enter as a long file name and splits it apart (parses it) so that part of it can be used as a corresponding short file name. The rest of the name is stored for later rebuilding, and the alias pointer is associated with all the pieces of the file name.

If you have a file called "1998 Fooferaugh + My list of stuff" and another file called "1998 Fooferaugh and Dave's stuff," IFS Manager will truncate the two files to an 8.3 name. Theoretically, that would result in two files called 1998foof.era at the same time—*totally* illegal by DOS rules, the United Nations Resolution 439 on International Tom Foolery, and a breach of the 1927 Zambian nuclear arms treaty!

When IFS Manager finds two files that will truncate to the same name, it uses the first six characters (minus spaces) and adds a tilde (~) plus incremental numbers (beginning with 1). If any periods are in the long file name, IFS Manager uses the first three characters after the last period as the DOS extension. Otherwise, it uses the next three characters it finds. In our example, the files would be named 1998fo~1.era and 1998fo~2.era for the short DOS name.

Note: The default use of the tilde can be changed by editing the Registry.

Short Names And Aliases

A typical way for a file system to come calling on the disk is when a DOS VM is created to run a DOS application in Windows. Windows 3.x applications also make calls to the file system, and both use Interrupt 21. The file system works to find room on the disk, store a file name (in the DAT), and help the disk controller move the hardware around. The DAT is an index for the longer FAT.

By the time the proposed Windows 95 long file name reaches the file system, IFS Manager has parsed it and added a pointer number. Meanwhile, DOS hasn't a clue that anything unusual is happening and still thinks it's running the same as it did back in 1981. DOS dutifully lays down the file, stores what it was told to store in the DAT, and goes back to sleep. The file is stored in clusters all over the disk, and IFS Manager makes sure that anything and everything in Windows 95 sees the file name that it's supposed to see.

Along with the short name in the FAT, the parsed long file name is given the pointer to hang onto. When anything calls the file system, IFS Manager goes back to DOS and presents the request. DOS hands IFS Manager the file location information, and IFS Manager looks at the associated alias number to find the rest of the file name. IFS Manager then shows the user the long file name.

Note: In certain circumstances, the VFAT and the 16-bit DOS FAT can become partly unsynchronized. In this strange situation, Explorer (not the File Manager, though) can end up showing two files with exactly the same name in the same directory. This is rare, but it results from the fact that the names being presented in Explorer aren't the actual file names any more than the name being presented in any other Windows 95 application is the actual name.

The DIR command in a DOS window is stolen by IFS Manager and returns the DOS directory with the long file name set aside in the IFS name space (to the far right of the DIR listing). Restarting the computer in DOS mode shuts down the entire Windows environment and eliminates the IFS and IFS Manager, along with LFN support. A DIR command at a plain DOS prompt (e.g., Option 6 from the F8 Startup menu) will show only the short name of the file as it's actually registered in the DAT.

Saving Long File Names

As you can see, the only thing keeping track of the long file names is IFS Manager. The Novell Netware OS/2 name space is an option that a network administrator might or might not decide to use. If you decide to store all the files from a Windows 95 computer on a network, the long file names will be stored only if the OS/2 name space has been enabled. If name space isn't enabled, the long file names are lost in the river of history.

A little-known (and hardly referenced) utility that comes with the Windows 95 CD-ROM is the LFNBK.EXE utility (for "long file name backup"). LFNBK.EXE is found in the ADMIN\APPTOOLS\LFNBACK folder, along with LFNBK.TXT that describes the basic operations and switches. Perhaps the program is hard to notice because Microsoft says that it's for experienced users and shouldn't be relied on for day-to-day maintenance.

The most immediate problem with long file names is that they're stored within Windows 95. In addition, part of that storage is the alias map that connects the physical location of the file to its corresponding IFS long name. Suppose that you decide to use a defragmenting utility from the DOS prompt. Part of the defragmenting process involves moving file clusters around. Naturally, the utility is in constant communication with the file system's DAT, which keeps track of the clusters, no matter where they end up. But who's telling all this to IFS Manager? No one!

Using a DOS-based file maintenance program can disassociate the short file name from the long file name, causing the long file name to be lost forever.

 IFS Manager is the Windows 95 file system manager that controls the way in which a long file name is stored. Anything involving files and their storage, naming, movement, and maintenance is intercepted by IFS Manager.

Reformatting a hard drive and reinstalling Windows 95 will not keep previous long file names associated with the short file names held by DOS. Keeping the original long file names requires a complete backup of the existing Windows 95 environment. For emergency purposes, the LFNBK utility has been shipped with the Windows 95 CD-ROM installation disk.

An interesting problem arises when long file names disappear from the system. Certain program instructions that are internal to Windows 95 program files make calls to other files by their specific long file name. The files exist on the drive but only in short-name form. Because Windows is looking for the exact file name of a program and expecting IFS Manager to have that name, it can't find the file because it can only see the short name. At that point, Windows fails to run.

Windows 95 Networking

One of the most powerful capabilities of Windows 95 is its integration of peer-to-peer networking. The certification exam will have a few questions relating generally to networks and specifically to networking with Windows 95.

Network Overview

Networks allow users to share computer resources, including printers, disk drives, and data. The two basic types of network are *client-server* and *peer to-peer*. In a client-server network, one or more PCs called *servers* are dedicated to data and program storage. PCs that access the server for data and programs are called *clients*. Servers are like waiters and waitresses, in that they serve up files, applications, and processing to their clients.

Network file servers provide an excellent way to share data among many workstations and eliminate the need for redundant storage at each PC. Furthermore, because data is stored at one location, increased security and control can be implemented. Most client-server networks provide similar functions for sharing printers and other peripherals.

Peer-to-peer networks don't have dedicated servers. In this type of network, each PC is allowed to share its resources with other PCs connected to the network. For example, you might access Sue's hard drive to retrieve a spreadsheet template, and she might choose to print a document using your printer. Although security is provided to determine who can use what, peer-to-peer networks don't have the same level of security or control provided by client-server networks.

 Windows 95 provides built-in peer-to-peer networking. The feature must be enabled, and the Installation Wizard will look for a network interface card.

Most networks transfer data in one of two ways. Token passing, as used in IBM's token ring network, connects PCs into a ring and passes a token (i.e., an emptied data packet) from PC to PC. When a PC requires data from another PC, it waits for the token to come around, places its request in the token (which then becomes a data packet), and passes the packet along the ring to the appropriate PC.

A token ring network is like a group of people sitting at a dinner table. If someone wants mashed potatoes, they wait for a pause in the conversation and pass their request around to the person nearest the potatoes. That person hands the potatoes to the first person in the ring, and everyone passes the mashed potatoes along. When the person who requested them gets the bowl, they dish out some potatoes on their plate—their local hard drive.

The second method, used in Ethernet networks, incorporates a *bus*. Initially, the bus was a long piece of coaxial cable with a resistor on either end called a *terminator*. PCs were connected to this coaxial cable, which they shared for communications. Because all the PCs shared one cable, only one PC could transmit at any one time. All PCs on the bus would hear the transmission, but only the addressed PC would copy the transmission into its buffer for processing. The terminators prevented signals from being reflected back and forth along the coaxial cable and creating all kinds of problems.

Ethernet is more like the old telephone party lines: However many people were talking on the phone, each person could hear every other person. The trick was to listen for the specific voice of the caller you were trying to have a conversation with and ignore the rest. Networks are a little more sophisticated than that, but the image serves its purpose.

A unique network address is entered into the ROM of a network interface card (NIC) when it's manufactured. In most cases, this address cannot be changed. When you place a NIC in your PC, the PC takes on the network address of the NIC. Therefore, if you change the NIC in your PC, you'll change its address.

The first coaxial cable used in Ethernet was referred to as *Thick net* or *10Base5*. In this case, the *10* at the beginning specifies transmission speed (10 megabits per second); *Base* stands for *baseband*, where one signal at a time is transmitted; and *5* at the end equates to 500 meters—the maximum length of the cable. Thick net was replaced by *Thin net*, which was much easier to install. Thin net, or *10Base2*, cable ran at 10 megabits per second, was baseband, and could be slightly less than 200 meters long at a maximum.

Both 10Base5 and 10Base2 require terminators at the end of the cable. If the cable breaks or a terminator isn't installed, the entire network can perform erratically and fail.

Because of the limitations in length and the difficulty of installing coaxial cable, most Ethernet networks today are 10BaseT—*twisted pair*. These installations use pairs of wires twisted together (similar to telephone cable) to connect the PC's NIC to a *hub*, or *concentrator*. The hub is a small box that contains an Ethernet bus, connectors, and terminators, all of which are prewired and protected from damage.

The "T" in 10BaseT stands for "twisted" pair wiring. Although it was unusual, we did see some questions that asked for this sort of low-level historical knowledge. Remember that the 10 stands for the transmission rate (10 megabits per second) and the 5 or the 2 at the end of the name represents the maximum length of the coaxial cable (in meters).

Setting Up A Windows 95 Network

Adding a NIC and activating the necessary Windows 95 components are the only requirements of networking a PC that runs Windows 95. Everything, except the NIC and the wiring, is included in Windows 95.

 PCs must use the same protocol, or language, to communicate successfully on a network. The most common network protocols in use today are NetBEUI, IPX/SPX, and TCP/IP. The Internet uses TCP/IP as its main networking protocol.

To set up a Windows 95 network, follow these steps:

1. Insert the NIC into an ISA or a PCI expansion slot. The NIC provides connectivity to the network through a cable and is almost always PnP.

2. Double-click the My Computer icon. Select Control Panel, then Network, and then Add Client For Microsoft Networks in the Configuration tab.

3. Add a network protocol or protocols. A protocol is like specifying a language and must be the same for all PCs on the network.

4. Add File and Print Sharing. If you don't add this, you won't be able to share printers and files.

5. Give your computer a name and description and identify the work group you'll be a part of, in the Identification tab.

6. Choose a security method in the Access Control tab. This will be either Share-Level or User-Level, depending on whether you want to control access by individuals or resources such as printers and drives.

7. Go back to My Computer and right-click on each of the resources you want to share under My Computer. Select Sharing to activate sharing, privileges, and passwords (printers are found in the Printers folder).

That's all there is to networking a PC running Windows 95. Of course, choosing the appropriate type of network, physically installing it, and managing it requires a great deal of planning and knowledge that exceeds the scope of A+.

 Resources that are shared across networks are usually printers, CD-ROM writers, hard drive directories (and their applications or data files), and modems. Monitors, mice, desk lamps, or scanners aren't generally something people share this way. If you wouldn't have to get out of your chair to go use the resource, then it's probably a good candidate for a network resource.

External Networks

Windows 95 also provides access to external networks such as the Internet and America Online through Dial-up Networking, which can be found in the properties menu for the My Computer icon. The certification exam will ask you one or two questions relating to the Internet, so you should know the following information.

The Internet uses TCP/IP (Transmission Control Protocol/Internet Protocol) as its protocol, and you'll need to add this to your protocols under Network Configuration choice in Control Panel. Windows 95 can use multiple protocols and automatically switch between them as long as they have been added to the network configuration. (The IFS Manager recognizes the requested protocol by reading information in the file packet.)

In most cases, you'll be using a domain name server (DNS) on the Internet and can address communications using the domain name rather than a numeric IP address. Numeric IP addresses are 12 digits long and are difficult to remember. Domain names are cross-referenced to a numeric address on the domain name server and allow people to use names that are much easier to remember.

Email Addresses

An email address requires a user name and a domain name. The separator between the two is the @ sign, with the user name being to the left and the domain name to the right. A typical email address would be jimjones@jamesgjones.com. The user name is the *jimjones*, then comes the separator. In this case, the domain name is jamesgjones.com with the .com appended as the type of domain.

World Wide Web addresses, called universal resource locators (URLs), use the familiar www. to indicate that the part of the internet being used is the Web. The http:// prefix indicates a hypertext transfer protocol. In the URL **http://www.jamesgjones.com**, once again the James G. Jones domain shows up (jamesgjones). This is a "commercial" domain, and therefore has a .com suffix. **http://www.comptia.org** indicates that CompTIA is an "organization," having the .org suffix. Government agencies typically use .gov as their suffix.

 An email address has a user name and a domain name (which includes the .com, .org, .gov, or other suffix).

Exam Prep Questions

Question 1

> Windows 95 differs from previous Windows versions in that it is a true 32-bit multithreading, multitasking system.
>
> ○ a. True
>
> ○ b. False

False. Windows 95 still includes significant portions of 16-bit code and uses DOS for file management and disk partitioning. Windows 95 can be thought of as a transitional system between DOS and Windows NT, which is a true 32-bit multithreading, multitasking operating system.

Question 2

> The 10Base2 cable of an Ethernet network breaks. What happens next?
>
> ○ a. The network segments into two fully functional networks
>
> ○ b. The segment containing the server continues to function normally
>
> ○ c. The entire network stops functioning reliably with no warning
>
> ○ d. The NICs on either side of the break go into backup mode

The answer is c. There is no connectivity between the remaining segments, and without terminating resistors at the break, the signals on each segment begin reflecting, causing unreliable communications on the segment.

Question 3

How is the Windows 95 Registry edited?

○ a. By using the system editor in a DOS window

○ b. By opening the Registry in Notepad and using the
file editor

○ c. By selecting Run from the Start menu and entering
"Modify Registry"

○ d. By selecting Run from the Start menu and entering
"REGEDIT"

The answer is d. The Registry is modified using a special editor called REGEDIT, which is usually started by entering REGEDIT in the Run field under the Start menu.

Question 4

What is Windows 95 Safe mode?

○ a. A mode in which only one program can run at a time

○ b. A mode that was designed for mission-critical applications

○ c. A diagnostic mode in which only keyboard, mouse, and
VGA drivers are loaded

○ d. The standard mode of operation, providing protection
from program-to-program interference

The answer is c. Safe mode is a diagnostic mode that loads the minimum number of drivers required for system operation.

Question 5

Windows 95 is provided on a CD-ROM for convenient backup should system files become corrupted.

○ a. True

○ b. False

False. The Windows 95 CD-ROM is not a backup. If system files become corrupted, you might not have access to your CD-ROM drive to read the Windows 95 CD.

Question 6

How would you start Windows 95 in Safe mode?

○ a. Press the Ctrl and Esc keys simultaneously after
     Windows 95 starts

○ b. Press the F3 key following POST

○ c. Double-click Safe Mode Operation under System in
     Control Panel

○ d. Press F8 prior to startup of Windows 95 and select Safe
     Mode from the menu

The answer is d. Safe mode is entered by selecting it from the menu presented
when F8 is pressed prior to the startup of Windows 95.

Need To Know More?

Chellis, Perkins, and Streb: *MCSE Networking Essentials Study Guide.* Sybex Network Press, San Francisco, CA, 1996. ISBN 0-7821-1971-9. This book goes into more detail than you'll need for the certification exam but is a good place to start if you're considering a career as a network engineer.

Derfler, Frank J.: *PC Magazine Guide to Connectivity.* Ziff Davis, 1995. ISBN 1-56276-274-5. This book is easy to read and provides a good introduction to networking.

Microsoft Windows 95 Resource Kit. Microsoft Press, Redmond, WA. ISBN 1-55615-678-2. This is the definitive resource for all Windows 95 questions. It assumes that you have a good working knowledge of Windows 95.

Norton, Peter, and Mueller, John: *Complete Guide to Windows 95.* Sams, Indianapolis, IN, 1997. ISBN 0-672-30791-X. This very good introduction to Windows 95 explains the "why" as well as the "how."

Tidrow, Rob: *Windows 95 Registry Troubleshooting.* New Riders, Indianapolis, IN, 1996. ISBN 1-56205-556-9. This book goes into more detail than you'll need for the certification exam, but if you really want to get into it, this is your source.

Trulove, James: *LAN Wiring.* McGraw-Hill, New York, NY, 1997. ISBN 0-07-065302-x. This book addresses every aspect of physically wiring and testing a LAN. It is easy to read and provides a wealth of information that is rarely covered in books on networking.

Troubleshooting

Terms you'll need to understand:

✓ Beep codes

✓ CMOS

✓ File attributes

✓ IRQs and interrupts

✓ Ports and port addresses

Concepts you'll need to master:

✓ Boot sequence

✓ File locations

✓ Device drivers

✓ Hexadecimal numbering

✓ Direct memory access (DMA) channels

✓ IRQ lines and I/O addresses

✓ Environment variables

You've probably heard the story about a young musician who encounters an accomplished older musician on the street and asks for directions: "How do I get to Carnegie Hall?" The older musician replies, "Practice." The intent of this book is not to teach you how to repair computers. The field of repairing and configuring computers is so large that we can touch on only its main areas. We expect you to spend time working with Windows 95 and practicing on your own. Before you take the exam, you should be comfortable with the general workings of the mouse and with navigating Windows 95.

Due to certain constraints having to do with the organization of a topic as vast as that covered by the A+ certification exam, we've created a special, standalone appendix. We strongly urge you to turn to that section and read the scenario and ensuing discussion before reading this chapter, because the appendix is where we pull together much of the conceptual framework for the entire book. The appendix is a way for you to examine your own knowledge from a different perspective. This chapter, along with the appendix, takes a different tack than previous chapters.

Although there are many ways to memorize simple facts, we've found that passing an exam such as the A+ certification exam takes more than rote memorization. The exam is a complex combination of both psychologically devious questions and a test for underlying conceptual knowledge of PCs. We've taken the approach that hanging various facts on a tree of your imagination will better prepare you in your endeavor. To that purpose, the appendix is designed to offer you a chance to step back a few paces and evaluate your current knowledge base.

This chapter will prepare you to answer exam questions dealing with diagnosing and resolving system problems (troubleshooting). We've made it a sort of catchall for diagnostic topics we've seen on the exam and for topics that don't quite fit into any other chapter of the book. We focus on the topics involved in solving the most common problems. These topics will be on the exam. Some customer service issues that apply to troubleshooting make a brief appearance here and work in conjunction with the basic framework we initiate in the appendix scenario.

Once again, we hope you'll read the appendix first, and if you have trouble with the material presented there, that you'll go back and review the areas we point you to. When you're comfortable with your understanding of the Kingdom of Aeyre and the technology there, then you should read this chapter to solidify what you've learned.

Basic Troubleshooting Theory

People have been solving problems ever since the first human picked up a stick to knock some fruit out of a tree. Over time, a theory of problem solving has evolved, and the basic steps of that theory apply to computer problems as easily as anything else. The basic steps to solving any problem include:

1. Defining the symptoms

2. Identifying and isolating the problem

3. Repairing or replacing

4. Retesting

5. Marking as "solved" or returning to the symptoms

Tech Support

Earlier we spoke about the systems analyst, the systems integrator, and the needs assessment/client interview. Once a system is working, the person who comes in to solve problems or configure specific components is called by many names. For the purposes of this discussion, we refer to the technical (tech) support person, or systems administrator, as the one who performs hands-on diagnostics, troubleshooting, and repair.

The key customer service point to remember about tech support is that any customer with a problem is frustrated and upset that things aren't working right now! A customer wants someone to answer a phone immediately, and to provide an exact solution to the problem instantly. Where phone support isn't the mode, the customer wants a live human being to teleport to his or her location, wave a magic wand, and instantly make the system work perfectly again. The attributes of a skilled systems administrator include:

➤ Professional demeanor

➤ Competence

➤ Control over the professional environment

➤ Imagination

➤ Organization

➤ Focus

➤ Patience

➤ An ability to extract important information about a problem through guided questions

➤ Efficiency

When a commercial client makes a call to tech support, the technician who arrives on-site must understand that the call is costing the client money by the minute. The customer has no interest whatsoever in whether the technician had an interesting weekend, had a fight with a date, or heard a funny new story. The employees at the site are being paid to work, and any customers at the site are there to do business of some kind. Distractions cost money, and anything other than direct attention to the problem at hand is a distraction.

The Jargon Problem And Body Language

If you don't understand by now that computers are incomprehensible to most people, you might want to engrave that in the mirror you use to comb your hair in the morning. Some people have a knack for understanding *jargon* (the technical terms associated with a specialized field). Most people have no idea what you're talking about when you mention CPUs, megahertz, cards and boards, or apps (applications).

If you watch people at all, you've probably noticed their *body language*. Body language is the way people signal their emotional state of mind and their inner thinking process. Typical body language indicating that a person is "turning you off" includes:

➤ Crossed arms

➤ A frowning expression

➤ Yawning

➤ Checking a watch or rummaging through papers in the middle of your sentence

➤ Turning or looking away

➤ Irritable movements (e.g., tapping feet, fiddling with things, or drumming fingers)

If you're explaining a problem, talking in a continuous stream and pointing to the PC, you have *no idea* how your customer is reacting to what you're saying. Keep an eye on your customer's body language and facial expressions. Every time you make a statement about anything involving the PC, look up and see what kind of reaction you get in response.

As soon as you see the first signs of puzzlement, confusion, irritation, or impatience, STOP! Immediately ask the customer whether you've lost him or her and reconsider whether what you're talking about has any real purpose. In commercial environments, the person using the computer you're working on generally couldn't care less whether it works. In fact, in many cases that person would be just as happy if the computer never worked again and he or she could go home for the day.

Scatterbrained Approach

Take a moment to think objectively about your overall way of dealing with a large number of variables. Think about when you need to organize a party, an excursion, a shopping errand, or anything else that involves many variables needing to come together at the same time. What do people say about your organizational skills? How proficient are you at *logistics* (putting materials and resources together for a specific purpose)?

One of the features distinguishing a systems administrator from a low-paid technician is the administrator's ability to quickly isolate the essential information about a problem and then to put all the steps involved in solving that problem into an immediate, organized, prioritized sequence.

Almost invariably, you can use the rule of thumb that if a problem were easy to solve, the person using the computer would have solved it. By the time you arrive on the scene, many of the obvious remedies have been tried. Furthermore, some of the attempted fixes that have been applied have probably both worsened the original problem and made it harder to find.

When you decide to make your first professional statement to the customer (after a courteous greeting), you should be completely clear about what you want to say. Attorneys use the general rule of never asking a witness on the stand a question that they don't already know the answer to. A modification of this rule as it applies to tech support is that you don't ask a technical question that you don't have a reason for asking.

If your problem-solving process is to "just jump right in and start messing around," you might do well in the back room of a large service facility, but you probably will never become a systems administrator or technical support provider. You should use your brain, your experience, and your imagination before you ever touch the system. If your chosen area is telephone support, you'll want to develop a pleasant, trusting relationship with customers on the other end of the phone. Those people must be willing to turn control of their eyes, ears, and hands over to you.

If you don't know what you want, or if you keep backtracking to fix a statement you blurted out without thinking, no one will be willing to follow your direction at all.

IRQs, DMA, And I/O Ports

The certification exam has a number of questions about IRQs (interrupt requests), COM and LPT port addresses, and DMA (direct memory addressing) channels. Remember that an IRQ is the way in which a device interrupts the CPU. A DMA channel is a shortcut around the main expansion bus that allows a device to access RAM directly.

The following definitions apply to IRQs and DMA channels:

➤ AT motherboards have two DMA memory controllers. Prior to the AT-class PC, the XT motherboard had one DMA controller.

➤ Each DMA controller has four channels.

➤ AT and ATX motherboards have eight DMA channels; XT motherboards had four.

➤ DMA channels are used by devices to send data in and out of memory.

➤ Interrupts are generated by a device to request the CPU's attention. When the interrupt handler has finished, the CPU returns to what it was doing (by looking in the STACKS).

➤ An *interrupt routine* is the instruction set within a device driver (software) that processes commands to the device.

➤ An *interrupt service routine* is an instruction set in BIOS that services IRQs coming from devices or software.

➤ An *interrupt vector* is an area of conventional memory that contains addresses to each of 255 interrupts. The *interrupt vector table* is an index of those vector addresses.

➤ *IRQ lines* are used by the device to send an interrupt to the CPU.

➤ 80286 and later CPUs have 16 interrupt lines; the 8088 had 8.

DMA channels and IRQ lines interconnect the components (devices), the CPU, and memory. You should document the current devices and their IRQs and

Device	IRQ	Handler
Table 11.1 A typical MSD.EXE report of IRQ usage.		
Timer output	0	WIN386.EXE
Keyboard	1	Block device
Cascade from IRQ 9	2	BIOS
COM2, COM4 (serial ports)	3	BIOS
COM1, COM3 (serial ports)	4	BIOS
LPT2 (parallel port, XT drive)	5	BIOS
Floppy disk controller	6	Default handler
LPT1 (parallel port)	7	System
Real-time clock	8	Default handler
Redirected IRQ2 (video, network)	9	BIOS
(Reserved)	10	BIOS
(Reserved)	11	BIOS
(Reserved), built-in mouse	12	Default handler
Math coprocessor	13	BIOS
Primary fixed disk controller (IDE)	14	BIOS
Secondary fixed disk controller	15	Default handler

DMA settings before you install and configure a new device. Table 11.1 lists IRQ lines and their default device services. MSD.EXE includes a report under IRQ Status that shows which IRQs are being used on a specific PC.

 Remember that 16 IRQs are available to devices. Because the IRQs are numbered in the common technical format (i.e., hexadecimal), the first IRQ is 0. The upper limit is IRQ 15. There are 16 IRQs to conform with hex memory addressing (base 16) and the 16 segments of conventional memory.

IRQ 14 is set aside for the primary IDE (AT) drive controller. However, terminology might refer to a master drive, the primary hard drive, or the first hard disk. An IDE (or EIDE) controller can have two devices chained to it, and a second hard drive is the slave. IRQ 15 (the last IRQ) is typically set aside for the secondary IDE drive *controller*, not a second drive.

Ordinarily, a second disk is chained to the IDE controller. Remember that IDE controllers allow for a daisy chain of two devices, so the master and slave usually connect to a single controller.

Remember that the default IRQ 14 is used for the primary hard disk IDE controller. IRQ 15 most likely is used for a *third* physical disk. More typically, two physical disks use the primary controller on IRQ 14. Adding a third disk requires using a second IDE controller, which then uses IRQ 15.

Be sure you don't get confused by a response on the exam that refers to IRQ 16. There isn't any number 16. If you can remember that hex (Latin for *6*, e.g., *hexa*gon) numbering uses 16 numbers starting at 0, at least the numbers assigned to the last IRQs make sense; 14 is primary and 15 is secondary for the disk controllers.

I/O Addresses

We know that a PC has a number of I/O devices connected to the motherboard. Each device requires a unique I/O hardware address. Programs and the operating system send instructions to, and read instructions from, the hardware by calling to the I/O addresses. The first megabyte of conventional memory has room for one million *real* addresses used by data (Real mode). Extended memory allows for millions more data addresses. Usually, only about 800 addresses can be used as hardware addresses.

Some memory addresses are reserved for system use, and a typical device uses 4, 8, or 32 bytes of address information. Some of the hardware addresses have been predefined as available for use by the most common devices (though they might not always be used for that purpose).

We did see questions having to do with the origin of a hardware address. During the POST, the BIOS checks the CMOS tables for the existence of an I/O port interface. If this port exists, the CPU assigns a hardware memory address and stores the address in memory for the length of the running session. The main I/O ports (e.g., COM ports) have common default settings.

Once the device has a hardware memory address (from the CPU), the operating system uses the low-memory IRQ vector table to point to their addresses when moving instructions back and forth between the device and the software.

User-configurable devices store configuration settings that tell the device to use a particular port and an I/O address. Often, the I/O address is described in either the CONFIG.SYS or the AUTOEXEC.BAT file.

Cascaded IRQs

The XT BIOS provided for eight IRQ lines (0 through 7). The AT BIOS adds eight more (8 through 15). Instructions for controllers designed to work on an

AT motherboard usually are located at IRQ 9. However, these instructions typically are *redirected*, or *cascaded*, to IRQ2.

Make a note that if IRQ 2 is being used by BIOS instructions, IRQ 9 is also being used. IRQ 9 is *cascading, vectoring*, or *redirecting* to IRQ 2. All three words refer to the same process of pointing to somewhere else. This is a typical question on the exam. When source information is *redirected* to a destination, the destination receives *cascaded* information from that source.

COM And LPT IRQs

Most modern computers have two serial interfaces built into the motherboard. The two serial controllers are on the motherboard. Each controller interface has a cable connecting them to the port connectors on the back panel of the casing (what you see from the back of the box). Many times, COM1 is a PS/2 mouse connector and COM2 is a nine-pin serial connector.

Return to the diagram of the motherboard in Chapter 2(Figure 2.2). Note that both serial ports have their own sockets on the board. The controller sockets are connected to the back of a connector on the back panel of the PC with a cable (usually a ribbon cable). You will see a similar exhibit on the exam and be asked to identify I/O interfaces or other parts of the motherboard.

The two physical interfaces are broken up into four logical COM ports. Each logical port has its own default address. COM1 and COM3 go together with the first serial interface. COM2 and COM4 go together with the extra serial interface.

In the real world, you'll be able to research memory addresses such as those of the COM ports on a given PC. MSD.EXE prints out whether a device is attached to either of the serial ports and which address the device is using. For the purposes of the exam, Table 11.2 lists the default memory addresses assigned to each COM port.

Table 11.2 Default COM port addresses and IRQs.			
I/O Serial Interface	**Port**	**Address (Hexadecimal)**	**IRQ**
Controller 1	COM 1	03F8	4
Controller 1	COM 3	03E8	4
Controller 2	COM 2	02F8	3
Controller 2	COM 4	02E8	3

Here's a mnemonic that might help you build COM addresses during the exam. Observe that the only changing address values are "2-3" and "F-E." All four default addresses begin with 0 and end with 8. The only IRQ choices are 4 and 3.

It might help to think of COM3 and COM4 as "Extra," with an "E" hex address. COM1 and COM2 are "First," with an "F" hex address. The exam is multiple choice, so you won't really need to remember the 0 or the 8.

Using an odd/even trick, COM1 and 3 use the "3" (odd address) and COM2 and 4 the "2" (even address). In other words:

➤ Port 1 (odd), COM1 and 3, use odd "03".

➤ Port 2 (even), COM2 and 4, use even "02".

➤ First (Ph)ysical interfaces 1 and 2 use "F" for First.

➤ Extra logical interfaces 3 and 4 use an "E" for Extra.

➤ The only place the rule reverses is the IRQs 3 and 4 (odd port—even IRQ4, even port—odd IRQ3).

Aside from the COM ports, the default printer (LPT) ports and their IRQs are also considered testable knowledge. The good news is that although the default COM port memory addresses are considered common knowledge, the LPT addresses aren't. LPT ports have a range of addresses, though they commonly try for a default address. Table 11.3 lists the two LPT ports and their default IRQs.

LPT2 is rarely used these days, except on network print servers (PCs under the control of a network operating system and dedicated to managing a shared printer). IRQ 5 is much more often assigned to a sound card on standalone systems. In fact, IRQ 5 is the default for SoundBlaster cards, with LPT1 going to IRQ 7. If LPT2 is being used, it is usually assigned to IRQ 5 and 278h.

Note: LPT2 comes first because IRQ 5 was originally the XT hard drive controller's IRQ. Later PCs have a normal configuration of two parallel ports, so LPT2 took over from the obsolete XT controller.

Table 11.3   LPT2 and LPT1 and their default IRQ lines.

Parallel Interface	IRQ
LPT2 (parallel port)	5
LPT1 (parallel port)	7

We've tried to come up with some ways to help you remember the proper order of the LPT ports and their default IRQs. Here are some suggestions, though you might have your own method:

➤ You have 2 hands with 5 fingers (LPT2-IRQ 5).

➤ "When I was 17 (1-7) It Was a Very Good Year" (LPT1-IRQ 7, and therefore LPT2-IRQ 5).

➤ LPT is 3 letters. If you add "2" (LPT+2) you have "5" (LPT2-IRQ 5).

➤ Parallel printer ports are 25-pin (2-5) connectors (LPT2-IRQ 5).

➤ "There's only 1 God and only 1 heaven, and LPT1 uses IRQ 7."

DMA Channels

Modern (AT-class) PCs have two DMA controllers, each of which provides four channels for fast DMA. Again, a device can use a DMA channel to bypass the CPU and directly access main memory, allowing for faster performance.

The original 8088/86 (8-bit/16-bit) processors provided 4 DMA channels that were capable of supporting both 8- and 16-bit cards. The 80286 added 4 more 16-bit-only channels. Table 11.4 lists the DMA channels and the most common devices configured to use them.

Note: IRQ 5 and IRQ 7 are usually taken by a printer. Typically, IRQ 7 is always taken (LPT1), but IRQ 5 might be available in a configuration situation (e.g., for a sound card).

It's very good policy to follow the instructions for setting IRQs, DMA channels, and I/O ports according to the manufacturer's recommendation, especially

Table 11.4	Direct memory accessing channels.	
DMA Channel	**Bus Width (Bits)**	**Common Device**
1	8 or 16	Sound cards
2	8 or 16	Sound cards; network (LAN)
3	8 or 16	Floppy drive
4	8 or 16	ECP or EPP parallel port
5	16	Cascade channel
6	16	Not assigned
7	16	Not assigned
8	16	ISA IDE hard drive controller

with sound cards and scanners. Install the sound card first and then let it find the IRQ and DMA channel it needs. Install everything else next. Install the sound card before CD-ROM drives as well, then let the CD take whatever DMA channel is open.

> *Note: Windows 95 provides a listing of the in-use DMA channels by selecting the My Computer properties and then the View Resources tab.*

Environment References

Once a sound card is installed, it uses a series of environment variables to know which DMA channels and IRQs to use. The Windows SYSTEM.INI file contains a DEVICE= reference to load the specific driver, and Windows uses the DOS environment variables to complete the card's configuration. The following two lines are taken from an AUTOEXEC.BAT file:

```
SET SOUND=C:\SB16
SET BLASTER=A220 I5 D1 H5 P300 E620 T6
```

The first SET= line from the AUTOEXEC.BAT file creates an environment variable that tells the device that auxiliary files are found in the C:\SB16 subdirectory. The second SET= line uses configuration switches to set environment values for the specific values we're talking about (A220 I5 D1 H5 P300 E620 T6). The environment variables are:

➤ A220, indicating that the address is 220h (hex)

➤ I5 (not 15), indicating IRQ 5 (replacing LPT2)

➤ D1, indicating DMA channel 1

➤ H5, indicating high DMA channel 5

➤ P300, indicating port address 300h

> *Note: Note that the E refers to extended wave audio tables and the T to the type of card. Also note that the lowercase h following a number typically means that the number is a hexadecimal number.*

The following lines are taken from the SYSTEM.INI file under the [386enh] section:

```
device=vcache.386
device=vshare.386
device=vsbawe.386
device=*int13
```

The device=vsbawe.386 reference is the Sound Blaster AWE (sbawe) card driver. The *v* indicates that Windows is using a virtual device driver (VxD). This driver is a 16-bit Windows driver, which in Windows 95 would be a VxD virtual device driver. (*int13 on the following line is a reference to interrupt 13—INT13h.)

The System Is Screwed Up

In many cases, your first contact with a PC will be when someone says, "I don't know what the problem is. Everything was working just fine yesterday, and now it [fill in the exam question]." Typically, the system won't boot up, or the operating environment (DOS, Windows 3.x, or Windows 95) won't start.

Another common situation is where the PC is an unknown system requiring some sort of identification and repair, or optimization. In most cases, a user will be attached to the system. However, in other cases, only a written problem-description will be taped to the box. One of the more interesting problems is when *no information at all* is attached to the computer. This is interesting because a computer can be made to report almost everything about itself (remember MSD.EXE).

 Remember that the two most important steps to take in working with a problem computer are:

1. Making sure that all data is backed up on the hard drive if necessary

2. Making sure to have a bootable disk with the main system files and critical configuration files

The Bootable Disk

Back when every PC used DOS, making a bootable disk was a simple process. You would insert a disk into drive A: and format it with system files (FORMAT A: /S). You would copy over a few useful DOS utilities, and from that point on you could access just about any machine that could spin the floppy drive. Today there are different purposes for bootable disks, and they're created in different ways, depending on the operating system and the user interface.

Make A DOS-Bootable Disk

On a working PC, insert a 1.44MB standard floppy disk into drive A:. Exit all applications or otherwise set the system to a DOS prompt (command line).

Enter "FORMAT A: /S /U" and press Enter to format drive A: and transfer the system files, formatting the disk unconditionally. Allow the process to complete.

Leave the new disk in drive A: and restart the machine. If the machine successfully boots up, you will be asked for the date (press Enter) and the time (press Enter) and arrive at an A: prompt.

Once the bootable floppy has all the files we've talk about, make the disk write protected to prevent the transfer of viruses to its boot sector.

Making a disk bootable means that the three system files (IO.SYS, MSDOS.SYS, and COMMAND.COM) are copied to the disk. Along with the system files, the bootstrap loader (see Chapter 8) is placed in the boot sector. If the disk can start the operating system, the disk is bootable.

SYS.COM

The boot *sector* includes the *master boot record* (MBR). You can't just copy the DOS system files using the COPY command because of the specific location of both the files and the special bootstrap loader. Additionally, both IO.SYS and MSDOS.SYS are hidden files, and COPY won't see them.

SYS.COM is a special DOS program that has one purpose only: to copy the system files to another bootable disk. The destination disk must first have been formatted as a bootable disk. Use SYS.COM to replace corrupted system files on a hard drive by copying clean versions of the system files from a working, virus-free bootable floppy.

SYS.COM is indicated when a hard drive stops (following the POST) and the message "Bad or missing command interpreter" appears. The command to copy the system files from drive A: (bootable disk) to drive C: (with corrupted files) is SYS C: or SYS A: C:.

An even more frightening message following the POST is "Non-system disk or disk error" when you're booting from a hard drive. Boot from your emergency boot disk and see whether you can log on to drive C:. If you can, try SYS.COM.

A bootable floppy will start the operating system and provide a way to test for access to the hard drive. If the system boots and you enter "C:" and press Enter, you should log on to drive C: regardless of whether that drive is bootable. If you can't log on to drive C:, a more serious problem exists.

Make A DOS-Bootable Disk From Windows 3.x

Insert a disk into drive A:. From within Windows 3.x, execute the WINFILE.EXE program or double-click on the File Manager icon.

From the Main menu in File Manager, select DISK/Format Disk. The default drive is A:, so click on OK. In the Format Disk dialog box, make sure that you click on the Copy System Files radio button. Click on OK or press Enter.

Creating a bootable disk in Windows is a fun way to work in the graphical environment, but you don't have the opportunity to choose the /U (unconditional) switch, nor do you have as much control over the process as you do in DOS.

Make A DOS-Bootable Disk From Windows 95

Insert a disk into drive A:. From within Windows 95, execute the EXPLORER.EXE program or select START/Programs/Explorer. One way or another, call up Windows Explorer. Windows 95 won't allow you to format a hard drive, and the Format Disk option will not appear unless you have a disk in drive A:.

With a disk in drive A:, right-click on the drive A: icon in Windows Explorer. In the Properties dialog box, select Format. Make sure that you click on the Copy System Files radio button.

Remember that you can create an emergency startup disk in Windows 95 by selecting START/Settings/Control Panel/Add Remove Programs and clicking on the Startup Disk tab.

Neither Windows 3.x nor Windows 95 will allow you to format a disk unconditionally (completely wiping out any preexisting information). Windows 95 won't allow the format option when you right-click on a nonremovable drive. Fortunately, we still have the option of either going to an MS DOS prompt in a window, or restarting the machine in DOS mode. As long as you can get to a command line, you can still format any disk unconditionally.

Note: The technical geek's term for right-clicking (on the exam) is alternative-click. Don't confuse this with Alt click or the Alt key.

Bootable Disk Utility Files

You can assume that the only time you'll need a bootable disk is in an emergency, in which case you'll need to do some detective work and probably some repair work as well. The repair work could simply be editing a CONFIG.SYS file, or it could be as drastic as performing an FDISK (re-partitioning) on the hard drive.

The Windows 95 emergency startup disk isn't quite the same as a DOS bootable disk. The emergency disk will boot the system using IO.SYS, MSDOS.SYS, and COMMAND.COM. However, it includes a number of utility programs that are automatically copied to the emergency disk by the process. If Windows 95 is workable and the problem involves accessing the hard drive, the emergency startup disk will boot the system and try to load Windows.

 When you run FDISK and partition a hard disk, you totally and irrevocably wipe out all information on the disk. You remove not only applications and data but also the logical drives themselves.

FDISK is used *only* to view the existing partition setup of a hard disk or to completely destroy all information on the hard disk—there is no in-between! If you can think of *any* other option for solving a problem, you should attempt that before using FDISK to completely reinstall the disk.

If Windows 95 can be loaded at all, the emergency startup disk will attempt to load in Safe mode if it can't load normally. The emergency disk contains a number of programs that can be run only from within Windows 95 (e.g., ScanDisk).

Note: If Windows 95 can't load, IO.SYS will still produce a "Starting Windows 95" message, but the start sequence will end at a plain DOS prompt. In this case, no text-based F8-type startup menu will appear, and you'll need to know DOS commands to continue solving the problem.

Some of the utility files that should be copied to the DOS bootable disk include:

➤ FORMAT.COM

➤ FDISK.EXE

➤ EDIT.COM (for editing ASCII startup files)

➤ SYS.COM

➤ SCANDISK.EXE (DOS version) or CHKDSK.EXE

➤ ATTRIB.EXE

➤ DEBUG.EXE (for destroying a boot sector)

Note: DEBUG.EXE is a program for creating assembler (COM) files. In very special cases, the only way to ensure that a boot sector virus has been totally destroyed is to use assembler language. Also note that if you use EDIT.COM on any system prior to Windows 95, you must include QBASIC.EXE as the support file for the editor (or it won't run).

Bootable Disk Configuration Files

A specific PC should have its own dedicated bootable disk. That disk should include up-to-date copies of critical startup files used to start the PC in a normal condition. If the PC has a CD-ROM drive, a device driver must load in the CONFIG.SYS file. References to the device driver might exist in the AUTOEXEC.BAT file as well.

If the PC has a sound card, scanner, mouse, printer, or any peripheral that isn't absolutely critical, the device drivers can probably be replaced in the event of an FDISK-type catastrophe. You should examine the system for SCSI device drivers and other driver files that will be necessary when the problem is fixed.

Note: Make sure that you have copies of any device drivers on the hard drive (if you can access the drive). If you can't find original installation disks for SCSI, sound card, mouse, or other devices, back up copies of any subdirectories with driver files to disk.

Important configuration files to include on a PC's bootable emergency disk include:

➤ CONFIG.SYS

➤ AUTOEXEC.BAT

➤ CD-ROM device drivers (manufacturer-specific), or MSCDEX.EXE (generic CD driver)

➤ WIN.INI and SYSTEM.INI (if necessary)

Place the PC's emergency boot disk in that PC's *system binder* along with a current printout of MSD.EXE. If you had to back up driver files in subdirectories, put those disks in the system binder as well.

Note: A system binder is a three-ring binder containing configuration printouts, unusual instructions relating to a PC, and a number of vinyl disk-sized pocket pages. These vinyl pages hold critical installation disks for drivers, the operating system, and other important devices. The system binder is a good place to keep current backup copies of the SYSTEM.DAD and USER.DAT Registry files.

MSD Report

In the appendix, we discuss MSD.EXE and the idea that a full configuration can be printed as a report. The report is generated as a file, then the file is brought into a word processor or text editor. The MSD report:

➤ Can be run by using the MSD /P [*drive:*][*path*]*filename* to write an MSD report to the specified file without first requesting input (MSD /F requests identifying information for the top of the report.)

➤ Stores a full printout of the current Windows SYSTEM.INI and WIN.INI files

➤ Stores a full printout of the current DOS CONFIG.SYS and AUTOEXEC.BAT files

 Remember that the SYSTEM.INI file contains detailed configuration settings for 16-bit Windows and Real mode device drivers for Windows 95 and Windows 98. The WIN.INI file contains environment settings for 16-bit Windows. Every time the Windows environment or configuration changes, the SYSTEM.INI and WIN.INI files might change.

Although MSD.EXE is a basic diagnostics program found on most PCs today, it can't compare with third-party diagnostics utilities. A number of these utilities are available, and people servicing PCs should have at least one program suite in their black bags.

CMOS Problems

The CMOS can store a machine password that will prompt the user for a password on completion of the POST. Some PCs offer separate passwords for the machine and general access to the operating system. The default option in the CMOS Password setting is to disable the password completely (with the None or Disabled selection). If the machine password is disabled, the POST will automatically hand off to the operating system.

An enabled CMOS password is stored below both the disk and the operating system. In other words, the CMOS password is asked for at the end of the POST and before the boot process begins. If the user forgets the password, the recommended way to recover the system is to remove the CMOS battery to clear the chip, or reconfigure a jumper on the motherboard to clear the chip. These steps will clear all CMOS settings and require reconfiguring the CMOS when the battery is replaced. In the field, some technicians have been known to short-circuit the CMOS jumper to clear the chip. However, although this could be the only available option on the exam, this procedure is not recommended.

Another important setting in CMOS is the order of the drives the POST will check for an operating system. Keep in mind that a *default* setting is the value that will be set if no manual configuration change takes place. In other words, if you don't specify some value for a setting, the default value will be true. The default in most PCs is that the system will search drive A: first and then drive C:. Other settings include disabling the checking of drive A: completely.

> *Note: In the event that drive C: becomes disabled, the operating system can often be booted from drive A:. If the CMOS has disabled the checking of drive A:, there will be no way at all to access the hard drive. Again, the only way to change the CMOS will be to remove the battery (or reset the jumper on those motherboards that provide a jumper).*

CMOS Error Messages

If no operating system is found, POST will return an error message to the screen and pause the system. The two typical messages about a missing operating system are "Bad or missing command interpreter" or "Non-system disk or disk error." These errors indicate that you should try to use SYS.COM to reinstall the DOS system files.

Remember that CMOS errors often can be generated after someone has changed the settings for the computer. Adventuresome people might decide to enter the CMOS and experiment with the settings there. This situation can lead to anything from an inability to boot the machine to a simple pause at the POST screen. Some errors might allow the machine to continue booting after a key (often F1) is pressed.

CMOS Display Type Mismatch

This error indicates that the video settings don't apply to the actual monitor installed on the system. The first step is to reenter CMOS and verify that the correct monitor has been selected.

CMOS Memory Size Mismatch

On many machines, this error will appear when more memory has been added. Autodetection will usually reconfigure the CMOS with a pause during the POST to make sure that what CMOS saw matches reality.

 Displays and hard disks are considered devices, and any one of the attached devices can generate a *CMOS device mismatch error.* Most likely, these errors mean that the wrong device is listed in CMOS for the physical device attached to the machine.

CMOS Checksum Failure

We've seen how parity checking uses an odd-or-even comparison to verify memory chips. In a similar way, checksum validation works with files. A number is read when the file is created and stored. The number can be appended (added on to) the file and stored for later checksum verification. When the file is read again later, the same process runs and should generate the same number. If the new number doesn't match the stored number, there is a *checksum error.* This process is a first step toward identifying a possible virus.

The CMOS checksum failure indicates that corruption exists in the CMOS memory. The memory is storing settings in a sort of file. The settings file has a stored checksum, and when the CPU reads the CMOS internal file, the numbers don't match. Often this can happen with a bad battery or a loose connection to the battery. If changing and checking the battery doesn't solve the problem, it might be a motherboard going bad.

Viruses

A computer virus is a set of instructions (a program) that tells the PC to execute a series of actions without the owner's consent or knowledge. A virus can operate only by running the instructions held within a program. Even the modern macro viruses are a series of instructions. The difference between a program virus and a macro virus is that the macro virus uses an application (MS Word or MS Excel) rather than the operating system as the command interpreter.

Note: Some versions of Windows and DOS offered the Microsoft Anti-Virus (MSAV) utilities as a primitive defense against viruses. Third-party virus protection programs are far better choices because they constantly upgrade their virus databases. Often, these third-party virus-fixing updates can be downloaded from an Internet site.

A virus program usually waits for an event to take place, then executes its instructions. That event might be a specific date and time in the system clock, or a set of keystrokes. A virus also works by attaching itself to a particular program. When the program is run, the virus executes. Each virus program has its own program code, called a *signature*.

Note: Many email messages are clogging the Internet, warning of deadly email viruses. Opening and reading a text email message provides no opportunity to execute a binary program. Only the attachments that come with email messages can be suspect as virus carriers.

Types Of Viruses

A virus is classified according to how the virus is transmitted and how it infects the computer. No matter which kind of virus is involved, it can't be spread by coughing on a machine or by placing a PC too close to another PC (or a VCR). Another common myth (with no basis in reality) is that viruses can enter a PC through some sort of sub-band channel of a modem connection.

The main categories of viruses are as follows:

➤ **Boot sector** Overwrites the disk's original boot sector with its own code. Every time the PC boots up, the virus is executed.

➤ **Master boot sector** Overwrites the master boot sector's partition table on the hard disk. These viruses are difficult to detect because many disk examination tools don't allow you to see the partition sector (head 0, track 0, sector 0) of a hard disk.

➤ **Macro viruses** Written in the macro language of applications, such as a word processor or spreadsheet. Macro viruses infect files (not the boot sector or partition table) and can reside in memory when the specific application's document is accessed. Usually, the virus is triggered by an autorun feature in the application that runs a macro, much like an AUTOEXEC.BAT file. Otherwise, the virus runs by user actions, such as certain keystrokes or menu choices.

Macro viruses can be stored in files with any extension. Most modern applications can recognize their own files by information stored in the header of the file. An MS Word document might have the default .DOC extension or an .XYZ extension. Regardless of the extension, it's still a Word document and is capable of running macros. Macro viruses are spread through file transfers and email. However, they can be executed only by the program that interprets the macro commands. Once again, until email programs include some sort of macro capability, plain email messages can't contain viruses.

How Viruses Work

Viruses of different types work in different ways. Some viruses keep the same code and attach to programs or load into memory. Newer viruses are aware of antivirus programs and make an effort to change their code while continuing to do their damage.

Functional characteristics of viruses include the following:

➤ **Memory-resident viruses** Load themselves in memory, take control of the operating system, and attach themselves to executable files (e.g., .EXE, .COM, and .SYS). These viruses often change the file attribute information and the file size, time, and date information.

Note: Viruses can't attach to .BAT files, because these files are text-based lists of commands. A virus may, however, be attached to a program file called by a batch file.

➤ **Nonresident file viruses** Infect other programs when an infected program is run. They don't remain in memory, so they don't infect the system. These viruses often change the file attribute information and the file size, time, and date information. Like memory-resident viruses, nonresident viruses attach themselves to executable files.

➤ **Multipartite viruses** Combine the characteristics of memory-resident, nonresident file, and boot sector viruses.

 Remember that COMMAND.COM is a program. If a virus attaches itself to the main command interpreter, executing any of the DOS internal commands (e.g., DIR, DEL, or MD) will cause the virus to execute. Inserting a disk infected with a boot sector virus in drive A: and running a simple DIR command often will cause the virus to be copied to the hard drive's boot sector.

➤ **Polymorphic viruses** Modify their appearance and change their *signatures* (their program code) periodically (for example, by changing the order of program execution). This allows the virus to escape signature-scanning detection methods.

➤ **Stealth viruses** Hide their presence. All viruses try to conceal themselves in some way, but stealth viruses make a greater effort to do so. This type of virus can infect a program by adding bytes to the infected file. It then subtracts the same number of bytes from the directory entry of the infected file, making it appear as if no change has taken place.

 It seems that the exam capitalizes on the bizarre and complex names and acronyms used in the PC world. If you know only that polymorphic and multipartite are weird names that you don't hear much at all, you'll have a tool for deciphering any questions that throw these terms at you. Keep in mind that the most deadly viruses tend to affect the boot sector, master boot record, and partition table.

Beep Codes

We've seen that the power-on/self-test routine resides in ROM BIOS and executes when power is supplied to the motherboard at startup. During the time the POST runs and completes, no operating system is loaded, and no device drivers have been put in memory. Therefore, the PC has no way of working with a disk, a monitor, floppy drives, or any other device that requires a driver. There's practically no way for the POST to communicate with you.

The POST produces a pattern of sounds, depending on the exit condition it finds on completion of the program. These sounds access the motherboard's speaker and produce a *beep*. Most programs provide a way to tell the world what happened when the program finished. In DOS, the ERRORLEVEL batch command uses these *error codes* produced by many DOS programs. An error code can include a code for successful completion with no errors.

Table 11.5 lists some of the main beep codes (sound patterns) associated with a POST exit. The PC's speaker beep is a DOS bell control signal (decimal .007, or ^G). *Bell* refers to the old teletype machine bells.

If you hear more than four beeps at startup, you have a precarious situation. The motherboard could be smoking or the CMOS could have lost its mind. Generally, a repeating series of beeps indicates that a network configuration file or user's logon script is failing to find various devices and drives.

HIMEM.SYS And EMM386.EXE

We covered these two memory managers in Chapters 8 and 9, but they're worth mentioning again here because the exam contains some questions about memory. These two driver files are used very differently in 16-bit Windows and Windows 95.

These two files are DOS memory management devices that allow the system to access memory beyond the conventional 1MB of RAM. HIMEM.SYS manages *extended* memory, whereas EMM386.EXE manages *expanded* memory.

Table 11.5	The main AMI BIOS beep codes.
Number Of Beeps	**Meaning**
None	There must always be at least one beep. If you don't hear a beep when the POST has completed, then the PC speaker may be bad. Otherwise, the motherboard has failed or the power supply is bad.
1	Successful: The POST has completed successfully. If you can see everything on the monitor, then the system started okay.
	The most common problem for a successful POST but no monitor is lack of power to the monitor. Check the monitor's fuse and power supply. If the monitor still has no picture following a 1-beep successful POST, then the video card may have a bad memory chip.
	To check the video memory, try reseating the SIMMs and rebooting the machine. If the SIMMs are in tightly and there's still no image, then you'll probably need to buy a new video card, because the SIMMs are usually soldered onto the IC board.
2, 3, or 4	Memory: The POST checks the first 64K of main memory. If you hear 2, 3, or 4 beeps, then either video or main memory has a problem. If the video is working, then there was a parity error in the first 64K of system memory (low memory). Try switching SIMMs between memory banks. If a reboot generates 1 beep, then you have a bad memory module in the switched bank.
4	Clock: 4 beeps can also mean a bad timer oscillator.

Because expanded memory on modern PCs is usually a part of extended memory, HIMEM.SYS must open the door for EMM386 to follow.

 Do whatever you need to do to separate the correct names and characteristics for expanded (EMS) and extended (XMS) memory from conventional memory. The exam will contain a number of questions about how each type of memory works and their correct names. You might use the *386* in EMM386.EXE to think of the old days, back when the 80386 processor was a hot item. Today, practically nothing uses expanded memory, so perhaps you can associate *expanded* with *old* and *386*.

Upper Memory Blocks

DOS and Windows 3.x machines want to have as much base memory (640K application memory) as possible for running DOS applications. DOS 5.0

introduced a change to COMMAND.COM that allowed it to use high memory and upper memory blocks (UMBs) to store parts of itself.

Upper memory blocks are managed by EMM386.EXE, which can run only after HIMEM.SYS has opened the door to extended memory. Therefore, the only way the DOS=UMB directive can be used is if the HIMEM.SYS driver is used first.

After HIMEM.SYS opens access to all memory over the 1MB of conventional memory, COMMAND.COM can be loaded into the high memory area. DOS=HIGH places most of the command processor into high memory (above 640K). To utilize even more extra memory, the UMBs can be made accessible only through the expanded memory driver (EMM386.EXE).

 EMM386.EXE allows high memory and UMBs to be used for applications and drivers. High memory can hold programs by using DEVICEHIGH= (in CONFIG.SYS) and LOADHIGH= (in AUTOEXEC.BAT).

EMM386.EXE

In Chapter 8, we discussed how commands are used. The syntax of any command includes the command and the variables (switches) that can be used to set various configuration values. EMM386.EXE offers a good example of the convention used to describe a command's syntax. The complete syntax for EMM386.EXE is as follows, where each of the settings enclosed in square brackets ([ ]) can either have a value or represent a value:

```
EMM386.EXE [memory] [L=minXMS] [NOEMS] [RAM] [ON|OFF|AUTO]
[I=address-address] [X=address-address] [W=ON|OFF] [Mx]
[FRAME=address] [/Paddress] [Pn=address] [B=address] [A=altregs]
[H=handles] [D=nnn] [N=path]
```

Note: EMM386.EXE RAM (using the RAM switch) provides whatever expanded memory is needed for any DOS applications that require it.

 Conventional memory technically refers to the full 1MB of RAM installed on almost every computer sold in the last 10 years. The lower 640K of application memory is technically called *base* memory. The upper 360K is technically called *high* memory.

DEVICEHIGH and LOADHIGH can take advantage of high memory and UMBs to store device drivers. DOS=HIGH,UMB can load parts of COMMAND.COM into high memory and upper memory blocks.

The certification exam generally uses the conventional memory designation to mean the first 640K and the high memory designation to mean the upper 360K, including UMBs.

Complex CONFIG.SYS

The following CONFIG.SYS file was processed by MEMMAKER, the DOS memory-optimization utility. Let's again discuss the fundamental directives and what they do using a real-world example.

Be sure that you don't get caught saying that MEMMAKER speeds up the overall system performance. MEMMAKER only increases the amount of conventional memory available to DOS applications by moving whatever it can into high memory and UMBs (if they're available). Technically, this can speed up some applications, but for the exam MEMMAKER affects space, not performance.

```
DEVICE=C:\DOS\SETVER.EXE
DEVICE=C:\WINDOWS\HIMEM.SYS /TESTMEM:OFF
DEVICE=C:\WINDOWS\EMM386.EXE RAM I=B000-B7FF WIN=CD00-CFFF
BUFFERS=40,0
FILES=70
DOS=UMB
LASTDRIVE=K
FCBS=16,0
DOS=HIGH
STACKS=9,256
SHELL=C:\COMMAND.COM /P /E:1024
DEVICE=C:\BUSLOGIC\BTDOSM.SYS /D
DEVICEHIGH /L:3,19344 =C:\BUSLOGIC\BTCDROM.SYS /D:MSCD0001
DEVICEHIGH /L:1,22576 =D:\IOMEGA\ASPIPPM1.SYS FILE=SMC.ILM SPEED=10
DEVICE=D:\IOMEGA\SCSICFG.EXE /V
DEVICE=D:\IOMEGA\SCSIDRVR.SYS
DEVICEHIGH /L:1,5888 =C:\DOS\RAMDRIVE.SYS 2048 /E
DEVICE=C:\WINDOWS\IFSHLP.SYS
```

A quick (but subtle) way to see that this PC is not running Windows 95 is the fact that EMM386 has no REM (remark) in front of it, and the existence of the line DOS=UMB. In the analysis of Windows 95, we saw that SETUP.EXE automatically removes any expanded memory drivers from an existing CONFIG.SYS file during the Windows 95 installation process. Windows 95 has its own virtual expanded memory management.

Remember that Windows 95 requires HIMEM.SYS to access extended memory for virtual memory management. HIMEM.SYS has been hard-coded into the IO.SYS file, which took over configuration from CONFIG.SYS. Windows 95 also will cancel with REM any reference to SMARTDRV or EMM386.EXE.

Points Of Interest

Notice that the DEVICEHIGH= directive has been put in by MEMMAKER. The /L:# value is automatically configured when MEMMAKER optimizes the specific addresses. The BusLogic SCSI adapter driver controlling the CD-ROM has been moved to high memory, as has an Iomega driver.

EMM386 (expanded memory) has been told that Windows 3.x is present and to include (/I=) a range of memory addresses for use by devices. This is the I=B000-B7FF switch on the EMM386 line.

A RAM drive has been installed using the DEVICEHIGH /L:1,5888 =C:\ DOS\RAMDRIVE.SYS 2048 /E line. The /L:1,5888 was added by MEMMAKER to put the device driver in high memory. RAMDRIVE.SYS loads the RAM drive device driver and creates a 2MB RAM drive in extended (/E) memory. A companion line in the AUTOEXEC.BAT file could then be used (SET TEMP=G:\) to tell DOS to use the RAM drive for temporary files.

Note: RAMDRIVE.SYS comes with both DOS 6.x and Windows 95.

Finally, HIMEM.SYS is used with an unusual /TESTMEM:OFF switch. During bootup, when the HIMEM extended memory driver is loaded, it tests the memory in almost the same way that the parity check is done during the POST. With 32 or 64MB of RAM installed in many PCs today, this second memory integrity check takes enough time that it can be turned off. /TESTMEM:ON|OFF is the settings switch to either turn off the memory checking or force it (useful with nonparity memory).

DEVICE= And DEVICEHIGH=

This system is not running Windows 95. We can immediately see this by the fact that EMM386.EXE is present. Windows 95 removes any reference to expanded memory drivers during its installation. A typical statement in the above CONFIG.SYS file appears as follows:

```
DEVICE=D:\IOMEGA\ASPIPPM1.SYS FILE=SMC.ILM SPEED=10
```

The DEVICE= directive means that there is a device attached to the system. In this case, the device driver (usually a .SYS file) can be found on drive D: in the \IOMEGA subdirectory. The specific name of the device driver file is ASPIPPM1.SYS. With a little experience, we might guess that this refers to an Iomega Zip, Jaz, or Ditto (tape) drive.

Remember that the CONFIG.SYS file is executed prior to the AUTOEXEC.BAT file during the boot process. The PATH environment variable can be set only after the system is under the control of the operating system. The PATH command can be run only in a batch file or at the DOS command line. PATH= is always found in the first few lines of the AUTOEXEC.BAT file.

Because no search path has been set when the CONFIG.SYS runs, every device must have its full path and file name in the directive. Because no path has been set, DOS can look for the driver file only in the root directory of the bootable disk in the boot drive. This is the directory that DOS is logged in to as the current directory at bootup.

If there were enough memory available in high memory (above conventional memory, according to the exam), the DEVICEHIGH= directive (DOS 5.0 and later) would attempt to load the Iomega (device) driver above the 640K of base memory. In this case, the DEVICE= directive means that the driver is intended to load into conventional (base) memory.

MEMMAKER automatically runs hundreds of configuration settings to see which programs can make the most efficient use of high memory, UMBs, or both. In this case, it determined that the Iomega driver should stay in conventional base memory.

DOS marks an intentional space between characters with an equal sign (=), a semicolon (;), or a space (spacebar or ASCII decimal .0032 scan code). An equal sign or a semicolon is used most often to ensure that a space is marked and to leave no room for misinterpretation. ".0032" can be entered using the Alt key at the same time as the digits are entered on the numeric keypad of the keyboard.

Again, the line we're examining is:

```
DEVICE=D:\IOMEGA\ASPIPPM1.SYS FILE=SMC.ILM SPEED=10
```

A space and more information follow the device driver. FILE=SMC.ILM probably refers to a data file in which either further configuration settings are stored through customer configuration or the device reads factory-configured values.

During SETUP.EXE (all Windows versions) or INSTALL.EXE (DOS) for a new device, a typical detection program uses simple tests to check for the existence of certain hardware and software. This is not the same as the POST looking at CMOS settings.

Depending on whether Yes or No returns from a setup test, the new device's installation routine often chooses one of several files containing factory-configured values. These files are usually taken from the installation disk that comes with the device. Some knowledgeable guesswork would indicate that SMC.ILM is one of these factory configuration files relating to some device made by Iomega.

 The exam might ask you to explain why Windows 95 notices a particular device attached to the system but can't provide the manufacturer's information and settings. Windows 95 has a large internal database of many devices made by today's hardware manufacturers.

If Windows 95 can read settings information from a BIOS chip on a PnP-compatible device, it will configure the device with its correct settings. If Windows 95 can recognize that a generic type of device is attached to an I/O port, it will try to use generic settings, which might work.

If Windows 95 notices only that a device exists at an I/O port but can't even tell which general class (Registry) the device falls into, it will try to prompt the user for specific configuration settings by using the Have Disk option dialog box during installation.

If neither PnP processing nor generic device awareness takes place, the device is ignored in a full PnP-enabled configuration. If PnP is not enabled, Windows 95 resource management stops short of managing device resources.

MSDET.INF

Windows 95 uses detection modules called by MSDET.INF during setup. These DLL modules contain general settings information about classes (general categories) of devices. The specific DLL files that MSDET.INF calls try to read information from a device through PnP BIOS chips on the device. If PnP won't work, the DLL generates common settings for that class of device. The settings are stored in the Registry following completion of the setup routine. This so-called auto-detection became available starting with Windows 95.

The data resulting from the checking process is stored in the DETLOG.TXT file (detection log text file), and the device will have either a manufacturer's name and settings stored in the Registry or a generic class name. To distinguish between true PnP compatibility and the best-guess capabilities built into Windows 95, we use the term *autodetect* here, although it is not the formal name of a feature in Windows 95.

At the end of the SMC.ILM file name is yet another space and the SPEED=10 setting value. Note that no internal way exists of knowing what this refers to beyond some sort of speed setting with 10 being the value. The SPEED setting is explained only in the device's technical reference documentation.

A classic way to troubleshoot a PC is to bypass every reference to any device from all configuration files. Inexperienced technicians tend to use the Delete key to delete the entire file or to delete a line in a configuration file. In this situation, if it should turn out that the device was a critical system driver (such as a SCSI controller), the technician is left with only his or her memory to replace the line.

Regardless of whether CONFIG.SYS supports the REM statement, entering "REM" followed by a space at the beginning of any line in CONFIG.SYS or AUTOEXEC.BAT will cause DOS to bypass the line without executing any instructions. In Windows INI files, use the semicolon (;) followed by a space to accomplish the same bypass.

If it should turn out that a configuration line is necessary, it can be reactivated by deleting the REM or the semicolon, removing the necessity of trying to remember what you've deleted at a later date.

SET=

The DOS environment is a small, 256-byte area of memory set aside to store configuration settings for the operating system to use. We won't discuss how the 256 bytes can be used up, but we will mention that they can be used up by running several instances of COMMAND.COM. Entering the SET command and pressing Enter at a DOS command prompt will produce a report of the current settings. For example, a typical environment report shows the following:

```
TMP=C:\WINDOWS\TEMP
winbootdir=C:\WINDOWS
COMSPEC=C:\COMMAND.COM
WINPMT=$P$G
PROMPT=Type EXIT to$_Return to Windows$_$p$g
PATH=C:\WINDOWS;C:\WINDOWS\COMMAND;C:\;C:\DOS;D:\UTILS;D:\BATCH;
D:\WINUTILS
```

An interesting property of the DOS environment is that the names of the environment variables are automatically converted to uppercase in all instances.

Once you've passed the certification exam, you might be interested in researching how the *winbootdir* variable can show up as lowercase.

Meanwhile, the important variables to note are COMSPEC=, PATH=, PROMPT=, and TMP=. All of these are set manually, except for COMSPEC=, which tells DOS where COMMAND.COM is located. When we say *manually*, we mean either that the user enters a SET [*variable*]=[*value*] command at the command line or that the SET commands can be listed in the AUTOEXEC.BAT batch file. DOS 5.0 introduced an installation routine that created a basic search path, prompt, and TEMP= or TMP= variable.

 The COMSPEC= environment variable is automatically set by COMMAND.COM during the boot process. The value for this variable setting will always be the drive containing the boot disk and the name of the command interpreter file (almost always COMMAND.COM).

We'll discuss the TMP= variable next, but right now you need to know that both DOS and Windows can work with the environment. COMMAND.COM looks in the environment for a number of variable settings whereas DOS batch files move information in and out of the environment in a rudimentary programming capability.

 Batch files are ASCII text files containing DOS commands on separate lines. Batch files must have a .BAT extension. COMMAND.COM contains a number of internal commands that can be used by batch files. Some of the internal commands include the ECHO, @, ERRORLEVEL, PAUSE, FOR, and IF commands.

The exam will sometimes refer to COMMAND.COM as a "batch command processor," although the proper name is "command interpreter."

TMP=

Both Windows and DOS applications use a temporary directory to store overflow files, swap files, and other temporary files. DOS and Windows know where to put those files by looking at the TMP= or the TEMP= setting.

The temporary directories are not required to be called \TMP or \TEMP. They can be called anything you like and be located anywhere on any accessible drive. The important thing is that the SET TEMP= line of the AUTOEXEC.BAT file placed the "TEMP" variable in the environment and named the variable's setting. Windows and DOS look for a variable called TMP or TEMP, but the directories being used can be any valid directory on a local hard drive.

An environment variable can be manually set by entering "SET [*variable name*]=[*value setting*]" (without the quotes) at the command line. To change the PROMPT variable at any time, enter "SET PROMPT=Hello World" (without the quotes) at the command line and press Enter. This would mean that instead of the DOS command line starting with C:\WINDOWS>_, it would start with Hello World_. Entering "PROMPT=$p Hello World$g" (without the quotes) and pressing Enter would cause the command line to start with C:\WINDOWS Hello World>_.

To change the search path to only the \Windows and the \Exam98 directories, enter "PATH=C:\WINdows;c:\eXAm98" (without the quotes) and press Enter.

The SET command itself is required only from within a batch file. Entering only the variable's name and a DOS character separator and then the specific value you want to use is sufficient at the command line. Note that in the PATH variable, the case of the letters is ignored. The semicolon is the formal separator used. The equal sign or a space is the formal character separator following the variable name.

SHELL=

The AUTOEXEC.BAT's SET command sneaked in before we got to the SHELL= directive because this CONFIG.SYS file happens to have a directive to increase the DOS environment. Ordinarily, 256 bytes is enough to handle the few configuration settings DOS uses during a session. In some cases, a larger environment is used for tweaking the speed of the machine (enhancing performance by experimental settings changes). The DOS environment is technically called the DOS *shell*. The line that changes the environment size is:

```
SHELL=C:\COMMAND.COM /P /E:1024
```

The SHELL= environment variable can be set only from within a batch file (like the AUTOEXEC.BAT). In this case, the shell is set to the COMMAND.COM interpreter. The /P switch loads COMMAND.COM and keeps it permanent. The /E: switch tells COMMAND.COM to change the environment, and 1,024 is the value for the number of bytes. The environment has been increased from the default of 256 bytes to 1,024 bytes.

LASTDRIVE=

Certain DOS settings are automatically set to a default value. The DOS shell is 256 bytes by default, and the prompt is C> or A> by default. The default number of logical drives that DOS will accept as valid is set to five. Drives A:

and B: are automatically set as floppy drives, and the first nonremovable disk (drive 0) is set to C:.

> The default setting for LASTDRIVE leaves D: and E: open as additional logical drives, following drives A:, B:, and C: found on a system with a hard disk.

The reason for the limit of 24 logical drives is that drives A: and B: always exist in the system, even if they don't physically exist on the PC. There are 26 letters in the alphabet, so 26 minus 2 (A: and B:) leaves 24. The example we've been using includes the directive:

```
LASTDRIVE=K
```

This line means that DOS has been told to become aware of 11 logical drives. An interesting fact to keep in mind is that Novell uses the default drive F: to search for the LOGIN.EXE command. However, during the installation, Novell requires that the LASTDRIVE be set to Z:. Note that whereas drives are always accessed by using the drive letter and a colon, the LASTDRIVE= statement doesn't require a colon.

> LASTDRIVE is an important (though not required) CONFIG.SYS file directive for networks and is important when many partitions exist on a big hard drive. If no line for LASTDRIVE exists, DOS assumes that only five logical drives exist on the system.
>
> Be sure to remember that COMMAND.COM can recognize 24 drives beyond drives A: and B:, but that an extended DOS partition can contain a maximum of only 23 logical drives. Drive C: must be a primary partition.

If a disk is partitioned into 12 logical drives (two primary partitions and an extended partition with 10 logical partitions), you must create a CONFIG.SYS file (with a text editor) and include the LASTDRIVE=N line. Whether you use DOS, 16-bit Windows, or Windows 95, the extra drives can be made visible only in a CONFIG.SYS file.

In the 12-drive example, the actual value for LASTDRIVE= can be any letter from N to Z; however, if it appears earlier in the alphabet than N (e.g., L), DOS won't see whatever drives exist that would have had the letters you forgot. In this case, the last drive is N (the fourteenth letter) because A: and B: are the floppy drives; therefore, 12 logical drives exist in addition to the floppies.

While today's PCs often come with more than 16MB of RAM, the DOS environment is still only a small area, measured in bytes. Each drive letter takes a small amount of memory, and the elegant way of setting up a system is to use as few letters as necessary rather than arbitrarily setting the last drive to Z in all cases.

DOS Commands

The main thing to remember about DOS is that COMMAND.COM is the command processor (command interpreter) and that it uses MSDOS.SYS and IO.SYS to make up the trio of the DOS operating system. COMMAND.COM has a number of commands (programs) contained inside the overall code making up its COM file. Those mini-programs inside COMMAND.COM are the *internal* commands, which include DIR, COPY, DEL, MD, CD, and TYPE.

 In some cases, an operating system is referred to as the combination of command processor, system files, and user interface. In DOS, COMMAND.COM is the command processor, IO.SYS and MSDOS.SYS are the system files (though COMMAND.COM is technically part of the system files), and the DOS prompt (C:\>_) is the user interface. Although this form of reference is really a set of informal nicknames, you might see this form of reference on the exam.

DOS comes with many other programs besides the main trio. FORMAT.COM, FDISK.EXE, SYS.COM, ATTRIB.EXE, CHKDSK.EXE, and EMM386.EXE are some of the *external* commands. Anything that comes with DOS but that isn't inside COMMAND.COM is an external command. If it can be entered on the DOS command line (MS DOS prompt) or used in a batch or an AUTOEXEC.BAT file, it's a command. Device drivers (.SYS) could be called commands, but they're more accurately called drivers.

Finally, DOS comes with some generic device names that can be used to instruct the basic devices that come with any PC. Some of these devices are PRN (printer), CON (video console), COM (communications), and LPT (line printer). When you enter "COPY FILENAME.TXT PRN" (without the quotes) and press Enter, you tell DOS to copy a file called filename.txt to the printer. The file will then be printed.

Files

When data is created either in programs or in the files created by programs, the result is a file. Files, which are stored on disks, contain the data and instructions that a user has created, as well as additional data that can be used by the operating and file management systems.

A file's header information generally contains identification data that other programs can read. This is how file viewing applications (e.g., Quick View and

Outside-In) can identify the correct viewer to show the file. Every file has an important piece of data, its *attribute bit*, attached to it.

ATTRIB.EXE

Attributes come in four flavors: (H) hidden, (S) system, (R) read-only, and (A) archive. Each attribute can be turned on or off using the plus (+) or minus (-) sign associated with the external ATTRIB command. If an attribute is turned on, it shows in the results of issuing the command. The syntax for ATTRIB.EXE is:

```
ATTRIB [+R | -R] [+A | -A] [+S | -S] [+H | -H] [[drive:][path]filename] [/S]
```

```
 +   Sets an attribute.
 -   Clears an attribute.
 R   Read-only file attribute.
 A   Archive file attribute.
 S   System file attribute.
 H   Hidden file attribute.
 /S  Processes files in all directories in the specified path.
```

The results of using the ATTRIB command show the current attribute of a given file or set of files. DOS 6.x added several switches to the DIR command, where specific files could be shown on the basis of their attribute. For example, the DIR /A:H shows a listing of all hidden files in a directory. Another switch added to DIR is the /S for subdirectories. Prior to these changes in DIR, the only way to see every file in every subdirectory was to use ATTRIB, CHKDSK, or TREE.

Look at the following example of the ATTRIB command:

```
    SHR    IO.DOS        C:\IO.DOS
    SHR    MSDOS.DOS     C:\MSDOS.DOS
A   H      BOOTLOG.PRV   C:\BOOTLOG.PRV
      R    COMMAND.DOS   C:\COMMAND.DOS
      R    WINA20.386    C:\WINA20.386
A          CONFIG.DOS    C:\CONFIG.DOS
A          AUTOEXEC.DOS  C:\AUTOEXEC.DOS
    HR     SUHDLOG.DAT   C:\SUHDLOG.DAT
    H      MSDOS.--      C:\MSDOS.--
    H      SETUPLOG.TXT  C:\SETUPLOG.TXT
A          COMMAND.COM   C:\COMMAND.COM
```

Note that examples of all the types of attributes are listed by entering "ATTRIB" and pressing Enter. In this case, IO.DOS is a system, hidden, read-only file. The DIR /A:[*option*] command lists only those files with the specific attributes you state. The ATTRIB command also shows the subdirectory where the file is located and can use the /S switch to list subdirectories. In older as well as modern PCs, issuing the ATTRIB *.* /S >PRN command is one of the only ways to get a full printout of every file on the disk. The > redirector sends the results of the command to the printer.

> *Note: The TREE command in versions of DOS prior to 7.0 could be used to produce a full listing of files or a graphical report of all directories on a logical drive. Microsoft removed the TREE command in DOS 7.0, leaving shareware utilities as the only way to meet this need.*

Hidden Files

Certain files on a drive are so important that if they don't exist, the system will fail to boot. On the other hand, the Delete command is so easy to use that it is very easy to delete the files. One of the more dangerous aspects of Windows File Manager and Windows Explorer is that files can be easily deleted regardless of whether they are hidden or otherwise protected.

The R (read-only) attribute means that a file can be opened and read but not changed. Read-only does *not* protect the file from being deleted. The hidden and system attributes make the file undeletable by DOS. If you enter "DEL IO.SYS" (without the quotes) and press Enter, the result will be "File(s) not found." IO.SYS is hidden, and you can't delete a file unless DOS can see it.

 Remember that a hidden file is only more difficult, but not impossible, to delete. Windows Explorer, File Manager, or changing the attribute to -H will make the file visible to DOS, after which it can be deleted easily.

Windows Explorer

The default installation of Windows 95 configures EXPLORER.EXE to show only files that DOS can see. These are the files with read-only and archive bits. The configuration can be changed by going to the VIEW/Options/View tab and selecting Show All Files. Unfortunately, Windows Explorer lost the ability to show the file attributes in the listing window.

The only way to see the attributes in Windows Explorer is by clicking on a single file and then right-clicking to the Properties option. At the bottom of the General tab is the particular set of attributes for just that file. ATTRIB or WINFILE is the only way to see an overall listing of attributes, and only ATTRIB.EXE comes with DOS 7.0.

Naming Conventions

An odd reference we came across recently had to do with the Windows 95 file-naming conventions. We know that Windows 95 allows long file names and characters usually not allowed in DOS file names. We also know that DOS uses the 8.3 file name format under Windows 95.

Windows 95 can allow strange characters in a file name, but because DOS uses only specific characters, we've made the assumption that any exam question pertaining to file-naming conventions applies to the DOS process. DOS doesn't allow periods, quotation marks, semicolons and colons, question marks, and asterisks in file names. For detailed information on DOS characters, see Chapter 8.

Printer Problems

Problems with printers are so common and, in many cases, so complicated that many corporations have a dedicated information systems person assigned to working with printers. The only questions we saw on the certification exam dealing with printer problems related to cleaning, paper jams, and the printing process.

 Be sure to review the entire laser printing process in Chapter 7. The technology involved in capturing an image to a drum and putting it onto a piece of paper is an important part of the exam.

Cleaning

Electronic components made of plastic usually come with a reference manual of some kind. Somewhere in the beginning of these manuals is always a short statement about cleaning the components with a damp cloth and mild detergent. This instruction applies to computer parts and external printer parts as well.

Paint and lacquer thinners are designed to take paint and grease off metal or wood that you're about to paint. Electronic components are *delicate,* so use some common sense when answering questions dealing with how to clean devices such as printers. If the component is delicate, you don't use hydrochloric acid to clean it!

Friction

If you remember back to your basic science classes, *friction* is the tendency of certain materials to stick to other materials. When you go skiing, you use polished skis and put wax on the bottoms. Both snow and skis are slippery. When the two come together, the goal is to have a zero-friction event, in which you ski down the slope as fast as possible and are slowed down as little as possible by the friction between the skis and the snow.

Print rollers, on the other hand, are designed to rub against a piece of paper and pull it through a printer. Print rollers need friction to work, so they're often made of rubber. Rubber against paper tends to produce a lot of friction. Grease on rubber is like wax on a ski. The more grease buildup, the less friction the rubber has.

Rubbing alcohol is a grease solvent that evaporates into the air, leaving no residue. Use alcohol on parts that need to retain their friction. Use alcohol on any parts that can't have any liquid residue on them (electronic or electrical conducting parts).

> *Note: Always be sure that you've disconnected components from all electrical power sources before cleaning them with liquids. Liquids tend to conduct electricity and can lead to electrocution.*

Paper Jams

A likely cause of paper jams in printers is either the wrong type of paper (inkjet) or too many sheets of paper trying to get into the printer (laser). A laser printer uses a paper pickup roller and registration rollers to grab a piece of paper from the paper bin. A *rubber separation pad* prevents more than one sheet of paper from entering the printer at a time.

 Remember that laser printers tend to develop paper jams if the separation pad fails to prevent more than one sheet of paper at a time from being pulled into the printer.

Dot Matrix

Remember that dot matrix printers use either a tractor-feed or pressure roller (friction) method of pulling paper through the printer. The pressure rollers press down on a piece of paper and hold it tight against the *platen* (the big roller behind the paper that backs the paper and ribbon). When the print head pushes the pins into the ribbon and paper, the platen takes the pounding. Once the line of characters has been printed, the platen turns, as do the tractor gears on the sides of the platen. As the gears turn, they pull the paper forward one line.

The platen has no real effect on moving the paper, so it doesn't need to be cleaned. However, the tractor gears don't always turn at the same speed, so if the paper isn't lined up exactly and the tractor wheels don't turn at the same speed, the paper begins to develop a slant as it moves through the printer and eventually will jam.

Cleaning a dot-matrix printer is usually a preventative maintenance measure. Naturally, vacuuming out dust and debris periodically, or using a can of compressed air to blow out dust, is a simple process. The internal tractor belts and the rubber parts of the pressure rollers can often be cleaned with a proper chemical rubber-cleaning compound. Keeping torn pieces of paper out of the internal drive mechanism is another periodic cleaning task.

In addition, you should always check the instructions on rubber-cleaning chemicals. Some chemicals are destructive to various types of rubber. Check the printer's reference manual as well before using solvents.

Home Position

Dot matrix and many inkjet printers require the printhead to start in an exact location—the *home* position. Some printers use a system of counting a series of pulses sent by the printer's motor. When the correct number of pulses has been counted, the printhead is in the home position. Other printers use an optical sensing device to locate the printhead in the home position.

Typically, when power is supplied to a printer at startup, part of the initialization procedure is to set the printhead to its home location. When the printhead is aligned, many printers will sound two beeps to let you know the printer is ready to accept print jobs.

Exam Prep Questions

Question 1

> What is the highest IRQ number that can be used in an AT system?
>
> ○ a. IRQ 16
>
> ○ b. IRQ 15
>
> ○ c. IRQ 12
>
> ○ d. IRQ 9

The answer is b. Sixteen IRQs are available to devices in an AT system. Because the IRQs are numbered in the common technical format (i.e., hexadecimal), the first IRQ is 0. The upper limit is IRQ 15. There are 16 IRQs to conform with hex memory addressing (base 16) and the 16 segments of conventional memory.

Question 2

> How many DMA controllers do AT systems have?
>
> ○ a. Two
>
> ○ b. One
>
> ○ c. Four
>
> ○ d. Eight

The answer is a. AT systems are provided with two DMA controllers running four DMA channels each.

Question 3

> What is the default address of COM 2?
>
> ○ a. 02E8
>
> ○ b. 03E8
>
> ○ c. 03F8
>
> ○ d. 02F8

Answer d is correct. The default address of COM 2 is 02F8.

Question 4

> What is the default IRQ for LPT1?
>
> ○ a. 5
>
> ○ b. 7
>
> ○ c. 3
>
> ○ d. 2

The correct answer is b. The default IRQ for LPT1 is 7.

Question 5

> What would be the best way to recover from a lost CMOS password?
>
> ○ a. Order a new CMOS from the factory.
>
> ○ b. Download system settings and flash the CMOS.
>
> ○ c. Momentarily remove power from the CMOS and then reconfigure it.
>
> ○ d. Use a boot disk to boot the system and change the password file.

Answer c is correct. An enabled CMOS password is stored below both the disk and the operating system. In other words, the CMOS password is asked for at the end of the POST and before the boot process begins. If the user forgets the password, the recommended way to recover the system is to remove the CMOS battery to clear the chip or reconfigure a jumper on the motherboard to clear the chip. These steps will clear all CMOS settings and require reconfiguring the CMOS when the battery is replaced.

Question 6

> What type of computer virus can modify its appearance and change its signature?
>
> ○ a. Multipartite
>
> ○ b. Polymorphic
>
> ○ c. Stealth
>
> ○ d. Nonresident file

Answer b is correct. Polymorphic viruses modify their appearance and change their signatures (their program code) periodically (for example, by changing the order of program execution). This allows the virus to escape signature-scanning detection methods.

Question 7

> Print rollers should be cleaned with what type of solvent?
>
> O a. Alcohol
>
> O b. Mild soap and water
>
> O c. Thinner
>
> O d. Print rollers are brushed clean, solvents are not
>   recommended

Answer a is correct. Print rollers need friction to work properly. Therefore, they must be cleaned with a solvent that will dissolve grease and leave no residue. Alcohol has these properties and is an excellent solvent for cleaning print rollers.

Need To Know More?

Aspinwall, Jim: *IRQ, DMA & I/O*. MIS Press, New York, NY. 1995. ISBN 1-55828-456-7.

Bigelow, Stephen: *Troubleshooting, Maintaining, and Repairing Personal Computers*. TAB Books, New York, NY. 1996. ISBN 0-079-12099-7.

Bigelow, Stephen: *Troubleshooting & Repairing Computer Printers*. TAB Books, New York, NY, 1996. ISBN 0-07-005732-X.

Karney, James: *Upgrade and Maintain Your PC*. MIS Press, Indianapolis, IN. 1996. ISBN 1-558-28460-5.

Minasi, Mark: *The Complete PC Upgrade and Maintenance Guide*. Sybex Network Press, San Francisco, CA. 1996. ISBN 0-782-11956-5.

Sample Test

You're ready to take the test. The following test is as accurate a representation as we've been able to make in terms of what you'll see in the exam room. The only difference is that you will be taking the exam in two parts, and we have combined those parts into one.

We covered many test-taking strategies in the Introduction and Chapter 1 of this book, and you should feel comfortable about your knowledge before you take this sample test. After you complete the sample test, you can turn to Chapter 13 to check your answers.

You only get one chance to be surprised in a book like this. No matter how much you pretend to be surprised, if you skim the answers and take the test again, it won't be the same. You can read the end of a novel, then go back and experience some excitement by finding out how the ending was brought about. It isn't the same with a sample test.

Give yourself 90 minutes to complete this sample exam. Sit at a table or desk, and try to make the table as clear of any other items as possible. Lay down a piece of paper and a pencil and spend five minutes writing down the facts that you most want to have handy (from the Cram Sheet and your notes). Try to re-create the exam rooms you remember from your past. The more accurate you create a virtual final environment, the more comfortable you'll feel when your scheduled exam day comes around.

Picking The Right Answer

Go back and refresh your memory with the Introduction and Chapter 1, and think about the types of questions you're about to encounter. Keep in mind that the people creating the test (ourselves included) take a sort of twisted pleasure in making things difficult. We've been where you are, and we made it through, so you can, too!

Keep your eyes peeled for the following:

➤ Words like *best*, *required*, and *most appropriate* These are red flags telling you that there are multiple possibilities based on how an unstated industry standard might apply.

➤ **Long lists of commands** These can easily be read in the wrong order if you don't have your eyes focused. Write them on your scratch paper, and put numbers next to them to ensure the proper order.

➤ **Questions that try to draw images in your mind** Let the image come, and try to see it clearly. Add sound and action. These questions are usually "customer service" questions.

Confusing Questions

By the time this test reaches your hands, many people read it through, reviewed it, made suggestions, and researched every single word and punctuation mark. This test has been designed with psychology in mind and with a full knowledge of many other tests. If there's confusion about a particular question, you can pretty much bet your next paycheck that the confusion was specifically designed into the question.

We found a number of questions on the exam that really *were* confusing. To that end, we've tried to highlight those areas of knowledge in this book, and to give you our thoughts and how we analyzed the questions. In our own version of the exam, we've tried to cause you some confusion as well, but in a very specific manner.

Part of our preparation methodology is based on the idea that if you've read the book and you're feeling comfortable, you should have a fair amount of intuition going for you. Based on that assumption, we still want to throw a few curve balls at you so that you'll be somewhat familiar with the "Yikes!" feeling when it hits you in the real exam (and it will!).

Just remember—trust your instincts. If you get some of our most confusing questions right, then you'll probably do extremely well on the CompTIA exam. If you get them wrong, don't feel bad. They're *designed* to be difficult. After you check your answers using Chapter 13's answer key, the likelihood that you'll remember where you got tripped up is far greater than before, and we've crammed just that much more into your head.

The Exam Framework

The questions you're about to work with have been organized in a general order. We've made no attempt to follow the progression of this book, nor to follow any other sort of logical order. This is a general test of your overall knowledge of microcomputers.

The real world comes at you from every direction at once, and, frequently, you have to juggle many important problems at the same time. This test has also been designed with possible job interviews in mind, where you're brought back to a technical repair environment and turned loose for an hour or so.

Many of the questions use jargon phrasing and shortened versions of terminology. Throughout the book, we've tried to highlight how many concepts can be restated in different ways. We've varied the words used to refer to similar concepts and included both acronyms and fully spelled-out phrases throughout the text. Repeatedly, we've tried to prepare you for the varying ways that technical professionals refer to problems and to the tools of the trade.

The A+ exam was created by a committee of professionals, each of whom has a different way of talking about computers. We've tried to extract as many of those styles as possible and to jumble them together to simulate the A+ exam. Life is rarely simple, and this exam (in our opinion) is quite difficult.

Begin The Exam

From the time you complete your notes on the blank sheet of paper, you have 90 minutes to complete the test. Take your time, and imagine you're ship-wrecked on a desert island and have all the time in the world. Read every word carefully, and then read the whole question a second time before you look at the responses.

Read each response on its own, and don't try to fit it in with the question. When you've read each response as though it were a random statement of fact, go back and read the question one more time.

A common flaw in the human mind is that it immediately attempts to make sense out of incoming data. This flaw is often used against you on various exams. By reading the question on its own and then reading each response without thinking about the question, you overload the "surprise circuit." Once your mind stops trying to puzzle over the question, you're ready to actually read the question as it stands.

Start your timer, and begin the exam now.

Question 1

Your primary controller is connected to a disk with one active and one extended partition formatted as one logical drive. You connect a second disk drive to the secondary controller and create two partitions. Which drive letter will be assigned to the first of the new partitions?

○ a. C

○ b. D

○ c. E

○ d. F

Question 2

How many devices can be attached to a SCSI chain?

○ a. 5

○ b. 6

○ c. 7

○ d. 8

Question 3

If you use IRQ 2 in an AT system, which IRQ cannot be used?

○ a. IRQ 13

○ b. IRQ 5

○ c. IRQ 9

○ d. IRQ 8

Question 4

You are upgrading Windows 3.1 to Windows 95. What should you do with regard to SMARTDRV?

○ a. Expand its size to speed loading.

○ b. Disable SMARTDRV.

○ c. Change the settings for SMARTDRV to protected mode.

○ d. Activate the write through option for SMARTDRV.

Question 5

What is MEMMAKER used for in DOS 6.2?

- ○ a. MEMMAKER is used to free up more conventional memory.
- ○ b. MEMMAKER loads Microsoft's expanded memory driver.
- ○ c. MEMMAKER autoconfigures newly added RAM.
- ○ d. MEMMAKER is not used in DOS 6.2.

Question 6

What function key stops the automatic loading of Windows 95 and provides you with a menu of options for loading?

- ○ a. F1
- ○ b. F8
- ○ c. F9
- ○ d. F3

Question 7

Which of the following would aid system cooling?

- ○ a. Remove the expansion covers in the back of the system case for increased airflow.
- ○ b. Attach covers to any open expansion slots on the back of the system unit.
- ○ c. Place the system unit against a cool inside wall.
- ○ d. Open windows to increase airflow in the room.

Question 8

Which is the common, default IRQ used for LPT2?

- ○ a. IRQ 5
- ○ b. IRQ 9
- ○ c. IRQ 7
- ○ d. IRQ 14

Question 9

Choose the appropriate response to fill in the blanks. When a piece of paper comes out of a laser printer almost completely black, the _____ has failed to properly _____ the _____.

- ○ a. separation pad, separate, paper
- ○ b. heated roller, fuse, toner
- ○ c. primary corona, charge, EP drum
- ○ d. transfer corona, charge, paper

Question 10

What is true of XT system boards?

- ○ a. They use ZIF sockets for processor mounting.
- ○ b. The expansion bus width is limited to eight bits.
- ○ c. Configuration settings are stored in a battery backed up CMOS.
- ○ d. Processor voltage is set by jumpers on the system board.

Question 11

What parts of a dot matrix printer should never be lubricated?

- ○ a. Nonmetallic platen drive gears
- ○ b. Print head ballistic wires
- ○ c. Print head carriage guide
- ○ d. Tractor feed drive gears

Question 12

The thermal fuse fails in a laser printer. What is the most probable cause?

- ○ a. The fuser overheated.
- ○ b. The corona wire shorted.
- ○ c. The drum overcharged.
- ○ d. The laser diode needs changing.

Queston 13

Which of the following components is a common source of powerful static build-up?

○ a. An ESD

○ b. A resistor

○ c. A chassis

○ d. A monitor

Question 14

The print from a dot matrix printer is erratic, with some characters only partially printed. What needs to be done?

○ a. The ribbon needs to be replaced.

○ b. The print head needs to be aligned.

○ c. A lighter-weight paper needs to be used.

○ d. The tractor feed needs adjusting.

Question 15

HIGHMEM.SYS is reported missing or corrupted as Windows 95 loads. What will happen?

○ a. Nothing. Windows 95 does not require HIMEM.SYS.

○ b. Windows 95 will load in Safe mode.

○ c. Windows 95 will fail to load.

○ d. Windows 95 will load but only have access to the first 1MB of RAM memory.

Question 16

Windows 95 recognizes a new modem as a "standard modem" and does not identify the type and manufacturer. Why?

○ a. Windows 95 does not have a driver for this modem.

○ b. The modem is not PnP.

○ c. The SYSTEM.DAT does not have a listing.

○ d. The modem is not seated correctly.

Question 17

Safe mode for Windows 95 loads which of the following display drivers?

○ a. SVGA

○ b. VGA

○ c. EGA

○ d. CGA

Question 18

A DOS file with the .TXT extension is best edited with which of the following?

○ a. MS Word

○ b. MS Write

○ c. MS Paint

○ d. WordPad

Question 19

You have decided to edit CONFIG.SYS on a Windows 3.1 system, using MS Works. Clicking on "SAVE" saves the CONFIG.SYS with a .SYS extension in a Works format. The most likely effect of this will be:

○ a. The system will read the file faster.

○ b. The system runs a spell-check at POST.

○ c. The system ignores the CONFIG.SYS file.

○ d. The system produces a "File(s) not found" message.

Question 20

ATTRIB C:*.SYS /S /-H will cause the following:

○ a. Delete SYS files from the C: drive

○ b. Archive SYS files in the root directory

○ c. Unhide SYS in the root directory

○ d. Unhide SYS on the entire drive C:

Question 21

The CONFIG.SYS file contains the line LASTDRIVE=F. The system uses a CD-ROM, one primary partition, and three logical DOS drives. A loaded CD-ROM disk will:

○ a. Install a program

○ b. Become the G: drive

○ c. Become the F: drive

○ d. Do nothing at all

Question 22

To bypass the execution of a line in a configuration file, the following two choices are used:

○ a. REM and ;

○ b. REM and :

○ c. : and ERASE

○ d. // and REN

Question 23

What device would best protect a PC against erratic power and blackouts?

○ a. A line conditioner

○ b. A surge protector

○ c. UPS

○ d. ATA

Question 24

Two files that are part of the Windows 3.11 kernel are:

○ a. IO.SYS and GDI.EXE

○ b. KERNL386.EXE and MSDOS.SYS

○ c. GDI.EXE and USER.EXE

○ d. KERN386 and WIN.COM

Question 25

What are the default interrupts and addresses for COM1?

○ a. IRQ 4 and 27F8h

○ b. IRQ 5 and 03F8h

○ c. IRQ 4 and 03F8h

○ d. IRQ 3 and 02E8h

Question 26

The small "h" following an address indicates:

○ a. The address should be read in hexadecimal.

○ b. The address uses a high-order bit.

○ c. The address is a default address.

○ d. The address uses hard coding.

Question 27

The standard VGA monitor has a horizontal resolution of:

○ a. 640 pixels

○ b. 480 pixels

○ c. 300 dpi

○ d. .28 dot pitch

Question 28

A monitor that draws every other line on the screen, then returns and draws skipped lines is called:

○ a. Interfaced

○ b. Noninterfaced

○ c. Interlaced

○ d. Noninterlaced

Question 29

A cable in a 10BaseT Ethernet network breaks. What is the most likely result?

○ a. The entire network crashes

○ b. Only the PC attached to that cable loses connectivity

○ c. The network operating system forces a system shutdown

○ d. Nothing

Question 30

What is the default networking protocol used on the Internet?

○ a. IPX/SPX

○ b. DNS

○ c. TCP/IP

○ d. MIME

Question 31

The following files are executable:

○ a. .EXE, .COM, .BAT, .DRV

○ b. .COM, .BAT, .PIF, .EXE

○ c. .EXE, .DBF, .OVL, .ZIP

○ d. .BAT, .COM, .DLL, .INI

Question 32

How would you run two separate applications at the same time in DOS?

○ a. Run the applications in Protected mode.

○ b. Run in 386 Enhanced mode.

○ c. Enable multithreaded multitasking.

○ d. None of the above.

Question 33

Which command will list all files in the directory where the third character of the extension is the underscore (_)?

○ a. DIR *._

○ b. DIR *.*_

○ c. DIR *.?_

○ d. DIR *.??_

Question 34

The Windows 95 REGEDIT.EXE program is used to edit which file or files?

○ a. SYSTEM.DAT and MSDOS.SYS

○ b. WIN.INI and SYSTEM.INI

○ c. REG.DAT

○ d. SYSTEM.DAT

Question 35

The following seven files are run in what sequence to start Windows 3.1?

○ a. IO.SYS, MSDOS.SYS, COMMAND.COM, CONFIG.SYS, AUTOEXEC.BAT, SYSTEM.INI, WIN.INI

○ b. IO.SYS, MSDOS.SYS, CONFIG.SYS, COMMAND.COM, AUTOEXEC.BAT, SYSTEM.INI, WIN.INI

○ c. IO.SYS, MSDOS.SYS, CONFIG.SYS, AUTOEXEC.BAT, COMMAND.COM, SYSTEM.INI, WIN.INI

○ d. IO.SYS, MSDOS.SYS, CONFIG.SYS, COMMAND.COM, AUTOEXEC.BAT, WIN.INI, SYSTEM.INI

Question 36

A polymorphic virus cannot change the:

○ a. Boot sector

○ b. Master boot record

○ c. IRQ sector

○ d. Partition table

Question 37

How many DMA controllers and DMA channels are on an AT system board?

○ a. 2 controllers and 8 DMA channels

○ b. 1 controller and 16 DMA channels

○ c. 1 controller and 4 DMA channels

○ d. 2 controllers and 16 DMA channels

Question 38

What switch would you add to the DOS FORMAT command to make a floppy disk bootable?

○ a. /B

○ b. /U

○ c. /S

○ d. /A

Question 39

Which of the following would be a time to use the DOS FDISK command?

○ a. You would use FDISK to optimize hard drive access time.

○ b. You would use FDISK to view hard drive partitions.

○ c. You would use FDISK to format a disk.

○ d. You would use FDISK to correct errors in the FAT.

Question 40

A user has set a password in CMOS and then forgotten it. What would you do to gain access to the system?

- ○ a. Use one of the password-breaking programs available on the Internet.

- ○ b. Remove battery power to CMOS to clear it, reconnect the battery, and then reconfigure the CMOS.

- ○ c. Boot the system from a floppy disk, and check the file USERPASS.INF for the correct password.

- ○ d. Call the BIOS manufacturer, and ask for the master password.

Question 41

There is no beep code at system startup. What is the most likely problem?

- ○ a. The speaker is disconnected.
- ○ b. There is no beep code for a normal system start.
- ○ c. The system clock is not working.
- ○ d. A memory module failed the POST.

Question 42

The best cleaning solution to use on a dirty system case is:

- ○ a. Alcohol
- ○ b. Carbosol
- ○ c. Mild soap and water
- ○ d. Diluted muric acid

Question 43

What device uses electrical current levels that can be potentially lethal?

○ a. CD drives

○ b. Power supplies

○ c. SCSI hard drives

○ d. Internal tape backup units

Question 44

What electrical component found in computers can hold an electrical charge even when disconnected from power?

○ a. A resistor

○ b. A capacitor

○ c. A diode

○ d. A potentiometer

Question 45

A good fuse will give what kind of reading when tested with a standard multimeter?

○ a. High DC volts value

○ b. Low ohm value

○ c. High ohm value

○ d. High capacitance value

Question 46

To reduce possible ESD damage while repairing a PC, what is the most effective way to ground yourself?

○ a. With a copper strap attached to the workbench

○ b. With a copper strap attached to the PC

○ c. By touching the chassis while replacing components

○ d. None of the above

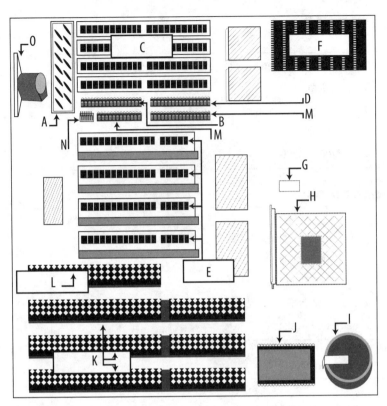

Exhibit 12.1   Use this motherboard diagram to answer questions 47 through 51.

Question 47

What are the two items pointed to by the letter "M"?

○ a. Serial interface

○ b. ISA bus slot

○ c. L2 cache chips

○ d. Batteries

Question 48

What is the item pointed to by the letter "H"?

○ a. Modem

○ b. Battery

○ c. CPU

○ d. Parallel interface

Question 49

What are the three items pointed to by the letter "K"?

○ a. 8-bit ISA slots

○ b. 50-bit SCSI slots

○ c. LPT ports

○ d. 16-bit ISA slots

Question 50

What is the letter "C" labeling?

○ a. PCI bus

○ b. SIMM slots

○ c. ZIF socket

○ d. BIOS chip

Question 51

What does the letter "O" point to?

○ a. AT keyboard connector

○ b. Orientation chip

○ c. Power supply

○ d. LPT connector

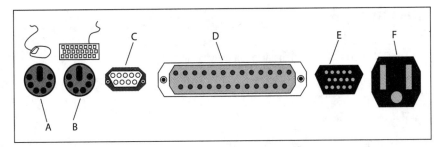

Exhibit 12.2   Use this chassis back panel diagram to answer questions 52 through 54.

Question 52

A parallel printer cable connects to which item (designated by a letter)?

○ a. C

○ b. D

○ c. E

○ d. F

Question 53

What is the item pointed to by the letter "E"?

○ a. Serial interface connector

○ b. Parallel interface connector

○ c. Video interface connector

○ d. AC power connector

Question 54

A COM port is shown in the diagram by what letter?

O a. B

O b. C

O c. D

O d. E

Question 55

You are currently logged in to the C:\UTILITY directory. At the command line, you type "RUNME" and press Enter. That PATH environment variable has been set to PATH=C:\WINDOWS;C:\DOS; C:\BATCH. When you press Enter, the message "File(s) not found" appears on the screen. Which is the most likely reason?

O a. RUNME.COM is in the C:\BIN directory.

O b. RUNME is not a proper word.

O c. You failed to type "PATH=RUNME".

O d. The SET command wasn't issued first.

Question 56

On the way to a client site, you have a vehicle accident that delays your arrival by two hours. When you arrive at the client's offices, you should:

O a. Show the client your copy of the police report and describe why the accident took two hours to clean up.

O b. Explain to the client that you were not at fault but that you had to fill out a police report.

O c. Tell the client you feel upset and that you need a quiet place to collect your thoughts.

O d. Apologize for being late and ask where the problem computer is located.

Question 57

You greet a customer, and they tell you that they've been to your location three times now, and their computer still doesn't work. They tell you that "You people are incompetent idiots, and we don't know why we brought the darn PC here in the first place." Your most appropriate response should be:

○ a. Tell them it wasn't your fault that the previous technician doesn't know what he's doing.

○ b. Tell them to keep their voice down to avoid a scene.

○ c. Empathize with them, and tell them you want to bring the lead technician out to take a look at the PC.

○ d. Offer them a coupon for a free disk of clip art.

Question 58

You are assigned to the main counter in a retail store that provides technical support and repair. You have five customers whom you're helping and the phone rings. When you pick up the phone, the caller tells you they have a problem installing some software. The most appropriate response would be to:

○ a. Tell the caller to hang on, and put them on hold.

○ b. Ask the caller if you can return their call within 30 minutes, and get their phone number.

○ c. Ask the caller if they purchased the software from your store.

○ d. Tell the caller that the store is closing and to call back the next day.

Question 59

When a PC is powered on, the POST routine completes with one beep. This means that:

○ a. The system is testing the PC speaker.

○ b. The system has a nonsystem disk in Drive A:.

○ c. The system has completed the POST with no errors.

○ d. The system CMOS has a bad battery.

Question 60

> A common ribbon cable used to connect a SCSI device has how many pins?
>
> ○ a. 25
>
> ○ b. 36
>
> ○ c. 50
>
> ○ d. 9

Question 61

> When you save a file to a disk, the information about which sectors and clusters the file is using is placed in the:
>
> ○ a. PAT
>
> ○ b. FAT
>
> ○ c. DIR
>
> ○ d. ROM

Question 62

> The Windows 95 default installation process removes which file reference from a CONFIG.SYS file?
>
> ○ a. EMM386.EXE
>
> ○ b. HIMEM.SYS
>
> ○ c. SETVER.EXE
>
> ○ d. MSDOS.SYS

Question 63

> In the first megabyte of RAM installed on a machine, the following types of memory are used by DOS:
>
> ○ a. Expanded, UMBs, High
>
> ○ b. Conventional, High, Extended
>
> ○ c. Low, High, Conventional
>
> ○ d. Extended, Conventional, Base

Question 64

Which of the following best describes an I/O address?

- ○ a. The location of a device on the motherboard
- ○ b. The address used by the device to bypass main memory
- ○ c. A memory address used by a TSR
- ○ d. A memory address used by a COM port

Question 65

IRQ 14 is the default IRQ assigned to which of the following?

- ○ a. Secondary disk controller
- ○ b. Primary disk controller
- ○ c. Master slave disk controller
- ○ d. XT drive controller

Question 66

A cable has a 25-pin male connector at one end and a Centronics 36-pin male connector at the other end. A common use for this cable is best described by which of the following choices?

- ○ a. A parallel printer connection
- ○ b. A modem connection
- ○ c. A serial printer connection
- ○ d. A SCSI device connection

Question 67

The message "Bad or missing command interpreter" appears on the monitor following the POST. Which of the following is the best procedure to follow?

○ a. Use FDISK C: to examine the partition table of the hard disk.

○ b. Use SYS C: to transfer system files to the hard disk.

○ c. Use FORMAT C: /S to transfer system files to the hard disk.

○ d. Use FDISK /MBR to re-create the master boot record.

Question 68

The last five in the 10Base5 standard refers to:

○ a. The maximum length of the cable in hundreds of meters

○ b. The width of the cable in centimeters

○ c. The width of the center conductor in millimeters

○ d. The maximum number of connections per meter

Answer Key
To Sample Test

1. c	24. c	47. a
2. c	25. c	48. c
3. c	26. a	49. d
4. b	27. a	50. b
5. a	28. c	51. c
6. b	29. b	52. b
7. b	30. c	53. c
8. c	31. b	54. b
9. c	32. d	55. a
10. b	33. d	56. d
11. c	34. d	57. c
12. a	35. b	58. b
13. d	36. c	59. c
14. a	37. a	60. c
15. c	38. c	61. b
16. a	39. b	62. a
17. b	40. b	63. c
18. d	41. a	64. d
19. c	42. c	65. b
20. d	43. b	66. a
21. d	44. b	67. b
22. a	45. b	68. a
23. c	46. d	

Here are the answers to the questions presented in the sample test in Chapter 12.

Question 1

The answer is c. Drives A: and B: are automatically installed on a PC. The primary controller has a C: drive for the active partition and a D: drive for the extended partition. The second disk will start with the E: drive regardless of how many logical drives are installed on the disk. The question says that "one active and one extended partition with one logical drive" are on the first disk. Therefore, the entire extended partition on the first disk is a logical D: drive.

Question 2

The answer is c. Up to seven devices can be daisy-chained to a SCSI controller, each with a unique ID number.

Question 3

The answer is c. The AT BIOS cascades IRQ 9 to IRQ 2.

Question 4

The answer is b. Windows 95 doesn't use SMARTDRV. If you don't remove or comment out the SMARTDRV line from your CONFIG.SYS file, SETUP.EXE will do it for you.

Question 5

The answer is a. MEMMAKER optimizes the first megabyte of conventional memory. The optimization is commonly referred to as "freeing up more memory" by allowing device drivers and TSRs to be loaded into high memory and UMBs.

Question 6

The answer is b. The F8 key, pressed between the time the "Starting Windows 95" message and the Microsoft Windows 95 logo appear, interrupts the load process and produces the text-based Start menu.

Question 7

The answer is b. The expansion slot covers are part of the internal space's engineering design and allow for optimal airflow within the case. Removing unused slot covers causes cooling air to flow out of the case and generally increases the temperature inside the case.

Question 8

The answer is c. LPT2 uses IRQ 7, while LPT1 uses IRQ 5. IRQ 9 redirects to IRQ 2, and IRQ 14 is the primary disk controller.

Question 9

The answer is c. The primary corona wire is used to place a negative charge on the electrophotosensitive (EP) drum. This removes toner from those areas that will not produce an image. The secondary corona places a charge on the paper to attract toner to the correct locations. If the paper fails to charge, no toner will stick to the paper for fusing. If the drum fails to charge correctly, the entire drum will take on toner and transfer it to the whole piece of paper.

Question 10

The answer is b. Although the XT used both the 8088 and the 8086 CPU, both processors connected to an eight-bit expansion bus. The ZIF (zero-insertion force) CPU socket is a recent development. The AT motherboard introduced the CMOS chip for storing configuration settings. Processor voltage has nothing to do with system board jumpers.

Question 11

The answer is c. Nonmetallic parts are rarely lubricated. The print head does not provide for general maintenance. Tractor feed drive gears are passive parts. The print head carriage guide requires the smoothest possible movement of the print head to avoid character printing problems.

Question 12

The answer is a. The fuser step of the printing process involves high amounts of heat to melt the toner and fuse it to the paper. For safety, a thermal fuse is inserted in the circuit to prevent possible fire hazards.

Question 13

The answer is d. A monitor builds up a heavy static charge.

Question 14

The answer is a. The clue is that some characters are only partially printing. The immediate diagnostic test would be to replace the existing ink ribbon. The weight of the paper has no direct connection to the print quality. The tractor feed could cause misalignment of characters. Print head alignment is not a common cause of partial character printing.

Question 15

The answer is c. Windows 95 requires HIMEM.SYS and a minimum of 4MB of extended memory. HIMEM.SYS is a memory manager that allows access to all memory above the first 1MB of conventional memory. If HIMEM.SYS fails, Windows 95 cannot access anything more than 1MB of memory and will fail to load.

Question 16

The answer is a. If Windows 95 can access the device and understand that the device is a modem, it will attempt to find an internal device driver for the specific modem. Windows 95 will use PnP BIOS to read the manufacturer's name and the model of the modem, if available. However, whether or not the device is PnP, Windows understands it is a modem. If there is no named internal device driver, Windows 95 will assign a generic device driver and call it a "standard modem." Once the name and settings are assigned, they are written to the SYSTEM.DAT file.

Question 17

The answer is b. In Safe mode, Windows 95 installs a keyboard driver and a standard VGA display driver and bypasses network connections without loading network drivers.

Question 18

The answer is d. A TXT file is a plain ASCII text file. WordPad is a plain ASCII text editor applet that comes with Windows 95.

Question 19

The answer is c. The CONFIG.SYS file must be a plain ASCII text file, located in the root directory of the bootable disk. Saving the file in MS Write format changes the format to the proprietary MS Write format, which DOS cannot read. Because the CONFIG.SYS file cannot be read, it is bypassed.

Question 20

The answer is d. The /S switch tells ATTRIB to operate on all subdirectories. The C:*.SYS tells ATTRIB to operate on all SYS files on the C: drive, beginning at the root directory. The -H switch tells ATTRIB to turn the hidden attribute off or to unhide the file.

Question 21

The answer is d. The default CONFIG.SYS file has no LASTDRIVE= statement, and DOS can read a default maximum of five drives. The system has an A: and a B: drive; a C: drive primary partition; and D:, E:, and F: drives as logical DOS drives. The CD-ROM would become the default G: drive and require the addition of a LASTDRIVE=G statement in a CONFIG.SYS file. This CONFIG.SYS file tells DOS that a maximum of only six drives exist, meaning that the G: drive of the CD-ROM would be unavailable to DOS.

Question 22

The answer is a. The comment signal is REM in DOS (remark) and the semi-colon (;) in Windows. A colon is used for drive letters, and // is commonly used as a directory statement in networking operating systems.

Question 23

The answer is c. An uninterruptible power supply (UPS) contains a battery backup to provide power to the PC during power interruptions and blackouts.

Question 24

The answer is c. Whereas KRNL386.EXE is part of the kernel, neither IO.SYS, WIN.COM, nor MSDOS.SYS is part of the kernel.

Question 25

The answer is c. COM1 uses IRQ 4 and address 03F8h for the default installation. (COM1 is odd and uses even IRQs.) Answers a and b are not COM addresses. Answer d is the default address for COM4. COM ports 1 and 3 use IRQ 4, whereas COM ports 2 and 4 use IRQ 3.

Question 26

The answer is a. A common indicator that a number or address is a hexadecimal unit is either a lowercase or an uppercase h before or after the unit.

Question 27

The answer is a. A standard VGA monitor has a resolution of 640 × 480. The word *horizontal* refers to left and right. *Pixels* (picture units) is a designation for graphic resolution in displayed images such as monitors or graphics. *Dots per inch* (dpi) is a designation for printed or scanned resolutions. *Dot pitch* is used to define an electronic specification of a cathode ray tube.

Question 28

The answer is c. Monitors are either interlaced or noninterlaced. When the electron gun at the back of a CRT monitor redraws every other line, it is noninterlaced.

Question 29

The answer is b. 10BaseT is a twisted pair wiring configuration. Twisted pair allows each PC to connect to a hub directly. If the wire breaks, only the specific PC connected by that wire will be affected. The overall network connection is designed in such a way that each PC has its own connection, and the wiring integrity is not dependent on a functional connection between all the PCs.

Question 30

The answer is c. The Internet is a Unix-based network using TCP/IP networking protocols. IPX/SPX is typically used in a local area network. MIME is an email protocol.

Question 31

The answer is b. Whereas DOS uses .EXE, .COM, and .BAT for executable file extensions, Windows uses .PIF and .DLL extensions as well. A .ZIP extension commonly means an archive file, and .DRV is usually used for device drivers. A configuration file commonly has an .INI extension. Archive files, device drivers, and configuration files are not executable.

Question 32

The answer is d. DOS versions 1 through 7.x do not support multitasking in any form.

Question 33

The answer is d. The ? wildcard is used to represent a single, unknown character. The question indicates a three-character extension. DIR *._ will find all files with only the underscore character following the period. DIR *.*_ will find any file with any extension. DIR *.?_ will find any file with a two-character extension ending with an underscore.

Question 34

The answer is d. The Windows 95 REGEDIT.EXE program is a Registry-editing utility. SYSTEM.DAT is the main Registry file. REG.DAT is the Registry file used in Windows 3.11. MSDOS.SYS, WIN.INI, and SYSTEM.INI are not Registry files.

Question 35

The answer is b. CONFIG.SYS always runs before COMMAND.COM. AUTOEXEC.BAT always runs after COMMAND.COM. SYSTEM.INI always runs before WIN.INI.

Question 36

The answer is c. A polymorphic virus or any other type of virus cannot make changes to the IRQ sector because IRQs are held in a table contained in ROM BIOS or low memory.

Question 37

The answer is a. XT motherboards contained one DMA controller with four channels. The AT system board added a second controller and four more channels making a total of two DMA controllers with eight channels (four channels per controller).

Question 38

The answer is c. The /S (system files) switch formats a disk and transfers the DOS system files to the disk. The /U switch formats a disk unconditionally. There is no /B or /A switch for the FORMAT.COM command program.

Question 39

The answer is b. FDISK.EXE is used to partition a disk or to view the current partitioning scheme. FDISK has nothing to do with optimizing a disk, formatting a disk, or affecting changes to the file allocation table (FAT).

Question 40

The answer is b. CMOS is the low-level area containing system-level settings. CMOS cannot be accessed by programs that require an operating system to be loaded because operating systems work only after a PC has been configured. There is no generic, master password for CMOS, and the password is contained within the SRAM CMOS chip. The only way to clear the password is to clear the CMOS by removing all power to the chip.

Question 41

The answer is a. Beep codes are always generated by the POST. Regardless of the number of beeps generated, there will always be at least one. If no beeps are heard, the most likely problem is that the speaker is disconnected or broken.

Question 42

The answer is c. Mild soapy water is noncorrosive and provides the best cleaning solution for plastic, vinyl, or metal cases. Alcohol is used mainly where no residue should be left, such as certain internal metal or plastic parts. Carbosol and muric acid are fictional terms.

Question 43

The answer is b. The power supply contains a number of capacitors that store electricity at very high levels. Although the power supply might be disconnected from the wall, the capacitors are like batteries and can produce a lethal shock if touched incorrectly.

Question 44

The answer is b. Capacitors store electricity for later release.

Question 45

The answer is b. A fuse is a breakable part of a circuit line. Ohms are used to measure resistance. If the circuit enters a condition beyond a specified tolerance, the fuse breaks and the circuit line is interrupted. If the fuse is unbroken, it appears as a normal part of the circuit line and has no more resistance than any other part of the circuit line.

Question 46

The answer is d. Ground straps must have a resistor placed in the line to avoid electrocuting the technician in the event of a short.

Question 47

The answer is a. There are usually two serial (COM) interface controllers on a motherboard. The serial interfaces are smaller than drive controllers such as B and D. Note that serial controllers are typically located closer to the center of the board on many motherboards.

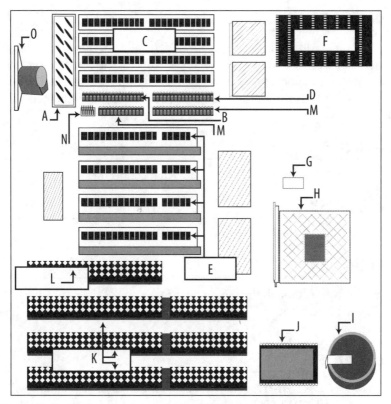

Exhibit 13.1   Diagram used to answer questions 47 through 51.

Question 48

The answer is c. Typically, the CPU is the largest chip on a motherboard and, for AT boards up through the Pentium Pro, is usually large and square.

Question 49

The answer is d. Although the diagram does not show 16 connector points, the general shape of an expansion slot is fairly accurate. The responses in the question define either an 8-bit ISA or a 16-bit ISA slot. Because the 16-bit connections are longer than 8-bit connections, and many modern motherboards have at least four ISA connectors, these are 16-bit ISA slots.

Question 50

The answer is b. The SIMM memory modules are usually closer to the outer edge of the motherboard. The letter E points to a PCI bus, which is often closer to the center of a motherboard.

Question 51

The answer is c. Although a power supply is generally not shown on a diagram of a motherboard, the outline of the cooling fan makes it a clear representation. There is no "orientation" chip (another fictional term). Note that an LPT connector or AT keyboard connector could also be located on an outer edge near this area.

Question 52

The answer is b. The parallel printer is a 25-pin connector.

Question 53

The answer is c. The video connector is a 15-pin connector.

Question 54

The answer is b. Although the mouse might take one of the COM ports, the letter A is not listed. Letter C is the only other nine-pin serial connector choice available.

Question 55

The answer is a. RUNME is most probably a program. A program will be searched for in the PATH. The clue that this is a PATH question is the care taken to specify the search path. The only answer that refers to a location of a program is answer a.

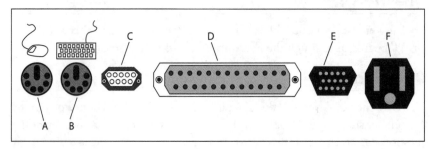

Exhibit 13.2 Diagram used to answer questions 52 through 54.

Question 56

The answer is d. A client has no interest in your personal life and is concerned only that the PC system is working correctly and continually. The time you spend on explanations is time taken away from doing business. A two-hour delay has already cost money, and the less time added to that delay, the better.

Question 57

The answer is c. This customer is obviously questioning the overall competence of the organization. The reference to a lead technician indicates that you are in a nonmanagement position. Empathy will open the door to a short relationship with the customer, who apparently has decided to try one more time with the organization, and any decisions relating to overall corporate policy will need to be made by a manager. Additionally, bringing in the "top person" is reassuring the customer that their problem is worth serious consideration and increases their perception that something concrete will be done to solve their problem.

Question 58

The answer is b. Although these kinds of situations are subject to different interpretations, the best policy is to let the calling customer know that they are important enough that the corporation will come to them to help. Placing a customer on hold for an undefined period of time is bad policy. Answers c and d essentially refer to telling a customer to go away and leave you alone.

Question 59

The answer is c.

Question 60

The answer is c. SCSI cables typically use 50 pins. A parallel cable typically uses 25 pins. A Centronics parallel connector typically uses 36 pins. A serial connector typically uses nine pins.

Question 61

The answer is b. The FAT is the file allocation table used for storing the physical location data of a file on a disk. PAT is a fictional term used to confuse you with a reference to a partition. DIR is the DOS directory listing command. ROM is read-only memory.

Question 62

The answer is a. EMM386.EXE is an expanded memory manager, and Windows 95 does not use an external memory manager. Windows 95 will automatically place a REM and a space before any line containing EMM386.EXE references.

Question 63

The answer is c. The first megabyte of memory *never* refers to either extended or expanded memory.

Question 64

The answer is d. An I/O address is a hardware address. TSRs are programs, not hardware. The physical location of a device on a motherboard is irrelevant. Devices use DMA channels to bypass main memory, not addresses. The only remaining answer that involves both hardware and memory is the COM port address.

Question 65

The answer is b. IRQ 14 is the primary disk controller. IRQ 15 is the secondary disk controller. IRQ 2 was originally assigned to the XT drive controller, but now contains cascaded instructions from IRQ 9.

Question 66

The answer is a. The clues here are both the 25-pin connector and the Centronics connector. Because the parallel port at the back of the chassis is 25-pin female, a 25-pin male connector fits into that port.

Question 67

The answer is b. SYS.COM is a single program dedicated to transferring system files to a disk formatted as bootable. FDISK cannot transfer system files or install them. FORMAT C: /S will reformat the hard drive and destroy any data contained on the logical drive. FDISK /MBR is an undocumented switch used to possibly repair a master boot record. The master boot record does not contain the system files.

Question 68

The answer is a. Originally, the last digit in network wiring referred to the maximum length of a cable in hundreds of meters. 10Base5 refers to a cable with 500 meter maximum length. 10Base2 is a thinner cable, with a maximum length of 200 meters. When 10BaseT wiring was introduced, the last character changed to reflect the type of wiring. T refers to twisted pair.

Configuration And Customer Service

We've set aside this particular segment of this book for both customer service and configurations. We hope you'll read through this appendix before you take the test. Much of what we've discussed throughout the book has been on a fairly simplistic level. We've taken time to explain many terms and concepts, along with giving you an overview of the framework behind the questions you'll see on the exam. In this segment, we move into more of a real-world discussion of computers.

If you take the time to read through the scenario presented here, we think you'll find that you can better gauge your level of preparedness before scheduling your exam. Along with your knowledge of PCs, you will be tested on how you think a service environment should operate, and here is where we try to give you some underlying principles of good customer service. Your score in customer service won't affect whether you pass or fail the exam, but your passing certificate will include a customer service notation to prospective employers.

Preparation

Imagine that you've been assigned to travel to the Kingdom of Aeyre to modernize the country's computer technology. The kingdom's technology consists of a few computers from the Stone Age of technology and a few newer PCs. The king and the queen, who have many diamonds and jewels to pay for the project, have asked you to examine everything they have and to put together a working computer environment.

The entire kingdom has only about 12 PCs, most of which are old 386s and 286s, along with a few 486 machines and an XT. You've been asked to report on the state of the kingdom's computer technology and to make recommendations regarding how to best use the existing resources. The king wants you to install new computers for himself and his wife, but they'll let their cabinet ministers have the old machines.

Tools

Preparing for the trip, you pack your clothes and belongings and the basic tools you know you'll need during the project. Some of these are a set of screwdrivers (flat head and Phillips head), a pair of large tweezers, a small flashlight, needle-nose pliers, and maybe a chip extractor for pulling CPUs out of sockets without damaging the pins. A box of jeweler's screwdrivers and a small set of socket wrenches wouldn't hurt. You'll want to bring a multimeter to check voltages, circuit continuity, and resistance, and you'll probably want to bring a bottle of aspirin. Don't forget your ESD kit with its ground strap and ground mat. You don't want to fry a motherboard with electrostatic discharge. If you have some antistatic storage bags, bring those along as well.

Software

Because you have no idea what condition you'll find the computers in, you should pack as much diagnostic and utility software as you can. Be sure to pack a copy of the *Micro House Technical Library* on CD-ROM. If anyone can answer a question about what the jumper settings are on some unknown motherboard, *Micro House* probably can. The *Micro House* database is the industry-standard diagnostics and repair resource. It's sophisticated enough that you can enter a description of what you're looking at, and the database will return the proper configuration settings and any other repair data you might need, even if you don't always have a model number or a brand name.

You'll want to bring installation copies of DOS (3.3 and 5.0 or 6.2) just in case you need to set up an old PC for the Minister of the Interior. DOS 6.2 can run on an XT, but 3.3 is smaller and won't use up as much space on the 10MB hard drive the XT probably has. Definitely pack a copy of Windows for Workgroups 3.11 and Windows 95.

Many third-party diagnostics utilities (e.g., Norton Utilities, Check-It, and First-Aid) are available for checking out problems with PCs. Usually, these software programs can access components and run test sequences designed for each component type. However, because the utility programs are software based, they're rarely able to find or resolve problems related to intermittent hardware failures (such as heat-related problems). Typically, software diagnostics utilities are used to uncover configuration and operations problems. You'll want to bring whatever utility software you can fit in your luggage.

Web-Based Tech Support

Many service companies, consulting firms, and large corporate information systems divisions provide Internet access to specialized service sites within their own organization. These sites request a user ID and a password from a technician, then grant access to the site. Other Internet resources (e.g., vendor sites) allow technical service people to register with their companies for specialized access to links within the site.

These Internet sites provide software patches, technical white papers, email support, and other helpful information and services. Usenet *list servers* offer specialized newsgroups that run discussion groups pertaining to widely used applications. An example of a Usenet discussion group is a newsgroup devoted to maintaining a dedicated network email server.

Systems Analyst

A PC doesn't exist in a vacuum. There is always a human being who makes a decision to buy a computer and to do something with it. These are your customers (clients). A customer interview (needs assessment) should be conducted before any components are purchased, installed, and configured. Regardless of the customer's level of knowledge and ability to use technical jargon, the customer interview is where customers try to communicate their needs—the reason they came to you. You might configure a PC to enable a sound card, only to discover that the customer absolutely hates hearing any noise while he or she is working. Simply because a normal computer has a working sound card doesn't mean that the customer wants sound on his or her machine.

> *Note: When a customer comes to you with an existing system or with questions about purchasing a new one, you take on some of the responsibilities of a systems analyst.*

In the computer services field, you can wear many hats and perform many functions. No matter what area you're working in, you should be skilled at matching a specific customer need to an appropriate computer system. A systems analyst is the person who analyzes a technology environment in relation to what that technology is expected to do. After the analysis, the systems analyst reports how the existing system meets the customer needs or what changes will need to be made to meet those needs.

Sometimes a client will describe what kind of work he or she wants to do on a computer. The systems analyst will then describe the available technology that might help the client do that work. At other times, a customer might want a specific device or application. The systems analyst then must examine the existing configuration to see whether it will support the new device or software. In all cases, the systems analyst works with customers to try to understand what they want a computer system to accomplish. The systems analyst doesn't *invent* new work; rather, *customers* decide what work they want to do with their computers.

You're going to interview the king of Aeyre, and if you make him feel foolish you could end up in front of a firing squad. Before you do anything, make sure you understand both what the king wants and what you can promise to deliver. A classic poem about installing a new system for a client ends with the line "… it's just what we asked for, but not what we want."

 When a customer with a 286 PC and 20MB hard drive wants Windows installed, the appropriate way for a systems analyst to deal with the situation is to begin a customer interview. Ask about the work the customer expects to perform and what particular features he or she is looking for in Windows. *Suggest* (don't lecture) that either a different method of doing the work could be installed on the existing configuration or that a different system configuration will be required to run Windows. Blurting out that the existing system can't possibly run Windows and falling over laughing is simply unprofessional and not the way for a systems analyst to act.

Needs Assessment

There are thousands of PCs and thousands of ways they can be configured. Because of continued backward compatibility in so much of the industry, a system can (and often does) have components you've never even heard of. You can't just pop off a computer's cover and know what's inside the *box* (how field technicians often refer to the case containing the motherboard, expansion buses, I/O ports, connectors, power supply, and drives). In many cases, you won't be able to find a technical reference manual for the components you're looking at.

Talking with the PC's owner, you can get a lot of great information about what you might have to work with. Of course, you don't *have* to talk with anyone, but if you don't, you will increase the amount of work you'll need to do and come across as unfriendly. The king of Aeyre is very touchy, and he has his own army, so perhaps being friendly is worthwhile.

Don't waste time gabbing about irrelevant topics. Make an active attempt to discover what sorts of things the customer enjoys doing. Information about hobbies might point to unusual configuration needs. If the customer is a farmer, a discussion about the weather and crops might lead to the need for a specialized database that will require a specific configuration.

Make sure that you understand *exactly* what a person wants you to do with his or her system. If you understand that, you should be able to paraphrase those needs and receive a smile and nod of agreement. If you can't paraphrase those needs, ask questions until you do understand them. Almost always, the sign that you're on the right track is a smile and a nod.

It's always better to spend time clarifying what the customer wants than to create an unusable system or one that performs worse than it did when you first saw it. Like in the Hippocratic oath, the first rule of configuration and troubleshooting is "Do no harm."

Although installation and configuration are two different processes, most people refer to a working PC by its configuration (e.g., having a minimally configured system or a server configuration). It's best to write down all the components that a system will require so as to meet the stated customer needs. Once you've described the necessary configuration, the customer can decide how to prioritize his or her needs. Customers decide what money they want to spend, and the systems analyst's job is to describe the best system for the money while meeting as many customer needs as possible.

Building A System

After the needs assessment, take a physical inventory of what kinds of computers and peripherals the kingdom has. Write down as much information as you can about each PC, then sit and think about what has to happen next. Relaxed, focused thinking is very beneficial when it comes to computers (and exams) because computers can't think, and this gives you an edge. The computers and the components will do whatever they can to make your life difficult, so you should take advantage wherever you can.

We've reached the point where the king has generally described the customer needs and where you have created an inventory list of the existing PCs. If the two lists don't match, either the king will need to change his desires or the computers will need to be changed. The king has already told you that money is available, so it looks like the PCs will change. Both the king and the queen want a new computer, so the next step is to describe the new types of PCs available and to explain what each feature provides.

The king has been using a 486 system and the queen a 386 system. Both PCs were running Windows 3.1, and both the king and the queen have been using

MS Word 6.0. The Kingdom of Aeyre primarily uses Word and Excel for correspondence and spreadsheets, though some of the cabinet ministers have been using Word 2.0 for DOS.

The Systems Integrator

We can split the process of configuring a system into two broad categories:

➤ The set of decisions about particular components and their capabilities

➤ The installation of a specific component into a PC

A systems integrator works with both configuration types to match specific components with the performance requirements reported by the systems analyst.

We said previously that a systems analyst doesn't invent new work. On the other hand, a systems integrator might describe new technology to a customer that could modify or enhance his or her environment. Perhaps the customer is approaching a problem in a limited way because of an inability to ask the right questions. Part of a systems integrator's job is to know when to introduce new knowledge to the customer.

> *Note: When you answer customer questions about specific hardware or software, you take on some of the characteristics of a systems integrator. When you demonstrate new products that your customer might be interested in, you work with knowledge that you acquired during the customer interview.*

You can't really configure a CPU or an expansion bus. However, the CPU that you decide to install or the type of expansion bus that you put on a motherboard are parts of the *overall system configuration*. A systems integrator is the person with technical knowledge of component specifications and capabilities and an understanding of how the components will function together in a real-world scenario.

You know you're going to need a box, a keyboard, and a monitor as part of a minimum configuration. However, the king and the queen have stated that they want a *maximum* configuration, so you'll need a mouse, a printer, a scanner, and everything else we're going to talk about. You'll probably need to connect some PCs together in a network eventually, so enough expansion slots for future capabilities need to be available.

A PC is just a decoration if it doesn't have an operating system and some software applications to perform work, so you'll need to ask your customer what kind of operating system he or she wants installed. Both the king and the queen want the latest and greatest of everything. They've read about Windows 98 and want you to install it on both of their machines.

If you simply install Windows 98 on the king's and the queen's computers, you will have failed as a systems analyst. If you don't explain some of the compatibility issues involved with the computers, you will have failed as a systems integrator.

Your needs assessment and inventory showed you that most of the computers in the environment (context) can't run Windows 98. Therefore, those PCs will have installed applications that create and read data differently from Windows 98 applications. Although Windows 98 can likely read the older application data, the older PCs probably won't be able to work with output from all the applications on the king's and the queen's computers.

Explain compatibility issues first; then explain how a PC can have more than one operating system on the same hard disk. In this case, new knowledge will change the way the customer approaches the decision about an operating system.

Features Decisions

The foundation of any PC is its motherboard, which is where everything comes together (connectivity) to move data through circuits and over buses. The motherboard controls the overall timing of the data movement, so you'll want to get a fast motherboard. The king has decided to go with two different systems and then see which one is easier and faster to work with. On the basis of what you've told him, he chooses a Pentium Pro for the queen and a Pentium II for himself.

Pentium Pro

The Pentium Pro motherboards support either one or two (parallel processing) Intel Pentium Pro processors. The motherboards can be configured with speeds ranging from 150 to 366 MHz. The queen's PC will have a Baby AT motherboard with four PCI slots, three ISA slots, and four SIMM sockets. The system board comes with two EIDE ports for a total of four hard drives and/or CD-ROM drives. It also has a floppy (drive) port, two serial (COM) ports, and a parallel (LPT) port. The BIOS is made by Award, and it is Flash BIOS (flash memory) for easy upgrading. The BIOS also features full PnP support and energy-saving features.

Intel Pentium Pro configurations produce CPU speeds of 150, 166, 180, or the full 200 MHz. The most common Pentium Pro CPUs are 180 and 200 MHz.

The queen's machine will be configured with a Pentium Pro 200 MHz CPU with MMX technology (instruction set), using the Intel 430TX chipset. You'll reinstall a 2GB EIDE hard drive as well as a 24x CD-ROM drive. She'll have 32MB of EDO parity RAM installed and a 512K SRAM (static RAM) secondary L2 cache. The system will have a 15-inch noninterlaced SVGA color monitor (.28 dot pitch) and a graphics accelerator card with 2MB of onboard DRAM. Along with the 3½-inch floppy drive, her system will have an internal IDE Iomega 100MB Zip drive installed with ROM BIOS support for the new Zip drive right on the motherboard.

The Chipset Is Not The CPU

CPUs include the 80386, 80486, and Pentium (among others) processors, which we've discussed throughout this book. The CPU is one of a number of integrated components on a motherboard that work together to perform instructions. The super I/O chip is a reference to the continuing integration of more components as miniaturization and manufacturing techniques improve. The super I/O chip is usually referred to as a *chipset*.

The queen will use an inkjet-technology printer for producing photographic-quality output from her digital camera. The camera allows for 1,224×768 pixel resolution, and she would like 1,440 dpi printer resolution. She wants as sharp an image as possible, and although the king thinks that a laser printer will produce the sharpest possible image (600 dpi), the queen prefers an ink jet printer. Her PC will have a 33.6K internal modem.

The PC will come from the vendor installed with Windows for Workgroups 3.11, MS Office 4.3, DOS 6.2, and all the software and reference manuals in the shipping carton. The sound card and the CD-ROM drive will include software drivers and reference manuals as well.

Pentium II

The king is going to try a leading-edge computer that uses the new Pentium II technology from Intel. His machine will have a 400 MHz Pentium II microprocessor using Intel's 440LX chipset. The Pentium II architecture means that it can plug into only an ATX form factor motherboard (specified by Intel). The ATX board supports Intel's new Accelerated Graphics Port (AGP) technology, which moves the graphics accelerator off the PCI bus to a faster, direct connection with the CPU. The motherboard will have both a PCI and an ISA expansion bus, but his machine will have a SCSI card and controller for the hard drive (taking up one slot in the PCI bus).

The king's hard drive will come preinstalled with Windows 95 OSR/2, MS Office 95 Professional, and a multimedia tour of the system. The system will include a CD-ROM of Windows 95 and a Microsoft CD-ROM bootable disk.

The king's machine will be configured with a Pentium II 400 MHz CPU with MMX and a 5.5GB SCSI hard drive as well as a 24x SCSI CD-ROM drive. The PC will have 64MB SDRAM with ECC installed but no L2 cache. During your on-site stay, you'll be keeping an eye on both systems to see whether the SDRAM outperforms the EDO RAM with its L2 SRAM cache.

The system will have a 17-inch noninterlaced color SVGA monitor (.28 dot pitch) and a graphics accelerator card with 4MB of onboard VRAM. Along with the 3½-inch floppy drive, the king's system will have an Ultra SCSI interface and an Iomega 1GB Jaz drive connected to the parallel port with a pass-through 25-pin connector on the back of the Jaz unit. The king's PC will have a 56.6K external modem.

The king's machine will have a 600 dpi laser printer attached to the pass-through DB25 port of the Jaz drive and another internal SCSI card for a scanner that the king and the queen will share. The scanner is a 600×600 dpi optical resolution 32-bit color scanner with 9,600 dpi max resolution using software interpolation. Generally, they will use the scanner to scan artwork that the princess brings home from kindergarten, so they rarely need more than 97 dpi. They would like to be able to put their daughter's drawings up on a Web page.

Both the king's and the queen's machines will have 16-bit Sound Blaster sound cards, each using one ISA slot. Along with the sound card, each machine will have a pair of audio speakers with a rated frequency response of 100 to 20,000 Hz. Each PC will have a 24x CD-ROM and a three-button mouse. Each machine will have a standard 101 keyboard (though the queen was asking about an ergonomic keyboard).

If you find yourself describing a system to a customer in technical jargon, you can assume that the customer has no idea what you're talking about. Although this is how many systems are outlined in catalogs and sales materials, real human beings need varying amounts of background and detail to understand a list of specifications. Talking beyond a person's ability to understand

and using jargon serves no purpose beyond personal ego gratification.

Reality Check

We interrupt this appendix to advise you that the preceding section has been a test of the Emergency Brain-Cramming Network. If this had been an actual exam, you would have been notified that you're not allowed to use this book during the exam. Relax. Lighten up! You're scheduled for the exam tomorrow, right? Plenty of time. Besides, you might be surprised at how much you already know. If you're worried, nervous, tense, and generally in a bad mood, you're not going to enjoy taking the exam, and that's no good. Life should be fun!

The certification exam is a multiple-choice exam with a single correct response to every question. The only real scenario-type questions we've seen have dealt with customer service. However, a few questions contained a sentence with a number of blanks that you would fill in with response choices in a correct sequence. The scenario of the Kingdom of Aeyre is designed to provide you with an imaginative framework for understanding the fundamental concepts of computers.

You might see a few questions that ask for numbers in their responses. These questions almost always deal with the addresses, interrupt requests (IRQs), or the number of pins on a cable or connector. The connectors are usually the most common ones (i.e., 9-pin, 15-pin video, 25-pin, 36-pin Centronics, and 50-pin SCSI).

Other number questions might involve amounts of memory, such as the 640K of conventional (base) memory or the 384K of high memory. We saw no deep-level questions involving which pin number manages which instruction for a device.

Now take a break, go for a walk, eat an ice cream cone, or do whatever it is that you do that doesn't require a lot of thinking. While you're doing that, think about the king and the queen of Aeyre and the configurations of their two computers. Can you think of anything in your configuration list that we haven't already covered in this book?

Try to remember what the configurations specified. Did you just pass by all the letters? Did you read that the queen's machine has 32MB of *hmnehmmeneh* RAM, or did you catch that it was *parity* RAM? Did you read each feature and have a pretty good idea of what it related to?

What things made absolutely no sense to you at all? There shouldn't have been any, other than the specific name of the Intel 430TX and 440LX chipsets, and the exam won't test you on their names. Everything else is the way a computer configuration is listed in the real world, and everything should have been familiar enough to you to point you to an area of system performance. If it wasn't, go back and read it again and make a note of what you're having trouble with.

Once you've passed the certification exam, you'll have the entire world as a resource for looking up things such as the speed of an SRAM chip and whether a hard drive has a seek time of 16 or 18 milliseconds. You won't even need to know most of these specific numbers during the exam—they're there only to help you remember that RAM is measured in nanoseconds but that drives are measured in milliseconds.

Reviewing The Features

Even if you didn't go for a walk, we're going to rearrange the two configurations that the king and the queen will have. The first time around, everything was all jumbled together in paragraphs, much the way you're presented with information in the real world. Table 1 puts the same features in a side-by-side list. Consider which is easier for you to follow. If a list is easier for you, it will also be easier for a customer. Read through the table and think about what each feature will do for overall system performance. Who has the better machine? Can you show a point-by-point reason that the king's machine might be better?

Table 1 Side-by-side configuration comparison of the king's and the queen's machines.	
The King's Machine	**The Queen's Machine**
Pentium II 300 MHz CPU	Pentium Pro 200 MHz CPU
MMX instruction set	MMX instruction set
ATX motherboard	Baby AT motherboard
PCI and ISA buses	PCI and ISA buses
AGP (accelerated graphics port)	-
5.5GB SCSI hard drive	2GB EIDE hard drive
Ultra ATA hard drive interface	Ultra ATA hard drive interface
64MB of SDRAM with ECC	32MB of EDO parity RAM
-	512K SRAM secondary L2 cache
17-inch noninterlaced .28 SVGA color monitor	15-inch noninterlaced .28 SVGA color monitor
Graphics card with 4MB of onboard VRAM	Graphics card with 2MB of onboard DRAM

(continued)

Table 1 Side-by-side configuration comparison of the king's and the queen's machines (continued).

The King's Machine	The Queen's Machine
1 GB Iomega Jaz drive with external SCSI interface	IDE Iomega internal 100MB Zip drive with ROM BIOS support
24x CD-ROM	24x CD-ROM
Three-button mouse	Three-button mouse
Standard 101 keyboard	Standard 101 keyboard
600 dpi laser printer	1,440 dpi thermal ink printer
56K external modem	33.3K internal modem
600 dpi optical 32-bit color scanner, SCSI internal interface	-
Windows 95, Office 95 Professional	Windows for Workgroups 3.11, DOS 6.2, MS Office 4.3

Better And Worse

We use *superlatives* (e.g., good, better, best, bad, worse, and worst) to describe how closely something matches its defined purpose. If you say that the king's machine is better than the queen's, you must know the purpose for which the king's machine was defined. If you don't know the exact purpose, you can't use a word like *better*.

Feature Comparison

Several important distinctions can be made between the king's and the queen's PCs. The memory on the king's machine has ECC error correction, whereas the queen's uses parity checking. The king's monitor uses VRAM on the graphics card, whereas the queen's uses DRAM. VRAM has two paths to the same memory address, whereas DRAM can create a bottleneck during read-writes to the address. Review Chapter 4 if you can't describe the differences in memory checking or VRAM. If you're having a hard time visualizing noninterlaced monitors, review Chapter 7 and restudy the workings of a display monitor.

The king's machine requires an Intel-specified ATX motherboard to accommodate the change in the Intel-specified changes to the Intel Pentium's design. Intel decided to make the Pentium II vertically oriented rather than the previous flat design of every other CPU. The design change means that the Intel

Pentium II chip is the only (no other brand of CPU) one that will fit into the ATX board's socket. The queen's PC uses a standard Baby AT motherboard. The king's and the queen's motherboards are not interchangeable between cases. If you need to, review Chapter 2 and note the differences.

The king's machine uses SDRAM memory, whereas the queen's uses EDO memory with an L2 cache. The exam won't test you on how SDRAM functions, but you will need to know the difference between DRAM, SRAM, and EDO RAM. The important thing to note about EDO RAM is that it keeps data in a memory address for multiple reads rather than discharging the address after every read. The L2 cache on the queen's machine will supply the main memory with 10 nanoseconds of cache memory. The king's machine should (theoretically) have 10 nanoseconds of *main* memory. Review Chapter 4 if you're having a hard time separating what each type of memory does.

The king's hard drive uses a separate SCSI controller card and therefore won't utilize the EIDE controller at all. The SCSI drive on the king's machine will use an installed SCSI card plugged into the PCI bus. Once installed, both the 5.5GB hard drive and the scanner will interface with the PC by using the SCSI controller. Finally, the resolution of the queen's camera is in pixel units, whereas the printer resolutions are in dots per inch (dpi). Display output devices measure a graphic image in terms of the smallest part of the image that can be displayed (*pixels*, or *picture units*). Print and scan devices measure an image by the smallest part of a printed image (dots). For the details on printers, review Chapter 7. If you don't recognize the phrase "600 dpi optical resolution (scanner)," review Chapter 5. The exam won't test you on the resolution of digital cameras, but it will test you on typical resolution modes of images and monitors.

Setting Up The System

Both the king's and the queen's new PCs came out of their shipping containers with an operating system and software installed and the disks configured. The king's machine has its SCSI adapter card and CD-ROM drive installed and configured. The first thing that you must do is physically set up both systems.

Remember that SCSI adapter cards use one slot in an expansion bus. SCSI is often used to install an external device to the PC and can have up to seven devices on a single SCSI daisy chain. The SCSI hard drive controller is usually ID 7, leaving six other devices available. The king's PC has a CD-ROM drive attached to the SCSI adapter, using another ID number.

Pick a place where there's room around the boxes and where there are no extreme temperature changes. The PCs and video monitor work best with good air circulation and a fairly dust-free environment. Heat buildup can cause intermittent system freezing. The early Pentium microprocessors ran very hot and often used a CPU fan to cool down the chip. Over time, the CPU fan might fail and lead to sporadic lockups. This kind of problem can be difficult to resolve. Later Pentium chips run cooler and have heat sinks and CPU fans or (on ATX form factor boards) use the air circulating from the power supply fan.

Remember that the POST routine runs any parity checking that might be installed on the PC. The POST parity check tests only whether a memory cell is working at the time of the check. Some SIMMs develop cells that work with a cool temperature but that fail in the heated environment of a running PC. The parity check can't test for potential problems that might arise when the system has been running for a while.

Only if a cell fails between the time the data is written and the time the data is read *and* if parity checking or ECC has been installed can the parity check report a crashed memory cell.

Heat-Related Problems

As long as we're discussing heat and dust, you should know that most modern PCs are designed with very high tolerances for changing conditions. The hard disk is hermetically sealed (i.e., in a vacuum), and the remaining components are designed to take a wide swing in electrical voltages, as well as changes in temperature and humidity, for a short period of time. Although most components run at 3.3 volts DC, a lot of heat is generated inside the box.

Remember that the inside of a PC is designed with airflow in mind. To promote good air circulation, you should keep at least six inches of free space around the ventilation holes in the case and around the monitor. The metal slot covers are both a protection for unused expansion slots and part of the ventilation system. Keep any unused slot covers in place rather than unscrewing and removing them. This will allow the cooling air to flow through the inside of the box rather than escaping from a missing slot position.

A good habit to develop is to periodically blast out the inside of the case and power supply with compressed air to get rid of the dust buildup that can also restrict air flow.

Power Blackouts

Periodically, the electrical power supplied to the PC can be suddenly interrupted (a *blackout*). An uninterruptible power supply (UPS) provides a battery backup for power and conditions the power to be a single, steady voltage. Surge protectors are designed only to block sudden high-voltage spikes of short duration.

The electrical grid in the Kingdom of Aeyre uses old technology. As such, brownouts and blackouts often occur. During brownouts, the power can drop from 110 to 85 volts. In some cases, line surges can boost the incoming voltage to as high as 125 volts. Fortunately, you've purchased 300 watt UPS units for both the king's and the queen's PCs as well as for all the older PCs in the kingdom.

 Remember that the most important thing to be concerned about following a power interruption is the soon-to-follow surge of electricity into every component of the system. If a blackout lasts more than a few seconds, the system should be turned off until the power returns.

Connecting Devices

Gather all the hardware and cables, AC cords, reference manuals, and software that might have come with the system. You should already know how to plug the standard components into the back of the PC, so you won't need a reference manual for those items. Figure 1 is a graphic outline of the rear view of a typical desktop PC chassis. We refer to the various items by their letter designation.

Figure 1 is a basic outline drawing of the back of a box and is meant to approximate the type of exhibits you'll see on the certification exam. You should also be familiar with a basic motherboard outline (see Chapter 2) and the connectors *coming from* the PC. The exam distinguishes between *coming from* the PC and *on* the PC. A connector on the PC is usually a port, whereas a connector coming from the PC is usually the end of a cable.

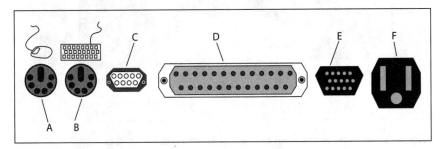

Figure 1   Back panel of a PC showing port connectors.

The exam will likely test your visual recognition of the 25-pin parallel port (D), the 9-pin serial port (C), and the 15-pin video interface (E). On this PC, both the keyboard and the mouse (B and A, respectively) use a PS/2-style 6-pin mini-DIN connector. Remember that the mouse is often taking COM1 even though it isn't a 9-pin serial connector. In Figure 1, the following letters identify the interfaces:

➤ A = PS/2 mouse connector (COM1)

➤ B = keyboard connector

➤ C = serial port (COM2 port interface)

➤ D = parallel port (LPT1 port interface)

➤ E = video connector interface

➤ F = AC electrical wall connector (male with ground pin)

Always remember that on the PC motherboard, the parallel interface is 25-pin female and the serial interface is 9-pin male. Logically, then, on a printer cable (coming from the PC), the DB25 parallel connection is a 25-pin male configuration.

Figure 2 is a line diagram of a typical parallel cable designed to attach a PC to a printer. Note that the end that connects to the PC is a DB25 male 25-pin connector. The end that connects to the printer is a male 36-pin Centronics connector.

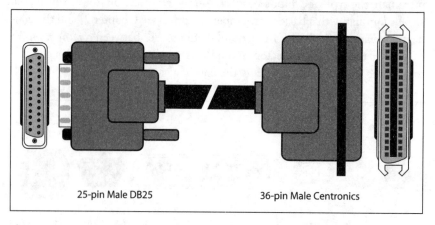

25-pin Male DB25   36-pin Male Centronics

Figure 2 A typical parallel cable connecting a PC to a printer.

Be sure to carefully read any exam question that asks about cables and connectors. When a typical parallel *cable* is used, you might see the first connector described as "coming from the PC" and the other end of the cable as "connecting to the printer."

Because the LPT interface connector on the PC is female, its corresponding cable connector must be male. Throughout this book, we've been consistent in our reference to the interface port connectors on the back of the PC. Use logic and careful reading to distinguish between the connectors.

Backing Up The System

Whether you work with a PC that has preinstalled software or an existing system with software and user data, you should be careful when changing the configuration that you have a full backup of the hard drive. Backup devices can be tape machines, removable hard disks, CD-ROMs, or floppy disks. A change to the CMOS or CONFIG.SYS file can sometimes make the system inaccessible. *Always* make a backup of anything you won't be able to reinstall from original disks.

Disk Images

A disk image is a file containing an exact replica of a floppy disk. The file is in a special format that requires a compatible imaging program. The imaging program reads a floppy disk and makes the image file. Later, the imaging program reads the file and writes an exact copy of the tracks, sectors, and clusters to a blank floppy. A disk image can re-create a bootable floppy and sometimes can even copy an original disk serial number.

Many modern PCs with preinstalled software contain a folder with disk images of the software programs installed on the hard drive. Check the reference manual for how to make the actual disks or look for a program (e.g., an EXE file) related to images or the brand name of the computer.

On both the king's and the queen's PCs, you'll be repartitioning the entire hard disk. FDISK irrevocably destroys all file data on a hard disk. Some viruses can protect themselves from FDISK, but aside from that, the hard disk information will be completely deleted.

Files To Back Up

Typically, you should back up an AUTOEXEC.BAT file, a CONFIG.SYS file, and both the SYSTEM.INI and the WIN.INI files (if they exist). On Windows 3.x systems, you should back up PROGMAN.INI and all GRP files. On Windows 95 systems, back up the SYSTEM.DAT and USER.DAT files. You should also back up a CD-ROM driver, if one exists somewhere in a folder. The CD-ROM device driver should be located on an original software disk that came with the drive.

Windows 95 new installation CD-ROMs should include a 3½-inch floppy with a generic device driver for the CD. This is a critical disk, because you won't be able to access the CD drive without first having a driver running.

Many times, the vendor assumes that Windows 95 will manage the CD-ROM drive and therefore won't include a device driver. This is fine until you need to reinstall Windows 95 on a clean disk. If you have only the CD-ROM installation disk, you might have a problem.

In the case of the king's machine, a bootable floppy was included with an AUTOEXEC.BAT routine that uses MSCDEX.EXE to install the CD-ROM driver. This is sufficient to allow for the Windows 95 installation. Windows 95 will then take over the management of the CD-ROM drive.

> *Note: MSCDEX.EXE is the Microsoft CD Extensions program file that contains generic instructions for running a CD-ROM drive. In many cases, this will provide basic access to the drive. Unusual or off-brand drives may not work with MSCDEX.EXE, so you should spend some time making sure you have a correct CD installation disk available.*

All the previously listed files should fit on one 1.44MB floppy, except the Windows 95 Registry files (i.e., SYSTEM.DAT and USER.DAT). The SYSTEM.DAT file might not fit on a single floppy, in which case you could use an Iomega Zip disk or a third-party archiving program (e.g., PKZip or WinZip) that will allow an archive to span multiple disks.

Windows 3.x And PROGMAN.EXE

The queen's new hard drive has been preconfigured with Windows for Workgroups 3.11. You'll definitely want to take a backup copy of the SYSTEM.INI and the WIN.INI files. Although Windows for Workgroups can start without a WIN.INI file, the desktop colors and other user-configured Windows settings are in the file. Don't forget the GRP files that Windows 95 will read to recreate the program groups as cascading menus during the upgrade.

PROGMAN.EXE (Program Manager) is the default shell interface used with Windows for Workgroups. It contains the icons and organization of Program Manager, which contains a number of subwindows (program groups) held in GRP files. You'll want a backup of all those files as well as PROGMAN.INI, which keeps track of how Program Manager loads.

PROGMAN.EXE (Program Manager) contains the icons and program groups for the main Windows 3.x user interface. The program groups that a user creates with File|New|Program Group are contained in the GRP files in the \WINDOWS subdirectory.

In case the system is upgraded from 16-bit Windows to Windows 95, the installation can read GRP and INI files that have been restored from a backup of the previous configuration. An upgrade installation of Windows 95 will read the existing GRP files in the \WINDOWS folder. An original installation of Windows 95 will require the creation of a \WINDOWS subdirectory and restoration of the GRP files.

For the moment, the queen will continue to use Windows for Workgroups, having learned it on her old 386 machine. However, the new hard drive doesn't contain all her data files. The king was using a 486 and also has many data files that were created in MS Office 4.3. Your three primary customer needs are to:

➤ Repartition and reinstall all the hard disks

➤ Reinstall all the data files from the previous PCs

➤ Ensure compatibility between the two new PCs and the other PCs in the kingdom

CMOS Settings And BIOS Instructions

The king's and the queen's PCs are modern systems, so they'll store critical configuration settings in CMOS. Before you reinstall the hard drives and software, boot the computers to see whether the screen offers any information on how to get into CMOS. The reference manual should tell you which keystroke combination will access CMOS, but the on-screen prompt is usually easier to find. The kingdom has a trade agreement with several countries, so the king's and the queen's machines come from two different suppliers.

On the king's machine, pressing F2 during the POST will access CMOS. On the queen's machine, pressing Ctrl+Delete will do the same. Either way, getting to the CMOS settings means accessing a screen that's presented after the POST but before the operating system.

The CMOS chip is an SRAM chip and requires a small amount of electricity to remember the stored settings. When the CMOS battery dies, the basic settings for the computer disappear. Changing the battery requires removing the battery, and the settings will vanish at that time as well, with varying results.

Hard Drive Configuration

The CMOS stores the specific details about any nonremovable disks (hard drives) installed in a PC. If more than one disk will be installed, each disk will have its own DIP switch or jumper settings that will define which disk is the *master* (first) disk (drive 0) and which is the *slave* (drives 1, 2, 3, and so on). The CMOS settings for a hard drive include the:

➤ Number of cylinders

➤ Number of heads (read-write)

➤ Number of sectors per track

➤ Cylinder capacity

➤ Maximum storage capacity

Note: The formal reference to the location of data on a disk uses cylinders, tracks, sectors, and clusters. Field technicians tend to refer to the locations by cylinders, heads, and sectors. A master boot record on cylinder 0, track 0, sector 0 is almost the same thing as saying head 0, track 0, sector 0.

To make future problem solving easier, access the CMOS on a working PC and write the exact setting numbers for the hard disk on a small piece of paper. Tape the disk's model number and settings to an easy-to-see area inside of the case.

MSD.EXE—Microsoft Diagnostics

Beginning with DOS 6.0 and Windows 3.1, Microsoft began providing a utility program for analyzing most of the PC system. Microsoft Diagnostics (MSD.EXE) can usually be found in either the DOS directory or the Windows directory on 16-bit systems. MSD.EXE can also be downloaded from the Microsoft Internet site (http://www.microsoft.com) and comes on the Windows 95 installation disk(s) in the \OTHER\MSD subfolder.

Although MSD can be used in both a configuration and a troubleshooting context, we tend to use it first in the configuration phase. The MSD /F [*file name*] switch is very useful for keeping a written copy of the current configuration of a given PC. To that end, we introduce it here.

MSD is a DOS-based program that can run in a window under both Windows 3.x and Windows 95. The most accurate way to run the program is by entering "MSD" at a command prompt. It will usually run because either DOS or Windows (or both) is in the search path. Once the program starts, it tries to analyze the computer as best as it can.

> *Note: When you are in Windows, it's better to restart the machine (Windows 95) in DOS mode or to exit Windows (3.x) before running MSD.EXE. Otherwise, MSD tends to report an incorrect description of memory and other areas.*

MSD Report

No matter how smoothly most installations go, a time will come when you need to get your hands dirty and run a trial-and-error configuration using open IRQs. MSD can print a report (to a file, a printer, or the screen) of the existing state of the machine, which includes the following details:

➤ The type of computer

➤ The amount of memory and its organization

➤ The type of video, drivers, and resolution

➤ Which (if any) network is running

➤ Other adapters that are in place (e.g., joysticks)

➤ Which logical disk drives exist and what their sizes are

➤ How many LPT and COM ports exist and details about their configuration (This is one place to find out which UART chip is installed on the machine.)

➤ Which version of DOS and Windows is installed

➤ Which TSR (terminate-and-stay-resident) programs are loaded into memory addresses

➤ Default IRQ status

➤ CONFIG.SYS and AUTOEXEC.BAT printed reports

➤ SYSTEM.INI and WIN.INI printed reports

The IRQ status report often indicates which IRQs are open. This should help you find an open IRQ when it comes time to configure the king's scanner. Finding an open DMA channel is usually simply guesswork.

Be aware that the MSD.EXE is mostly a main memory and systems information report. You can use the reports for configuring COM ports and IRQs and to discover which types of CPU and video are on the system. You can't use MSD to analyze hit ratios for SmartDrive or any other cache programs.

Another real-world point about MSD is that it generally describes default IRQs. Don't count on the accuracy of the listing, and use either a third-party program (Windows 3.x) or the Windows 95 Device Manager or HWDIAGS.EXE program.

CONFIG.SYS And IO.SYS

Observe that, for the moment, we haven't mentioned running software utilities (other than MSD.EXE), opening boxes, pulling out wires, installing software, or anything that changes an existing configuration. Too often a technician fails to *document* the existing configuration of a fully functional PC. *Documentation* is a formal process of making a precise, written record of an event or of a condition. In this case, the written record will be the configuration settings for the king's and the queen's new PCs. After all, the PCs came out of their shipping containers fully configured and working. Why lose all that information and have to paw through reference manuals for low-level settings?

CONFIG.SYS Directives

We discussed the function of the CONFIG.SYS file in Chapter 8. CONFIG.SYS loads Real mode device drivers for DOS and 16-bit Windows. Most of the functions of CONFIG.SYS were taken over by the Windows 95 version of IO.SYS.

The specific *directives* (file-specific commands) in the CONFIG.SYS file define the configuration of any devices running in DOS or a Windows 3.x virtual machine (VM). Most of the default directives in CONFIG.SYS were moved to IO.SYS in Windows 95. However, Real mode (16-bit) device drivers still often require a setting in the CONFIG.SYS file in Windows 95.

Note: Aside from an MSD.EXE report, the CONFIG.SYS, AUTOEXEC.BAT, SYSTEM.INI, and WIN.INI files are ASCII text files. They can be printed at any time using any text editor, word processor, or the COPY [file name] PRN command from a DOS prompt.

Each device attached to the motherboard has some sort of device driver. In 16-bit systems, the device is loaded either from a CONFIG.SYS file used by DOS or from a SYSTEM.INI file used by Windows 3.x. Windows 95 uses an internal VxD but sometimes needs a Real mode setting in either a CONFIG.SYS or SYSTEM.INI file (as we saw in Chapter 10).

The device driver usually has configuration settings that determine how the device will fit into the specific context of a specific system. These configuration settings are often set from a line in the AUTOEXEC.BAT file. Sound cards often use a device driver in SYSTEM.INI. Sound cards, scanners, and CD-ROMs are notorious for their manual configuration requirements for IRQs and DMA settings.

Remember that the CONFIG.SYS and AUTOEXEC.BAT text files must be located in the root directory of the bootable disk in the bootable drive. Note that a CONFIG.SYS file and an AUTOEXEC.BAT file are not required to boot the DOS operating system.

In case the CONFIG.SYS file or AUTOEXEC.BAT file has necessary device drivers and configuration settings but ends up "File(s) not found" by COMMAND.COM during bootup, the system will still probably start. However, when the system completes the boot process in this situation, some devices will be inoperable.

Basic CONFIG.SYS File

The king's PC (having come with Windows 95 installed) doesn't use a CONFIG.SYS file because IO.SYS installs all the basic configuration drivers and HIMEM.SYS to access extended memory. However, both the king's and the queen's previous machines *will* have a CONFIG.SYS file. When you install a CONFIG.SYS and an AUTOEXEC.BAT file on the new machines, Windows 95 will comment out all real drivers during its setup routine. The following is a typical CONFIG.SYS from a Windows 3.1 PC upgraded to Windows 95:

```
DEVICE=C:\WINDOWS\HIMEM.SYS
REM DEVICE=C:\WINDOWS\EMM386.EXE RAM
DOS=HIGH
REM DOS=UMB

BUFFERS=40,0
FCBS=16,0
SHELL=C:\COMMAND.COM C:\ /P /E:1024
REM DEVICE=C:\BUSLOGIC\BTDOSM.SYS /D
REM DEVICE=C:\BUSLOGIC\BTCDROM.SYS /D:MSCD0001
REM DEVICE=SMARTDRV.EXE
```

```
REM DEVICE=D:\IOMEGA\ASPIPPM1.SYS FILE=SMC.ILM SPEED= 10
REM DEVICE=D:\IOMEGA\SCSICFG.EXE /V
REM DEVICE=D:\IOMEGA\SCSIDRVR.SYS
```

Partition The Disk

You've created and printed a full MSD report and written the CMOS settings of the new PCs. All the software on the new machines is available on disks, and both systems have a CD-ROM driver installation disk. You're ready to re-partition the king's 5.5GB hard drive and the queen's 2GB hard drive.

You have a bootable disk with FDISK.EXE and FORMAT.COM and the DOS and Windows 3.x installation disks that you brought with you (for more on bootable disks, see Chapter 11). You'll need to make sure that you purchase individual copies of DOS and Windows for the king's PC because you must have a licensed copy of any software you put on a PC. You'll need to purchase a copy of Windows 95 for the queen's machine because it came only with Windows for Workgroups 3.11. Since you're adding either Windows 95 to the queen's machine or WFW 3.11 to the king's machine, you'll be short one copy of each operating system when you're done.

FDISK Main Menu

Boot the system to the floppy disk and run the FDISK program by typing "FDISK" (without the quotes) at the command line and pressing Enter. The first screen will present you with the main FDISK menu as follows:.

```
Microsoft Windows 95
Fixed Disk Setup Program
(C)Copyright Microsoft Corp. 1983 - 1995

FDISK Options

Current fixed disk drive: 1
Choose one of the following:
1. Create DOS partition or Logical DOS Drive
2. Set active partition
3. Delete partition or Logical DOS Drive
4. Display partition information

Enter choice: [4]
```

Note: Note that Option 4 is used to display partition information. Before you can create new partitions, you must delete both the logical DOS

drives and the extended partitions containing them. Extended partitions
contain logical DOS drives. Also, make a note that this PC has only one
physical hard disk installed. If there were more than one disk, Option 4
would offer the ability to view disks 1 and 2 or however many disks were
installed. Physical disks are not the same as drives.

Partition Information

The king's 5.5GB drive could be efficiently configured with separate partitions
for both operating systems and with separate 16-bit and 32-bit partitions for
application software. Finally, it might be useful to have two partitions for the
data created by each of the two operating systems.

The larger the partition, the larger the clusters in the sectors. This is a 5GB
disk, so even with six partitions, the clusters would be very large, resulting in a
lot of wasted space (slack). Suppose we make a 1GB partition for DOS and
Windows 3.1, and a 1GB partition for Windows 95. That uses 2GB in two
primary partitions.

The next step would be to create a 3.5GB extended partition using the rest of
the available disk space. Choosing Option 1 from the main FDISK menu moves
to the following menu:

```
Create DOS Partition or Logical DOS Drive

Current fixed disk drive: 1

Choose one of the following:

1. Create Primary DOS Partition
2. Create Extended DOS Partition
3. Create Logical DOS Drive(s) in the Extended DOS Partition

Enter choice: [1]
```

 An extended partition can contain a maximum of 23 logical DOS
drives. Drives A: and B: are assigned on every modern PC. The C:
drive is always the primary partition. The alphabet has 26 letters,
so when you subtract the A:, B:, and C: drives, you're left with 23
letters.

When you partition a disk with multiple operating systems, only one primary
partition will be active at a given time. The primary active partition is the C:
drive. Because there can't be two C: drives, one of the primary partitions will
be *hidden*. All other partitions will be visible to the operating system and will

start with the D: drive. If there are two data partitions, either one can be used by whichever operating system has booted the system. Note that DOS can't hide a partition, though Windows 95 and various third-party utilities can (e.g., PowerQuest's *Partition Magic*).

| If there are two bootable primary (active) partitions, only one can be visible at a time. Neither primary partition will see the other. A boot manager program (e.g., Boot Manager or System Commander) must control the hiding and unhiding of one of the primary partitions.

For the moment, let's look at the existing partition information on a similar system with a smaller disk. Choosing Option 4 from the main FDISK menu produces the following report:

```
Display Partition Information

Current fixed disk drive: 1

Partition     Status  Type    Volume Label   Mbytes System Usage
         1    A       Non-DOS                 2             %
         2            Non-DOS                 300           29%
C:       3            PRI DOS W95_5-8-97      200    FAT16  19%
         4            EXT DOS                 528           51%

 Total disk space is 1030 Mbytes (1 Mbyte = 1048576 bytes)

 The Extended DOS Partition contains Logical DOS Drives.
 Do you want to display the logical drive information (Y/N)......?[Y]
```

In this example, the 2MB partition (partition 1) is the IBM Boot Manager that controls whether partition 2 or 3 is the active partition. Partition 2 is a 16-bit DOS/Windows partition that has been hidden. FDISK sees it as a *non-DOS* partition under Boot Manager's control.

Partition 3 has the C: designation and is primary. In this case, the Boot Manager is the A (active) partition that controls whether partition 2 or 3 is bootable. In case only one primary partition is available, the A would be next to C: 3, making the C: drive active, primary, and therefore bootable.

> *Note: Observe that partition 4 is the EXT DOS partition, which is short for extended DOS partition. Note that the total size of the partition is 528MB.*

Logical Drive Information

In the previous example, the extended DOS partition contains logical drives, and we have the opportunity to display information about them. The default choice is Y (Yes), so pressing Enter produces the following report:

```
Display Logical DOS Drive Information

Drv     Volume Label    Mbytes  System  Usage
D:      ALL-DATA        350     FAT16   66%
E:      DATA            178     FAT16   34%


        Total Extended DOS Partition size is 528 Mbytes (1 MByte =
        1048576 bytes)
```

Looking at the last line of the report, we can see that the size of the total extended DOS partition (528MB) is the same as that shown on the preceding screen for partition 4.

If you've followed this scenario and were able to understand each of the notes, tips, and exam alerts, you've seen much of what you'll see on the certification exam. Our intent has been to help you create images of people and places with specific PCs. We've left out some of the things that you would do in a real-world situation, concentrating on important points rather than details. As a result, we hope that you have been able to concentrate on the two different systems and have not found your mind wandering to some vague set of abstract machines.

The main purpose of the appendix up to this point has been to give you a way to gauge your understanding of PC configurations and to create a story line where we could focus on what you'll see on the exam. Next, we'll cover some principles of customer service, common customer concerns, and maintaining professionalism.

Customer Service

This book isn't really the place for a complete discussion on the philosophy and principles of how to work with people. Neither is there room to discuss hundreds of examples of good or bad customer service. However, we'll touch on a few principles of good customer service as something for you to think about before you take the exam. Try to think of a place where you received excellent service and another place where you were made to feel like an idiot. If you think about it, you can probably figure out what made the difference.

Here are some interesting service statistics from the U.S. Department of Labor to think about while you're reading this section:

➤ Only 4 percent of disgruntled customers complain, preferring to leave rather than fight.

➤ Twenty percent of your customers account for 80 percent of your problems.

➤ Of the customers who register a complaint, between 54 percent and 70 percent will return if their complaint is resolved. That figure goes up to 95 percent if the complaint is resolved quickly.

➤ The average customer who has a problem will tell 9 to 10 other people about it, and 13 percent will tell more than 20 people.

➤ Customers who complain and have problems resolved satisfactorily will tell an average of five people about the treatment they received.

➤ Between 68 percent and 82 percent of customers leave because of neglect or an attitude of indifference toward them.

A fact of human nature is that when things go well, we don't usually comment about it. When things go badly, we usually tend to make a lot of noise about it. As they say, "Good news doesn't sell newspapers."

Principles Of Customer Service

Customer service is a business term that sometimes is referred to as *quality assurance, people skills, customer relations,* or *customer satisfaction.* Customer service is a conceptual abstract that describes the ways in which people work with one another toward a satisfying end by solving problems. However, customer service is not simply solving problems.

> *Note: Customer service involves the "how" of working with people as opposed to the "what" of fixing a problem. In this case, the problem is a computer problem, and you are the person who'll meet the problem, solve the problem, or both.*

The basic principle of customer service is to ask your customer, "What can I do right now, at this moment, to make you feel that things are going to work out right and that you are being taken care of righteously?" Although you could ask the person that question outright, you're expected to be able to act toward reaching this goal without necessarily asking each customer.

Although the task at hand might be simple and merely a matter of mechanics or a mundane task such as selling someone a parallel cable, make each customer feel that his or her request is a personal one. Requests *are* personal because the customer is personally requesting something from *you*. Present people with an air of experience, expertise, general know-how, and a willingness to offer that know-how. Your customers should always feel that they are being taken care of.

Imagine what would happen if you acted bored, or smirked or laughed at your customer's problem, and then went back into the service area and made fun of that customer where the customer could see you through a glass wall. Suppose that customer happens to be a friendly police officer who just happens to stop you for a broken taillight on your way home from work. You have no way of knowing who a person is when you're speaking with him or her. Remember that you, too, once had a lot of "dumb" computer questions.

Some of the specific actions to take toward the goal of good customer service are the following:

➤ Use the word *we* rather than *I* or *you*. Both of you are trying to solve a problem with a dumb machine.

➤ *Show* what you're going to do, don't just tell someone. If you can, involve the person in the diagnostics process by showing him or her how you're going to do it. Don't lecture, but explain how you plan to go about solving his or her problem.

➤ Explain that there's no such thing as a dumb computer question, only common knowledge and uncommon knowledge.

Customer Concerns

Customers will have three basic areas of worry: their wallets, their watches, and their egos. The customer is worried about how much this will cost, how long it will take, and how to keep from looking stupid. You can go a long way toward reducing the concerns in all three of these areas, and that is where your responsibilities in customer service come into play.

> *Note: The least important concerns in a customer encounter are* your *time,* your *money, and* your *ego.*

Money

We all know someone who bought a computer and expected it to work perfectly forever. The machine cost a lot of money, and they think, "For that amount of money, the machine should darn well work perfectly!" Suddenly, it stops! On the other hand, we've all been in situations like this where we feel forced to spend a lot of money for something that already cost too much. It isn't fair, but some things just must be done.

Have some empathy (emotional sympathy) by imagining how you would feel if your car's transmission blew up tonight on your way home from work. How would you want your tow-truck driver and mechanic to treat you? Would you want them to point out, in excruciating detail, just how you could have prevented the problem?

> *Note: Fix the problem first, then show the customer what he or she can watch out for as a preliminary symptom if the problem should begin to creep up again. Don't treat the customer like a child; explain the problem and solution as you would explain them to a friend. Patronizing someone is not only bad customer service, but bad policy in general.*

Time

One of Murphy's laws states that anything that can go wrong *will* go wrong, at precisely the worst time for it to go wrong. Most people don't feel or don't know that they ought to tune up a computer regularly (e.g., through defragmenting or running ScanDisk). Often they're under pressure of a deadline, and their reputation and bank account will be affected by what they wanted to do with their computers. Suddenly, the computer stops, and all they have in mind is the future, and at the moment it looks homeless!

When you first come into contact with a customer in an over-the-counter situation:

➤ Acknowledge people waiting for your help with a friendly "How can I help you?" (not with "What's the problem?"). If they knew what the problem was, they wouldn't be consulting you in the first place!

➤ Don't just look out over a countertop and yell, "Next!"

➤ Acknowledge that you're busy by letting someone know, as soon as possible, "I'll be with you in just a moment."

➤ If you expect to be busy longer than five minutes, interrupt what you're doing and work out a compromise with waiting customers. Remember that even the CPU must work with interrupts and use a STACK to keep everything flowing smoothly.

➤ Don't put people on hold without some sort of explanation or asking them first.

➤ The customer's time is *always* more important than yours in the work environment—no exceptions.

Ego

Expensive studies (by phone companies) have shown that if you have a smile on your lips, the tone of your voice is made more friendly. When you talk with a customer, you should put a smile on. You don't have to think something is funny, and you want to watch out that you don't have a smirk on your face. Think about how you'd want to look if you were asking someone to dance for the first time. Remember, *you* chose to present yourself as a problem solver— no one's holding a gun to your head and forcing you to work with customers, clients, and people.

Many people are intimidated by computers because they don't feel competent to understand them. You have a reputation as someone who can understand computers. That doesn't mean that you can do anything else in particular, but by taking the job, you've presented yourself to the world as having a certain amount of expertise. A person standing in front of you or talking with you on the phone is taking a personal risk by letting you in on a dark secret: They don't know what to do about something.

When talking with a customer or a client:

➤ Be completely honest in your assessment of *your* abilities. If you don't know something, don't lie, and don't make up an answer just to make someone shut up or go away.

➤ Don't blame customers for messing up their computers. After all, they're paying you money to fix it, not make them feel worse.

➤ Don't patronize customers. You're not a priest or a magician, and the knowledge you have is of something that someone else created. You had to learn too, and knowledge is something that should be shared, not hoarded.

Don't Take It Personally

People who might be shouting in your face are angry at life and its events. They're looking for someone to blame, and you happen to be handy at the moment. If you honestly think that you can solve their problems, direct their attention to how you expect to do it. If you think you can't solve their problems, let them know right away and work together with them to find someone who can.

Note: When you become a professional computer technician, you take on the responsibility that any problem that comes to you will be your problem, not just the customer's problem.

There's a saying that the customer is always right. Obviously, this can't be true all the time. Instead, remember that you have volunteered to present yourself as an expert. The customer has a right to expect that you *are* an expert. Because you can't be an expert in everything involving computers, the customer has a right to be told *immediately* whether you are or aren't what you say you are.

You or your employer put up a sign that told people to come see you for help, so when people come to you for help, they have a right to expect it. When people get angry and start shouting, it's probably because they feel that they've been lied to.

Always be 100 percent honest with a customer who's asking you for help. Think how you would feel if a mechanic told you that he had fixed your car, but he hadn't, and your car died at two in the morning in the middle of nowhere! A person's computer is often the single repository for much of what they care about in life. Respect the person, and respect the computer.

Professionalism

Your personal opinion about life, love, God, human rights, or anything other than an opinion about a computer problem is off limits in a professional environment. After hours, you can talk about anything you want, but when you're working with a customer, you're being paid for your expertise in diagnosing and solving computer-related problems.

The difference between a professional and a hobbyist or an amateur is a sum of money exchanged for services or knowledge. Get paid for what you do, and do what you get paid for. Remember that a friendly conversation about how a computer is working and what the customer uses it for should be geared toward possibly uncovering what went wrong or what's causing the problem.

If customers knew enough to tell you what caused a problem, chances are they would fix it themselves. You need to develop a sense of trust with customers so they'll give you clues and extra information about what led to a problem. Being a professional means being *approachable* in that people feel comfortable talking with you. It doesn't mean presenting yourself as "the ogre behind the counter."

Bad Reputations

At some point in your professional career, you will come into contact with customers or clients who have had previous experience with your firm or business. They had a bad experience, and they confront you with an aggressive complaint about that past. They tell you that you probably don't know what you're doing and that they expect you'll probably cause even more problems. This is a situation on the verge of getting out of control.

If you are a professional, everything customers say to you on a personal level is irrelevant. They don't know you or your family, your history, or where you went to school. They're taking someone else's unprofessional conduct and incompetence and assigning it to you.

The best way to handle this kind of situation is to:

➤ Keep your mouth shut until the customer pauses to take a breath.

➤ Make a polite acknowledgment that you're aware of his or her frustration. For example, "I'm sorry to hear you've had some frustrating experiences. Tell me what I can do right now so we can get you up and running. When I've done that, I will personally look into your past complaints and have someone call you within the next two days."

If you're in a situation in which you're the brunt of someone else's lack of ability, a supervisor or manager must be somewhere in the loop. Unless the managing person has no interest in customer service, you can almost always guarantee a return phone call within two business days. Then it's up to you to *follow through* and make sure that the call was made, even if you make a call yourself to tell the customer that you haven't forgotten him or her.

Final Notes On Customer Service

If you say you're going to do something, do it! If you think you won't do it for whatever reason, don't say you'll do it. You have only one chance to lie to someone. If you do lie, you'll never have their respect again. A corporation might go back on written promises, but an individual person lies. It takes a lot of dissatisfied customers to bankrupt a corporation, but only one lie to one customer to get you fired.

Acronym Glossary

. . . .

AC (alternating current)—Changes from a positive voltage to a negative voltage during one cycle. The most common example is household electricity, which is 110 volts at 60 hertz in the United States.

ADC (analog-to-digital converter)—An electronic device, usually packaged in a chip, that converts analog signals, such as speech, to a digital bit stream.

AGP (accelerated graphics ports)—Provide the video controller card with a dedicated path to the CPU. Found on newer PCs.

ANSI (American National Standards Institute)—One of several organizations that develop standards for the information technology industry.

ASCII (American Standard Code for Information Interchange)—Specifies a seven-bit pattern used for communications between computers and peripherals.

AT (Advanced Technology)—IBM's name for its 80286 PC, which it introduced in 1984.

ATA (Advanced Technology Attachment)—The ANSI standard for IDE drives.

ATAPI (ATA Packet Interface)—The ANSI standard for EIDE drives.

ATX (Advanced Technology Extensions)—A system board form factor that incorporates an accelerated graphics port. It is designed for the Pentium II and is mounted vertically.

Basic (Beginner's All-Purpose Symbolic Instruction Code)—A popular programming language developed in the 1960s at Dartmouth College.

BIOS (Basic Input Output System)—A set of detailed instructions for PC startup that usually are stored in ROM on the system board.

CCD (charge-coupled device)—A semiconductor that is sensitive to light and is used for imaging in scanners, video cameras, and digital still cameras.

CD (compact disc)—A plastic disk measuring 4.75 inches in diameter that is capable of storing a large amount of digital information.

CGA (Color Graphics Adapter)—An IBM video standard that provides low-resolution text and graphics.

CMOS (Complementary Metal Oxide Semiconductor)—The type of chip commonly used to store the BIOS for a PC. It is usually backed up with a small battery for times when the PC's power is off.

COBOL (Common Business Oriented Language)—A high-level programming language commonly used on mainframe and minicomputers.

CompTIA (Computing and Industry Trade Association)—A nonprofit organization made up of over 6,000 member companies that developed the A+ certification program.

CP/M-86 (Control Program for Microcomputers)—The first operating systems developed for microcomputers.

CPU (central processing unit)—The main chip where instructions are executed.

CRT (cathode ray tube)—The picture tube of a monitor.

DAC (Digital-to-analog converter)—An electronic device that converts digital signals to analog.

DC (direct current)—Electricity that flows in only one direction. The power supply in a PC converts alternating current from the wall socket to direct current at voltages needed by PC components.

DDE (Dynamic Data Exchange)—A message protocol within Windows that allows applications to exchange data automatically.

DIMM (dual inline memory module)—A popular form factor for RAM in which each side of the edge connector has separate connections.

DIN (Deutsche Institut für Normung)—The German Standards Institute, which developed standards for many of the connectors used in PCs.

DIP (dual inline package)—A common rectangular chip housing with leads on both of its long sides.

DMA (direct memory access)—Specialized circuitry, often including a dedicated microprocessor, that allows data transfer between memory locations without using the CPU.

DOS (Disk Operating System)—The most widely used single-user operating system in the world.

DRAM (dynamic RAM)—The most common type of computer memory.

DVD (Digital Video Disc)—The next generation of high-capacity CD-ROMs. These double-sided, double-layered CDs have capacities approaching 10GB.

ECC (error correction code)—Tests for memory errors, which it corrects on the fly.

ECP (Enhanced Capabilities Port, or IEEE 1284)—The standard for enhanced parallel ports that are compatible with the Centronics parallel port.

EDO (extended data output) RAM—A type of memory that approaches the speed of static RAM by overlapping internal operations.

EEPROM (electrically erasable programmable memory)—Holds data without power. It can be erased and overwritten from within the computer or externally.

EGA (Enhanced Graphics Adapter)—A medium-resolution IBM text and graphics standard. It was superseded by today's VGA standard.

EIDE (Enhanced Integrated Drive Electronics)—An extension of the IDE interface that is compatible with more devices and offers increased transfer rates.

EISA (Extended Industry Standard Architecture)—Expands the 16-bit ISA bus to 32 bits and provides bus mastering.

EMI (electromagnetic interference)—An adverse effect caused by electromagnetic waves emanating from an electrical device.

EPP (Enhanced Parallel Port, or IEEE 1284)—A high-speed ECP capable of bidirectional speeds approaching 2MB per second.

ESD (electrostatic discharge)—Electrical current moving from an electrically charged object to an approaching conductive object.

FAT (file allocation table)—The part of DOS that keeps track of where data is stored on a disk.

FPU (floating-point unit)—Commonly called a math coprocessor, it was available as an optional chip for Intel CPUs up to and including the 80386. The unit was internally integrated in the 80486 and Pentium processors.

GUI (graphic user interface)—Implemented with Windows, it incorporates icons, pull-down menus, and the use of a mouse.

HTML (Hypertext Markup Language)—A standard for defining and linking documents on the World Wide Web.

IDE (Integrated Drive Electronics)—A popular hardware interface used to connect hard drives to a PC.

IEEE (Institute of Electrical and Electronic Engineers)—An organization with an overall membership of over 300,000 members that is highly involved in setting standards.

IRQ (interrupt request)—A hardware interrupt generated by a device that requires service from the CPU. The request is transmitted through one of 8 to 16 physical lines on the system board, with one device typically allowed per line.

ISA (Industry Standard Architecture)—An expansion bus commonly used on PCs. It provides a data path of 8 to 16 bits and is sometimes referred to as an AT bus because of its use in the first IBM AT computers.

LED (light-emitting diode)—A small electrical device that generates light when current passes through it.

LIM (Lotus/Intel/Microsoft)—Three companies that jointly developed a standard for memory management above 640K.

LPX (Low Profile Extensions)—An AT system board form factor used in small desktop cases.

MCA (Microchannel Architecture)—A 32-bit expansion bus developed by IBM. The bus requires specially designed cards that are not interchangeable with other popular bus designs.

MDA (Monochrome Display Adapter)—The first IBM standard for monochrome video displays for text.

MMX (Multimedia Extensions)—An expanded CPU instruction set optimized for multimedia applications.

NIC (network interface card)—Provides the physical connection of a PC to the cable of a local area network.

NTFS (New Technology File System)—The preferred file system used by Windows NT.

OS/2 (Operating System 2, second generation)—IBM's single-user, multitasking operating system for PCs.

PCB (printed circuit board)—A board where electrical paths are etched on the board as opposed to connected with wires.

PCI (Peripheral Component Interconnect)—A popular expansion bus that provides a high-speed data path between the CPU and peripherals.

PCMCIA (Personal Computer Memory Card Industry Association)—A nonprofit industry association that standardized the 16-bit socket, allowing portable computers to utilize credit-card-size expansion cards.

PnP (Plug 'n' Play)—An Intel standard that allows components to be automatically configured when added to a PC. The standard requires support from the BIOS, the expansion card, and the operating system.

POST (power on self-test)—A series of built-in tests that are performed at system startup.

RAM (random access memory)—The computer's main workspace. Data stored in RAM can be accessed directly without having to read information stored before or after the desired data.

ROM (read-only memory)—A memory chip that permanently stores instructions and data.

SCSI (Small Computer System Interface)—A hardware interface that allows the connection of up to seven devices.

SIMM (single inline memory module)—A narrow printed circuit board that holds memory chips. The connector is integrated into the edge of the board so it can easily be added to sockets on the system board.

SRAM (static RAM)—Requires power to hold content but does not need refreshing like other types of RAM. Because of this, it is very fast.

UART (Universal Asynchronous Receiver Transmitter)—A semiconductor device that transmits and receives data through the serial port.

UPS (uninterruptible power supply)—Provides backup power when the main power fails or moves to an unacceptable level.

USB (Universal Serial Bus)—A new standard that allows 128 devices to be daisy-chained to a cable running at 1.5MB per second.

VESA (Video Electronics Standards Association)—An organization composed of PC vendors that is dedicated to improving video and multimedia standards.

VFAT (virtual file allocation table)—A 32-bit file system used in Windows for Workgroups and Windows 95. The VFAT is faster than the DOS FAT and provides for long file names.

VGA (Video Graphics Array)—The IBM video standard that has become the minimum standard for PC displays. It provides 16 colors at 640×448 resolution.

VRAM (video RAM)—Differs from common RAM in that it utilizes two ports to simultaneously refresh the video screen and receive data for the next screen.

VxD (virtual device driver)—Runs in the most privileged CPU mode and allows low-level interaction with hardware and internal Windows functions.

WYSIWYG (What You See Is What You Get)—Refers to the ability to display text and graphics on a monitor using the same fonts and size relationships as will be printed in the final document.

XT (Extended Technology)—The first IBM PC with a hard drive. It used the same 8088 processor and 8-bit expansion bus as the original PC.

ZIF (zero-insertion force)—A socket that uses a lever to grasp the pins of a chip once it is inserted. This eliminated bent pins and became very popular for mounting CPUs.

Index

R